发现中国系列

总主编 陈建国
副总主编 马荣 周莉萍 赵晓峰

教育部新文科建设项目
"数智化时代经济学人才培养改革与专业建设实践"项目成果
普通高等院校数字素养与创新型复合人才培养
现代经济学专业课程"十四五"规划系列教材
华中科技大学"十四五"本科规划教材

中国经济

（双语版）

主　　编：欧阳红兵
副 主 编：刘亚清　赵晓峰

英文翻译：严　薇　熊苒苒

华中科技大学出版社
http://press.hust.edu.cn
中国·武汉

图书在版编目(CIP)数据

中国经济：双语版：汉英对照 / 欧阳红兵主编. -- 武汉：华中科技大学出版社，2024.9. --（发现中国系列）. -- ISBN 978-7-5680-9750-5

Ⅰ．F12

中国国家版本馆 CIP 数据核字第 2024AC8435 号

中国经济（双语版） 欧阳红兵 主编
Zhongguo Jingji(Shuangyu Ban)

总 策 划：	阮海洪
策划编辑：	杨玉斌
责任编辑：	左艳葵　严心彤
封面设计：	清格印象
责任校对：	刘小雨
责任监印：	朱　玢
出版发行：	华中科技大学出版社（中国·武汉）　电话：(027)81321913
	武汉市东湖新技术开发区华工科技园　邮编：430223
录　　排：	华中科技大学惠友文印中心
印　　刷：	湖北金港彩印有限公司
开　　本：	787mm×1092mm　1/16
印　　张：	23.25
字　　数：	578 千字
版　　次：	2024 年 9 月第 1 版第 1 次印刷
定　　价：	158.00 元

本书若有印装质量问题，请向出版社营销中心调换
全国免费服务热线：400-6679-118　竭诚为您服务
版权所有　侵权必究

总序

纵观人类历史,教育兴则国家兴,教育强则国家强。如今,随着经济全球化的深入推进,教育对外开放已成为推动国家发展的重要战略。党的十八大以来,有关高等教育国际化发展的重要文件密集出台,国际交流与合作已被列入高校五大职能之一,华中科技大学积极响应号召,发布一系列纲领性文件,深入推进国际化办学,高度重视来华留学生教育工作。"发现中国系列"正是在这一背景下为来华留学生打造的经典著作,可以说既是时代之需,也是责任之举。

我们身处的时代,是一个交通高度发达、人员往来密切、文化交流日益频繁的时代。在这个时代,如何讲好中国故事,让世界更好地了解中国,成为摆在我们面前的重要课题。我们深知,来华留学生具有"贯通中外"的优势,是中外友好往来的特殊使者,是沟通中国与世界的重要桥梁。向来华留学生全面系统讲述中国经济社会发展情况,有助于赋能来华留学生讲好中国故事,增强中华文明的国际传播力和影响力。

近年来,习近平总书记多次饱含深情给海外学子、留学归国人员、来华留学生回信,认真学习这些回信让我深受启发,倍感鼓舞。一方面,我曾是海外学子,于1995年出国留学,先后在德国、美国学习工作6年多,这些经历让我更了解来华留学生的学习和生活需求;另一方面,留学归国20多年来,我一直在高校从事科研教学和管理工作,在担任华中科技大学副校长期间更是分管国际交流与合作工作多年,来华留学生教育工作是我的重要工作职责之一。我见证和亲历了我国高等教育事业和科技事业的飞速发展,面对日益庞大的来华留学生队伍,深感骄傲和自豪,同时也感到责任重大。

当前,我国社会正处于高质量发展的新阶段,以高水平对外开放促进高质量发展已成为时代要求,在经济领域如是,在教育领域亦然。我相信,高水平的教育对外开放既是推动高校"双一流"建设的动力,也是开辟高校国际合作新领域的契机。因而,在国际化工作中,我们始终坚持从国际维度布局,在国际坐标定位,以国际名校为标杆,大力拓展与国际顶尖大学的实质性合作,在扩大我校来华留学生规模的基础上,进一步提升来华留学生教育质量。

"发现中国系列"正是为广大来华留学生打造的经典著作。该系列选取了中国的经济发展、医疗卫生、数字化建设等民生热点,通过阐述各大领域的发展历程、技术创新、政策演变、深层逻辑、国际合作等内容,全面介绍现代化建设的中国质量和中国速度,不仅是对中国现代化建设的生动记录,更是对中华文明精神标识和文化精髓的提炼展示。

该系列每一本书都由相关领域的权威专家担任主编,在这里,我要特别感谢各位主编的大力支持与辛勤付出。他们既是深耕科研的顶尖专家学者,对我国乃至国际的经济与科技发展态势有敏锐的感知,具有丰富的图书编写经验,对内容的把握高屋建瓴,又是拥有丰富教学经验的一线教师,了解来华留学生的需求,深谙授业之道,在人才培养上有独特的见解。我相信,这样一套契合时代背景、精选热点主题、洞悉读者需求的双语系列图书,能很好地向广大来华留学生展示全面、立体、真实的中国,赋能他们讲好中国故事,当好友谊使者,搭起合作桥梁。

据我所知,"发现中国系列"已与世界知名出版机构施普林格达成英文版出版协议,将面向全世界出版发行。这也意味着,我们将站在一个更为广阔的舞台上讲述中国故事,宣介中国智慧、中国方案,有助于推进对外文化交流、加强国际传播能力建设,构建中国叙事体系。

未来,"发现中国系列"还会陆续编写、出版,为来华留学生的教育工作逐步夯实基础,一步一个脚印、稳扎稳打做好我校国际化建设工作。我很期待来华留学生和海外读者能从"发现中国系列"中认识中国、了解中国、爱上中国,也很希望该系列能够成为中外文化交流的一道亮丽风景线,为推动构建人类命运共同体贡献我们的智慧和力量。

陈建国

华中科技大学原副校长

目录

1 中国经济的自然条件和基础 ... 001
   1.1 地形 ... 001
   1.2 气候与环境 ... 002
   1.3 行政区划 ... 004
   1.4 自然资源 ... 006
   1.5 基础设施 ... 007

2 中国经济的历史发展（1949年以前） ... 010
   2.1 古代和近代中国的小农经济 ... 010
   2.2 现代化的开端（1912—1937年） ... 012
   2.3 战争状态下的经济（1937—1949年） ... 013
   2.4 新中国建立时的经济基础 ... 014

3 中国经济的发展和探索（1949—1978年） ... 015
   3.1 国民经济恢复时期（1949—1952年） ... 015
   3.2 "一五"计划与"三大改造"（1953—1957年） ... 015
   3.3 "大跃进"和人民公社化运动（1958—1960年） ... 017
   3.4 国民经济的调整（1961—1965年） ... 018
   3.5 "文化大革命"时期（1966—1976年） ... 018
   3.6 决定性的转折（1977—1978年） ... 019
   3.7 1949—1978年经济发展和探索的总结 ... 020

4 中国经济的改革和转型（1978年以后） ... 022
   4.1 1978年的伟大历史转折 ... 022
   4.2 改革启动和局部试验阶段（1978—1984年） ... 023
   4.3 改革全面探索阶段（1984—1992年） ... 026
   4.4 初步建立社会主义市场经济体制阶段（1992—2000年） ... 028
   4.5 完善社会主义市场经济体制阶段（2000年至今） ... 031

5 改革开放以来中国的经济与社会发展 ... 033
   5.1 改革开放以来中国的经济发展成就 ... 033
   5.2 经济结构调整与增长方式转变 ... 035

  5.3 改革开放以来的中国社会发展 037
  5.4 改革开放以来中国经济社会发展的主要经验与启示 039

6 中国的对外开放与国际贸易 041
  6.1 对外开放政策的基本内涵 041
  6.2 中国对外开放的进程 043
  6.3 中国国际贸易的发展 047
  6.4 中国对外贸易政策的演变 055

7 中国的农村改革 057
  7.1 家庭联产承包责任制 057
  7.2 农产品流通体制改革 060
  7.3 中国农村改革的经验与思考 065

8 农业生产与农业产业化 066
  8.1 中国的农业现代化 066
  8.2 乡村振兴与中国农业的未来发展 071

9 中国特色的国有企业制度改革 074
  9.1 社会主义计划经济体制和国有企业制度的建立 074
  9.2 改革开放初期国有企业改革探索:放权让利和承包经营责任制改革 078
  9.3 20世纪90年代初期国有企业改革:股份制改革和现代企业制度 080
  9.4 新时代中国特色现代国有企业制度全面完善:混合所有制改革 082

10 工业化进程与城市发展 085
  10.1 社会主义工业化道路的形成 085
  10.2 改革开放后社会主义市场经济下的工业化 089
  10.3 2012年以来中国特色社会主义工业化建设 091
  10.4 改革开放以来中国的城市发展:工业化与城镇化 093

11 中国的宏观经济政策和财税体制 097
  11.1 中国宏观经济政策的演变 097
  11.2 中国的公共财政体制 101
  11.3 财政收入和财政支出 103
  11.4 财政体制改革 107

12 中国现代金融体系的改革与建立 110
  12.1 中国金融体系改革的阶段性回顾 110
  12.2 中国的金融体系 113
  12.3 中国金融体系改革的基本经验 120
  12.4 中国金融体系发展的趋势和未来展望 122

13 中国特色的经济发展模式 124
  13.1 中国特色社会主义市场经济模式 124
  13.2 经济增长和社会发展的"中国奇迹" 128

14 新时代的发展理念与发展格局 132
  14.1 新发展理念的提出及其内涵 132
  14.2 新发展格局的内涵和特点 134

Contents

1 Natural Conditions and Foundation of the Chinese Economy   137
    1.1 Terrain   137
    1.2 Climate and Environment   139
    1.3 Administrative Division   142
    1.4 Natural Resources   145
    1.5 Infrastructure   147

2 Historical Development of the Chinese Economy (Before 1949)   152
    2.1 The "Small-Scale Farming" in Ancient and Modern China   152
    2.2 The Beginning of Modernization (1912-1937)   155
    2.3 The Economy under the State of War (1937-1949)   157
    2.4 The Economic Foundation at the Establishment of New China   157

3 Development and Exploration of the Chinese Economy (1949-1978)   159
    3.1 The Period of National Economic Recovery (1949-1952)   159
    3.2 The "First Five-Year Plan" and "Three Socialist Transformations" (1953-1957)   160
    3.3 The "Great Leap Forward" and the People's Commune Movement (1958-1960)   162
    3.4 Adjustment of the National Economy (1961-1965)   164
    3.5 The "Cultural Revolution" Period (1966-1976)   165
    3.6 The Decisive Turning Point (1977-1978)   165
    3.7 Summary of Economic Development and Exploration from 1949 to 1978   167

4 Reform and Transformation of the Chinese Economy (after 1978)   170
    4.1 The Great Historical Turning Point of 1978   170
    4.2 The Stage of Reform Initiation and Experiment (1978-1984)   172
    4.3 The Stage of Comprehensive Exploration of Reform (1984-1992)   177
    4.4 The Stage of Establishing the Socialist Market Economy (1992-2000)   180

	4.5	The Stage of Improving the Socialist Market Economic System (2000 to Present)	185
5	**Economic and Social Development in China since the Reform and Opening Up**		189
	5.1	Achievements of Economic Development in China since the Reform and Opening Up	189
	5.2	Adjustment of Economic Structure and Transformation of Growth Pattern	192
	5.3	Social Development in China since Reform and Opening Up	195
	5.4	Main Experience and Enlightenment of China's Economic and Social Development since the Reform and Opening Up	199
6	**Opening Up to the Outside World and International Trade of China**		202
	6.1	Basic Connotation for the Policy of Opening Up to the Outside World	203
	6.2	The Process of China's Opening Up to the Outside World	205
	6.3	Development of China's International Trade	211
	6.4	The Evolution of China's Foreign Trade Policies	220
7	**Rural Reform in China**		223
	7.1	Household Contract Responsibility System	224
	7.2	Reform of the Agricultural Product Circulation System	228
	7.3	Experience and Thoughts on China's Rural Reform	236
8	**Agricultural Production and Agricultural Industrialization**		238
	8.1	Agricultural Modernization in China	238
	8.2	Rural Revitalization and the Future Development of China's Agriculture	246
9	**Reform of the State-Owned Enterprise System with Chinese Characteristics**		250
	9.1	Establishment of the Socialist Planned Economic System and the State-Owned Enterprise System	250
	9.2	Exploration for Reform of the State-Owned Enterprise in the Early Stage of the Reform and Opening Up: Decentralization of Power and Transfer of Profits and Contract Management Responsibility System Reform	256
	9.3	Reform of State-Owned Enterprises in the Early 1990s: Shareholding System Reform and Modern Enterprise System	261
	9.4	Comprehensive Improvement of Modern State-Owned Enterprise System with Chinese Characteristics in the New Era: Mixed-Ownership Reform	264
10	**Industrialization Process and Urban Development**		269
	10.1	The Formation of Socialist Industrialization Path	269
	10.2	Industrialization under the Socialist Market Economic System after the Reform and Opening Up	275
	10.3	Construction of Socialist Industrialization with Chinese Characteristics since 2012	279
	10.4	Urban Development in China since the Reform and Opening Up: Industrialization and Urbanization	283

11	**China's Macro-Economic Policies and Fiscal and Taxation System**	288
	11.1 The Evolution of China's Macro-Economic Policies	288
	11.2 China's Public Fiscal System	296
	11.3 Fiscal Revenue and Expenditure	299
	11.4 Restructuring of the Fiscal System	305
12	**Reform and Establishment of China's Modern Financial System**	309
	12.1 The Stage Review of China's Financial System Restructuring	309
	12.2 China's Financial System	314
	12.3 Basic Experience of China's Financial System Reform	327
	12.4 The Development Trend and Future Prospects of China's Financial System	330
13	**The Economic Development Model with Chinese Characteristics**	333
	13.1 The Socialist Market Economic Model with Chinese Characteristics	333
	13.2 "China's Miracle" of Economic Growth and Social Development	339
14	**Development Philosophy and Pattern in the New Era**	346
	14.1 The Proposal and Connotation of the New Development Philosophy	346
	14.2 The Connotation and Characteristics of the New Development Pattern	349

参考文献
References   354

1 中国经济的自然条件和基础

中国位于全球最大的大陆——欧亚大陆的东部和全球最大海洋——太平洋的西岸。中国领土辽阔广大,陆地总面积约960万平方千米,仅次于俄罗斯、加拿大,居世界第三位。中国陆地边界长度约2.2万千米,同14国接壤。中国大陆海岸线长度约1.8万千米,海域总面积约473万平方千米,自北向南环绕大陆边缘的海依次为渤海、黄海、东海和南海,沿海分布有台湾岛、海南岛、崇明岛、舟山群岛、南海诸岛等7 600多个大大小小的岛屿,与8国海上相邻。

中国的疆土南北相距约5 500千米,东西相距约5 200千米,大部分位于中纬度,其中处于温带、暖温带和亚热带的幅度最宽,水热条件良好,自然资源物种众多,季风强盛,有利于农业生产发展。中国海域辽阔,海洋资源丰富,有利于对外经济贸易往来。中国自然条件复杂、生物品种繁多、资源类型丰富,是世界上少数矿产种类比较齐全、矿产资源丰富的国家之一。但是,中国人口超过14亿,人均资源量少,地域分布不均,可再生资源趋向负荷极限。

本章将基于上述背景,从地形、气候与环境、行政区划、自然资源、基础设施五部分,具体介绍中国经济的自然条件和基础。

1.1 地　　形

中国地势西高东低,自西向东倾斜,呈阶梯状分布。中国地形多种多样,其中山地面积约占国土面积的33%。几千万年以来,随着印度板块不断向北推进,并不断向欧亚板块下插入,世界上最年轻的高原——青藏高原逐渐被抬升形成。由于板块碰撞产生的力量向外围不断扩散,青藏高原形成的同时也带动了其周缘地势的变化。青藏高原的隆升对中国整体的高原、山系和盆地分布产生了极大影响,从而直接促进了中国地势西高东低,三级阶梯状分布特征的形成。第一级阶梯主要是青藏高原,平均海拔4 000米以上,其中就包括喜马拉雅山脉和柴达木盆地。第二级阶梯以一系列高原及盆地为主,平均海拔在1 000~2 000米。这一区域占中国陆地面积的1/3,与第一级阶梯的分界线为昆仑山脉—阿尔金山脉—祁连山脉—横断山脉,大部分深居于内陆,干旱少雨,盆地中荒漠广布,包括中国北部内蒙古高原和黄土高原,中国西南部云贵高原和四川盆地以及中国西北部塔里木盆地和准噶尔盆地。第三级阶梯与第二级阶梯以大兴安岭—太行山—巫山—雪峰山为界,地形以平原和丘陵为主,平均海拔低于500米,主要包括东北平原、华北平原、长江中下游平原,以及辽东丘陵、山东丘陵和江南丘陵。东部平原大体相连,大多是冲积平原,地势低平,土壤肥沃,有利于农耕作业等生产发展,也成了中国开发程度高、经济文化发达、城镇密集、人口稠密的地区。

正由于中国地形的多样和地质结构的复杂,其河流水系的类型也较为丰富,主要有树枝状水系(如闽江水系)、扇状水系(如海河水系)、羽状水系(如钱塘江水系)等。西高东低的地势使中国大多数河流流向为自西向东,中国三条重要河流——长江、黄河和珠江——都自西向东流淌。中国的地形地势影响到河流分布,继而影响到人口分布。在中国诸多的地理格局中,有一条著名的分界线——黑河—腾冲线,该线从中国东北边境的黑龙江省黑河市一直延伸到中国西南边境的云南省腾冲市,大致为呈45度角倾斜的直线状。这条分界线也被称为中国人口地理分界线,体现了中国东南和西北的人口分布之悬殊差异。黑河—腾冲线西北部面积约占全国土地总面积的57%,其人口却只约占全国总人口的6%,且集中分布于少数几个盆地和分散的绿洲,整体而言地广人稀,平均每平方千米不足10人。水资源的短缺是该地区人口如此稀少的主要原因,极大地限制了该区域的人口发展。而黑河—腾冲线东南部面积约占全国土地总面积的43%,人口却约占全国总人口的94%。这一区域的主要地形为丘陵——东南丘陵,包括江南丘陵、浙闽丘陵及两广丘陵三部分,其中零星分布着平原和山地。季风气候的丰沛降水为该区域提供了丰富的水资源,推动了该区域的人口发展。中国东部沿海地区人口密度较大,平均每平方千米多于400人。中国人口密度高于世界平均水平,但远低于韩国、印度、荷兰、日本、英国等人口密度排名靠前的国家。

全球陆地地形的五种基本类型在中国均有分布,这为中国工农业的发展提供了多种选择和条件。中国山地和丘陵面积约占全国陆地面积的43%,这使得交通运输业和农业发展存在一定困难。据勘测,中国1类宜居面积不足两成,其中约半数是耕地,人均耕地面积较少。优良农业耕地多位于肥沃的平原以及由山丘与山脉分割开来的河谷中。第三次全国国土调查数据显示,截至2019年底,中国耕地面积为19.18亿亩①,位居世界第三,但人均耕地面积只有1.36亩,不足世界平均水平的40%。但2021年中国的粮食总产量在世界上位居第一,中国利用不足世界耕地总面积10%的耕地,养活了约占世界22%的人口。

1.2 气候与环境

中国幅员辽阔,纬度跨度广,距海远近差距大,加之呈三级阶梯状分布的显著地形特征,导致中国的气候复杂多样,季风气候显著,大陆性气候强。中国受冬夏季风交替影响的地域广,是世界上季风最典型、季风气候特征最显著的地区,因而夏季潮湿、高温多雨,冬季干燥、寒冷少雨。冬季盛行偏北风,由亚洲内陆上空形成高压带而产生,带来寒冷、干燥的空气,所以普遍降雨少,气温低,北方更为突出。到了夏季,亚洲内陆上空形成与之相对应的低压带,位于东南方向的太平洋和西南方向的印度洋向内陆送来温暖、湿润的空气,温暖的空气在进入中国东南部时受山脉阻拦,与冷空气发生摩擦,从而形成丰沛的降雨,雨热同期。因此,当夏季的内陆盆地地区以及西部沙漠地区极为炎热的时候,沿海地区相对凉爽。

夏季季风由东南沿海登陆后,在向西北方向推进的过程中势头会不断减弱,因而降水量

---

① 1亩≈666.67平方米

也呈明显减少趋势,造成了中国南北地区极具特色的降水差异,即北方干旱少雨,南方河道纵横。在中国古代战争中,南北气候差异也形成了"南方善水,北方善马"的固有印象。受全球气候变暖影响,这种长期存在的南北差异也越来越显著。季风行进过程中,途经长江与黄河之间的山脉时,会为中国北方带来适度的夏季降雨。值得重视的是,如果季风太弱,无法抵达黄河河谷附近,而是逗留在中部山区,中国大陆将面临北方遭受干旱,南方发生洪涝的挑战。因此,秦岭—淮河一线也就成为雨水丰沛的南方和长期缺水的北方的又一分界线。

如果对中国的水资源情况进行定位的话,那么中国是一个严重干旱缺水的国家。中国北部的黄河流域几乎全部都是干旱与半干旱地区。黄河是中国第二大河,全长约5 464千米,流域总面积约79.5万平方千米(含内流区面积约4.2万平方千米),但黄河的水量只是中等水量,天然年径流量仅占全国河川年径流量的2.1%,位居全国七大江河的第四位,小于长江、珠江、松花江。黄河流域大约70%的面积为黄土高原,其表层覆盖着数十米至数百米的黄土层,土质疏松,抗冲能力低,遇水极易崩解。而南方的长江是中国水量最丰富的河流,年径流量高达9 600亿立方米,约占全国河流年径流总量的36%,为黄河的20倍。虽然珠江长度不到黄河的一半,但其水量是黄河水量的7倍之多。正因为如此,中国启动了南水北调工程,以实现中国水资源南北调配、东西互济的合理配置格局。

中国外流河的水文特征深受季风气候的影响。随着夏季风的到来,雨带由南向北推移,河流水流骤增,水位上涨,形成汛期;随着冬季风的加强,雨带南撤,河流进入枯水期。中国各地枯水期一般由秋季开始,延续到次年春季,南方较短,北方较长。

与世界上绝大多数国家相比,中国的经济发展面临着更为严峻的资源限制。而未来中国的极端天气气候事件发生频率仍可能增大,这也将对中国的经济社会发展和人们的生产生活造成很大的影响。

近几十年,中国经济的快速发展对环境造成了不同程度的污染,特别是以城市为中心的环境污染不断加剧,并逐步向农村蔓延。尤其是在经济发达、人口稠密的地区,环境污染问题更为突出。虽然通过采取植树造林、防治沙漠化、水土保持、国土整治、草原建设及天然林资源保护等一系列措施来整治环境问题,中国部分地区的生态环境明显改善。但其治理速度远远赶不上破坏速度,生态赤字逐渐扩大,这主要表现在水土流失加剧、沙漠化面积不断扩大、草原退化严重、大气污染问题日益严峻等多个方面。其中大气污染是中国第一大环境污染问题,大气环境面临的形势仍然非常严峻,大气污染物排放总量居高不下。造成空气污染的原因主要有工业污染、交通污染、生活污染等,其中工业污染和交通污染是主要因素。中国是世界上水土流失最严重的国家之一,由于特殊的自然地理和社会经济条件,中国绝大多数省区存在不同程度的水土流失现象。水土流失既是土地退化和生态恶化的主要形式,也是土地退化和生态恶化程度的集中反映,对经济社会发展的影响是多方面的、全局性的和深远的,甚至是不可逆的。北方地区主要表现为沙漠化严重,沙漠、戈壁、沙漠化土地已超过149万平方千米,约占国土面积的15.5%。在中国的天然草原中,目前约有90%的可利用草原出现了不同程度的退化,其中覆盖度在5%～20%的地区明显减少,草原退化、沙化、盐碱化形势堪忧。同20世纪50年代相比,目前中国草原的产草量下降了30%～50%。

面对日益严峻的生态破坏和环境污染问题,中国必须也不得不走上绿色发展的道路,必须大力倡导以可持续发展为核心的绿色发展理念,在绿色经济的框架下,推动包括循环经济、低碳经济、生态经济、合理消费等在内的各领域的发展,同时调整产业结构,转变经济发展方式,淘汰落后产业,发展新兴节能绿色产业。

1.3 行政区划

中国国土面积巨大,为便于管理,中国的行政区划分为省级行政区、地级行政区、县级行政区以及乡级行政区四个级别。中国现有 23 个省、5 个自治区、4 个直辖市、2 个特别行政区,合计共 34 个省级行政区。根据 2022 年的数据,澳门特别行政区是中国常住人口最少的省级行政区,约 68 万人;常住人口最多的省级行政区是广东省,常住人口约 12 657 万人。图 1-1 是中华人民共和国行政区划图。

图 1-1 中华人民共和国行政区划图
图片来源:中华人民共和国自然资源部

中国的省级行政区划最早可追溯至元朝的行省制度,但是其并不总是划分中国经济空间的最自然的方式。根据人类学家施坚雅的方法,首先把中国区域土地作为一个整体,按照其特点划分成几个大区,每个大区由一个以上的省份组成,以便于进行地理、气候、经济、军事、通信、交通和行政等方面的研究和管理。综合地理位置、自然地理、人文地理的特点,可以把中国划分为四大地理区域,即北方地区、南方地区、西北地区和青藏地区;而在行政分区上则是设立华北、东北、西北、华东、中南和西南六大行政区。在科学的基础上，综合历史、民族等多种维度，遵循相关的区划原则进而开展的区划工作，也称为行政地理分区，据此，中国可分为华中、华南、西南、西北、华北、东北、华东七大区域。华北地区的京津冀地区是中国北方经济规模最大、最具活力的地区。华北平原也是中国三大平原之一，是中国人口密度最大、人口最多的平原。中华人民共和国的首都北京，与其拥有约 1 387 万常住人口（第七次全国人口普查数据）的姊妹城市天津，形成了华北地区的城市中心，但华北地区的城市化水平总体上略低于全国平均水平。华北地区气候主要为温带季风气候，夏季高温多雨，冬季寒冷干燥，年平均气温为 8～13 摄氏度，年降水量为 400～1 000 毫米，其中内蒙古自治区降水量少于 400 毫米，为半干旱区域，但是这并不影响农业成为华北地区的重要产业。华北地区发展综合性农业，以麦、棉等传统作物为主，是全国重要的商品粮基地，同时也大力发展近郊农业、节水农业、机械化生产等。2019 年，华北平原以 24.2% 的中国总人口，创造了 25.4% 的国内生产总值。

中国最发达的地区是长江中下游地区，面积 5 万平方千米的长江三角洲是中国最大的河口三角洲。长江三角洲以种植小麦、水稻、大豆、玉米为主，农耕条件优越，农业历史悠久，农业生产水平高，是举世闻名的鱼米之乡和丝绸之乡。长江中下游地区由于长江中下游平原肥沃的土地和适宜的水热条件，开发历史悠久，早在隋唐时期即开始大规模开发。晋朝到宋朝曾出现北方人口、文化和经济南移的高潮，长江中下游地区很快成为中国经济发展的重心。近代，长江中下游地区又以其优越的区位条件和便利的长江水道运输条件，成为中国近代工业的摇篮，其中上海是中国近代工业的发祥地，是中国的经济、金融、贸易和航运中心。2020 年，长江三角洲地区生产总值为 24.5 万亿元，常住人口城镇化率超过 60%，以不到 4% 的国土面积，创造出中国近 1/4 的经济总量、1/3 的进出口总额。长江三角洲地区包括上海市、江苏省、浙江省、安徽省，共 41 个城市，截至 2021 年底，长江三角洲地区人口为 23 647.83 万人，区域面积 35.8 万平方千米。2021 年，长江三角洲地区生产总值为 27.6 万亿元，在中国占比达到 24.1%。2019 年，长江三角洲地区铁路路网密度达到 325 千米每万平方千米，是全国平均水平的 2.2 倍，并规划于 2025 年达到 507 千米每万平方千米。

与长江三角洲地区相呼应的便是位于中国华南地区的珠江三角洲地区，它是中国改革开放的先行地区，是中国重要的经济中心区域，也是中国经济发展的重要引擎和南方对外开放的门户，是辐射带动华南、华中和西南发展的龙头，同时也是中国人口聚集度最高、创新能力最强、综合实力最强的三大城市群之一，有"南海明珠"之称。珠江三角洲地区总面积达 55 368.7 平方千米，2021 年常住人口总量超 7 860 万，地区生产总值突破 10 万亿元，约占中国国内生产总值的 8.8%，珠江三角洲地区虽然只有 9 个城市，却创造了广东省全省 80% 以上的生产总值，其中深圳、广州占比较高。而随着珠江三角洲地区发展日渐成熟，一个新的发展格局逐渐形成，即建立囊括珠江三角洲地区 9 个城市在内，联合香港特别行政区以及澳门特别行政区所形成的粤港澳大湾区。该地区地理条件优越，"三面环山，三江汇聚"，具有漫长的海岸线、良好的港口群和广阔的海域面。该地区经济腹地广阔，辐射范围大，与福建、江西、湖南、广西、海南、四川、贵州、云南等形成区域合作，被称为"泛珠三角区域合作"，区域内拥有中国约 1/5 的国土面积、1/3 的人口和 1/3 的经济总量。截至 2020 年 12 月，粤港澳大湾区常住人口达 8 617.19 万人；截至 2022 年 2 月，粤港澳大湾区 11 个城市的生产总值达到 12.63 万亿元。粤港澳大湾区以香港、澳门、广州、深圳四大中心城市作为区域发展的核心引擎。而中国打造粤港澳大湾区,建设世界级城市群,也有利于丰富"一国两制"的实践内涵。

中国西部地区包括西北五省区(陕西、甘肃、宁夏、青海、新疆)、西南五省区市(西藏、云南、贵州、四川和重庆)和内蒙古、广西,拥有土地面积约687万平方千米,约占全国总土地面积的72%。由于地形条件和气候条件比较差,根据第七次全国人口普查数据,西部地区人口总数约为3.8亿人,只占到中国总人口的27.12%,同时,该地区土地资源中平原面积占42%,盆地面积不到10%,剩下约48%的土地资源则是沙漠、戈壁、石山和海拔3 000米以上的高寒地区,这使得西部地区的整体人口密度较低,平均每平方千米不足60人,远远低于中国的平均水平。但西部地区有两大天然优势:一是拥有丰富的自然资源;二是西部地区与10多个国家接壤,陆地边境线长约1.8万千米,如此长的陆地边境线,无疑为西部地区发展边境贸易展现了诱人的前景。昔日历史上穿越西部地区的"丝绸之路"曾是中国对外交流的第一条通道,今日的西部地区定然会随着西部大开发的进程再现辉煌。

1.4 自 然 资 源

中国的国土面积仅占世界陆地面积的6.44%,而人口则占到了世界总人口的约18%,中国自然资源总量及种类非常丰富、潜力巨大,但是人均资源不足。根据第三次全国国土调查的数据,中国耕地面积为12 786.19万公顷,其中黑龙江、内蒙古、河南、吉林、新疆五个省区的耕地面积较大,占全国耕地面积的40%;园地面积为2 017.16万公顷,主要分布在秦岭—淮河以南地区,占全国园地面积的66%;林地面积为28 412.59万公顷,其中四川、云南、内蒙古、黑龙江四个省区的林地面积较大,占全国林地面积的34%;草地面积为26 453.01万公顷,主要分布在西藏、内蒙古、新疆、青海、甘肃、四川六个省区,占全国草地面积的94%。尽管中国的土地资源绝对数量较大,但人均占有量少。首先,中国人均土地面积只有大约10亩,不到世界平均水平的1/3。其次,中国土地资源分布不均衡,90%以上的耕地分布在东南部的湿润、半湿润地区,全部耕地总面积中中低产耕地约占2/3。最后,宜开发为耕地的后备土地资源潜力不大。

截至2021年底,中国已发现173种矿产,其中能源矿产13种,金属矿产59种,非金属矿产95种,水气矿产6种。中国主要能源矿产储量方面,煤炭储量约为2 078.85亿吨,石油储量约为36.89亿吨,天然气储量约为63 392.67亿立方米。中国石油储量和天然气储量分别约占世界已探明总储量的1.5%和4.5%,"富煤、贫油、少气"是中国能源资源的鲜明特点。中国页岩气富集地质条件优越,页岩气储量约为5 440.62亿立方米,具有巨大的页岩气资源前景和开发潜力,但中国页岩气资源调查与勘探开发还处于探索起步阶段,至今尚未对其潜力进行全面估算。表1-1为2021年中国主要能源矿产储量。

表1-1 2021年中国主要能源矿产储量

序号	矿产	单位	储量
1	煤炭	亿吨	2 078.85
2	石油	亿吨	36.89

续表

序号	矿产	单位	储量
3	天然气	亿立方米	63 392.67
4	煤层气	亿立方米	3 659.68
5	页岩气	亿立方米	5 440.62

数据来源：《中国矿产资源报告（2022）》

中国的有色金属资源丰富，品种比较齐全，钨和稀土等7种金属的储量居世界第一位，铅、镍、汞、钼、铌5种金属的储量也相当丰富。尽管有色金属资源总量大，但人均占有量少，和中国土地资源的人均占有量情况如出一辙，因此中国也称得上是一个有色金属矿产资源相对贫乏的国家。其次，中国贫矿较多，富矿稀少，开发利用难度较大，共生、伴生矿床多，而单一矿床少。此外，中国矿产资源也存在分布范围广，地域分布不均衡的现象。

中国水能资源和矿产资源分布极不均匀，总体特点是分布广泛，相对集中在中国中西部。中国西部水能蕴藏总量占全国的82.5%，已开发水能资源占全国的77%，但开发利用尚不足1%；而矿产资源更是可观，根据《2022煤炭行业发展年度报告》，从中东西部地区原煤产量占全国比重变化看，西部地区占比由54.4%上升到60.7%，中部地区占比稳定在33.7%，东部地区占比由7.2%下降到3.2%，东北地区占比由4.7%下降到2.4%。自2011年起10年间，西部新增石油探明地质储量和产量分别占全国总量的62%和34%，天然气占85%和84%，其中鄂尔多斯累计探明地质储量石油近70亿吨和天然气超5万亿立方米。在中国已探明储量的159种矿产资源中，西部地区就有143种，一些稀有金属的储量名列中国乃至世界前茅。相比于能源矿产主要分布在西部地区，有色金属则主要分布在南方。同时南方的水资源十分丰富，东西部的地形落差较大，所以中国西南地区水电的潜力巨大。但是，经济增速极快的南方沿海地区基本没有能源储备，为使分布不均的资源在全国范围内有效地调配使用，急需加强交通运输建设。同时基于资源和土地密集型产业的发展战略并不可行，中国只能发展劳动密集型产业并最终走上发展知识密集型产业的道路，环境制约因素使得中国经济发展上的权衡变得更加困难和复杂。

1.5 基础设施

基础设施是经济社会发展的重要支撑，具有战略性、基础性和先导性作用，基础设施建设可分为交通运输、能源动力、数字通信和民生工程四个部分。

2012年至2022年，中国建成了全球最大的高速铁路网、高速公路网、世界级港口群。中国不仅在传统基础设施建设方面取得了迅速发展，还在新型基础设施建设方面实现了重大突破。本节将围绕交通运输、能源动力、数字通信、民生工程四个部分介绍中国的基础设施建设。

1.5.1 交通运输

截至2021年底，中国全国铁路营业里程达到15万千米，稳居世界第二，其中，高速铁路营业里程达到4万千米,稳居世界第一;铁路复线率为59.5%;电化率高达73.3%;西部地区铁路营业里程达6万千米。全国铁路路网密度高达156.7千米每万平方千米。中国的铁路、公路里程10年间增加了大约110万千米,相当于绕行地球赤道27圈半。铁路固定资产投资累计超过7万亿元,增产里程5.2万千米。

根据行政等级划分,中国公路分为国家公路、省级公路和农村公路三个等级,国家公路网包括国家高速公路网和普通国道网,是公路网中最高层次的路网。中国2013年发布的《国家公路网规划(2013年—2030年)》提出,到2030年,中国国家公路网总规模将达到40万千米,其中国家高速公路和普通国道总规模分别为13.6万千米和26.5万千米,截至2021年底,这两项的完成比例分别达到85%和96.5%。2021年底,中国公路总里程达528万千米,公路网密度达到55千米每百平方千米,位居世界前列,其中高速公路里程总量位居世界第一。目前以国家高速公路为主体的高速公路网络已经覆盖了98.8%的城区人口20万以上的城市及地级行政中心,连接了全国约88%的县级行政区和约95%的人口;普通国道基本覆盖县级及以上行政区和常年开通的边境口岸。此外,截至2021年底,中国境内运输机场总数达到248个,中国机场总设计容量超过14亿人次。

交通运输建设在打赢脱贫攻坚战和服务乡村振兴方面更是功不可没。2011年至2021年,中国农村公路总里程从356.4万千米增加到446.6万千米;1 040个乡镇、10.5万个建制村通硬化路的难题得到解决。交通基础建设使得城乡间的人流、物流、资金流加速互动,带动了农村的经济,提高了农民的收入。

此外,中国基础设施建设还走出了国门。中老铁路、亚吉铁路、蒙内铁路开通运营,雅万高铁正式启用,都有效推动了"一带一路"倡议的建设及发展。

1.5.2 能源动力

当代中国建设了一大批世界级的能源基础设施项目。围绕坚持保障能源安全的理念,中国加快推进能源安全新战略,着力构建清洁低碳、安全高效的能源体系,能源供应保障能力大幅提升。如今,中国可再生能源发电装机规模突破了10亿千瓦,绿色电力装机总量稳居世界第一;2021年底,风电光伏并网装机合计6.35亿千瓦,是2012年的近90倍。2021年10月,福清兴化湾59台风机全部并网发电,年发电量为14亿千瓦时,可满足70万个三口之家的正常用电需求。2021年1月,"华龙一号"核电机组——福建福清核电5号机组投入商业运行,标志着中国在三代核电技术领域跻身世界前列。

截至2021年底,中国发电总装机容量达到23.8亿千瓦,比2012年翻了1倍,平均年增速8.4%;中国220千伏及以上输电线路达到84.3万千米,变电设备容量达到49.4亿千伏安,分别是2012年的1.7倍和2.2倍。在川滇交界的金沙江下游,总装机容量达1 600万千瓦的白鹤滩水电站是当今世界在建规模最大、技术难度最高的水电工程。全面建成投产后,年平均发电量将达624.43亿千瓦时。此外,中国能源跨省跨区输送通道建设不断加强,截至2021年底,油气管道总里程达到18万千米,较2012年增长了1倍。

1.5.3 数字通信

随着中国通信技术的高速发展,中国信息通信业得以迭代跨越,中国建成了全球规模最大、技术领先的网络基础设施。其中,光纤网络接入带宽实现了从十兆到百兆再到千兆的指数级增长,移动网络实现了从"3G突破"到"4G同步"再到"5G引领"的跨越。

2012年,中国移动电话基站数刚刚突破200万个,而截至2021年底,这一数字达到了996万。截至2022年4月底,中国已历史性实现了全国行政村"村村通宽带",宽带网络平均下载速率提高了近40倍,4G基站规模占全球总量的一半以上,已建成的5G基站达到161.5万个。

遍及全国的信息基础设施为中国建设数字社会、数字政府提供了有力支撑,大幅提高了行政效率,提升了公共服务的流程透明度和数据共享程度,极大地缩减了居民的办事时间和精力。

发达的信息基础设施网络彻底改变了民众的生活习惯。在电信新技术的引领下,电子商务、电子政务、远程办公等互联网应用全面普及,移动支付年交易规模达527万亿元。

作为数字经济发展的核心生产力,算力基础设施已成为国民经济发展的重要基础设施。2022年2月,"东数西算"工程正式全面启动,通过将东部发达地区的数据传输到西部算力资源丰富的地区进行运算、存储,既缓解了东部能源紧张的问题,也给西部增加了新的发展机会。

未来,中国还将全面加强信息基础设施建设,扩大5G网络覆盖深度,加快5G等新兴技术规模化应用,以推动数字经济的发展。

1.5.4 民生工程

2012年前,在中国河北邯郸、邢台等一些地方,农村饮水氟超标问题十分严重,苦咸水、高氟水威胁着居民饮水健康。2014年底,中国南水北调中线一期工程全面通水。清澈的江水从位于汉江中上游的丹江口水库北上,流经上千千米,为极度缺水的华北地区带来甘霖。现在,南水北调受水区的家庭只要一打开水龙头,就能喝到千里以外的汉江水。

作为世界规模最大的调水工程之一,南水北调在建设中利用了明渠、渡槽、隧洞等多种技术,打造了世界最大输水渡槽、世界最大规模现代化泵站群。通水以来,南水已成为北京、天津、河北、河南等地40多座大中城市280多个县(市、区)超过1.4亿人的主力水源。

截至2022年5月13日,南水北调东线和中线工程累计调水量达531亿立方米,为沿线50多条河流实施生态补水85亿立方米,为受水区压减地下水超采量50多亿立方米。其他的民生基础设施工程,虽然体量不比南水北调工程的庞大,但同样为民众生活增添不少便利。2018年以来,中国政府部署了农村人居环境整治行动,推进农村"厕所革命",完善农村生活设施。截至2021年底,中国全国农村卫生厕所普及率超过70%,其中,东部地区、中西部城市近郊区等有基础、有条件的地区农村卫生厕所普及率超过90%。

2 中国经济的历史发展(1949年以前)

2.1 古代和近代中国的小农经济

中国自古以来推崇"大一统"的共同体理念,无论是"六合同风,九州同贯",还是"天下大同",都是这种思想理念的反映。但这种宏观层面"大一统"的背后,反映的是中国自古以来形成的、以无数分散的小农为基础的传统乡土社会。中国人讲究"安土重迁",传统乡土社会的稳定性,其实也对国家的稳定性和文化的稳定性起到了保障作用。

以乡土社会为基础的传统中国,超过九成的人口都在农村生活。人们"日出而作,日入而息",采用精耕细作的方式进行耕地劳作、繁衍生息,土地收成几乎是人们维持生计的全部来源。传统的农业体系,同时意味着没有机会实现大规模的机械化生产,因此所有的劳动基本上都必须通过人力来完成,这是一种较高的单位土地生产率与较低的人均劳动生产率并存的传统生产方式。

这样的生产方式又孕育了中国人民勤劳而富有智慧的特质。人们进行日复一日、年复一年的辛勤耕作,基本上所有的土地都经过了不同程度的人力改造。同时,人们不断摸索耕地劳作的经验,并代代相传,逐步形成了一种高效的传统农业生产体系。这一体系首先在黄河中下游和长江中下游形成,然后又逐步传播到有可能进行灌溉的低洼地和丘陵地区。适宜的生存环境也促进了人口增长,进而导致已有的耕地面积无法满足实际需要,于是,早在秦汉时期,农民就开始在山坡上构筑梯田(见图2-1),以解决粮食短缺问题。

中国地域广博,各个地方的自然资源和气候条件不尽相同,农作物产量和类别也具有很大差异。《晏子春秋》中就有"橘生淮南则为橘,生于淮北则为枳"的描述。随着生产生活的需要,人们开始进行交换和买卖,具有贸易往来的市场逐渐形成。陆路运输和水路运输是古代中国最主要的货物运输方式。隋朝时期,为了加强北方地区与南方富庶地区的联系,朝廷完成了贯通南北的京杭大运河,加强了南北经济的交流。当时人口密集的都市和较为发达的交通网络,实际上构建起了一个以农业为基础、具有竞争性市场和较为成熟的交易制度的高度商业化的社会经济体系。

中国传统农业的基础是个体小农家庭,不存在大农场或者大土地主。除了农业生产以外,其他非农业生产的规模也非常小,并由农户自己进行。例如,部分农户除了耕作农田外,还开设乡村小作坊,生产纺织品、铁制工具,以及酒、茶叶、糖、面条等产品,并拿到市场出售。因此,传统中国经济的基本模式是小农经济,它的基础是充满活力的家庭经济、个体经济。

自南宋起直到19世纪60年代,这一时期中国的出口都是享誉世界的,其中最主要的出

图 2-1　梯田景象

图片来源：新华社

口产品就是丝绸、瓷器和茶叶等。以丝绸和瓷器为代表的出口分别形成了陆上丝绸之路和海上丝绸之路，它们是古代中国对外贸易的主要渠道。在这段时期内，中国在世界贸易市场上一直保持着出口盈余，大量白银流入中国。由中国茶农生产、小型茶叶作坊进行加工的优质茶叶在世界市场上赢得了广泛赞誉。但是这种规模小而分散的生产方式，无法提供标准化的高质量产品，因此在 20 世纪初期之后，中国的出口商被迫退出了世界茶叶市场。

由此反映出，小农经济是一种稳定性较低但资源配置灵活性较高的经济模式。从积极方面看，资源和劳动力都非常高效地向具有最高回报率的地方流动，一旦回报率下降，资源和劳动力也立即退出，这有利于资源的有效配置。但从消极方面看，经济活动被细分为无数只有小资本参与的小生意，无法形成大规模的标准化生产方式，规模经济也无法形成。

中国传统小农经济"靠山吃山，靠水吃水"的自然主义生产生活方式，与近现代以来的工业化发展进程存在明显的不相适应的问题。富裕的劳动力和相对稀缺的土地资源，导致中国农民和手工业者更偏向于采取劳动密集型技术，而忽视了生产力进步和技术创新。小农经济的分散性、自私性和保守性，逐渐成为中国现代化和工业化的最严重障碍和阻力。

由于廉价工业品和鸦片的冲击，到 19 世纪 70 年代，中国对外贸易已经由顺差转为了逆差。鸦片的大量流入给中国社会和经济带来了严重危害，林则徐主持的虎门销烟成为鸦片战争的导火索。鸦片战争以中国失败告终，在 1842 年签订的《南京条约》中，中国被迫将香港岛割让给英国，并开放五个通商口岸。鸦片战争促进了小农经济的解体。自此，中国开始逐渐沦为半殖民地半封建社会。

19 世纪 60 年代到 90 年代，晚清洋务派掀起了一场旨在"自强""求富"的自救运动，史称"洋务运动"。在洋务运动中，西方的科学技术、军事装备、机器生产被大规模引进，刺激了中国资本主义的发展，推动了中国对于近代化道路的探索。洋务运动推动创办了一批企业，比较具有代表性的有曾国藩创办的安庆内军械所、李鸿章创办的江南制造总局和轮船招商局（见图 2-2）、张之洞创办的汉阳铁厂（见图 2-3）等。

图 2-2　轮船招商局

图 2-3　汉阳铁厂

从 17 世纪末到 19 世纪初，中国在人口增长、经济发展和疆域拓展方面表现得十分出色，直到鸦片战争之前的 1820 年，中国仍然是世界上最大的经济体，中国国内生产总值占世界生产总值的比重几乎达到 1/3。而此时，美国国内生产总值只占世界生产总值的 1.8%，整个欧洲也只占到 26.6%。然而，在此后一个多世纪的时间里，中国经济总量占世界经济总量的比重大幅下降，到 1949 年，中国经济总量占世界的比重不足 5%，世界排名第 13 位。

2.2　现代化的开端（1912—1937 年）

1911 年的辛亥革命结束了中国几千年的封建君主专制制度，此后，中国的制度发展和经济变化不断加速，进入了一个全新的阶段。随着现代运输业和通信业的兴起，其他行业也随之蓬勃发展,中国的现代产业逐渐发展完善起来。清末民初,中国处于军阀混战、政治分裂的时期,给经济带来了一定负面影响。从 1927 年南京国民政府成立到 1937 年日本发动全面侵华战争,这 10 年间,国内环境相对稳定,经济得到一定发展,教育投资和农业推广不断推进。

总体来看,从 1912 年到 1936 年,中国的工业化发展十分迅速。虽然基础相对薄弱,但是现代工厂的生产能够达到以每年约 9% 的速度增长。统计资料显示,截至 1933 年,近代工业生产总值占国内生产总值的比重达到 2%,雇佣的工人接近百万。

20 世纪初期,在工业发展的最初阶段,中国的工业化主要集中在通商口岸和东北地区。其中,通商口岸的现代工业是中国工业化的主导模式。外国商人在这里兴办工厂,主要集中在轻工业领域。统计资料显示,在 1933 年的全部工业产出中,纺织品占比达 42%,而上海、天津、青岛是主要生产地,70% 的纺织业都集中在这三个城市,其中,仅上海一座城市的产出就占到全部工业产出的 40%。东北地区的工业化模式则与通商口岸截然相反,这里最开始的投资者是日本政府及其半官方机构,东北工业化发展主要集中在重工业和以铁路为主的交通运输业。日本利用东北地区丰富的煤矿和铁矿资源,大力发展钢铁、冶金、机械等重工业,并兴建了一个密集的铁路网,以满足自己的经济和发展需要。

20 世纪 20 年代和 30 年代,中国的现代工业虽然总体规模仍然较小,但具有重大的意义和影响。从 1914 年到 1936 年,农业、手工业和传统运输业都有较大幅度的增长。现代小企业迅速增加,人均国内生产总值增长虽然缓慢但意义重大。显而易见的是,虽然这一时期的工业并没有从根本上改变中国经济的整体结构,但是工业化已经开始起步,并且为今后中国经济的发展打下了基础,提供了前提条件。

这一时期,社会上读书识字的人也有所增加。受对外开放的影响,有近 10 万名中国学生到海外长期学习。来华生活的外国人也在增加,1936 年,在中国居住的外国人达到了 37 万之多。中国和外国的人员交流也促进了技术、思想、文化等方面的交流互动。尽管中国社会由于政治的和社会的分裂而分化,但似乎也在迅速向前发展。

2.3　战争状态下的经济(1937—1949 年)

1937 年发生的"卢沟桥事变"标志着日本全面侵华战争的开始。抗日战争结束后,中国随即进入解放战争时期,直到 1949 年新中国成立。

抗日战争期间,国民政府迁往重庆,战争的压力导致国家对经济的干预日益增强。为了将工业从上海迁往内陆地区,并重新建立军工产业,国民政府设立了资源委员会,以促进政府主导型产业的发展。截至 20 世纪 40 年代初,资源委员会经营着共有 16 万人的多家工厂。在中国未沦陷土地上的全部企业中,国营企业的资本占比 70%,劳动力占比 32%。

20 世纪 40 年代末,由于手上已经拥有资源委员会经营的企业接收的日伪工厂,国民政府在短期内拥有了大笔资产,控制了约 2/3 的产业资本。据统计,截至 1947 年,国民政府已经控制了 90% 的钢铁产量、66% 的电力生产以及 45% 的水泥产量。此外,多数大银行和运输企业也在国民政府的控制之下。

为了支付战争费用,国民政府开始大量印刷钞票,以维持财政运行。但是,这一举措的后果是加速了通货膨胀,并最终导致了恶性通货膨胀。通货膨胀日益恶化、宏观经济的严重失衡使经济几乎陷入瘫痪,这也成为国民政府迅速垮台的重要原因。

2.4 新中国建立时的经济基础

战争严重破坏了经济基础设施,尤其是对工业资本和农业基础设施(特别是灌溉系统)的毁坏,极大地损害了经济发展。此时,短期实际产出远远低于产出能力。同时,恶性通货膨胀也反映出了金融领域的极度混乱局面。总体来看,连年的战争破坏了自20世纪20年代和30年代开始的极为脆弱的经济增长,中国此时仍然十分贫困。

统计数据显示,1949年,中国拥有人口5.4亿,人均预期寿命仅35岁,全国城乡就业人员18 082万人,其中城镇就业人员仅有1 533万人,城镇失业率高达23.6%。农业方面,耕地面积14.68亿亩,全国粮食总产量1.132亿吨;工业方面,钢产量15万吨,煤产量3 200万吨,石油12万吨,水泥66万吨。当时,中国国民总产值只有近123亿美元,人均国内生产总值约为23美元,人均国民收入只有27美元。广大人民群众生活条件恶劣,整个社会处在十分贫穷和落后的状态。

然而,脆弱甚至是近乎崩溃的经济可能在一定程度上促进了中国在1949年后相对顺利地采取社会主义计划经济制度、实施社会主义工业化战略。尽管截至1949年,中国依然非常贫困,但经济发展已经开始起步。中国拥有相对较好的人力资本禀赋,人口的识字率逐步提高。大学体系虽然很小,但已建立起来,技术人员也在国外受过训练。一些能够满足进一步经济发展之需的现代产业资本和运输资本也已经创建。

3 中国经济的发展和探索（1949—1978年）

3.1 国民经济恢复时期（1949—1952年）

新中国成立初期，中国人民面临着严峻考验。经济上，从国内来看，连年的战争极大地破坏了农业和工业生产力，恶性通货膨胀仍在蔓延；从国际来看，由于以美国为首的帝国主义国家的政治孤立和经济封锁，中国受到的贸易限制日益增多。在内忧外患的局面下，中国政府迅速采取行动恢复国内经济，严格管制货币，采取积极稳妥的态度推进经济建设。

在农村，土地改革运动在如火如荼地推进。在土地改革运动中，土地统一平均分配，由农户私人所有，激发了农民的生产积极性。截至1952年底，土地改革在全国范围内基本完成。在城市，中国政府接收了多数工厂，包括抗日战争后国民政府没收的日本人的工厂和国民党的工厂。这一时期中国政府的投资主要集中在对工业化发展战略有着重要意义的东北地区。到1952年底，中国的经济恢复和建设工作取得了极大成功，工业和农业发展都超过了1949年前的最高水平。据统计，1952年底，中国工农业总产值达810亿元，比1949年增长超过70%。国民经济的全面恢复和初步发展也意味着在全国范围内全面铺开社会主义工业化建设的时机已经相对成熟，中国即将迎来一个全新的发展阶段。

3.2 "一五"计划与"三大改造"（1953—1957年）

新中国成立后，中国经济发展的重点主要有两方面：一是工业化建设；二是社会主义计划经济体制的建立。在以毛泽东同志为核心的党中央领导下，中国不再走传统的、以家庭为基础的小农经济路子，而是通过直接的政府计划，大力发展大规模的社会主义工业联合体。在这一时期，中国的资源和精力主要集中在生产金属、机器、化工产品等产品的资本密集型企业。

1953年5月，中国和苏联在莫斯科签订《关于苏维埃社会主义共和国联盟政府援助中华人民共和国中央人民政府发展中国国民经济的协定》，规定苏联援助中国新建和改建91个工业项目，加上1950年已确定的50项和1954年增加的15项，合计156项。就这样，新中国第一个五年计划（简称"一五"计划）在苏联的支持下正式启动了。

"一五"计划的基本任务是"集中主要力量发展重工业，建立国家工业化和国防现代化的初步基础"。"一五"计划期间,中国的工业生产能力得到了极大发展,尤其是重工业生产部门的生产能力得到了显著提升。图 3-1 为第一批"解放"牌汽车试制成功。一方面,许多工业品产量大幅增加、技术水平明显提高;另一方面,工业部门内部结构逐渐完善,一些行业实现了从无到有、从有到优的突破和飞跃,为中国工业体系的全面发展奠定了坚实基础。从产量来看,与 1952 年相比,1957 年中国重工业产值增长了 210.7%,轻工业产值增长了 83.3%。从结构来看,1952 年,重工业和轻工业在全部工业中占比分别为 37.3%、62.7%,到 1957 年,重工业占比上升至 45%,轻工业占比下降至 55%。同时,轻重工业内部的结构也趋于合理。除了工业以外,农业生产的发展和农业基础设施的建设也具有明显进步。总的来说,"一五"计划期间,中国的工业化水平大幅提升,增强了中国的国防实力和综合竞争力。

图 3-1 "一五"计划期间,第一批"解放"牌载重汽车试制成功

图片来源:新华网

与"一五"计划几乎同时进行的是对农业、手工业、资本主义工商业的社会主义改造。从 1953 年至 1956 年,中国在短短 4 年内就完成了"三大改造",实现了把生产资料私有制转变为社会主义公有制,初步建立起社会主义基本制度。

具体而言,在"三大改造"中,对农业、手工业实行的是合作化,对资本主义工商业实行的是公私合营。农业的社会主义改造又称农业合作化运动,1953 年,中共中央先后发布了《中共中央关于农业生产互助合作的决议》和《中共中央关于发展农业生产合作社的决议》,中国农村开始走集体化和共同富裕的社会主义道路,农民个体经济逐步转变为社会主义集体经济。到 1956 年底,全国 96.3% 的农户加入了合作社。手工业的社会主义改造是通过合作化道路,把个体手工业转变为社会主义劳动群众集体所有制经济。到 1956 年底,91.7% 的全国手工业从业者加入了手工业合作组织。

公私合营是中国对民族资本主义工商业实行社会主义改造所采取的国家资本主义的高级形式,大体上分为个别企业的公私合营和全行业公私合营两个阶段。公私合营企业的特点是国家向私营企业投资和派遣管理人员,把双方合作深入到企业内部,即生产领域,生产资料为国家和资本家共有,社会主义经济成分处于领导地位。企业的利润按照"四马分肥"

的原则进行分配,大约34.5%以所得税的名义上缴国家,30%作为企业的公积金,15%作为工人福利费,20.5%作为资方红利。至1956年底,实行公私合营的工业企业已经达到原有资本主义工业总户数和职工人数的99%,占生产总值的99.6%。随着资本主义工商业改造的完成,中国建立起社会主义基本制度,并进入社会主义初级阶段。

3.3 "大跃进"和人民公社化运动(1958—1960年)

"大跃进"运动是党在探索建设社会主义道路过程中的一次严重挫折。过分夸大主观意志和主观努力的作用,忽视了经济发展的客观规律,高指标、瞎指挥、浮夸风、"共产风"等错误泛滥成灾,给工农业生产带来了极大的破坏,使得国民经济比例严重失调,人民生活遭受严重困难。

1958年5月,中国共产党(简称中共)第八次全国代表大会第二次会议通过了"鼓足干劲、力争上游、多快好省地建设社会主义"的总路线。会议号召全党和全国人民认真贯彻执行社会主义建设总路线,力争在15年甚至是更短的时间内在主要工业产品产量方面赶超英国和提前5年完成全国农业发展纲要的目标。会后,全国各条战线上迅速掀起"大跃进"高潮。同年8月,中共中央政治局在北戴河召开扩大会议,讨论1959年的国民经济计划,确定了一批工农业生产的高指标,并讨论和通过了《中共中央关于在农村建立人民公社问题的决议》。会后,全国掀起了"全民大办钢铁运动",农村出现人民公社化运动的高潮。

在1958年,经济领域出现了越来越多的"好消息",图3-2即为当年《陕西日报》的相关报道。这年秋天,粮食收成超过了前两年的水平,钢铁产量也出现了大幅增长。然而,几乎所有的报告都具有夸大的成分。统计报告的水分越来越大,并最终导致了经济几乎崩盘。不遵循经济发展客观规律的一味冒进造成了很多问题,例如大部分产品质量低劣、无法使用,劳动力从农业部门大量流失,资源消耗不可持续,等等。进入1960年后,地方粮食短缺已经发展成区域性短缺,相对恶劣的气候环境使得这一形势更加恶化,中国的粮食供给出现严重困难,国民经济陷入空前的萧条和低迷状态。

图3-2 "大跃进"时期的报纸

农村人民公社的设想和具体制度安排,是把农业(包括农林牧副渔业)、工业、商业、文化教育、军事国防等统一于农村基层社会组织之中。"政社合一"是人民公社的一个基本特点。客观来说,人民公社既存在消极的一面,也存在积极的一面。从消极方面来看,人民公社化运动出现了过急过猛、不尊重经济发展客观规律的问题,盛行"一平二调"的"共产风";从积极方面来看,人民公社化运动发挥集体力量使得中国农村面貌发生了极大的改变,客观上促进了农业经济的增长和农村生产条件的改善。

3.4 国民经济的调整(1961—1965年)

1960年11月,中共中央发出《关于农村人民公社当前政策问题的紧急指示信》,要求全党用最大努力坚决纠正"共产风"。不久之后,在1961年1月,中共八届九中全会召开,会议正式决定对国民经济实行"调整、巩固、充实、提高"的八字方针。以这两件事为标志,"大跃进"运动实际上已经被停止,国民经济开始转入调整的新轨道。

同时,毛泽东号召全党恢复实事求是、调查研究的作风,1961年也成为实事求是年和调查研究年,这为各个领域的调整奠定了坚实的思想基础。在工业方面,调整的重点是降低钢产量等指标和整顿企业秩序。1961年9月,中共中央出台《关于当前工业问题的指示》,明确指出必须把工业生产和工业基本建设的指标降到确实可靠、留有余地的水平上。此外,《国营工业企业工作条例(草案)》(简称"工业七十条")的发布试行,也为恢复和重建企业正常生产秩序起到了积极作用。在农村地区,人民公社虽然得到保留,但所有的人民公社都进行了整风整社,彻底检查和纠正此前的"共产风"、浮夸风等。同时,取消了公共食堂和供给制的原有规定,要求减少城镇人口和压缩城镇粮食销量。

一系列国民经济调整政策的制定和施行,使得中国的经济逐渐运行到正常轨道上。从1962年底开始,国民经济形势开始出现好转,工农业生产得到恢复,国家财政基本实现收支平衡,市场商品供应状况得到缓和,城乡居民生活水平也有所提升。统计数据显示,与1961年初相比,1963年6月,全国职工总数减少了1 887万人,全国城镇人口减少了2 600万人,吃商品粮人口减少了2 800万人。到1965年,国民经济调整任务基本完成。到1966年,全国基本完成了预定的国民经济调整任务,中国经济得到恢复和发展。

3.5 "文化大革命"时期(1966—1976年)

正当中国基本完成国民经济调整任务的时候,"文化大革命"开始了。"文化大革命"是一场给党、国家和各族人民带来严重灾难的内乱,留下了极其惨痛的教训。"文化大革命"的发动起因,其实是为了防止资本主义复辟、寻求中国自己的建设社会主义的道路。但是,由于对社会主义社会的建设发展规律认识不够清楚,加上"左"的方针占据了主导地位,最终酿成了10年内乱。从政治角度来看,"文化大革命"的影响是巨大的,但是从经济学角度来看,"文化大革命"时期经济领域的损失相对较小。与"大跃进"时期不同的是,"文化大革命"时期的经济运行相对而言较为有效:投资虽然在缩减,但是是一个相对有序的过程;农业生产受到的影响相对较小;工业生产虽然有所下降,但下降程度有限;重要的必需品和优先发展的项目仍在继续进行。与1965年、1966年类似,这一时期中国经济建设的重心仍然在三线地区。

3.6 决定性的转折(1977—1978年)

从1976年"文化大革命"结束到1978年中共十一届三中全会召开,这两三年的时间,对于中国经济来说是一个非常重要和关键的历史阶段。在这一时期,中国开始了经济思想领域的大解放和对计划经济体制的初步反思。如何确立党和国家的工作重点和中心任务,成了这一阶段的重要问题。

在这两三年的时间里,无论是在经济还是在思想等领域,中国都出现了极大的变化。全党开展了一场有关真理标准问题的大讨论,这为中共十一届三中全会胜利召开奠定了思想基础。中共十一届三中全会是新中国成立以来党的历史上具有深远意义的转折,全会作出把党和国家的工作中心转移到经济建设上来、实行改革开放的历史性决策。中共十一届三中全会召开之前,主要的一些议题,比如尊重客观经济规律、实行按劳分配、实行对外开放、引进外国资金和技术、尊重知识和人才、改革不合理的生产制度等,已经全盘提出来了。图3-3为当年的《人民日报》刊登的中共十一届三中全会公报。

图3-3 《人民日报》刊登的中共十一届三中全会公报

从新中国成立到改革开放前,经过近30年的积累和发展,中国经济也出现了一定增长。从经济总量看,1978年中国国内生产总值为3 679亿元,占世界经济总量的比重为1.8%。但是由于人口增长快,积累和消费关系不合理等,1978年全国居民人均可支配收入仅为171元,人均消费支出为151元。财政收入有所增加,1978年增加到1 132亿元。外汇储备仍然相当紧张,1978年末仅有1.67亿美元,居世界第38位。此外,1978年货物进出口总额为206亿美元,居世界第29位。从产业结构看,农业占比下降,工业占比上升。1978年,第一、二、三产业比重分别为27.7%、47.7%和24.6%。从社会和民生角度看,相较于新中国成立初期,此时的状况有所改善。1978年,基本普及小学教育,学龄儿童入学率达到94%;医疗卫生机构达到17万个,卫生技术人员达到246万人,但医疗卫生事业总体水平依然不高。此时仍有大量的农村贫困人口,如果按照2010年农村贫困标准衡量,1978年末中国农村贫困人口有7.7亿人,农村贫困发生率高达97.5%。

3.7　1949—1978年经济发展和探索的总结

3.7.1　1949—1978年中国经济建设的成就

从1949年新中国成立到1978年改革开放拉开序幕,这近30年的时间,对于中国来说是一个非常重要的历史阶段。在这个阶段,中国进行了社会主义经济体制的过渡,对经济建设进行了深刻的探索并积累了丰富的经验。

从社会性质和经济体制来看,我们可以大致将1949—1978年这近30年分为三个重要的阶段:一是新民主主义社会时期(1949—1952年);二是从新民主主义社会向社会主义社会过渡的时期(1953—1956年);三是单一公有制和计划经济体制时期(1957—1978年)。具体来看,在新民主主义社会时期,主要任务在于恢复和重建国民经济,通过没收官僚资本、进行土地改革等一系列经济举措,中国初步建立起高度集中的经济管理体制,为之后的大规模工业化打下了坚实的基础。在从新民主主义社会向社会主义社会过渡的时期,重点在于"一化三改"的过渡时期总路线,高度集中的计划经济体制逐步形成,"一五"计划取得了巨大且具有深远意义的成功。在单一公有制和计划经济体制时期,中国走过了十分曲折的经济建设之路,政治和经济因素交织,政策极其不稳定,工业化进程也多次受阻。

经过近30年的社会主义工业化建设,新中国取得了重大成就。一批新的工业基地在中国内地逐步建立起来,国防工业实现了从无到有的突破,尤其是"两弹一星"的成功发射,极大地维护了中国的国家安全。图3-4即为当年《光明日报》关于"两弹一星"的相关报道。此外,资源勘探开发和基础设施建设都取得了极大的进步和发展,一个独立的、较为完整的工业体系和国民经济体系基本形成。

图3-4　《光明日报》关于"两弹一星"发射成功的报道

总体来看,在这一时期,中国工业化道路的重点在于集中精力大力发展重工业,特点是政府作为投资主体、国家指令性计划作为配置资源的手段。在这个大背景下,中国不断探索如何正确处理国民经济结构关系、沿海和内地工业关系等一系列重要问题,逐步建立起独立的、较为完整的工业体系和国民经济体系,为改革开放后进一步加快社会主义工业化进程积累了宝贵的经验,打下了较好的物质基础和人才基础,尤其是重工业基础。

3.7.2 计划经济的特点与评价

实行社会主义计划经济是新中国成立以来的重要事件,社会主义计划经济体制也是近代以来中国工业化和现代化的重要转折点。就其本质来看,计划经济实际上是人类对于探索和试图掌握经济运行规律的一种积极尝试,许多国家对此都在进行不断的探索和实践。从更广泛的意义上看,计划经济已经超越了经济范畴,它不仅仅是资源配置、企业运行、收入分配的体制,而是成为国家动员所有资源的一种综合性体制。对于相对落后的大国来说,具有高度资源动员能力的计划经济体制有助于快速实现工业化和经济赶超。

邓小平在1992年视察南方期间的南方谈话提出的著名论断,对于我们理解计划经济与社会主义有着重大意义。他认为,计划经济和市场经济不是区分社会主义和资本主义的标准,计划经济不等于社会主义,市场经济也不等于资本主义。无论是社会主义,还是资本主义,都可以采用计划经济或者是市场经济的体制或者机制。

从具体实践来看,新中国从一个一穷二白的国家一跃成为具有较为雄厚的工业基础和较为完备的现代工业体系的国家,仅仅用了30年左右的时间,发展速度和效果是惊人的。因此,仅就这一点来看,那些认为计划经济是完全没有效率的落后经济的说法是不具有说服力的。今天,我们已经清楚地认识到,计划经济不等于单一的国家所有制,也不完全等于绝对的国家控制力,其在新中国经济发展过程中的作用应得到充分认识和正确评价。

4 中国经济的改革和转型（1978年以后）

1978年以后的中国经济体制改革极大解放了生产力，促进了经济增长，增强了发展活力，创造了"中国奇迹"。这种以市场化为导向的经济改革逐渐地放开了国家对经济活动和个人生活方式的控制。整个改革经历了大致四个阶段：第一个阶段是改革启动和局部试验阶段（1978—1984年），此时小规模的个体和集体之间零星的商品交易市场开始出现，国家在政策层面上把个体和集体经济的培育作为对社会主义计划经济的一个补充；第二个阶段是改革全面探索阶段（1984—1992年），在这一阶段，各类与市场制度相关联的改革政策和方案相继出台，计划经济体制和成分不断弱化，市场经济体制和成分不断加强，等价交换、供求关系、竞争等市场规则开始在经济生活中发挥重要作用；第三个阶段是初步建立社会主义市场经济体制阶段（1992—2000年），在该阶段，市场经济作为整体开始主导中国经济的发展格局，随着国有企业最终融入市场经济体系，以及劳动力、资本和土地资源市场化程度的加深，市场规则渗透到了整个经济领域、公共事业和社会生活领域；第四个阶段是完善社会主义市场经济体制阶段（2000年至今），该阶段逐渐建成完善的社会主义市场经济体制和更具活力、更加开放的经济体系，在强调继续深化经济体制改革的同时，开始重视对社会发展的政策制定和投入。

4.1 1978年的伟大历史转折

无论是在中国共产党发展史上，还是在中华人民共和国发展史上，甚至是在中华民族发展史上，1978年都是应当被永远铭记的一年。在这一年，邓小平推动实现了具有深远意义的历史性伟大转折。在这一年，通过关于真理标准问题的大讨论，人们冲破了"两个凡是"的束缚，解放了思想；党和国家顺应了人们要求改变生产力的落后状况的迫切心情，对内大胆地提出改革生产关系和上层建筑的意见，对外改善了与日、美等国的关系，确立了对外开放的方针；最后通过召开中共十一届三中全会，重新确立了党的实事求是的思想路线，实现了全党工作中心的转移。

要改革，首先需要确立正确的思想路线，推动实现党和国家工作中心的转移，并深刻认识改革开放的必要性和重大意义。可以说，中国经济体制改革的进程就是一次又一次的思想解放、理论突破与实践探索互动的进程。

1978年5月11日，《光明日报》发表的题为《实践是检验真理的唯一标准》的特约评论员文章，引发了一场全国范围的关于真理标准问题的大讨论，为拨乱反正、解决历史遗留问题创造了条件,为中共十一届三中全会的召开做了思想准备。

这一时期,中国还充分借鉴西方国家经验,迫切希望能突破禁锢,放下包袱,向一切先进的国家,包括政治制度不同的西方资本主义国家学习一切先进的东西。中共中央决策层当时已经下定对外开放的决心,他们思索和考虑的不是"要不要开放",而是"怎么搞对外开放"。

1978年7—9月召开的国务院务虚会,是为改革开放做准备的一次重要会议。这次会议以研究加快中国四个现代化建设的速度问题为主题。长达2个多月的国务院务虚会(总基调是"改革开放"),就加快中国现代化建设速度所发的议论、所提的办法、所拟订的措施,为中共十一届三中全会最终确定改革开放的总方针、总政策奠定了基础。

1978年12月18日至22日,中共十一届三中全会在北京召开,会议彻底否定了"以阶级斗争为纲"的错误理论和实践,作出把党和国家工作重点转移到经济建设上来、实行改革开放的历史性决策,拉开了中国改革开放的序幕,标志着中国进入了社会主义事业发展的新时期。从此,中共中央领导全国各族人民在新的历史条件下开始了新的伟大革命。这一伟大的历史转折表明,从20世纪50年代就已开始的对中国社会主义建设道路的探索,终于走上了正轨。

4.2 改革启动和局部试验阶段(1978—1984年)

中共十一届三中全会以后,党的十二大提出了"计划经济为主,市场调节为辅"的原则,第一次使市场调节在经济体制中取得了一席之地。这一时期的改革主要是在计划经济体制内部引入市场机制,以求引入市场机制完善计划经济体制。在实践方面,这一时期主要是在农村推行以家庭联产承包责任制为主的改革,以及对部分工业企业实行扩大自主权的改革。

4.2.1 农村经济改革兴起

改革过程中意义最为重大的变革是在国民经济最薄弱的环节——农业之中爆发的。家庭联产承包责任制、统分结合的双层经营体制取代"三级所有、队为基础"的人民公社制度,开始在全国农村普遍实行。

农业去集体化和家庭联产承包责任制的改革,是自下而上展开的。实行家庭联产承包责任制的开拓者来自安徽省的一个小山村——安徽省凤阳县小岗村。小岗村是当地有名的"乞丐村",1978年12月,该村18户农民冒着极大的政治风险,私下签署了一份包产到户协议,将集体土地承包到户,搞起了"大包干"。图4-1为部分大包干带头人合影。其做法是生产队与每户农民约定,先把该缴给国家的、该留给集体的都固定下来,收获以后剩多剩少都是农民自己的。到收获的季节,这些农民所获的粮食相较他们邻村的多得多,因而紧接着更多的农民也加入其中。小岗村18户农民的伟大壮举,奏响了中国改革的序曲。

然而,农业改革并非一帆风顺的,在一些地方,"农业学大寨"及"以粮为纲"仍旧是当时的农业指导思想,包产到户的做法引发了巨大的争论。在推行包产到户遇到重重阻力的关键时刻,邓小平站出来旗帜鲜明地给予支持。邓小平不仅对安徽农村改革表示巨大支持,也为全国农村改革指明了方向,对推动包产到户在全国的发展产生了重大影响。1980年9月,

图 4-1　部分大包干带头人合影
图片来源:《人民日报》

中共中央发出通知,第一次肯定了"大包干"的改革行动,农村改革由此全面铺开。其后,以家庭联产承包责任制为主要形式的新型农业生产关系在各地农村普遍确立。

1980 年,中国自然灾害频发,据统计,全国共有 4 733 万多公顷农田受灾,占播种面积的 30% 左右。灾情如此严重,群众忧心,党和国家领导人操心。但因为这一年农村政策好,大灾之年全国粮食产量高达 3.18 亿吨,这一年是新中国成立以来第二个高产年,家庭副业的优势也格外明显,人均纯收入比上年增长 42.2%。许多长期贫困落后的地区,农业喜获丰收。那些包产到户实施得早的地方,如安徽、四川、甘肃等地,则出现了更喜人的气象。大灾之年的生产实践,为这一年包产到户大争论作了很好的总结,"早包早富,晚包晚富,不包不富",已成了多数人的共识。

1982 年元旦,中共中央历史上第一个关于农村工作的"一号文件"——《全国农村工作会议纪要》正式出台,该纪要明确指出:"目前实行的各种责任制,包括小段包工定额计酬,专业承包联产计酬,联产到劳,包产到户、到组,包干到户、到组,等等,都是社会主义集体经济的生产责任制。"文件毫不含糊地给包产到户、包干到户正了名,不仅统一了人们对包产到户的认识,而且还把农村、农民和农业问题提到了一个高度重要的位置,极大地鼓舞了农村干部的干劲,提高了农民生产的积极性。1982 年,全国农业生产总值比上年增长 11%,粮食总产量比上年增长 8.7%,农民收入比上年增长 15%。实践再次证明,包产到户的政策合乎情理,中央文件顺应民心,农村经济充满了希望。

总体而言,家庭联产承包责任制的实行,对充分调动亿万农民积极性,打破农业长期停滞不前的困难局面,加快农业发展,改变农村面貌,产生了深远影响和极大推动作用。

4.2.2　扩大企业自主权

在农村之外,其他方面改革的试验也开始起步。在 1979 年以后的一段时间内,经济体制改革的中心环节是扩大企业自主权。中国开展了扩大企业自主权试点,推行两步"利改税",逐步推进"划分收支、分级包干"的财政体制改革,不断减少的集体经济和几乎绝迹的个体经济逐步恢复和发展。

扩大企业自主权的试点工作最初是在四川省开始的。1978年第四季度,四川省首先在6个地方国营工业企业进行试点,收到了较好的效果。1979年1月,四川省委、省政府总结了6个企业的试点经验,制定了《关于地方工业扩大企业权力、加快生产建设步伐的试点意见》,并决定从1979年起,把试点扩大为100个工业企业。这些改革措施给四川省的工业企业带来了前所未有的活力,取得了显著的经济效果。试点第一年,四川省84个地方工业企业的工业总产值比上年增长14.9%,利润增长33%,上缴利润增长24.2%,均高于非试点企业。

1984年5月,国务院颁发了《关于进一步扩大国营工业企业自主权的暂行规定》,在生产经营计划、产品销售等十个方面,给企业以应有的权力。1985年9月,国务院又批转了国家经济委员会(于1993年改为国家经济贸易委员会,于2003年撤销)、国家经济体制改革委员会(于1998年改为国务院经济体制改革办公室,于2003年改组为国家发展和改革委员会)制定的《关于增强大中型国营工业企业活力若干问题的暂行规定》的通知,通知作出了十四条规定,要求继续扩大企业自主权。

这一时期的改革把重点放在调整国家与企业关系上,着眼于调动企业和职工的积极性、主动性。通过这一阶段的改革,企业有了一定的生产自主权,开始成为独立的利益主体,企业和职工的积极性都有所提高,并将传统计划经济体制打开了缺口。但是,扩大企业自主权的改革思路是在计划经济的框架下进行的,这一阶段国有企业的改革仍没有动摇计划经济体制的基础。

4.2.3 兴办经济特区,逐步展开对外开放

中国兴办经济特区是根据对外开放的要求,参照国外经验提出来的。而创立经济特区这一重大决策的最初谋划,大致可以追溯到1978年5月《港澳经济考察报告》提出的把广东省宝安、珠海两县划成外贸基地的建议,以及1979年1月交通部(现交通运输部)和广东省关于选址宝安蛇口公社建立工业区的报告。

1978年5月31日,中共中央派出的港澳经济贸易考察团向中央提交了《港澳经济考察报告》。这份报告第一次提出了在深圳、珠海设立经济特区的设想,并且创造性地提出在两地实行有利于加快对外开放步伐的特殊政策,呼吁把它们作为工作重点来抓。可以说,这是中国创办经济特区的第一步尝试。

1979年1月6日,广东省、交通部联合向国务院报送了《关于我驻香港招商局在广东宝安建立工业区的报告》,表示"一致同意招商局在广东宝安境内邻近香港地区的地方建立工业区"。"招商局蛇口工业区"便先于深圳特区在1979年年初挂牌成立了。图4-2即为建设中的蛇口工业区。在质疑的声浪下,蛇口以占深圳2%的人口,创造了占全市16%的利润。从打破"大锅饭"到招商引资,从住房商品化再到全国人才招聘,在1979年到1984年的几年中,蛇口创造了"24项全国第一"。蛇口的成功经验被媒体誉为"蛇口模式",蛇口工业区成为经济特区的开路先锋。

1980年3月24日,中共中央在广州召开广东、福建两省会议,正式将"出口特区"定名为"经济特区"。1980年8月26日,《广东省经济特区条例》获准通过,标志着兴办特区有了法

图 4-2　1984 年 4 月，建设中的深圳蛇口工业区矗立着"时间就是金钱，效率就是生命"的宣传口号

图片来源：中国改革信息库

律上的依据。1981 年 11 月 26 日，全国人大常委会又授予广东、福建两省制定所属经济特区单项经济法规的权力，中国正式揭开了试办经济特区的序幕。

从区域空间看，中国对外开放经历了沿海经济特区到沿海开放城市、沿海经济开放区，再到内陆中心城市、沿边口岸及西部大开发全方位开放开发的转变。在空间拓展过程中，从 1979 年设立蛇口工业区开始，再到对广东和福建实行特殊政策与灵活措施，中国改革开放逐渐拉开序幕。1984 年，中国又进一步开放了北海、湛江、广州、福州、温州、宁波、秦皇岛、上海、南通、连云港、青岛、烟台、天津、大连 14 个沿海港口城市，并陆续批准建立了首批 14 个国家级经济技术开发区。

总体而言，经济特区的"特"可以概括为四个方面。第一，特区的经济发展，主要是依靠利用外资。第二，特区的经济活动，是在社会主义计划经济指导下，充分发挥市场调节的作用，或者说以市场调节为主。第三，对前来投资的客商，在税收、土地使用费、入境出境管理方面，给予特殊的优惠和方便，比如对外商投资的企业，企业所得税减按 15% 的税率征收。第四，国家给特区比较多的经济活动自主权，如重工业 5000 万元以下、轻工业 3000 万元以下，不需要国家平衡生产建设条件的建设项目，特区可以自行审批；基建指标可以在国家控制的指标之外另算；等等。

4.3　改革全面探索阶段(1984—1992 年)

这一阶段的改革主要是丰富所有制结构，尊重价值规律，进一步放权让利、激发市场活力，开始进行体制改革和运行机制改革以推动计划经济转向商品经济，为实行社会主义市场运行机制奠定体制基础。这一阶段改革的主要特征是以公有制为主体、多种所有制经济共同发展的格局进一步显露，国有经济实行承包经营责任制，我国现代化市场体系培育、宏观经济管理体制调整以及对外开放都获得了进一步发展。

4.3.1 发展有计划的商品经济和扩大改革开放

中共十一届三中全会后,中国经济体制改革首先在农村取得巨大成就。乡镇企业成为整个20世纪80年代中国经济发展最快的部分。与农村经济的迅速发展相比,中国政府自1978年来的重振国营企业的改革计划没有顺利实现。改革的初衷是给国营企业更多经营自主权,同时允许企业留有一部分收益自由支配,从而提高管理层和工人的积极性。但是企业本身必须同主管部门协商它们所得的权利,以及自己可以留下的利润。在讨价还价的过程中,政治和其他非经济因素往往会忽视经济规律,这导致很多高收益的企业将大部分收益交给了国家,而亏损的企业却持续接受政府的补贴。久而久之,效益好的企业的利润并不能继续增长,而效益差的企业也不会破产。此外,这些改革实行的是分权化的管理结构,导致地方政府会制造贸易壁垒以保护本地企业,以此换得自己控制企业运作的权力。从全国来看,地方保护主义几乎将经济运作推向了各自为战的封地经济。如果没有一个价格体系让所有企业都遵循同样的市场规范,国营企业改革将无法获得成功。

1984年10月,中共十二届三中全会讨论通过的《中共中央关于经济体制改革的决定》,深入阐述了加快以城市为重点的整个经济体制改革的必要性、紧迫性,规定了改革的方向、性质、任务和各项基本方针政策。该决定指出,改革计划体制,首先要突破把计划经济同商品经济对立起来的传统观念,明确认识社会主义计划经济必须自觉依据和运用价值规律,是在公有制基础上的有计划的商品经济。商品经济的充分发展,是社会经济发展的不可逾越的阶段,是实现中国经济现代化的必要条件。中共十二届三中全会标志着中国经济体制改革的重点由农村转向城市,改革进入全面探索时期。

到1987年中共十三大召开前后,城市经济体制改革和对外开放取得了明显进展,主要体现在六个方面。第一,在坚持公有制经济主体地位的前提下,调整所有制结构,形成了以公有制为主体,个体经济、私营经济、外资经济和其他经济为补充,多种经济成分共同发展的局面。第二,借鉴农村改革把生产资料所有权与经营管理权适当分离的成功经验,围绕增强企业活力这一经验,进一步扩大企业自主权。第三,逐步改革计划、财税、金融等政府宏观管理体制。第四,试行股份制改革。第五,改革流通体制,发展商品市场,改革不合理的价格体系。第六,改革工资和劳动制度。

经济体制改革的全面展开,使得中国经济出现了前所未有的活跃局面。1987年,中国国民生产总值达到10 920亿元,自1982年以来按可比价格计算平均每年增长11.1%;国民收入达到9 153亿元,自1982年以来按可比价格计算平均每年增长10.7%。中共十二大以后经过5年的发展,中国总体经济实力上了一个新的台阶。

4.3.2 改革开放在曲折中前进

到20世纪80年代末,中国改革开放和社会主义现代化建设加速发展,取得了显著成果,国家经济和科技实力得到显著增强。1987年,中国大陆人口超过10亿,绝大多数人过上了温饱生活,部分地区开始向小康生活迈进。然而,经过近10年的经济强劲增长后,随着改革开放的不断深入,经济发展中的一些深层次矛盾开始暴露,中国经济体制改革第一次面临危机和困难。

1984年中共十二届三中全会之后,经济体制改革在带来经济增长的同时,也埋下了通货膨胀的隐患。1984年货币供应增幅比1983年高出50%,比经济计划中设定的数额高出了45%。之后的1986年和1987年,通货膨胀率依旧居高不下,并且终于在1988年达到了两位数。产生通货膨胀的主要原因包括以下几点。第一,社会总需求远远超过社会总供给,国力和社会生产能力支撑不了庞大的建设规模和严重膨胀的社会消费需求。第二,产业比例失调,农业生产支撑不了过大的工业生产规模,能源、交通、原材料的供应能力无法支撑过大的加工工业规模。第三,生产、建设、流通领域中普遍存在着高消耗、低效益与高投入、低产出的现象。第四,工业生产与销售中的过程会牵扯到一长串的经济活动和众多企业的参与,使得政府对工业的管理和物价控制变得较为复杂,政策实行的效率也更低。

在此情况下,中国着手启动价格改革,期望帮助国营企业摆脱在价格双轨制下面临的困境。此前,中国已形成了一种"价格双轨制",即按计划指令生产的产品由国家定价,超计划增产的产品则按市场供求决定价格。这个过渡性的体制,在显著刺激增产的同时,也造成分配方面的混乱。1988年8月,中共中央政治局会议通过了《关于价格、工资改革的初步方案》,会议公报发表后,全国各地出现了居民抢购食品和生活用品、挤提存款的风潮,10天后,国务院宣布加强物价管理、不再出台物价调整项目、提升银行存款利息、全面整顿市场秩序。9月起,中国进入了为期3年的"治理整顿"期,主要任务是大幅度压缩需求,大刀阔斧地整顿流通领域,迅速抑制物价上涨。过旺的社会需求得到有效的控制,市场开始降温。但这也显著地对经济增长造成了负面影响,使这一时期经济改革面临巨大阻力。

4.4 初步建立社会主义市场经济体制阶段(1992—2000年)

在经济改革面临重重阻力的时刻,邓小平在1992年春天再次奋力推进中国改革。1992年邓小平视察中国南方,基本提出了建立社会主义市场经济体制的改革目标,并由此后的中共十四大确立。中国经济体制改革从此进入以制度创新为主要内容的新阶段。中共十四届三中全会通过的《中共中央关于建立社会主义市场经济体制若干问题的决定》指出,建立社会主义市场经济体制,就是要使市场在国家宏观调控下对资源配置起基础性作用,并勾画出社会主义市场经济体制的基本框架。1997年,中共十五大确立了公有制为主体、多种所有制经济共同发展的基本经济制度,实现了思想理论上的一系列新突破,推动以建立社会主义市场经济体制为目标的改革进一步向纵深发展。

4.4.1 改革开放的加速发展新阶段

20世纪90年代初,中国乃至世界都经历着重要社会与经济变动。彼时的世界经济形式出现重大转折,进入分化、改组时期。冷战结束后,以经济、科技为主的综合国力的竞争日益成为国际竞争的主要内容,经济代替军事成为世界各国交往和关注的重点,这是国际关系史的一个重大转折。此时中国也处于改革开放和现代化建设的关键时期。一方面,中共和中国政府成功抵制了国际上东欧剧变带来的压力,国内政局进一步稳定;而另一方面,改革开放中一些深层次矛盾和问题逐渐暴露,在对国内发展形势和东欧剧变的总结和反思中,出现了一些否定改革开放和"以经济建设为中心"的错误思潮,对中国改革和发展造成了困扰。

在改革开放事业可能面临最艰难挑战的关键时刻,邓小平视察南方,发表了重要的"南方谈话"。1992年1月18日至2月21日,邓小平视察了武昌、深圳、珠海、上海等地,沿途发表了重要讲话。通常人们把这些讲话称作"南方谈话"。"南方谈话"的思想精髓可以概括为如下几点:

第一,谈话指出,坚持中共十一届三中全会以来的路线,关键是坚持"一个中心、两个基本点"。不坚持社会主义,不改革开放,不发展经济,不改善人民生活,只能是死路一条。基本路线要管一百年,动摇不得。

第二,谈话把对社会主义的再认识问题加以集中提炼,突出了解放和发展生产力、走向共同富裕这两条。邓小平指出,革命是解放生产力,改革也是解放生产力。他指出,社会主义的本质,是解放生产力,发展生产力,消灭剥削,消除两极分化,最终达到共同富裕。

第三,明确提出社会主义本质、计划与市场关系、"三个有利于"标准、科技是第一生产力等理念,并最终得出"发展是硬道理"的结论。邓小平指出,要注意经济稳定、协调地发展,但稳定和协调也是相对的,不是绝对的。发展才是硬道理。经济发展得快一点,必须依靠科技和教育。科学技术是第一生产力。

第四,谈话强调抓住机遇,发展自己,切不可丧失机遇。邓小平指出,抓住时机,发展自己,关键是发展经济。要抓住机会,现在就是好机会。

第五,坚持社会主义必然代替资本主义基本观点。邓小平坚定不移地坚持社会主义必然代替资本主义观点。他强调,对社会主义的前途要充满信心,坚信社会主义必然代替资本主义。他提出"用一百年时间把我国建设成中等水平的发达国家"这一伟大战略目标,并指出实现这一目标需要埋头苦干。

从本质上来说,邓小平视察南方主要传达的信息就是鼓励进一步深化改革的第二次革命。随着邓小平南方谈话精神在全国的传播,消极对待改革甚至反对改革的思想开始消退,社会氛围再一次被改变。1992年也因此被称为"改革开放年"。

中共十四大于1992年10月12日召开,邓小平关于进一步深化改革的指示得到全面拥护。大会确立了邓小平建设有中国特色社会主义理论在全党的指导地位;明确中国经济体制改革的目标是建立社会主义市场经济体制;要求全党抓住机遇,加快发展,集中精力把经济建设搞上去。

此次会议第一次正式把建设社会主义市场经济体制确立为中国经济体制改革的目标。至此,人们对社会主义的认识就从传统的计划经济思想中彻底摆脱出来,市场经济开始与社会主义基本制度相结合,成为中国经济改革的基本目标。

4.4.2 社会主义市场经济体制的初步建立

中共十四大明确提出"中国经济体制改革的目标是建立社会主义市场经济体制",十四大后,党中央、国务院相继作出一系列重大部署,推动改革开放和现代化建设加速发展,并抓紧制定社会主义市场经济体制的总体规划。1993年11月,中共十四届三中全会通过的《中共中央关于建立社会主义市场经济体制若干问题的决定》把中共十四大提出的经济体制改革目标和原则加以具体化并进一步发展,勾画了社会主义市场经济体制的基本框架,成为20世纪90年代中国建立社会主义市场经济体制的行动纲领。

按照中共十四大和中共十四届三中全会的部署,1994年1月起,财税、金融、外汇、投资等方面以及住房和社会保障制度方面的改革全面展开,价格以及国有企业改革取得重要进展,使中国朝着社会主义市场经济体制的基本框架迈开了一大步。中共十五大以后,以国有企业改革为中心的各项改革进一步深化。到2000年底,中国社会主义市场经济体制初步建立。

具体而言,在价格改革方面,政府作出了一系列彻底解除价格管制的决定。涉及价格管理的原材料、生产资料及运输服务的项目由原来的737项削减至89项(到2001年被进一步削减至13项)。到1992年末,全国的粮食市场已完全放开。另外,国家计划委员会(于1998年更名为国家发展计划委员会,并于2003年改组为国家发展和改革委员会)将1993年的指令性生产计划减少了一半,大大增加了市场力量的发挥空间。1994年,价格管制大范围取消,对主要生产资料价格实行计划内外"并轨":统配煤价格全部放开,由市场进行调节;成品油、化肥也实现了价格"并轨";适度调整价格结构,大幅提高了原油的出厂价格和粮食购销价格;等等。绝大多数商品价格放开,市场调节的份额不断扩大,国家综合运用经济、法律手段和必要的行政手段加强宏观调控和市场管理。

在国有企业改革方面,通过建立现代企业制度,使企业成为独立的商品生产者和经营者全面参与市场竞争,成为真正的市场主体。中央和地方选择若干有代表性的国有企业进行了建立现代企业制度的试点,从战略上调整国有经济的布局,使国有资本逐渐集中到关系国民经济命脉的重要行业和关键领域。多种形式的国有资产监督管理体制的探索在一些地方积极展开,以适应国有企业改制和国有经济布局和结构调整的需要,并取得了良好效果。

在财税方面,建立了以增值税为主体的流转税体系,确立了以分税制为核心的新的财政体制框架。1993年12月,国务院发布《国务院关于实行分税制财政管理体制的决定》,决定从1994年1月1日起实行分税制改革和工商税制改革。分税制是指将国家的全部税种在中央和地方政府之间进行划分,借以确定中央财政和地方财政的收入范围的一种财政管理体制。新的分税制政策对消除之前存在的市场扭曲起到了关键作用,让企业不再受到财政政策对其直接而快速的过度影响,同时将微观经济环境从政府的宏观经济政策中分离了出来,为企业创造了一个富有竞争性的微观经济环境。

在金融、外汇外贸和投资等配套体系改革方面,强化了中央银行对货币供应的调控能力和金融监管方面的职能,开始分离政策性金融与商业性金融。中国建立了以市场供求为基础,单一的、有管理的浮动汇率制度,实现了人民币在经常项目下可兑换;国家计划管理从总体上的指令性计划向总体上的指导性计划转变;推行项目法人制、资本金制度和招投标制度,加强投资风险约束。

社会保障制度改革迈出了重要步伐,探索建立了多层次的社会保障制度。在试点的基础上,逐步建立起社会统筹和个人账户相结合的养老、医疗保险制度。适应深化企业改革的需要,建立了失业保险、社会救济制度及城镇居民最低生活保障制度。

此外,科技、教育、卫生体制改革取得重要进展。按照"稳住一头,放开一片"的方针,推进科技体制改革;以调整学校布局结构,改革高校招生和分配制度为重点,加快教育体制改革步伐;实行医疗机构分级分类管理制度,扩大卫生机构的经营管理自主权。与此同时,农村经济、对外贸易、城市住房等方面的改革,也取得了新的进展。经过全国人民共同努力,社会主义市场经济体制初步确立。

4.5 完善社会主义市场经济体制阶段(2000年至今)

从经济体制改革的进程看,到2000年,中国社会主义市场经济体制初步建立,至此中国进入以完善社会主义市场经济体制为基本任务的新阶段。

这一时期,在理论上进一步肯定了建立和完善社会主义市场经济体制的必要性。2002年召开的中共十六大提出,21世纪头20年改革的主要任务是完善社会主义市场经济体制,即在2020年建成完善的社会主义市场经济体制和更具活力、更加开放的经济体系。2003年中共十六届三中全会通过了《中共中央关于完善社会主义市场经济体制若干问题的决定》,对建立完善的市场经济体制进行了全面部署。此后围绕市场经济体制改革等问题形成了"科学发展观"重要思想。在科学发展观的指导下,提出了"五个统筹""构建社会主义和谐社会""社会主义新农村建设"等一系列新的发展理念,大大促进了改革实践的深化,为完善社会主义市场经济体制提供了理论指导。

中共十八大以来,在以习近平同志为核心的党中央领导下,中国在前30多年发展的基础上,又取得了全方位、开创性的成就,发生了深层次、根本性的变革。中共十九大报告指出,中国经济已由高速增长阶段转向高质量发展阶段,正处在转变发展方式、优化经济结构、转换增长动力的攻关期,建设现代化经济体系是跨越关口的迫切要求和中国发展的战略目标。这意味着新的经济发展阶段需要新的经济体系支撑和以新发展理念为指导的现代化经济体系。所谓现代化经济体系,就是具有现代性的经济系统,当今时代对现代性的要求是要与现代化进程中高质量发展阶段相适应,建设与高质量发展阶段相适应的现代化经济体系。

在这一阶段,对内改革的目标是深化国有企业改革,重塑政府与国有企业的关系,国有企业改革进入攻坚阶段。中共十六大首次提出"必须毫不动摇地巩固和发展公有制经济"和"必须毫不动摇地鼓励、支持和引导非公有制经济发展"的方针。中共十六届三中全会明确提出"大力发展国有资本、集体资本和非公有资本等参股的混合所有制经济,实现投资主体多元化,使股份制成为公有制的主要实现形式",以及"建立归属清晰、权责明确、保护严格、流转顺畅的现代产权制度",推动国有企业改革从承包制转向产权制。该轮国有企业改革的对象是不具备比较优势的国有中小企业,改革方式为企业产权制度改革和职工身份置换补偿,对中国经济产生了深远的影响。一方面国有中小企业在短期内大规模退出,促进了非公有制经济的发展,从根本上改变了国民经济的所有制结构;另一方面,国有大中型企业在国家支持下建立了现代企业制度,重新焕发经济活力。

对外开放的目标是加入WTO(World Trade Organization,世界贸易组织),开启全球市场。2001年,中国正式加入WTO,自此中国加入了庞大的世界贸易体系。图4-3即为中国正式加入WTO签字仪式的照片。加入WTO首先解决了美国给予中国最惠国待遇的问题,营造了良好的国际环境。在WTO框架下,国际粮食价格的长期低位运行,导致部分粮食国内外价格出现"倒挂"现象,对农业等弱势产业构成一定挑战,推动国内粮食收储制度改革,即从国家托市向"市场化收购"加"定向补贴"机制转变。同时,加入WTO意味着进一步参与国际经济合作和分工,国际资本大量流入,尤其是外国直接投资通过外溢效应与学习效应,使中国经济的技术水平、组织效率不断提高,进而提升全要素生产率。

图 4-3 2001 年,中国正式签署加入世界贸易组织的协议
图片来源:《中国日报》

与此同时,非公有制经济发展的体制环境进一步改善。非公有制经济的市场准入逐步放宽,非公有资本被允许进入法律法规未禁入的行业和领域;清理和修订限制非公有制经济发展的法规、规章和政策性规定,加强了对私有产权的依法保护,为非公有制经济发展提供制度保障。

此外,社会主义市场经济体制进一步完善,财税、金融、投资体制改革不断深化。公共财政体制不断健全,增值税转型试点和出口退税机制改革稳步推进;金融体制改革力度加大,国有商业银行股份制改革加快推进;汇率形成机制改革迈出重大步伐;政府投资的范围进一步缩小,企业投资自主权逐步扩大,投资审批制度不断规范。市场体系建设步伐进一步加快,商品市场的种类和数量逐年增加,土地、劳动力、技术、产权、资本等要素市场进一步发展,水、电、石油和天然气等重要资源价格的市场化步伐加快。

1978 年开启的波澜壮阔的改革开放事业,打破了传统计划经济体制,新型的社会主义市场经济体制的基础得到确立。经过对中国特色社会主义市场经济体制从目标到框架、从建设到完善的 40 多年的艰辛探索,中国成功走出了一条具有中国特色社会主义的渐进式改革发展之路,中国经济增长也取得了举世瞩目的伟大成就。2017 年以来,中国经济从高速增长转向高质量发展的新阶段,基于改革开放的经验,进一步完善社会主义市场经济体制和推进全面对外开放新格局,是推进中国转向高质量发展的必然选择。

5　改革开放以来中国的经济与社会发展

自1978年至今的40多年来,中国的经济发展取得累累硕果,可以称得上是经济发展的"奇迹"。这一经济奇迹体现在中国经济发展的规模和质量上。中国40多年来的经济发展不仅为中国社会带来巨大的变化,同时也对世界经济的增长和发展产生了深远影响。

中国改革开放的成就是全方位的,40多年来中国经济体制改革取得了重大的成就:经济发展实现飞跃,对外开放程度不断加深,综合国力显著增强;由落后失衡变为协调发展,经济结构不断优化;由温饱不足迈向全面小康,人民生活实现历史性跨越。这并非意味着中国已经找到一条完整的经济发展新道路。中国需要正确对待自身在改革开放40多年中所取得的成就,并在新时代加快经济发展转型升级,从而为世界经济可持续发展作出更大贡献。

5.1　改革开放以来中国的经济发展成就

改革开放40多年来,中国实现了世界罕见的持续高速的经济增长。中国经济发展水平显著提高,经济发展质量不断提升,综合国力日益增强,取得了社会主义经济建设的辉煌成就。

第一,中国经济实力大幅跃升,中国从"一穷二白"发展成为世界第二大经济体。近代以来,中国经济发展长期落后于世界,中国共产党自建党之日起,就自觉肩负起强国富民的历史使命。新中国成立初期,中国民生凋敝、百废待兴,中国共产党领导全国人民用3年时间实现了国民经济的全面恢复,为开始进行大规模的经济建设创造了前提条件。改革开放后,中国经济发展驶入快车道,1986年经济总量突破1万亿元,2000年跨越10万亿元大关,超过意大利成为世界第六大经济体。2001年加入WTO后,中国经济开始融入全球发展大潮,并进入新一轮快速发展期,到2010年中国经济总量超过日本,跃升至世界第二大经济体。2020年,尽管遭遇百年不遇的新冠肺炎疫情冲击,中国国内生产总值仍然可观,高达101.4万亿元,首次突破100万亿元大关(见图5-1)。中共十八大以来,中国经济持续较快发展,经济增速大大高于世界平均水平。2013—2021年,中国经济年均增长6.6%,大大高于2.6%的同期世界平均增速,也高于3.7%的发展中经济体平均增速,经济增长率居世界主要经济体前列。根据中国国家统计局数据,2013—2021年,中国对世界经济增长的平均贡献率达38.6%,超过七国集团(G7)国家贡献率的总和,成为拉动世界经济增长的重要引擎。中国创造了世界罕见的经济快速发展奇迹。

第二,经济发展质量不断提升,从要素驱动型粗放增长向创新驱动型集约发展转变。改

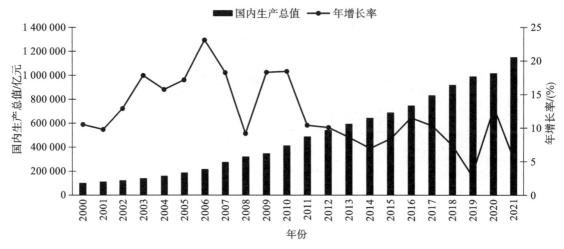

图 5-1 2000—2021 年中国国内生产总值变化情况

数据来源：中华人民共和国国家统计局

革开放以来，依靠资本、劳动力和土地等优势，中国经济实现了高速增长。但随着人口红利逐渐消失、投资效应减弱和土地约束增强，依靠要素扩张的粗放型经济发展模式难以为继。中共十八大作出"实施创新驱动发展战略"的重大部署，经济增长动力加速从"要素驱动"向"创新驱动"转变。中国坚持以推动高质量发展为主题，把实施扩大内需战略同深化供给侧结构性改革有机结合起来，增强国内大循环内生动力和可靠性，提升国际循环质量和水平，加快建设现代化经济体系，着力提高全要素生产率，着力提升产业链供应链韧性和安全水平，着力推进城乡融合和区域协调发展，推动经济实现质的有效提升和量的合理增长。

第三，统一开放、竞争有序的现代市场体系初步形成，市场机制对资源配置的基础性作用显著增强。多层次、多门类、多形式的商品市场格局已经形成，以连锁经营、物流配送、电子商务为代表的现代流通方式发展迅速。资本、土地、劳动力等要素市场化程度明显提高，股票、债券等多层次资本市场体系不断发展，劳动者自主择业、市场调节就业的体制已经建立，土地使用权有偿转让市场迅速发展，知识产权交易规模迅速扩大。根据 2020 年颁布的新版《中央定价目录》，中国商品价格基本上由市场决定，中国已形成以市场调节为主的价格机制，市场调节价的比重超过 97%。

第四，市场主体培育成效明显。改革开放以前，在计划经济体制下，国有经济一统天下，不允许非公有制经济的发展。这一时期，市场主体单一，国有经济经营范围涉及生产、生活的方方面面。改革开放以来，中国非公有制经济是与市场经济体制改革同步产生和发展起来的。伴随着经济体制改革的深化，尤其是所有制结构的调整和国有企业战略性调整，中国个体、私营等非公有制经济经历了一个从无到有、从小到大的发展过程，非公有制企业在数量上、规模上、进入领域以及自身竞争力等方面都获得了较大的发展，成为国民经济发展最主要的推动力量。非公有制经济在稳定增长、促进创新、增加就业、改善民生的过程中发挥基础性作用，从在国民经济中的地位来看，其贡献了 50% 以上的税收、60% 以上的国内生产总值、70% 以上的技术创新、80% 以上的城镇就业岗位、90% 以上的市场主体数量。由此不难看出，非公有制经济是实现可持续发展、增强国际竞争力的基本力量。

第五，中国对外开放水平逐步提高，外向型经济不断发展，实现了从封闭半封闭到全方位开放的历史性转折。伴随着中国经济体制改革的深化,中国实现了国内外市场的衔接,推进了外向型经济的发展,加快了中国参与经济全球化的进程,对外贸易规模不断扩大,吸收外商投资稳步增长,对外经济合作保持了良好的发展趋势。改革开放后,尤其是2001年加入WTO后,中国对外贸易迅速发展,中国在2009年成为全球货物贸易第一大出口国和第二大进口国,2013年超越美国成为全球货物贸易第一大国。同时中国对外投资合作快速发展,全球资源配置能力显著增强。2002年,中共十六大明确提出"走出去"战略,中国对外直接投资进入了快速发展阶段。中共十八大以来,中国实施了新一轮全方位对外开放战略,大力推进"一带一路"建设,对外直接投资存量屡创历史新高。根据联合国贸发会议发布的《2020年世界投资报告》,2019年中国对外直接投资流量和存量分别居于全球第二位和第三位。不仅如此,自2016年10月1日起,人民币正式被纳入国际货币基金组织(International Monetary Fund,IMF)特别提款权(special drawing rights,SDR)货币篮子,从而获得国际主要货币的地位。随着中国经济实力的逐步增强,以及中国在全球市场中话语权的不断提高,中国的进出口贸易、对外投资将对全球贸易的增长产生越来越大的影响,并日益成为全球经济再平衡的重要力量。

5.2 经济结构调整与增长方式转变

经济结构是在时间和空间里反映一个经济整体的特性的那些比例和关系。一个或几个新的生产部门迅速增长是经济结构转变的强有力的核心引擎,因为这些具有新的生产函数的生产部门会发出各种扩散效应,从而使经济增长产生飞跃。在此过程中,当旧的生产部门减退时,新的生产部门便会诞生。经济结构与经济增长互为因果,相互影响且紧密联系,经济结构的不同形态反映了经济增长的不同模式,而经济增长模式的转型很大程度上是由经济结构调整所决定的。

从总体发展情况来看,当前中国产业结构持续优化升级,三次产业发展更为协调。旧中国是一个落后的农业国,不仅工业基础十分薄弱,而且主要以轻工业为主。1952年,中国基本完成国民经济的恢复任务时,第一产业增加值占国内生产总值的比重仍高达50.5%,第二、三产业增加值占国内生产总值的比重分别仅为20.8%和28.7%。改革开放以来,社会主义市场经济体制逐步建立,产业结构调整持续深入,农业基础巩固加强,工业和服务业发展水平不断提高。2011年,第三产业就业比重提高到35.7%,首次超过第一产业,成为吸纳就业最多的产业。2012年,第三产业增加值比重达到45.5%,首次超过第二产业,成为拉动国民经济增长的第一大产业。中共十八大以来,中国加快推进经济结构调整和转型升级,供给侧结构性改革不断深化,农业现代化水平稳步提高,工业体系更加齐全。2019年,中国成为世界上唯一拥有联合国产业分类目录中所有工业门类的国家,服务业发展方兴未艾,三次产业发展更为协调。2020年,第一、二、三产业增加值比重分别为7.7%、37.8%、54.5%。第一产业、第二产业、第三产业的结构日趋合理化,第三产业逐渐占据主导地位。

1949年以来,中国的经济结构发生了两次重要升级,第一次是农业经济向工业经济的结构性转型升级,第二次是工业经济向服务业经济的结构性转型升级。第一次经济结构转型升级的显著特征是农业所占比重下降,工业和服务业所占比重提升,工业逐渐成为经济的主导产业。这一阶段的主要特征为经济的增长与结构的高速变动相互影响、相互促进。工业化转型进程中的经济处于快速增长阶段,经济增长不仅表现为劳动力和资本等生产要素的投入增长效应,而且表现为需求结构与供给结构变动的增长效应。自"一五"计划开始,中国在高度集中的计划经济条件下推进工业化建设,在发展战略上实行优先发展重工业的方针。这一工业化道路在较短时间内改变了中国的落后面貌,实现了工业化水平的快速提升。1978年,中国三次产业的占比结构已经转变为27.7%、47.7%和24.6%。经过1949年以来70多年的工业化建设,中国已经基本形成结构合理、门类齐全的现代化工业体系。在工业化进程方面,中国的工业化水平已经进入到工业化后期,中国的工业化水平综合指数在2015年为84,2020年为93。也就是说,中国已基本完成工业化进程,依赖工业转型释放"工业化红利"促进经济增长的发展方式将难以维系。一旦步入后工业化时代,技术进步便成为劳动生产率和全要素生产率提升的主要形式,因为技术引进和吸收所带来的"技术红利"的边际效应在不断递减。

第二次经济结构转型升级的特征是农业和工业的比重均下降,服务业的比重持续上升,成为经济的主导产业。从动力转换视角看,随着"人口红利"的消失和投资回报率的下降,经济增长的动力更多地依靠技术创新,通过提升全要素生产率来促进经济增长,到了这个阶段中国产业急需实现从资本要素驱动主导转向知识要素驱动主导。从国际经验看,高速增长经济体在进入中高收入阶段后,都经历过经济明显减速和"换挡"的过程。而中国在经历一个时期高速增长后,经济发展也会出现新的阶段性特征,从高速增长进入中高速增长新常态。中国经济自2009年起进行了结构性减速,从工业化进程看,中国经济在这个阶段所呈现出的运行特征以及所面临的升级任务都与进入工业化后期是一致的,实际上中国工业化进程也正是在2011年前后进入工业化后期的。

经济新常态背景下,中国产业成长的重点从追求快速成长转向追求质量提升,这具体表现为通过供给侧结构性改革提高实体经济供给质量,积极顺应新一轮科技革命和产业变化趋势,大力培育新兴产业和利用新技术改造传统产业等方面。第一,从农业发展看,农业生产布局进一步优化,现代农业产业体系、生产体系和经营体系加快构建,粮食主产区稳产增产,新型农业生产经营主体和服务主体快速涌现。第二,从工业发展看,工业结构持续优化升级,工业结构总体呈现从资源和资金密集主导向技术密集主导转型升级的趋势。在制造业内部结构方面,供给侧结构性改革取得积极进展,一方面,积极淘汰落后产能工作全面深入推进,另一方面,装备制造业和高技术制造业发展迅速。第三,从服务业发展看,传统服务业与互联网融合加速,现代服务业蓬勃发展,新业态不断涌现,服务业发展迅速。

虽然这个阶段中国产业发展取得了上述成就,但如前所述,中国经济发展已进入全新的阶段,既是经济新常态,又是工业化后期。在当前发展方式转型和新旧动能转换的关键阶段,中国在经济发展的过程中仍面临供给侧产业结构不合理、创新能力不足和需求侧消费需求乏力、投资动力不足、对外贸易形势严峻等发展阶段性新特征。转变经济发展方式,是适应发展阶段演替的基本规律,是促进经济可持续发展的长效机制。通过为传统产业注入新活力,为经济增长注入新动能,促进全要素生产率提高,释放未来经济增长潜能,拓展经济发展空间。

5.3 改革开放以来的中国社会发展

经济发展并不仅仅包括经济增长的指标,还需要从社会福利的角度看待中国的经济发展问题。中国式现代化走的正是一条生产发展、生活富裕、生态良好的文明发展道路。

第一,人民生活水平和质量大幅提高,实现了从温饱不足到全面小康的历史性跨越。中国共产党诞生时,中国积贫积弱,人民贫困如洗。新中国成立后,面对战争留下的满目疮痍,中国共产党带领全国人民迅速恢复生产。改革开放以来,经过 40 多年经济体制改革,中国社会经济得到了快速、稳定的发展,广大群众收入不断增加,人民生活水平获得较大提高。从人均国内生产总值水平的角度看,1978 年中国人均国内生产总值为 385 元,是当时世界上典型的低收入国家;而 2021 年,中国人均国内生产总值已经高达 8.1 万元(超过 11 000 美元),已经跻身中等偏上收入国家行列。随着经济的不断增长,中国居民人均可支配收入不断上升,由 1978 年的人均 171 元,增加到 2020 年的 32 189 元。城镇居民人均可支配收入增长的幅度更大,从 1978 年的 343 元增加到 2020 年的 43 834 元。

第二,收入的提高带动消费的进一步增长。居民消费水平不断提高,人民生活品质得到极大改善。新中国成立前,中国长期处于战乱和社会动荡之中,人民流离失所,基本温饱都难以实现。新中国成立后,伴随着经济的快速发展,中国居民收入水平稳步提高,居民消费能力不断提升。改革开放后,中国居民消费水平得到进一步的提升,消费规模持续扩大,消费对经济发展的基础性作用不断增强,中国已经是全球第二大消费市场,最终消费支出自 2013 年后连续 6 年成为拉动中国经济增长的首要动力。2020 年,最终消费支出达到 55.8 万亿元,其中全国居民消费支出为 38.4 万亿元。与此同时,中国居民消费结构也在不断升级。从居民食物消费占总消费的比重来看,恩格尔系数不断下降。1978—1992 年的部分年份,中国城镇居民恩格尔系数在 50% 以上,农村居民恩格尔系数在 54% 以上,到了 2020 年,城镇居民恩格尔系数下降到 29.2%,农村居民恩格尔系数下降到 32.7%(见表 5-1)。

表 5-1　1978—2020 年部分年份中国城镇及农村居民人均可支配收入及恩格尔系数

年份	城镇居民人均可支配收入/元	农村居民人均可支配收入/元	城镇居民恩格尔系数/(%)	农村居民恩格尔系数/(%)
1978	343	134	57.5	67.7
1985	739	398	53.3	57.8
1989	1 374	602	54.5	54.8
1992	2 027	784	52.9	57.5
1995	4 283	1 578	49.9	58.6
1998	5 418	2 171	44.2	53.2
2001	6 824	2 407	37.0	46.7
2004	9 335	3 027	35.8	45.3
2014	28 844	10 489	30.0	33.6
2015	31 195	11 422	29.7	33.0

续表

年份	城镇居民人均可支配收入/元	农村居民人均可支配收入/元	城镇居民恩格尔系数/(%)	农村居民恩格尔系数/(%)
2016	33 616	12 363	29.3	32.2
2017	36 396	13 432	28.6	31.2
2018	39 251	14 617	27.7	30.1
2019	42 359	16 021	27.6	30.0
2020	43 834	17 131	29.2	32.7

数据来源：中华人民共和国国家统计局

第三，城乡居民收入差距明显缩小，脱贫攻坚取得重大成就。新中国成立以来，中国共产党带领人民持续向贫困宣战。经过改革开放以来的努力，中国成功走出了一条中国特色扶贫开发道路，使7亿多农村贫困人口成功脱贫，为全面建成小康社会打下了坚实基础。英国学者阿塔尔·侯赛因曾指出，中国农村上亿人摆脱贫困，实现粮食自给自足，这是人类发展史上一个了不起的事情，也是改善人权的巨大成就。脱贫攻坚从2015年开始，中共中央政治局审议通过《关于打赢脱贫攻坚战的决定》。从中共十八大以来，乡村振兴、精准脱贫政策陆续出台，农村居民人均可支配收入实际增速连续多年快于城镇居民，贫困人口脱贫步伐明显加快。2020年11月23日，贵州宣布最后9个深度贫困县退出贫困县序列。这不仅标志着贵州省66个贫困县实现整体脱贫，也标志着中国脱贫攻坚战取得了全面胜利，现行标准下9 899万农村贫困人口全部脱贫，832个贫困县全部摘帽，12.8万个贫困村全部出列，区域性整体贫困得到解决，完成了消除绝对贫困的艰巨任务，创造了又一个彪炳史册的人间奇迹。

第四，就业质量显著提升。2020年全年城镇新增就业1 186万人，全年年均城镇调查失业率为5.6%，就业结构持续优化。教育事业蓬勃发展，根据2021年全国教育事业统计主要结果，中国劳动年龄人口平均受教育年限达到10.9年，从人力资源大国向人力资源强国迈进。

第五，城乡基本医疗公共服务均等化水平不断提高，中国人均预期寿命居于中高收入国家前列，全民健身公共服务体系基本建立。社会保障惠及全民，中国已建成世界上规模最大的社会保障体系，"十三五"规划期间，基本医疗保险覆盖超过13亿人，基本养老保险覆盖近10亿人。

第六，科技事业不断取得重大成果。中国科技事业发生了历史性、整体性、格局性变化，"天问一号"火星探测器、"深海勇士"号等载人深潜器成功研制、量子科技计算能力不断突破……基础研究和战略高技术领域的世界级科技成果不断涌现，创新能力持续提升，科技创新成为支撑引领经济高质量发展和民生改善名副其实的第一动力。改革开放以来，中国不断加大科技投入，逐步加大科技体制改革力度。2020年，全社会研发经费支出达到2.44万亿元，占国内生产总值的比重达到2.4%；世界知识产权组织数据显示，中国全球创新指数排名世界第14位，创新型国家建设取得决定性成就。近年来中国载人航天、探月工程、量子科学、深海探测、超级计算、卫星导航等领域取得了重大成就，高铁、5G移动通信、新能源等高新技术产业进入了世界前列。

第七，文化事业得到长足发展。改革开放40多年，在中共中央的坚强领导下，各地区各部门坚持社会主义先进文化前进方向,深化文化体制改革,建立健全现代文化市场体系,构建完善公共文化服务体系,文化产业快速发展,文化事业普惠民生,文化强国建设稳步推进,文化改革发展取得令人瞩目的成就。基层公共文化设施不断完善,文化投资布局更趋合理,文化产业增加值占国内生产总值比重逐年提高,居民文化消费水平持续提升,对外文化贸易增长强劲,国际文化影响力日益增强。中共十八大以来,中国现代公共文化服务体系建设迈入快车道,标准化、均等化特征不断凸显。据中国国家统计局发布数据,截至2021年底,全国广播节目综合人口覆盖率为99.5%,电视节目综合人口覆盖率为99.7%;全国共有公共图书馆3 217个、文化馆3 317个、博物馆3 671个,其中90%以上的博物馆已经实行了免费开放,实现了"无障碍、零门槛"。

5.4 改革开放以来中国经济社会发展的主要经验与启示

总结40多年经济体制改革的经验,归纳出创造"中国奇迹"的关键要素,对更好地推进经济体制改革,推动国民经济又好又快发展具有重要的意义。中国的改革开放是史无前例的,中国政府大胆探索,稳步推进,不仅实现了经济体制上的重大转变和经济社会的巨大发展,而且形成了关于社会主义市场经济的丰富认识,积累了建设社会主义市场经济的一些重要的经验。主要有:

第一,坚持改革开放的基本国策。首先,改革开放是经济体制改革的强大动力。在建立和完善市场经济体制过程中遇到的矛盾和问题,无论是解决发展问题还是体制问题都是依靠深化改革来提供强大动力的。其次,对外开放为中国经济体制的建立提供了外在推动力。高度发达的国际市场经济关系和激烈的国际市场竞争成为国内改革经济体制、强化竞争机制的外在推动力,推动了中国市场经济的发展;开放型经济同国际市场接轨后,为各类市场的培育和完善提供国际标准,为国内加快建立相应的各类市场提供外部推力。此外,对外开放开拓了国际市场,为引进外资、学习先进的技术和管理经验提供了平台,为进一步深化经济体制改革奠定了基础。

第二,坚持以经济建设为中心的基本方针。改革开放40多年来,中国一直坚持以经济建设为中心的基本方针,这为市场经济体制的建立奠定了基础。首先,坚持以经济建设为中心为经济体制改革的实施提供了思想认识基础。坚持以经济建设为中心要求必须对束缚生产力发展的落后的生产关系进行改革,不断解放和发展生产力,这就要求必须对落后的经济体制进行改革,使其适应生产力的发展。其次,坚持以经济建设为中心为经济体制改革的实施提供了环境基础。以经济建设为中心要求政府为经济改革和发展提供全方位的服务,要求政府不断探索经济改革和发展的新路子和新模式,这些都为经济体制改革提供了良好的环境。

第三,不断创新改革理论,以科学的理论指导改革实践。改革首先是对传统理论和思想观念的革命,必须通过理论创新解放人们的思想,统一人们的认识,为改革开放的实践提供思想保证。改革实践证明,每一次重要的改革实践行动,都以思想理论的不断发展和革新为先导。思想理论的每一次革新,都带来了改革实践的突破性进展。没有正确的改革理论,就不可能有成功的改革实践。

第四,先易后难、循序渐进,实行重点突破与整体推进的有机结合。改革的复杂性及在中国改革的特殊困难性,使政府采取了从实际出发、先易后难、由浅入深、循序渐进的渐进式总体改革战略,抓住一些关键的环节进行重点突破,以此来带动全面改革。循序渐进的改革战略和整体推进、重点突破的改革方式,既使改革保持了必要的力度、速度和连续性,又使改革逐步适应社会承受能力,避免了大的社会动荡的发生。概括来讲,中国渐进式改革的特点是最小化政策贯彻执行的成本,而不是最大限度地提高经济效率,以最小化市场经济改革的政治阻力,逐步适应不断变化的经济环境,采取由易到难的改革顺序以试点方式逐步推动改革。

第五,坚持改革、发展与稳定相结合的原则。在改革初始,中国就确定了改革是动力、发展是目的、稳定是前提的基本原则。在改革过程中始终坚持把改革的力度、发展的速度和社会可承受的程度统一起来,把不断改善人民生活作为处理改革发展稳定关系的重要结合点,在社会稳定中推进改革发展,通过改革发展促进社会稳定。中国成功改革的实践印证了坚持改革、发展与稳定相结合原则的重要性,三者相辅相成,共同促进中国经济体制改革的实施。

除此之外,中国政府在经济体制改革中还采取了其他一些有效方式,如充分尊重人民群众的首创精神,始终维护人民群众利益;把握社会经济环境和条件的变化,灵活调整改革措施;在积极扬弃、科学对待原体制基础之上,着力增进新体制的优势;注意把经济体制改革与政治、科技、教育、文化等方面的体制改革结合起来,实现经济体制改革的实质性突破;在着力抓好某些新的单项改革时,注意经济体制改革的整体配套与协调性;等等。

6 中国的对外开放与国际贸易

对外开放思想是邓小平理论的重要组成部分。对外开放是中国在经济全球化背景下的历史选择,是生产社会化、经济生活国际化的客观要求,是国际生产分工、国际市场经济发展的必然结果。随着越来越多的国家参与国际分工,融入世界经济体系,世界经济逐渐一体化,各国之间的相互依赖程度越来越高。在经济全球化背景下,任何国家都不可能依靠自身的生产要素满足本国经济发展的全部需求,必须积极参与国际分工和贸易才能满足本国的经济发展。

中国对外开放之初,生产力水平低,资金严重短缺。现代化建设要求对国民经济进行技术改造升级,实现这一改造需要大量的资金,仅依靠国内资金积累和投资是远远不够的。中国必须对外开放,积极引进外资,利用外资弥补资本要素缺口。纵观历史,经济技术落后的国家能够在较短的时间内迅速赶上甚至超过发达国家,无一不是积极引进国外先进技术,同时敢于创新和善于创新的结果。对外开放可以更好地借鉴和学习国外先进的管理经验,借鉴和引进国外先进的经济管理方法和经营方式也是对外开放的一项重要内容。

市场经济是一种开放型经济,与封闭型经济是相对立的,如果要享受到国际协作带来的好处,就必须参与国际交换和合作。在建设社会主义市场经济的同时,中国也要面向世界,对外开放,发展对外经济贸易关系,使自身成为世界市场经济体系的重要组成部分。实行对外开放,通过国际市场充分利用国内外的资源要素,是市场经济作为资源配置方式的内在的本质要求,也是建立社会主义市场经济的必然选择。

6.1 对外开放政策的基本内涵

6.1.1 对外开放的含义

"对外开放"是中国的一项基本国策。对外开放有两方面的含义,一方面是指中国主动地扩大同其他国家和地区的经济往来,另一方面是指中国内部要放宽政策,放开限制,不再采取封锁国内市场的保护政策,而是发展开放型经济。中国对外开放是在坚持社会主义制度的基础上,根据独立自主、平等互利的原则,按照生产国际化、资本国际化、国际分工进一步深化和社会主义市场经济发展的客观要求,积极发展与世界各国或地区的经济贸易关系,以及科学、技术、文化、教育等方面的合作与交流,以促进社会主义物质文明和精神文明的发展。中国的对外开放是全方位的,是向全世界开放的,是在平等互利原则上同世界各国和地区在贸易、技术、经济、科学等领域的全面合作。

6.1.2 对外开放的内容

在过去40多年里,中国对外开放的相关政策形形色色,涉及方方面面。对外开放的内容也一直呈现动态变化。目前中国对外开放的主要内容可以概括为下述的六个方面。

第一,推动体制机制改革,支持对外开放。推动对外开放离不开完善的制度保障。对外开放涉及的体制改革涵盖农村经济、金融体制、所有制结构和外贸体制等领域。体制机制的改革将使制度更为有效,降低交易成本,深化对外开放,有助于形成统一的市场。

第二,积极引进先进技术和设备,特别是有助于企业技术改造的先进技术。吸引先进的科学技术是中国对外开放的初衷之一,也是助推经济快速增长的关键因素。

第三,由点到面实行全方位开放。中国遵循着"摸着石头过河"的理念,对内"先行先试",总结相关经验再逐步推广至全域,以充分拓展国内和国外市场。中国从设立经济特区,到开放沿海城市、沿边城市、沿江城市、省会城市,设立经济技术开发区、高新技术产业开发区、保税区等,由点到面,靠先行沿海开放城市和区域的发展带动内地的开放,实现了中国的广度和深度开放。

第四,积极参与区域贸易和金融合作。在国际舞台上,中国的对外开放主要体现在三个方面:一是积极参与亚太区域合作;二是建立中国—东盟自由贸易区;三是积极推进"一带一路"建设。

第五,大力发展对外贸易。对外贸易就是国家或地区之间的商品和服务的交换活动。自1978年实行对外开放以来,对外贸易就一直在中国国民经济中处于重要的战略地位,是其他开放形式的基础,是开展对外经济交流的中心环节。对外贸易对中国国民经济的作用表现为:弥补国内资源短缺,优化资源配置;利用国际分工,获取相对利益;增加外汇收入,提高国内居民收入,增加就业机会。

第六,坚持对外开放,稳步推进人民币国际化。中国在1996年实现了经常项目下的人民币可兑换,在2014年正式开始人民币国际化项目,逐步放开资本项目的可兑换程度。随着人民币在2016年正式被纳入国际货币基金组织的特别提款权货币篮子,并且权重越来越重,人民币在成为国际货币的道路上迈上了新的台阶。

6.1.3 对外开放的原则

6.1.3.1 独立自主、自力更生

中国实行对外开放,发展对外经济关系,始终坚持的原则是独立自主、自力更生。独立自主并不是闭关自守,自力更生也不是盲目排外。科学技术是人类共同创造的财富,在自力更生的基础上,大胆地实行对外开放,放手利用国外一切可以为中国所用的先进科学技术,迅速地提高中国的科学技术水平,对加速中国现代化建设是必不可少的。正如邓小平所说:"技术问题是科学,生产管理是科学,在任何社会,对任何国家都是有用的。我们学习先进的技术、先进的科学、先进的管理来为社会主义服务,而这些东西本身并没有阶级性。"自力更生为主,争取外援为辅,是中国实现对外开放坚定不移的方针。

6.1.3.2 平等互利

平等互利原则的含义是:所谓平等,即国家不分大小强弱,不论政治制度和经济发展水平如何,在贸易关系中都应当尊重对方的主权和愿望,不应当要求任何特权;所谓互利,即在

贸易中,要根据双方的需要和可能,互通有无,以促进彼此的经济发展,不能把对外贸易作为控制和掠夺别国的工具。

6.2 中国对外开放的进程

根据邓小平对外开放思想,中共中央和国务院确定了分地区、分阶段、分层次的对外开放战略。纵观中国改革开放40多年历史,中国对外开放可以分为四个阶段。

6.2.1 广度开放阶段(1978—1992年)

在对外开放初期,中共中央和国务院就确定了"重点开放沿海地区,逐步向内地开放"的经济发展战略。按照此战略,中国对外开放的层次可以分为经济特区,沿海港口城市,沿海经济开放区,沿江、内陆和沿边城市四个层次。

6.2.1.1 创办经济特区

创办经济特区是中国对外开放的突破口和开创性举措。创办经济特区作为中国对外开放的先行试点,为中国对外开放探明道路,为更全面、更深入的开放做准备。1980年5月,中共中央确定在深圳市、珠海市、汕头市、厦门市各划出一定范围的区域,试办经济特区。1983年4月,中共中央、国务院批转了《关于加快海南岛开发建设问题讨论纪要》,决定对海南岛也实行经济特区的优惠政策。1988年4月召开的第七届全国人民代表大会第一次会议正式通过了建立海南省和海南经济特区两项决定,海南岛成为中国最大的经济特区。创办经济特区迈出了中国对外开放的第一步。邓小平指出:"特区是个窗口,是技术的窗口,管理的窗口,知识的窗口,也是对外政策的窗口。"

6.2.1.2 开放沿海港口城市

开放沿海港口城市是中国对外开放的第二步。1984年5月,中共中央、国务院批转了《沿海部分城市座谈会纪要》,决定进一步开放中国沿海港口城市。从北到南,包括大连、秦皇岛、天津、烟台、青岛、连云港、南通、上海、宁波、温州、福州、广州、湛江和北海共14个沿海港口城市。

6.2.1.3 建立沿海经济开放区

1985年2月,中共中央、国务院批转了《长江、珠江三角洲和闽南厦漳泉三角地区座谈会纪要》,将长江三角洲、珠江三角洲和闽南厦漳泉三角地区划为沿海经济开放区,并指出这是中国实施对内搞活经济、对外实行开放的具有重要战略意义的布局。1988年初,中共中央又决定将辽东半岛和山东半岛全部对外开放,同已经开放的大连、秦皇岛、天津、烟台、青岛等连成一片,形成环渤海开放区。中共中央还提出在这些经济开放区形成贸—工—农型的生产结构。

6.2.1.4 逐步开放沿江、内陆和沿边城市

进入20世纪90年代以后,中国对外开放的步伐逐步由沿海向沿江、内陆和沿边城市延伸。1992年6月,中共中央、国务院决定开放长江沿岸的芜湖、九江、岳阳、武汉和重庆5个城市。沿江开放对于带动整个长江流域地区经济的迅速发展,对于中国全方位对外开放新格局的形成起了巨大推动作用。不久,中共中央、国务院又批准了共17个省会为内陆开放

城市。同时,中国还逐步开放一大批内陆边境的沿边城市。沿江、内陆和沿边城市的开放,是中国的对外开放迈出的第四步。

到1992年,经过多年的对外开放的实践,不断总结经验和完善政策,中国的对外开放由南到北、由东到西层层推进,基本上形成了"经济特区—沿海开放城市—沿海经济开放区—沿江、内陆和沿边开放城市"的对外开放格局。至此,中国的对外开放逐渐跨入深度开放阶段。

6.2.2 深度开放阶段(1992—2001年)

在邓小平南方谈话和中共十四大确立社会主义市场经济体制改革目标的背景下,改革开放全面深化,中国的对外开放程度不断提高,外向型经济对国民经济的影响日益呈现,对外开放在全国范围内展开,基本形成了全方位开放格局。中国对外开放进程如表6-1所示。同时,中国积极同国际接轨,积极深化国内贸易体制改革和对外贸易体制改革,加速国内市场和相关产业开放。保税区、出口加工区等海关特殊监管区域先后创立。整个20世纪90年代,中国抓住了国际产业特别是信息技术产业结构调整的机会,以开发浦东为新举措,大力引进海外直接投资,积极参与全球产业链重构,推进国内产业结构升级。

表6-1 中国对外开放进程

开放层次	开放时间	地域范围
经济特区	1980年 1988年	深圳、珠海、厦门、汕头 海南省
沿海港口开放城市	1984年	大连、秦皇岛、天津、烟台、青岛、连云港、南通、上海、宁波、温州、福州、广州、湛江、北海
沿海经济开放区	1985年 1988年	长江三角洲、珠江三角洲、闽南厦漳泉三角地区 山东半岛、辽东半岛
经济技术开发区	1990年	上海浦东
陆地边境市、镇	1992年	珲春、绥芬河、满洲里、黑河、二连浩特、伊宁、塔城、博乐、瑞丽、畹町、河口、凭祥、东兴
沿江开放城市	1992年	重庆、岳阳、武汉、九江、芜湖等沿长江港口城市
内陆省会城市	1992年	太原、合肥、南昌、郑州、长沙、成都、贵阳、西安、兰州、西宁、银川、昆明、乌鲁木齐、南宁、哈尔滨、长春、呼和浩特、石家庄
进一步扩大西部地区的对外开放	1999年	四川、贵州、云南、西藏、陕西、甘肃、宁夏、青海、新疆、内蒙古、广西、重庆

6.2.3 全方位开放阶段(2001—2012年)

2001年,中国正式加入WTO,这标志着中国对外开放进入一个崭新的阶段。此后,中国充分利用WTO框架下完备的法律规则和开放的市场体系,大力推动对外经济体制改革,形成了与国际惯例并轨的对外经济体制,为中国成为世界制造业大国和全球第二大经济体奠定了基础。

在世界经济一体化趋势越来越明显的背景下,不仅中国的市场将向全面开放的方向发展,使国际资本和商品更大范围地进入中国市场,而且中国的资本也将以更快的速度进入国际市场,中国将有更多的企业从事跨国生产和经营,"引进来"和"走出去"将成为中国对外开放的两个轮子,有力地推动中国对外开放向纵深发展。

6.2.4 全面开放新格局的形成(2012年至今)

中共十八大开启了中国对外开放新的历史阶段。结合国内经济转型、体制升级的需要,一系列重大经济外交和国际合作战略思想被先后提出,中国的开放型经济建设进入新的阶段,新布局初步形成,新体制不断完善。2017年,中共十九大报告明确指出"中国特色社会主义进入新时代",明确"推动形成全面开放新格局",再次强调"中国开放的大门不会关闭",标志着中国对外开放的新时代的到来。

该时期一个关键性的变化是中国在投资领域从"引进来"为主变成"引进来"和"走出去"并重。从贸易大国到投资大国,从商品输出到资本输出,从单向利用外资到双向利用投资,这实际上是开放型经济升级的必经之路。当经济发展到一定程度,必然要求通过对外投资整合全球资源,实现资源的最合理配置。2013年"一带一路"倡议的提出给中国的对外开放、对外投资带来了新的机遇。另一个关键性的变化是中国更加积极地参与全球治理,推动全球治理体系的完善。从博鳌亚洲论坛到亚洲相互协作与信任措施会议(简称"亚信会议")、上海合作组织峰会,再到"一带一路"国际合作高峰论坛,中国始终在不遗余力地提供中国式治理和贸易思路,推进世界各国的经济文化交流。从"一带一路"倡议到亚洲基础设施投资银行、丝路基金的建立,再到构建"人类命运共同体",各种丰富的中国式治理思路为全球治理体系的进一步完善提供了新的思路和方向。

经过40多年的对外开放,中国目前已经形成了全方位、多层次、宽领域的对外开放格局。截至2023年3月,中国已经同全球182个国家建立外交关系,同时已签订19个自贸协定,涉及26个国家和地区。2020年11月15日,东盟10国和中国、日本、韩国、澳大利亚、新西兰共15个亚太国家正式签署了《区域全面经济伙伴关系协定》,标志着世界上人口最多、经贸规模最大、最具发展潜力的自由贸易区正式启航。2023年6月2日,该协定对15个成员国全面生效,全球最大的自贸区将进入全面实施新阶段。2020年12月30日,《中欧全面投资协定》在经历了7年的谈判之后顺利完成签订。《中欧全面投资协定》的签订是中国坚持深化对外开放程度,坚持高水平、高质量开放的表现。

在开放层次上,中国近年来的开放重点在自由贸易试验区和自由贸易港的建设上。2013年,中国首次成立中国(上海)自由贸易试验区,自此拉开了自由贸易试验区建设的序幕。截至2022年,中国已经批准建设了21个自由贸易试验区。2018年4月13日,中国支持海南全岛建设自由贸易试验区,并探索建立海南自由贸易港。图6-1即为海南自由贸易港图片。发展自由贸易港对中国对外贸易极为有利。在海南实行更加积极主动的开放战略,将海南打造成为中国面向太平洋和印度洋的重要对外开放门户,展现了中国对外开放的决心和信心。

宽领域的开放格局是指对外开放不仅局限在经济领域,也涉及保险、邮电通信等服务贸易以及环保、科技、医疗卫生、体育、文化、教育等领域的开放。在经济方面,中国积极发展对

图 6-1　海南自由贸易港

外贸易,加强"一带一路"沿线国家的基础设施建设。在加强"一带一路"具体建设中,中国采取了许多具有贡献的措施来促进中国同其他国家的经济往来,例如中欧班列的建设以及中国国际进口博览会的举办。中欧班列作为共建"一带一路"的重要助力,已经成为连接世界多国的重要陆路交通工具。中欧班列助力国家之间的合作,对促进经济发展和强化日常交流有着极其重要的意义。图 6-2 展示了从中国郑州到芬兰赫尔辛基的中欧班列。

图 6-2　中欧班列

图片来源:新华社

2022 年 11 月 4 日,第五届中国国际进口博览会暨虹桥国际经济论坛开幕式在上海举行。图 6-3 为开幕式现场照片。中国国际进口博览会是世界上第一个以进口为主题的国家级展会,已连续成功举办六届。进口博览会让展品变商品、让展商变投资商,交流创意和理念,联通中国和世界,成为国际采购、投资促进、人文交流、开放合作的四大平台,成为全球共享的国际公共产品。

图 6-3　第五届中国国际进口博览会暨虹桥国际经济论坛开幕式
图片来源：新华社

6.3　中国国际贸易的发展

自 1978 年改革开放以来，中国对外贸易体制不断改革升级，对外开放程度不断扩大。1978 年至今，中国对外贸易有了质的增长，实现了跨越式的发展。中国对外贸易是中国对外开放中最为重要的内容。2021 年，中国的外贸发展取得了瞩目的成绩，货物出口量稳居世界第一，进口量稳居世界第二，服务贸易连续 8 年位居世界第二，实现了进出口并重的对外贸易战略。中国逐步构建起了自己的对外贸易网络，辐射"一带一路"周边国家，同多国建立了对外自由贸易区。即使在 2008 年全球金融危机的背景下，中国的对外贸易进出口表现仍然优于其他经济体。

1978 年改革开放之初，中国货物进出口总额仅为 355 亿元，同期美元换算为 206 亿美元，当年中国出口明显低于进口，处于贸易逆差的状态，并且中国货物进出口总额占当年世界货物进出口总额比重不足 1%。到 2021 年，中国货物进出口总额为 60 438.7 亿美元，出口额为 33 571.4 亿美元，进口额为 26 867.3 亿美元，处于贸易顺差的状态。

随着对外开放的不断深入，中国对外贸易情况总体有了质的变化，在货物贸易、服务贸易和跨境电商等方面都有了相当大的进展。

6.3.1　中国货物贸易的发展

改革开放以来，中国一直都强调"走出去"的战略，不断推进贸易体制改革创新，货物贸易实现跨越式发展，贸易结构持续优化，国际市场不断拓展。1981 年，中国的货物进出口总额仅为 440.22 亿美元，其中出口额为 220.07 亿美元，进口额为 220.15 亿美元。2021 年，中国货物进出口总额为 60 438.7 亿美元，约为 1981 年总额的 137 倍。中国的货物贸易规模增长迅速，如今中国已成为世界第一大贸易国。从表 6-2 可以看出，中国的货物贸易长期处于贸易顺差的状态。即使在2020年疫情严重、国际形势紧张的情况下，中国的对外货物贸易依然实现了增长，并且依然处于世界第一的位置。

表6-2 1981—2021年中国货物进出口情况

年份	中国进出口总额 金额/亿美元	同比增幅/（%）	中国出口额 金额/亿美元	同比增幅/（%）	中国进口额 金额/亿美元	同比增幅/（%）	差额/亿美元
2021	60 438.7	29.8	33 571.4	29.6	26 867.3	30.1	6 704.1
2020	46 559.13	1.7	25 899.52	3.6	20 659.62	−0.6	5 239.9
2019	45 778.91	−1	24 994.82	0.5	20 784.09	−2.7	4 210.73
2018	46 224.44	12.5	24 866.96	9.9	21 357.48	15.8	3 509.48
2017	41 071.38	11.4	22 633.45	7.9	18 437.93	16.1	4 195.52
2016	36 855.57	−6.8	20 976.31	−7.7	15 879.26	−5.5	5 097.05
2015	39 530.33	−8	22 734.68	−2.9	16 795.64	−14.1	5 939.04
2014	43 015.27	3.4	23 422.93	6	19 592.35	0.4	3 830.58
2013	41 589.93	7.5	22 090.04	7.8	19 499.89	7.2	2 590.15
2012	38 671.19	6.2	20 487.14	7.9	18 184.05	4.3	2 303.09
2011	36 418.64	22.5	18 983.81	20.3	17 434.84	24.9	1 548.97
2010	29 740.01	34.7	15 777.54	31.3	13 962.47	38.8	1 815.07
2009	22 075.35	−13.9	12 016.12	−16	10 059.23	−11.2	1 956.89
2008	25 632.55	17.8	14 306.93	17.3	11 325.62	18.5	2 981.31
2007	21 761.75	23.6	12 200.6	25.9	9 561.15	20.8	2 639.45
2006	17 604.38	23.8	9 689.78	27.2	7 914.61	19.9	1 775.17
2005	14 219.06	23.2	7 619.53	28.4	6 599.53	17.6	1 020
2004	11 545.54	35.7	5 933.26	35.4	5 612.29	36	320.97
2003	8 509.88	37.1	4 382.28	34.6	4 127.6	39.8	254.68
2002	6 207.66	21.8	3 255.96	22.4	2 951.7	21.2	304.26
2001	5 096.51	7.5	2 660.98	6.8	2 435.53	8.2	225.45
2000	4 742.97	31.5	2 492.03	27.8	2 250.94	35.8	241.09
1999	3 606.3	11.3	1 949.31	6.1	1 656.99	18.2	292.32
1998	3 239.49	−0.4	1 837.12	0.5	1 402.37	−1.5	434.75
1997	3 251.62	12.2	1 827.92	21	1 423.7	2.5	404.22
1996	2 898.81	3.2	1 510.48	1.5	1 388.33	5.1	122.15
1995	2 808.64	18.7	1 487.8	23	1 320.84	14.2	166.96
1994	2 366.21	20.9	1 210.06	31.9	1 156.15	11.2	53.91
1993	1 957.03	18.2	917.44	8	1 039.59	29	−122.15
1992	1 655.25	22	849.4	18.2	805.85	26.3	43.55
1991	1 356.34	17.5	718.43	15.7	637.91	19.6	80.52
1990	1 154.36	3.4	620.91	18.2	533.45	−9.8	87.46

续表

年份	中国进出口总额		中国出口额		中国进口额		差额/亿美元
	金额/亿美元	同比增幅/(%)	金额/亿美元	同比增幅/(%)	金额/亿美元	同比增幅/(%)	
1989	1 116.78	8.7	525.38	10.6	591.4	7	−66.02
1988	1 027.84	24.4	475.16	20.5	552.68	27.9	−77.52
1987	826.53	11.9	394.37	27.5	432.16	0.7	−37.79
1986	738.46	6.1	309.42	13.1	429.04	1.5	−119.62
1985	696.02	30	273.50	4.6	422.52	54.1	−149.02
1984	535.49	22.8	261.39	17.6	274.1	28.1	−12.71
1983	436.16	4.8	222.26	−0.4	213.9	10.9	8.36
1982	416.06	−5.5	223.21	1.4	192.85	−12.4	30.36
1981	440.22	—	220.07	—	220.15	—	−0.08

数据来源：中华人民共和国商务部

注：表格数据来源于中华人民共和国商务部网站，"差额"一列数值可能因四舍五入等原因与"中国出口额"减去"中国进口额"之差略有出入，特此说明。后文同类表格不再加注说明。

中国对外货物贸易规模在不断扩大的同时，中国货物贸易的商品结构也在不断优化。根据国际贸易标准分类（Standard International Trade Classification，SITC），进出口货物按照产业部门来源分为初级产品和工业制品。从中国的进出口总额来看，初级产品进出口总额小于工业制品进出口总额。从1995年开始，中国的工业制品进出口总额占货物进出口总额的比例高达80%（见图6-4）。

图6-4 1995—2021年初级产品与工业制品进出口总额构成

数据来源：中华人民共和国国家统计局

从1995年开始，随着中国经济的发展，中国的初级产品处于进口大于出口的状态。如图6-5所示，1995年初级产品的出口额占到初级产品进出口总额的46.8%，到2015年，占比降到18%。2021年初级产品出口额占比仅为12.5%。中国初级产品的出口额占比大体呈现下降趋势。

与初级产品不同，工业制品的贸易发展一直是出口大于进口的格局。如图6-6所示，从1995年开始，工业制品的出口额占到工业制品进出口总额的50%以上。1995年，工业制品出口额占比为54.18%，此后基本保持着缓慢增长的趋势。2021年，工业制品的出口额占比达到65.34%。

图 6-5　1995—2021 年初级产品进出口情况

数据来源：中华人民共和国家统计局

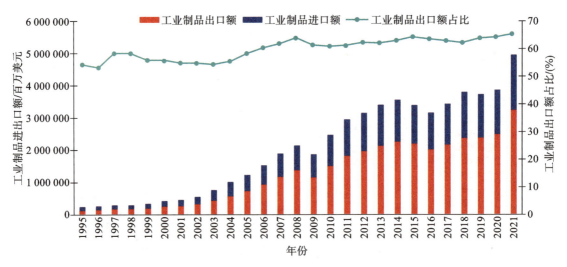

图 6-6　1995—2021 年工业制品进出口情况

数据来源：中华人民共和国家统计局

6.3.2　中国服务贸易的发展

中国自开放以来就一直积极参加国际服务贸易，服务贸易进出口规模迅速扩大。中国服务贸易进出口规模多年稳居世界第二。在 1982 年到 2001 年这段时间，中国的服务贸易进出口总额从 47 亿美元增长到 784 亿美元，增长 15 倍有余，年均增长速度为 16%。在此期间，出口额从 27 亿美元增长到 392 亿美元，进口额从 20 亿美元增长到 393 亿美元。中国服务贸易的规模在加入 WTO 之前已经实现了阶梯式的增长。加入 WTO 之后，中国对外贸易的各方面都呈现高速增长的状态，服务贸易规模也持续扩大。2002 年到 2021 年这段时间内，中国的服务贸易总额从928亿美元高速增长到8 212亿美元，总体规模扩大7倍有余，年均增长速度为12%。相比1982年，2021年服务贸易总额扩大了173倍有余。中国从1982年到2021年的服务进出口情况如表6-3所示。

表6-3 1982—2021年中国服务进出口情况

年份	中国进出口总额		中国出口额		中国进口额		差额/亿美元
	金额/亿美元	同比增幅/(%)	金额/亿美元	同比增幅/(%)	金额/亿美元	同比增幅/(%)	
2021	8 212	24.1	3 942	40.5	4 270	12.0	−327
2020	6 617	−15.7	2 806	−1.0	3 811	−24.0	−1 005
2019	7 850	−1.4	2 836	4.5	5 014	−4.5	−2 178
2018	7 965	14.5	2 715	19.0	5 250	12.3	−2 536
2017	6 957	5.1	2 281	8.9	4 676	3.4	−2 395
2016	6 616	1.1	2 095	−4.2	4 521	3.8	−2 426
2015	6 542	0.3	2 186	−0.2	4 355	0.6	−2 169
2014	6 520	21.3	2 191	5.9	4 329	30.9	−2 137
2013	5 376	11.3	2 070	2.7	3 306	17.5	−1 236
2012	4 829	7.6	2 016	0.3	2 813	13.5	−797
2011	4 489	20.8	2 010	12.7	2 478	28.2	−468
2010	3 717	22.9	1 783	24.2	1 934	21.7	−151
2009	3 025	−6.1	1 436	−12.1	1 589	0.0	−153
2008	3 223	21.4	1 633	20.7	1 589	22.1	44
2007	2 654	30.2	1 353	31.4	1 301	29.0	52
2006	2 038	21.1	1 030	22.1	1 008	20.1	21
2005	1 683	15.9	843	16.3	840	15.5	3
2004	1 452	36.2	725	41.3	727	31.5	−2
2003	1 066	15.0	513	11.0	553	18.9	−40
2002	928	18.2	462	18.0	465	18.5	−3
2001	784	10.2	392	11.8	393	8.6	−1
2000	712	16.7	350	19.3	362	14.3	−11
1999	610	17.6	294	17.2	317	17.9	−23
1998	519	−16.6	251	−26.8	268	−4.0	−18
1997	622	23.0	342	22.4	280	23.8	63
1996	506	1.9	280	14.6	226	−10.5	54
1995	496	36.0	244	20.9	252	54.7	−8
1994	365	37.1	202	38.5	163	35.4	39
1993	266	20.9	146	15.9	120	27.6	25
1992	220	61.0	126	31.7	94	128.9	31

续表

年份	中国进出口总额		中国出口额		中国进口额		差额/亿美元
	金额/亿美元	同比增幅/(%)	金额/亿美元	同比增幅/(%)	金额/亿美元	同比增幅/(%)	
1991	137	10.1	95	18.4	41	−5.3	54
1990	124	22.8	81	30.0	44	11.3	37
1989	101	16.2	62	21.6	39	8.5	23
1988	87	32.5	51	24.9	36	45.0	15
1987	66	7.0	41	5.7	25	9.2	16
1986	61	9.2	39	24.6	23	−9.8	16
1985	56	−5.5	31	0.3	25	−11.7	6
1984	59	24.9	31	11.7	29	43.3	2
1983	48	1.4	28	3.6	20	−1.5	8
1982	47	—	27	—	20	—	6

数据来源：中华人民共和国商务部

中国服务贸易除了整体规模上保持着高速增长，同时中国服务贸易进出口总额占世界服务贸易总额的比重（见图6-7）和中国服务贸易进出口总额占中国对外贸易总额的比重也呈现上升趋势。自1992年开始，中国的服务贸易开始快速增长，服务贸易占比开始上升。2014年中国的服务贸易已占世界服务贸易的6.79%，较1982年增长10倍有余，中国逐步成为世界上的服务贸易大国。目前中国已经成为世界第二大服务贸易国，2021年服务贸易进出口总额达8 212亿美元，同比增长24.1%。

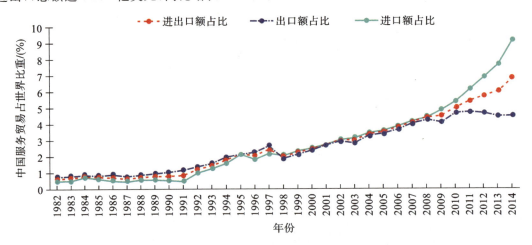

图6-7 1982—2014年中国服务贸易进出口额占世界比重
数据来源：中华人民共和国商务部

随着对外开放的不断深入和国际形势的不断变化，中国对外服务贸易的组成也发生了巨大的变化。中国的对外服务贸易从以运输服务为主转变为以运输、旅行、电信、计算机和信息服务并重的发展局面。2021年，运输服务、旅行服务、电信、计算机和信息服务分别占对外服务贸易的31.75%、14.91%和14.56%（见图6-8）。

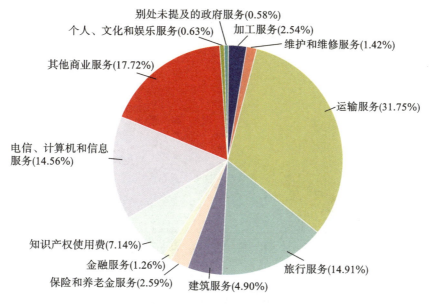

图 6-8　2021 年中国对外服务贸易占比情况

数据来源：中华人民共和国商务部

6.3.3　中国的对外贸易伙伴

改革开放以后,中国积极发展对外贸易,与世界上绝大多数国家和地区建立了贸易关系。中国的对外贸易伙伴从 1978 年的几十个国家和地区发展到 2023 年同 182 个国家建立外交关系并进行经济往来,几乎覆盖全球所有区域。欧盟、美国、东盟、日本、金砖国家等国家和地区成为中国的主要贸易伙伴。21 世纪以来,尤其是在中国加入 WTO 之后,中国与新兴市场经济体和发展中国家的贸易持续快速增长。

中国的贸易伙伴主要是美国、日本、欧盟、东盟、韩国、巴西等国家和地区,不同贸易伙伴占中国对外贸易的比重在过去几十年中发生了巨大的变化,2000 年至 2020 年中国同主要贸易伙伴的进出口额如图 6-9 所示。

图 6-10 展示了 2000 年、2010 年、2020 年中国主要贸易伙伴进出口总额占比情况。2000 年,日本是中国对外贸易的最主要国家,进出口总额为 8 316 399 万美元,占比高达17.53％。但此后中国同欧盟和美国的贸易往来更为密切,贸易总额及贸易增速远超日本,在 2004 年到 2019 年间,欧盟和美国交替作为中国的第一大贸易伙伴。2011 年之后,中国同日韩的贸易增速放缓,与此同时,中国同东盟、欧盟及美国的贸易依然保持着高速增长,东盟逐渐成为中国的第三大贸易伙伴。2018 年,由于美国挑起对华贸易摩擦,中美进出口贸易受到了较大影响。2019 年至 2022 年,美国从中国第一大贸易伙伴变为中国第三大贸易伙伴。自 2013 年中国提出"一带一路"倡议以来,中国同"一带一路"沿线国家的贸易往来变得更为密切,同东盟国家的对外贸易总额保持着高速增长,2020 年,东盟历史性地成为中国第一大贸易伙伴。2021 年,中国前五大贸易伙伴依次为东盟、欧盟、美国、日本和韩国。截至 2022 年,东盟已经连续 3 年成为我国第一大贸易伙伴,欧盟第二,美国第三。此外中国目前是 120 多个国家和地区的最大贸易伙伴。

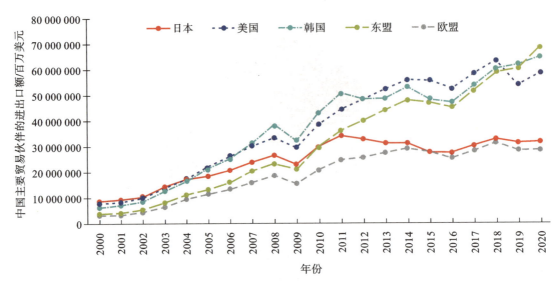

图 6-9　2000—2020 年中国主要贸易伙伴进出口总额

数据来源：中华人民共和国国家统计局

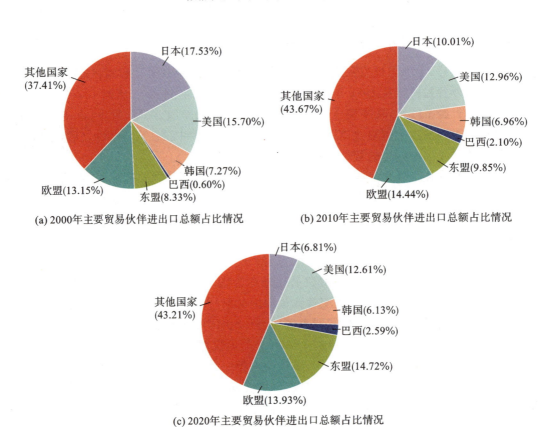

图 6-10　2000 年、2010 年、2020 年中国主要贸易伙伴进出口总额占比情况

数据来源：中华人民共和国国家统计局

6.4 中国对外贸易政策的演变

对外贸易在中国经济发展中的每一个阶段都扮演着重要角色,每个阶段的对外贸易政策都必须充分反映中国对外贸易发展的客观需求,同时契合当时的国际贸易经营环境。从1978年中国改革开放至今,中国对外贸易政策可以大致分为两个时期。

6.4.1 1978年到2000年的对外贸易政策

改革开放后,中国对外贸易开始实行进口替代与出口导向相结合的战略,引入了市场经济中比较优势的观点,在具有比较优势的劳动密集型产业采取鼓励出口的政策,引进外资增强竞争力。在不具有竞争优势的资本密集型和技术密集型产业,中国采取进口替代战略,满足国内产业发展需要的技术和资本。相应地,这个时期的对外贸易政策就有所调整。

这个时期的对外贸易的总政策目标是通过对外贸易政策促进出口,限制进口,保护与促进国民经济发展,保证国家关税收入。这个时期的对外贸易政策的主要特点表现为三点。第一,从单纯的保护转变为"奖出限入"。改革开放之前,中国实施的是"独立自主、自力更生"的建设方针。改革开放之后,中国意识到对外贸易对经济增长的促进作用,开始鼓励出口,利用国外资源发展经济,追求贸易顺差,贸易政策转变为"奖出限入"。第二,对外贸易政策从微观领域向宏观领域调整。中国对外贸易政策从最开始下放经营权、鼓励企业从事对外贸易,到改革外汇资源配置制度实现汇率双轨制,再到实现以市场为基础、有管理的浮动汇率制度,经历了从微观领域向宏观领域的调整。第三,以扩大出口为方针。这个时期每一次的政策调整都是在原先政策存在不利于扩大出口的因素情况下进行的,因而扩大出口成为对外贸易政策调整的基本方针。

6.4.2 2001年至今的对外贸易政策

2001年,中国正式加入了WTO。在这个阶段,中国对外贸易政策的制定与调整的总方向是融入世界贸易体系,充分参与国际竞争,同时中国的对外贸易政策要严格遵循WTO的要求。这样做是为了获得更公平的贸易地位,避免其他国家对中国实施不公平、不公正的待遇。在加入WTO后,中国签订了《中国加入世界贸易组织议定书》,承诺开放市场和按照世界贸易规则改革对外经贸体系,建立一套符合国际惯例的涉外经贸体系。在加入世界贸易体系的第一年,中国就按照WTO的要求清理了大量的旧的法律法规,制定了适应WTO的新法规。

中国的对外贸易政策总方向是走向贸易自由化。为保证中国经济发展的利益,保证在对外开放的背景下的经济运行,中国一直采取积极参与对外贸易的态度。同时中国结合自身发展情况,采取积极干预的贸易政策稳定中国的经济发展体系。积极干预的对外贸易政策是一种选择性的贸易保护政策,即对尚不具备国际竞争力的产业进行一定程度、一定时期的保护;对具有一定国际市场份额的企业或产业实施战略性贸易保护政策;对具有国际竞争力的产业或企业实施自由贸易政策。

在加入WTO之后,中国的市场准入管理政策与措施做出了调整。在进口方面,WTO

严令禁止高额关税,要求成员国逐步降低关税水平,走向贸易自由化。中国目前的关税水平已经低于发展中国家的平均关税水平,大大提高了中国的市场准入程度。尽管中国在加入WTO之后降低了关税水平,但中国依然可以借鉴保护关税的相关理论,实施阶梯式的关税结构,把关税水平设置在有利于中国产业发展和福利水平的最佳位置。在进口的非关税壁垒方面,中国在加入WTO之后,大部分传统的非关税壁垒贸易保护政策就不再适用,否则会违背WTO的约束。在加入WTO之后,中国可以使用的非关税壁垒贸易措施包括以下五类:第一,对限定产品的进口数量实施限制;第二,以WTO认可的形式进行政府采购;第三,对进口产品实施反倾销;第四,要求有关国家对其产品出口采取"自愿出口";第五,利用技术性贸易壁垒。

7 中国的农村改革

20世纪中后期,由于长期受"左"的思想束缚,中国农村实行的是"政社合一"的人民公社制度,其集中管理、统一分配的僵化体制严重挫伤了农民的生产积极性,阻碍了农村生产力的发展,农民的温饱问题得不到解决,农村经济处于停滞状态。因此,调整农村生产关系、改变农村政策成为广大农民的迫切需求。为此,中国开始了农村经济体制改革之路,纵观中国农村改革之路,主要可分为四个阶段。

第一阶段(1978—1984年):改革启动阶段。废除人民公社体制,实行家庭联产承包责任制,在土地公有制的基础上,把土地长期承包给农户使用,使农业集体生产变为分户自主经营,自负盈亏。通过基层的积极尝试和中央的政策推广相结合,包产到户迅速在全国扩展开来,农村经济由此得到了快速发展,实现了增产增收,农民经济状况和生活水平明显改善。

第二阶段(1984—1992年):市场化改革探索阶段。改革农产品流通体制,针对农业大丰收之下存在的卖粮困难的问题,取消了不再适应农村经济发展的统收派购的形式,农产品开始面向市场流通,产品价格实行"双轨制"。

第三阶段(1992—1998年):向市场经济全面过渡阶段。在中共十四大确立社会主义市场经济体制改革目标的推动下,建立适应社会主义市场经济发展要求的农村新体制,农村经济在这一阶段进入转轨时期,开始全面与市场接轨,并得到了快速发展。

第四阶段(1998年至今):社会主义新农村建设新时期。农村改革从经济改革向社会主义新农村全面改革过渡,中央也加大了对"三农"问题的重视程度,逐渐改变城乡二元制经济结构,把城市发展和农村经济发展紧密联系在一起,构建农村经济发展的长效机制,努力实现农村全面发展。

7.1 家庭联产承包责任制

农村改革,特别是家庭联产承包责任制的推行,是改革开放的第一步。中共十一届三中全会后,中国经济体制改革率先在农村取得突破,以包产到户、包干到户为主要形式的家庭联产承包责任制,破除了农村分配制度的平均主义,改变了人民公社"吃大锅饭"的制度弊端,逐渐成为党和国家农村政策的重要基石。

7.1.1 家庭联产承包责任制的兴起和变迁

中国是农业大国,农业生产和农民生活始终是党和政府高度重视的头等大事。新中国成立至"一五"计划结束,中国农业发展总体呈上升趋势。然而20世纪50年代末,情况开始恶化。从人口数量、耕地面积和粮食产量的相互关系看,中国农业生产存在的问题愈来愈突出。1957年至1978年,中国人口增长了三四亿,其中农业人口增量占总人口增量的60%以上;同期中国耕地面积不但没有随人口增长而增加,反而由于基本建设用地等原因而减少。尽管粮食总产量有所增长,但中国人均粮食占有量情况并没有得到根本改善,农业劳动生产率极低,贫困在农村普遍存在。

究其原因,主要是自20世纪50年代末后,人民公社化运动导致农业经营管理过于集中、分配上平均主义严重等弊端,严重挫伤了农民的生产积极性,在很大程度上抵消了中国对农业的投入,从而导致农业发展缓慢甚至停滞。

当时,中国农业落后的状况同人民改善生活的需要和四个现代化的目标之间,存在着很大的矛盾。究竟应该如何从根本上克服生产管理方面过分集中的弊端?应如何充分调动农民生产的主动性?这些问题已成为不可回避的现实问题。

1978年秋种时期,农业大省安徽遭遇大旱,安徽省委采取了"借地度荒"策略,即在特殊时期把集体土地借给农民,让农民自己耕种,以所得度灾年,而这种做法其实就是"包产到户"的前身。紧接着,凤阳县小岗村的18户农民首创了"包干到户"的做法,即缴够国家和集体的,剩下都是自己的,这一做法极大地调动了农民的生产积极性。1979年秋,小岗村油料作物总产量达到了17 600千克,大大超过150千克的任务量。图7-1展示了小岗村的丰收景象。

图7-1 小岗村的丰收景象

图片来源:《光明日报》

安徽省的做法影响了其他省份,一些地方纷纷放宽政策,采取类似做法,如四川省鼓励生产队包产到组,支持"以产定工、超额奖励"的试验,广东省在农村社队普遍推行"五定一奖"的经营管理制度。

包产到户、包干到户在多个地方的大胆尝试,改变了生产关系对农业生产力的禁锢,因时、因地制宜赋予农民生产自主权,激发农民生产积极性,是鼓舞广大农民在实践中创造新经验的大胆尝试。但是,也有人担心包产包干会瓦解农村集体经济,偏离社会主义方向。

在1980年的关键时刻,邓小平在谈话时明确指出,包产到户的方式效果很好,变化很快,这种做法不会影响集体经济。邓小平认为,只要生产发展了,农村的社会分工和商品经济发展了,低水平的集体化就会发展到高水平的集体化,集体经济也会巩固起来。邓小平的明确表态消除了人们的僵化思想和畏惧心理,推动了中共中央对包产到户、包干到户的公开肯定和支持。

1980年,中共中央印发《关于进一步加强和完善农业生产责任制的几个问题》,首次突破多年来把包产到户等同于分田单干和资本主义的观念,肯定了在生产队领导下的包产到户,不会脱离社会主义轨道,没有复辟资本主义的危险。1982年,关于农村工作的"一号文件"正式出台,明确指出包括包产到户、包干到户在内的各种责任制都是社会主义集体经济的生产责任制,反映了亿万农民要求按照中国农村的实际状况来发展社会主义农业的强烈愿望。

此后,农村改革更加迅猛地开展起来。家庭联产承包责任制迅速推广,充分调动了农民的生产积极性,促进了农业生产的迅速发展。如表7-1所示,主要农产品产量明显提高,农村面貌出现了可喜的变化。

表7-1 家庭联产承包责任制前后期中国主要农产品产量对比

指标	1977年	1978年	1979年	1980年	1981年	1982年	1983年	1984年
粮食产量/万吨	28 272.50	30 476.50	33 211.50	32 055.50	32 502.00	35 450.00	38 727.50	40 730.50
油料产量/万吨	401.58	521.79	643.54	769.06	1 020.52	1 181.73	1 054.97	1 190.95

数据来源:中华人民共和国国家统计局

经过这一时期的发展,家庭联产承包责任制不断释放红利,农业持续稳定增长。为了稳定民心,适应农村市场化改革,中共中央对家庭联产承包责任制进行了进一步明确和完善。

一方面,经营形式制度化。1991年,《中共中央关于进一步加强农业和农村工作的决定》明确提出,把以家庭联产承包为主的责任制、统分结合的双层经营体制作为中国乡村集体经济的一项基本制度长期稳定下来,并不断充实完善。1993年,家庭联产承包责任制作为农村经济的一项基本制度被载入《中华人民共和国宪法修正案》。

另一方面,通过合同规范家庭联产承包责任制,明确各主体间的权利和义务。1993年,《关于当前农业和农村经济发展的若干政策措施》提出,为了稳定土地承包关系,鼓励农民增加投入,提高土地的生产率,在原定的耕地承包期到期之后,再延长30年不变。从事开发性生产的土地,承包期可以更长。2002年的《中华人民共和国农村土地承包法》更是以法律形式保障农民长期的土地承包经营权。

7.1.2 家庭联产承包责任制的历史意义与局限性

作为中共在农村的基本政策,以家庭承包经营为基础、统分结合的双层经营体制突破了人民公社体制一大二公、高度集中的缺陷,在坚持生产资料集体所有的前提下,把土地承包给农户,确立了家庭经营的主体地位,赋予了农民充分的生产经营自主权和收益权。自此,被混淆了多年的集体同个人权益的关系,第一次得到了符合实际情况的明确划分。由于经营成果与生产者的利益紧密挂钩,"吃大锅饭"的弊端得到克服,农民生产积极性得到充分发挥,生产力获得大大解放,生产效率得到明显提高,农业产量迅速增加。

总结来看,家庭联产承包责任制解决了农业生产效率低下的问题,缓解了当时中国粮食产量不充足、农民无法满足温饱的问题,为接下来的改革开放奠定了坚实基础。更重要的是,家庭联产承包责任制改变了农业生产的现状和结构,为农业现代化发展奠定了基础。

以家庭联产承包责任制为标志的农村土地制度改革一度引领了农村的经济社会发展,在一段时间内农村面貌有了很大的改观。然而 21 世纪后,农村经济虽然仍在增长,但是城乡居民收入、城乡发展差距仍然不断拉大,究其深层次的几个原因,始终绕不开作为农村改革基石的家庭联产承包责任制。

第一个原因是土地规模狭小制约了农业规模化。中国土地地况复杂,加之家庭联产承包责任制要求人均耕地面积、土地质量等要公平分配,导致农户承包土地的地块在空间上处于割裂状态,农户经营零碎土地的现象较为普遍。土地规模碎片化又制约着农业规模化经营的实现,不仅从客观上限制了农户的生产投入,造成单个农户的农产品成本过高,经济效益低下,使农户在市场竞争中处于弱势地位,难以承担投资失败的风险,还从主观上限制了农户对规模生产投资的预期,反过来限制农业规模化经营的实现,形成恶性循环。

第二个原因是家庭联产承包责任制不能适应市场经济发展的需要。市场化是农业产业化经营的基本特征之一,但现有的土地经营分散化加之小规模的家庭经营,使农户难以克服其在生产上的盲目性,会出现跟风种植的现象,造成农产品供需不平衡。

第三个原因是土地使用权的流转不规范。国家允许土地使用权有偿转移,标志着土地可以作为生产要素进入市场,并借助市场优化配置。但土地使用权流转缺乏可信的市场中介,土地使用权转让的权益关系、交易程序、执行原则和定价方式等规定也较为模糊,导致土地流转不充分,土地使用效率不高。

7.2 农产品流通体制改革

农产品流通领域位于农业生产和居民消费之间。在市场经济下,流通决定生产,农产品流通模式僵化将直接影响农业生产,进而影响农业产业化、农民利益和新农村建设。

中共十一届三中全会后,在农村全面推行家庭联产承包责任制的同时,以市场为导向推行农产品流通体制的改革取得了较大成效。随着中国农业商品化和市场化程度不断提高,传统农业向现代化农业的转变步伐不断加快,农产品流通体制改革在推进社会主义农村建设方面发挥着越来越重要的作用。

7.2.1 农产品流通体制改革的历史回顾

改革开放前,中国农产品流通体制仍为计划经济时代的统购统销制度,即全社会所需要的粮食全部由国家供应,居民凭粮票领取粮食。除粮食外,国家还对生猪、鸡蛋、蚕茧、水产品等实行派购,品种多达 132 种。这些产品不能自由买卖,价格也由国家统一规定。城乡居民所需要的生活资料全凭国家印发的票证供应,票证达十几种,成了第二货币。图 7-2 为统购统销期间的部分票证。

该时期,农产品流通受到严格的行政限制,无法自由流通,农产品的生产、销售无法反映市场需求的变化,使农业生产、加工、流通与市场严重脱节。1978 年后,中国逐步探索农产

图 7-2　统购统销期间的部分票证

图片来源：金华党史网

品流通体制改革，主要经历了以下五个阶段。

第一阶段（1978—1984 年）：由计划经济向计划调节与市场调节相结合的过渡阶段。

随着家庭联产承包责任制的实施，农产品流通体制也开始突破传统的计划经济体制。中共十一届三中全会后，中国对农产品统购统销制度进行渐进式的改革。在从根本上不触动统购统销制度的条件下，有计划地提高农产品价格，逐步减少统购统销的农产品的品种，放开集市贸易，允许部分农产品议购议销和自由购销。

从 1979 年 3 月份起，中国国务院陆续提高粮食、油脂油料、棉花等 18 种主要农产品的收购价格。1982 年 1 月，《全国农村工作会议纪要》明确指出，农业经济"要以计划经济为主，市场调节为辅"。1983 年 1 月，中共中央在《当前农村经济政策的若干问题》中指出，对农民完成派购任务后的产品和非统购派购产品，应当允许多渠道经营。1983 年 10 月，国务院将商业部主管的一、二类农副产品由 46 种减少为 21 种，调整下来的 25 种降为三类，实行市场调节。1984 年 7 月，国务院又将一、二类农副产品由 21 种减少为 12 种。截至 1984 年底，属于统派购的农副产品由 1978 年的 100 多种减少至 38 种。农民出售农副产品总额中，国家按计划牌价统购派购的比重从 1978 年的 84.7% 下降到 1984 年的 39.4%。

与缩小统购统销范围相对应的是开放集市贸易，1979 年 4 月后，中国放宽对集市贸易的限制，规定三类农副产品和除棉花外完成统购任务的一、二类农副产品，均可实行议购议销和上市自由贸易。图 7-3 为青岛即墨路小商品市场。

第二阶段（1984—1992 年）：合同定购与市场收购并存的"双轨制"阶段。

在家庭联产承包责任制与农产品收购价格放开相配合下，农村经济迅速发展，一举解决了农产品供应长期匮乏的问题。为了防止由于市场价格的突然放开而导致价格剧烈变动，中国希望用计划价格满足社会的基本需求，追求经济的稳定，同时发挥市场的资源配置功

图 7-3 青岛即墨路小商品市场
图片来源:青岛日报社

能,促进生产,缓解社会矛盾。

1985年1月,中共中央发出的《关于进一步活跃农村经济的十项政策》规定,除个别品种外,国家不再向农民下达农产品统购派购任务,按照不同情况,分别实行合同定购和市场收购。粮食、棉花改为合同定购,生猪、水产品和大中城市、工矿区的蔬菜,也要逐步取消派购,自由上市,自由交易,随行就市,按质论价。至此,除少数品种外,农产品统购派购制度宣告结束。

这一阶段是农产品流通体制由计划经济向市场经济转变的阶段,农产品流通体制的改革打破了计划经济时代对农产品的限制,大大增强了农民的商品意识,农产品产量和品种迅速增加,标志农产品流通体制改革进入了市场取向的大跨步推进阶段。

第三阶段(1992—1998年):向社会主义市场经济转变阶段。

随着农业经营形式的完善,农业发展面临的主要矛盾是农业发展与社会主义市场经济不完全适应的问题。为解决这一主要矛盾,中共中央以建立农村社会主义市场体制为导向,通过农业政策不断改革农产品流通体制等,推动农村改革深化发展。

1992年,中国进入了社会主义市场经济的发展阶段,农产品流通体制改革也由开放搞活阶段进入到向社会主义市场经济转变发展阶段,以此推动农业结构调整。这一阶段主要目标是以市场经济为导向,加快粮食流通体制改革,放开粮食价格,实现以市场定价为主。

1993年,中国国务院颁发《关于加快粮食流通体制改革的通知》,要求农产品形成以市场购销为主、合同定购为辅的格局。我国取消粮票,实行了40年的粮食统购统销制度宣告终结,粮食价格随行就市。1998年,中共十五届三中全会通过的《中共中央关于农业和农村工作若干重大问题的决定》指出,要进一步搞活农产品流通,尽快形成开放、统一、竞争、有序的农产品市场体系,为农民提供良好的市场环境,保障农业和农村经济持续稳定发展。这也进一步明确了农产品市场体系的建设目标。

与此同时,中国积极建设农副产品批发市场。从1992年到1998年,各地兴起农产品批发市场建设的热潮,共建成农副产品批发市场近3 000个,涉及粮食、蔬菜、肉类和水产品等多个种类。批发市场成为全国农产品集散与资源配置中心,是带动农业经济发展的重要力量。至此,以批发市场为核心的农产品市场体系初步建立,为农产品流通体制深化改革打下了坚实的基础。图 7-4 展示了中国农副产品批发市场一角。

图 7-4　中国农副产品批发市场一角

第四阶段(1998—2004 年):全面市场化阶段。

农产品流通体制改革是中国改革开放深入进行的必要条件,也是逐步建立社会主义市场经济的重要途径,更是解决"三农"问题的重要突破口。从 1998 年开始,农产品流通体制进入全面改革时期,这一时期农产品流通体制改革重点在粮食领域。在粮食相对过剩的情况下,1998 年 4 月,全国粮食流通体制改革工作会议召开,提出实行粮食政策性经营和商业性经营分开的购销制度,完善粮食价格机制,实行粮食顺价销售;6 月,中国又出台了"三项政策、一项改革",即按保护价敞开收购农民余粮、国有粮食收储企业实行顺价销售、粮食收购资金实行封闭运行,加快国有粮食企业改革。

当然,农产品流通体制改革并不仅限于粮食领域,粮食以外的各类农产品流通的市场化改革进程都得到了持续的推进,并逐渐形成了较为稳定的市场化流通秩序。

第五阶段(2004 年至今):多元化农产品流通体系基本形成阶段。

2004 年,中国国务院办公厅发布《关于进一步做好农村商品流通工作的意见》,要求加快发展农产品批发、零售和物流等,搞活农产品流通。2005 年,中国商务部组织实施了以发展农村现代流通网络为主要内容的"万村千乡"市场工程。2006 年,中国商务部实施"双百市场工程",提高农产品流通企业的现代化水平,升级改造农产品批发市场。2006 年 5 月,中国商务部批准《农家店建设与改造规范》,促进和加强农产品现代流通体系的建设。如今,中国多元化农产品流通体系基本形成。

7.2.2　农产品流通体制改革的成就与启示

随着农产品流通体制改革的推进,农产品流通渠道也由过去的单一型转变为多元化,形成了多渠道的流通体系及公平竞争的市场格局,制度的变迁极大地激发了农产品生产和流通的积极性。通过逐步改革农产品流通体制,中国已经形成了多种经济成分、多种经营方式、多条流通渠道并存的农产品流通格局。

总结来说，中国农产品流通体制改革的成就体现在以下四个方面：

其一，农产品流通规模不断扩大。改革开放后，农产品流通体制改革使中国农产品的供应数量基本充足，品种丰富。如图7-5所示，1978年中国粮食总产量为30 477万吨，2021年中国粮食总产量为68 285万吨，水果、蔬菜、猪肉等生活必需品的产量也呈现几何式的增长，满足了现代中国居民的多元化需求。

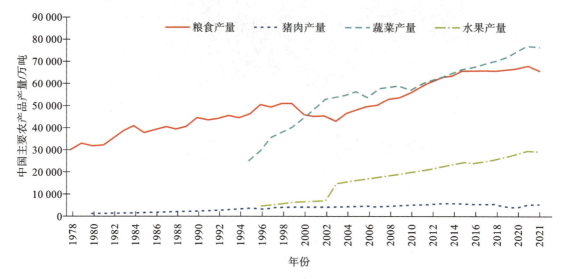

图7-5 中国主要农产品产量变化情况

数据来源：中华人民共和国国家统计局

其二，农产品流通市场体系不断健全。市场体系是市场经济的载体、纽带和渠道，农业向市场化发展必须充分发挥交易市场的作用，必要的市场条件不仅可以提高农产品交易和流通的效率，还能够提高农产品的效益。改革开放后，中国初步建立了包括集贸市场、批发市场和零售网点等在内的，以各类批发市场为中心、城乡农贸市场为基础、直销配送和连锁超市为补充的，产区、销区、集散地市场相结合的农产品市场体系，并使不同市场之间进行有机衔接，功能互补，协调联动，保障农产品顺利流通。不断完善的市场体系，不断改进的市场功能，不断健全的市场机制，成为中国农业发展的巨大推动力。

其三，农产品市场宏观调控机制不断完善。建立政府宏观调控机制是防范市场盲目性的重要手段。在农产品市场体系的建立过程中，在流通主体的培育过程中，政府宏观调控机制都应起到先导和支撑作用。改革开放后，中国中央政府和地方政府综合运用经济手段、法律行政手段和价格机制加强了对农产品市场的宏观调控能力，提高了应对突发事件及市场异常波动的能力和水平。这些宏观调控手段的运用都极大地改善了中国农产品流通的环境，促进了农产品市场的发展。

其四，农产品市场主体不断多样化，市场开放程度逐步提高。改革开放后，中国农产品市场主体由过去计划经济体制下国营商业和供销合作社等商业组织的单一格局逐步向多元化格局转变，农产品市场主体多元化趋势日益明显。国营商业和供销合作社等商业组织在农产品市场流通中的地位虽然下降，但仍然发挥着重要作用；农民个体日趋活跃；农民合作经济组织、农业产业化龙头企业日显重要。国内外农产品市场逐步接轨，农产品市场开放程度不断提高。

7.3 中国农村改革的经验与思考

农村改革后,农村社会生产力得到了极大解放和发展,农民的民主权利得到了充分尊重和保障,农村面貌发生了巨大变化。从根本上说,没有中国特色社会主义制度的优势和保障,中国农村改革不可能取得这样的成就。正是中国特色社会主义的根本制度及其优势,保证了中国农村改革的社会主义方向,也为新时代进一步深化农村改革、促进农村发展以及实施乡村振兴战略奠定了政治基础。从中国农村改革的实践过程来看,中国农村改革之所以能够取得巨大成就,主要有四点基本经验:

第一,坚持党对"三农"工作的集中统一领导。农村改革是中国共产党站在重大历史发展关头作出的正确选择,明确了中国式的农业现代化道路。农村改革初期,正是在中共中央的领导下,通过实行推广家庭承包经营、放开农产品价格、促进农民到非农部门就业等渐进式放活政策,逐步解除了计划经济体制约束,迅速释放出改革红利,既调动了农民的积极性,又优化了资源配置。进入21世纪后,中共中央提出要把解决好"三农"问题作为全党工作的重中之重,不断推动"三农"理论创新、实践创新、制度创新,逐步实现共同富裕。

第二,坚持市场化改革方向,通过市场化解决农业现代化的资源配置机制和市场主体激励问题。实践经验表明,农村改革必须坚持市场化的方向,通过深化改革全面激活要素、主体和市场,可以激发农村发展的内生活力和动力。市场化导向的改革明晰了农村产权和分配关系,促进了市场开放和要素流动,完善了价格形成机制,理顺了农民、集体与政府在市场中的功能和关系,从而使农村经济体制逐步向"发挥市场在资源配置中的决定性作用"趋近,对解放和发展农村生产力发挥了根本性作用,为农业农村现代化提供了坚实的体制机制保障。

第三,坚持"维护农民经济利益、保障农民政治权利"的基本主线。中国通过稳定并完善以家庭承包经营为基础、统分结合的双层经营体制,确保了农民在市场经营中的主体地位;通过农村劳动力流动制度改革,赋予了农民自由迁徙、择业等发展权利;通过农村集体经济组织运行机制和产权制度改革,提升了农民在集体经济发展中的主体地位。在此基础上,农村经济得到飞速发展。由此可见,确保农民是农村改革的主体和受益者是促进农村经济社会协调同步发展的基准主线,为农村改革与发展的持续推进奠定了坚实的社会基础。

第四,坚持基层创新与顶层设计相结合的农村改革"方法论"。包括农村改革在内,中国许多重大改革首先发端于基层,通过试点试验,再在全国范围内推广实施。实践证明,发挥基层人民的积极性、创造性,由基层人民推进改革是改革取得成功的核心要素。但是,单纯依靠基层创新是远远不够的。随着改革的不断深化,农村改革涉及的领域越来越广泛,所触及的矛盾的逻辑内涵更加深层,因而需要加强顶层设计,明确改革方向,优化实施路径等。经验表明,中国农村改革要想取得成功,就必须采取自下而上与自上而下相结合的方法,通过试点试验将基层创新与顶层设计有效地衔接起来,发挥农民的生产积极性。

8 农业生产与农业产业化

作为中国社会主义改革开放和现代化建设的总设计师,邓小平针对农业改革和发展提出了关于农业的"两个飞跃"的重要思想。第一个飞跃是废除人民公社,实行家庭联产承包为主的责任制。第二个飞跃是适应科学种田和生产社会化的需要,发展适度规模经营,发展集体经济。第一个飞跃着眼于变革农村生产关系,促进生产力的发展;第二个飞跃落脚于促进农业现代化,实现共同富裕。

随着改革开放的不断深入,中国的农业发展已经到了逐步实现"第二个飞跃"的阶段,农村改革从早期的以转变农业经营制度和引入市场机制为主要内容的经济体制改革逐步向覆盖农村政治、经济、社会、文化和生态等各方面内容的全方位改革推进,并取得了巨大的成就。

但是,中国城乡二元经济结构仍未彻底打破,农村土地、资金、人才等资源还在流失,制约农业和农村发展的深层次矛盾尚未解决,所以推进农村深化改革发展具有重要意义。

8.1 中国的农业现代化

在工业化、城镇化深入发展中同步推进农业现代化,既是转变经济发展方式、全面建设小康社会的重要内容,也是提高农业综合生产能力、增加农民收入、建设社会主义新农村的必然要求。

8.1.1 农业现代化的发展进程

农业现代化不是静态的,相反,它是一个不断发展变化的过程。时代背景和技术条件不同,农业现代化的内涵和目标都呈现出动态的演变。

20 世纪 70 年代末至 90 年代初,是农村改革与结构变革主导的农业现代化阶段。家庭联产承包责任制的确立与制度化使农民成为主人,并促进了农业的快速增长。80 年代中期以后,农村经济结构变革加速,乡镇企业发展吸纳了部分农业剩余劳动力,一定程度上缓解了农村人多地少的矛盾,但是,由于当时农村劳动力离土不离乡的制约,农村人地关系没有得到实质性的缓解,农业劳动生产率提高缓慢。

20 世纪 90 年代初至 2010 年前后,是农民离土出村的农业现代化阶段。农村土地流转市场开始发展,对农业的持续投入推动了土地生产率的稳步提高,加之大幅度提升机械化水平,农业劳动生产率快速提升。农业现代化朝着提高劳动生产率为主的模式转变。

2010 年后,农业发展进入历史转型期。2009 年,中国第一产业占生产总值比重首次下降到10%以下,2014年中国第一产业劳动力占比开始低于第二产业、第三产业的劳动力占比。除此之外,农业的内涵和功能都发生了变化,农业发展模式从满足温饱、提高土地生产率为主,转向显化乡村价值、提高农村劳动生产率为主。农业发展表现出明显的转型特征。

表现之一,是农民的代际分化。20世纪80年代和90年代出生的"农二代"开始成为进城务工的主力军。他们在经济社会等方面的行为特征出现一系列显著的代际性变化。"农二代"不仅如"农一代"那样,一如既往地离土出村,而且更多选择跨省份流动,前往东部地区以及大中城市务工经商,他们更期望融入现代化的城市生活体系之中。图8-1显示的为进城务工的农民群体。

图 8-1 进城务工的农民群体
图片来源:环球网

表现之二,是土地市场发展与规模化经营蓄势待发。在2007年以前的较长时期内,农村土地流转的规模基本保持稳定,农村土地流转面积占家庭承包耕地面积的比重基本上稳定在4.4%~5.4%。自2008年开始,全国各地农村土地流转速度陡然加快,土地流转面积逐年扩大,从2008年的1.1亿亩快速扩大到2020年的5.3亿亩。

表现之三,是农业经营主体的多元化。尽管农户仍是主要的农业经营者,但农业经营主体已经开始向多元化经营方向发展。家庭农场、农民合作社、从事农业生产托管的社会化服务组织等各类新型农业经营主体和服务主体快速发展。在应用新技术、增加农业生产投入、开拓新市场、融入现代农业产业链等方面,这些新型农业主体表现出不同于传统小农的新态势。

表现之四,是农业发展的动能发生了转变。以农业机械为代表的现代要素的投入,逐渐替代了农业劳动力等传统要素的投入,成为农业发展的新动能。全国农业机械总动力、主要农作物耕种收综合机械化率大幅提升,农业生产方式转为以机械作业为主和要素匹配阶段。图8-2显示的即为农业机械作业。农业科技进步在农业生产过程、农业资源配置以及农产品复杂化、专业化中具有显著贡献。

与此同时,农业发展的外部环境更加错综复杂。一是人和地的矛盾愈来愈突出;二是以户籍制度为基础的城乡二元经济结构的负面效应日益凸显。基于大国小农的基本国情农情,中国实现农业现代化难度较大。只有充分发挥多种形式适度规模经营的引领作用,才能不断提高土地、资本、劳动力等要素的生产效率,从根本上提高农业质量效益和竞争力。

图 8-2　农业机械作业

图片来源:《经济日报》

在中共十八大后,按照在工业化、城镇化深入发展中同步推进农业现代化的要求,中国坚持走中国特色农业现代化道路,以转变农业发展方式为主线,以保障主要农产品有效供给和促进农民持续较快增收为主要目标,以提高农业综合生产能力、抗风险能力和市场竞争能力为主攻方向,着力促进农业生产经营专业化、标准化、规模化、集约化,着力强化政策、科技、设施装备、人才和体制支撑,着力完善现代农业产业体系,提高农业现代化水平、农民生活水平和新农村建设水平,为中国现代化建设提供具有决定性意义的基础支撑。

8.1.2　农业现代化的主要成就

新中国成立以来,尤其是改革开放以来,中国农业现代化进程持续推进,农业发展取得了举世瞩目的成就,粮食和其他主要农产品生产能力稳步提高,农业经济效益和竞争力显著增强,农民收入水平大幅提升,农业可持续发展能力不断强化,中国逐步走上了具有中国特色的农业现代化道路,为促进世界农业发展作出了巨大贡献。

第一,农业经济平稳增长,粮食综合生产能力再创新高。中共十八大后,中国粮食产量连续 3 年保持递增状态,2012 年粮食总产量首次突破 6 亿吨,2015 年突破 6.5 亿吨,随后始终稳定在 6.5 亿吨以上。图 8-3 为中国近年来粮食总产量的变化情况。根据世界银行与联

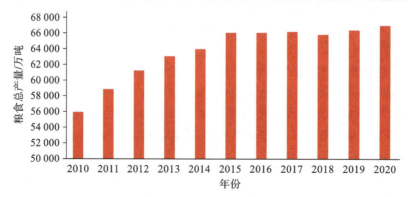

图 8-3　2010—2020 年粮食总产量的变化情况

数据来源:中华人民共和国国家统计局

合国粮农组织的数据,2017年中国谷物单产达6 029千克/公顷,与高收入国家相当。2020年,中国人均粮食占有量达到474千克,已经连续13年超过人均400千克的国际粮食安全标准线。中国已经连续多年实现口粮完全自给,用不足世界10%的耕地养活了约占世界22%的人口,为中国乃至世界的粮食安全作出了举世瞩目的贡献。

此外,在粮食产量连年增长的带动下,中国其他农产品的产量也实现了前所未有的增长。中国谷物、小麦、稻谷、花生、茶叶和肉类产量等多项指标位列世界第一,谷物、小麦和玉米产量占世界产量的20%以上,花生产量占世界产量的30%以上,茶叶产量占世界产量的40%以上。农产品的多元化增长结构,保障和优化了国内农产品的供应,丰富了中国居民的饮食结构。

第二,农业生产经营的质量和效益稳步提升。经过多年的发展,中国的农业实现了从单一以种植业为主的传统农业向农林牧渔业全面发展的现代农业的转变,农业发展由增产导向转向提质导向。2020年,在中国农林牧渔业中,农业总产值占比为52.1%,牧业总产值占比为29.2%,渔业和林业总产值占比逐步增加,分别为9.3%和4.3%,农林牧渔专业及辅助性活动产值占比为5.1%,产业结构进一步优化。农林牧渔结构日益合理的现代农业产业体系初步建立,粮食主产区稳产增产能力增强,经济作物进一步向优势产区集中,农业生产区域布局日趋优化。

第三,农业技术装备条件大幅改善,农业机械化、科技化、信息化水平不断提升。新中国成立初期,中国农业产业基础薄弱,1978年,中国农业机械总动力仅为1.2亿千瓦,全国农业综合机械化率仅有19.7%。改革开放以来,中国农业生产方式实现了从主要依靠人力、畜力到主要依靠机械动力的历史性转变,2020年,全国农业机械总动力10.6亿千瓦,农作物耕种收综合机械化率已超过70%,其中主要粮食作物耕种收综合机械化率超过80%。图8-4为中国2010年到2020年农业机械总动力的变化情况。

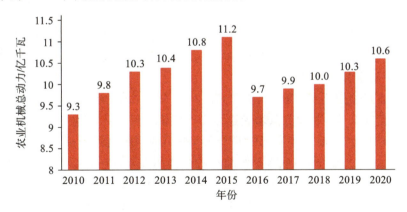

图8-4 2010—2020年农业机械总动力的变化情况

数据来源:中华人民共和国国家统计局

农业科技进步为农业现代化注入了强大动力。1978年,中国农业科技进步贡献率仅为27%,而2020年,农业科技进步贡献率已经达到60.7%,主要农作物良种基本实现全覆盖,自主选育品种面积超过95%。

农村信息化水平迅速提高,农业生产数字化起步。在新冠肺炎疫情防控期间,农村电商的作用更加凸显。图8-5为农产品电商直播情景。据中国农业农村部统计,2021年中国电

图 8-5　农产品电商直播

图片来源：南方网

商服务站行政村覆盖率在八成左右，县域农产品网络零售额超过 3000 亿元，增长迅速。在智慧农业领域，农业生产数字化方兴未艾，单品大数据，如油料、天然橡胶、棉花、大豆等产品全产业链建设已经起步，大数据系统应用领域不断扩展。

第四，农村集体产权改革完成阶段性任务，集体经济成为新增长点。随着中国农业供给侧结构性改革深入推进，现代农业经营体系也加快构建，全国范围内基本完成了农村集体产权改革任务，通过清产核资、成员界定、经营性资产量化以及建立经济合作社等举措，农村资产资源被大大盘活。农村承包土地流转面积比例大幅提升，多种形式适度规模经营实现新发展，新型经营主体不断丰富。农民合作社等新型农业经营主体数量增长迅猛。截至 2020 年底，中国依法登记注册的农民合作社达到 225.1 万家，是 10 年前的 5.9 倍，连续 4 年稳定在 220 万家以上。全国经县级以上农业产业化主管部门认定的龙头企业超过 9 万家，其中国家重点龙头企业 1 547 家。农村发展的内生动能显著提升，集体经济成为新增长点，为实现共同富裕目标奠定扎实基础。

第五，农民收入稳定增长，消费稳步提升。2004 年至 2020 年，农民收入增长实现"十七连快"；2010 年至 2020 年，农民收入增速连续高于城镇居民收入增速；2020 年的农民人均可支配收入达 17 131 元，提前一年实现中共十八大提出的"翻一番"目标。如图 8-6 所示，城乡居民可支配收入之比平稳下降，收入差距缩小的趋势明显。同时，农村居民消费升级趋势明显，2020 年，农村居民恩格尔系数为 32.7%，其中，主食消费比重逐年下降，副食消费比重上升，膳食结构日趋合理。整体上来看，农村居民饮食支出占比下降，"医""行""娱"等消费正不断升级，农村居民生活质量逐步提升。

到 2020 年，全国农业现代化取得明显进展。国家粮食安全得到有效保障，农产品供给体系质量和效率显著提高，农业国际竞争力进一步增强，农民生活达到全面小康水平。东部沿海发达地区、大城市郊区、国有垦区和国家现代农业示范区基本实现农业现代化。以高标准农田为基础、以粮食生产功能区和重要农产品生产保护区为支撑的产能保障格局基本建立。粮经饲统筹、农林牧渔结合、种养加一体、一、二、三产业融合的现代农业产业体系基本构建。

图 8-6 2010—2020 年城乡居民可支配收入之比变化情况

数据来源：中华人民共和国国家统计局

8.2 乡村振兴与中国农业的未来发展

农业是三大产业之本，是人类生存发展的根基，农产品则是人类最重要的物质生产资料。当前，中国顺利打赢了脱贫攻坚战，全面建成了小康社会，消除了中国乡村的整体性绝对贫困状况。"十四五"时期是向第二个百年奋斗目标进军的第一个五年，"三农"工作重心历史性地转向了全面推进乡村振兴，进一步消除相对贫困。而推进乡村产业振兴是实施乡村振兴战略的首要任务，也是加快构建新发展格局、促进农民农村共同富裕的重要途径。

8.2.1 乡村产业振兴之路

在乡村振兴的"五个振兴"中，产业振兴位于首位，它是乡村振兴的重中之重，是产业从发展走向振兴的核心载体，是整合城乡要素、促进乡村经济发展、激发乡村内生动力的重要驱动力，也是覆盖领域最大、带动人口最多、可持续性最强、巩固脱贫成果防止返贫、全面完成脱贫任务最有效的方式。

产业振兴通过挖掘区位优势，立足资源禀赋，整合市场资源，联结政府、农户、龙头企业、农村经济合作组织等主体，调整乡村传统产业结构，在农村地区形成一批现代化的集聚、共生协同产业，将资源优势转变为经济优势，进而带动群众增收，最终实现共同富裕。

在乡村产业振兴的实现路径上，可以针对区域因地制宜采取不同模式。产业基础薄弱的地区一般缺乏资源、区位优势，其产业振兴应以产业扶贫为第一目标，在产业扶贫实施过程中，为产业振兴奠定较好的物质、人才基础，并在制度安排上留好接口。而在已经有一定产业基础的地区，则其产业发展应以实现产业转型升级为目标，着力推动产业融合发展和产业一体化体系的形成。在发展模式上，资源禀赋条件较好的区域适宜走内生型发展模式；而在经济基础薄弱、资源优势不明显的区域，则需要从外部借力，通过外部资金、技术、劳动力等生产要素的注入，以及强有力的政策指导，即采用外部诱发型发展模式，才能有效促进经济发展。

总体来说,乡村振兴中的产业兴旺需要把握以下三个大方向。

一是坚持市场导向,打破"人、地"要素流动的制度障碍。

在激活人才要素流动方面,一是打破城乡经济社会二元体制,构建城乡命运共同体。按照统一的标准实施教育、就业、就医和保险等政策,城乡居民享受同样的公共服务,真正使城乡结成命运共同体。二是探索人才引进机制,针对产业需求加大人才培养力度,创新人才培养机制。在促进农村青年人才回流的同时,还应逐步吸引高素质人才入驻农村,帮助农民提高生产管理的科学化和规范化水平,提升农业的现代化水平,逐步形成一支技能型的专业劳动大军,为农业现代化和乡村振兴的全面实现提供不可或缺的人力资本基础。

在激活土地要素流动方面,国家在农村土地制度改革中扩权赋能,实行土地所有权、承包权、经营权分置并行,即"三权分置",并鼓励承包土地向新型农业经营主体流转。在扩权赋能方面,要求在依法保护集体所有权和农户承包权的前提下,平等保护经营主体依流转合同取得的土地经营权,保障其有稳定的经营预期。在鼓励规模化流转和经营方面,强调要大力培育新型农业经营主体和服务主体,通过经营权流转、股份合作、代耕代种等多种方式,加快发展土地流转型、服务带动型等多种形式规模经营。

二是优化产业链布局,重塑产业链利益联结机制。

各地需要因地制宜,选择具有本地特色、符合本地实际、能够促进农民增收致富的项目和产业。对产业进行合理引导、精细管理,实现生产和销售的有效衔接。大力塑造和推广区域农业品牌,发展电子商务,引入直播带货、短视频引流和社群营销等新型销售方式。逐步延长产业链,提高产品附加值,以对初级农产品进行深加工为主线,推动一、二、三产业融合发展,实现农业、工业和服务业的有机融合,并大幅提高农产品的价值增值水平,推动农民收入的提升和城乡共同富裕的实现。

在市场竞争中,应该发挥新型农村合作经济组织作用,利用农村专业合作经济组织公平、公开、公正的利益分配机制有效地保证农民收入稳定增加。在此基础上,积极探索和创建农村新型经济组织形式,鼓励和引导农民实行团体式专业合作经营模式,使农民形成风险共担的利益共同体,有效保障农产品商品化生产经营过程中农民利益的最大化。

三是促进三产融合,推进产业兴旺。

中国农村一、二、三产业融合发展还处于初级阶段,三产难以发挥联合效应。开展多元化产业兴旺工作,将农业与二、三产业结合起来,依托新型农业经营主体,推动农业内部重组融合,促进农业横向一体化经营,培育生态农业、设施农业。通过龙头企业、互联网平台等主体,创新共享理念,组织引导土地、劳动力、技术、资金等要素与乡村产业融合,打破城乡壁垒,引导城市要素流向农村,促进城乡要素双向流动。形成产业之间的集聚与联动、纵向一体化发展,使农业向二、三产业自然延伸,二、三产业向农业逆向渗透,形成发展合力,打造集旅游、电商、金融、服务等于一体的多功能产业园区。

8.2.2 中国农业农村的未来

《乡村振兴战略规划(2018—2022年)》实施5年来,中国乡村产业实现新发展,乡村生态展现新气象,广大农民获得感、幸福感、安全感大幅提升。

2021年,全国粮食产量稳定在6 500亿千克以上,棉油糖、肉蛋奶等主要农产品供给充裕。在这一年,农业科技进步贡献率达到61%,农作物耕种收综合机械化率超过72%,分别比2017年提高3.5个和6个百分点。全国农产品加工转化率达到70.6%,农村一、二、三产业深度融合,休闲观光、农村电商等新产业新业态蓬勃发展,农村创新创业活力不断迸发。农业绿色发展水平大幅提升,化肥农药施用量多年负增长,畜禽粪污综合利用率达到76%。农村人居环境明显改善,截至2021年底,中国农村卫生厕所普及率超过70%,农村社会综合服务设施覆盖率比2017年提高40多个百分点。2017—2021年,中国农村居民人均可支配收入实际增长28.9%,城乡居民收入倍差由2.71缩小至2.5。

未来,面对当前中国乡村发展不平衡、不充分的问题,中国将坚定不移地继续全面深化农村改革,破除阻碍乡村振兴的制度障碍,统筹城乡规划,深化土地制度改革,统筹推进农村政治建设、经济建设、文化建设、社会建设、生态文明建设和党的建设,加快推进乡村治理体系和治理能力现代化,加快推进农业农村现代化,落实产业兴旺,真正让农业成为有奔头的产业,让农民成为有吸引力的职业,让农村成为安居乐业的美丽家园。力争到2035年,乡村振兴将取得决定性进展,农业农村现代化基本实现;到2050年,乡村全面振兴,农业强、农村美、农民富全面实现。

9 中国特色的国有企业制度改革

国有企业①在中国国民经济中居于支柱地位,而国有企业的健康持续发展又依赖于有效的企业制度。企业制度作为生产关系的表现形态,随着生产力的发展而变化其形式或改变其性质,同时又反作用于生产力,影响有时甚至决定着生产力的发展进程。企业制度是社会基本经济制度的重要组成部分,也是实现基本经济制度目标的基础性制度安排,国有企业制度建设是中国特色社会主义基本经济制度形成和发展的重要组成部分。

总结新中国成立以来国有企业制度建设的历程和经验,以改革开放为转折点可以分为传统社会主义的国有企业制度形成与改革开放以来国有企业制度的探索,共经历了四个阶段:第一个阶段是1949年到1978年社会主义计划经济体制下国有企业制度的建立和调整探索;第二个阶段是改革开放之后,20世纪80年代的放权让利和承包经营责任制改革;第三个阶段是20世纪90年代初期开始的股份制改革与现代企业制度探索;第四个阶段是中共十八大以来的新时代中国特色现代国有企业制度全面完善。

9.1 社会主义计划经济体制和国有企业制度的建立

国有企业制度是整个计划经济体制最为基础的构成部分。从1949年新中国成立到1978年改革开放之前,是计划经济体制的形成和曲折发展时期。由于没有现成模式可以参考,新中国成立之后便开始了从企业所有权制度到企业内部治理制度的全方位探索,建立了"国有国营"的国有企业制度。如图9-1所示,1957年工业总产值中国有经济占53.77%,集体经济占19.03%,私营经济、个体经济、公私合营等占27.20%,国有经济占绝对优势。至此,社会主义生产资料公有制经济全面建立,"国有国营"成为计划经济时期最为普遍的企业制度形式。这种单一的企业所有权制度一直持续到20世纪70年代末。

9.1.1 社会主义公有制下国有企业制度的特征和重要组成体制

在这个阶段,国有企业制度的发展基础是生产资料社会主义公有制。中国社会主义生产资料公有制的快速建立,有其特殊的政治经济背景。新中国成立之初,农业落后、工业基础薄弱,面对美国等西方国家的政治和经济封锁,国家决策层选择了以重工业优先增长带动

---

① 国有企业即全部或大部分的财产属于国家所有和控制的企业。在我国,国有企业即社会主义全民所有制企业。原均由国家直接经营,通称"国营企业"。经济体制改革中,为增强企业活力,实行所有权和经营权分离,国家不再直接经营企业,改称"国有企业"。在本章中,为便于读者理解,统一称为"国有企业"。

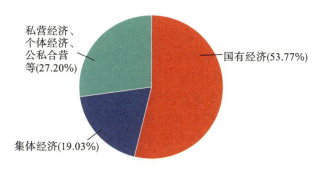

图 9-1 1957年中国工业总产值各类经济占比情况
数据来源:中华人民共和国国家统计局

整个工业化发展,以实现国民经济快速增长的发展战略,加快对私营工商业社会主义改造的进程。迅速建立的社会主义生产资料公有制,成为实施国家发展战略的基础性制度安排,国有企业制度成为服务国家经济体制目标的内生性制度,对社会主义公有制实现形式的探索,使得国有企业迅速发展并占据绝对优势地位。

以集中统一为特征的工业管理体制主要包括以下两个层次的内容。第一个层次,中央政府和地方政府在国有企业管理权限划分方面,实行统一领导、分级管理的基本原则。1950年中央人民政府政务院(简称"政务院",成立于1949年,结束于1954年)把凡属国家所有的工厂企业,分为三种办法管理:一是属于中央各部直接管理;二是属于中央所有,暂时委托地方管理;三是划归地方管理。适当扩大地方政府在发展地方工业方面的权力和责任,促进地方工业的发展,建立起一个集中统一的管理体制。这个体制的核心是要把中央和地方关系处理好,在中华人民共和国成立初期,强调既要保障中央的权威,又要扩大发展地方工业的权力,促进地方工业的发展,但主要还是以集中统一为主流。第二个层次,在国家和国有企业的关系上实行以统收统支为主要特征的集中统一的管理体制:一是在财政方面实行统收统支,国有企业需要的资金按照所属关系由各级人民政府预算拨款,超定额的流动资金由人民银行贷款,国有企业除缴纳税收之外还要将其大部分利润上缴政府;二是在物资供应和产品销售方面开始实行以计划调拨为主的物资供应和产品收购体制;三是在劳动方面着手建立集中管理体制,各公营企业人员均由各级编制委员会统一管理;四是在计划方面开始对国有企业进行直接计划即指令性计划管理。

国有企业领导和管理体制的建立是"国有国营"的国有企业制度的一个重要组成部分。由社会主义公有制性质所决定,国家与企业之间的关系又在很大程度上决定了国有企业制度的特征和运营机制。基于新中国成立之前革命根据地时期公营企业供给制的传统,特别是出于实施国家工业化战略的迫切需要,新中国成立之后就开始建立中央计划经济体制下的国有企业领导和管理体制,包括主要国有企业由中央各部门直接管理,关系国计民生重要工业品的生产和分配、绝大部分工业基本建设项目、重要工业生产资料都由中央部委统一分配,中央管理之外的企业由地方政府统一管理,整体上形成了由物资分配管理、财务管理、干部管理、劳动工资(福利)管理等计划经济管理制度所组成的国有企业制度。

企业党委领导下的厂长负责制是当时国有企业制度中的内部治理体制。"一五"计划期间,国有企业内部治理制度建设取得了明显进展。其中,在企业内部领导体制探索方面主要实行厂长负责制与民主管理相结合的制度,通过采用工厂管理委员会的形式达到民主管理的目的。生产行政工作实行厂长负责制,企业党委主要负责政治思想领导,对企业生产行政工作发挥保证监督作用,对工会、青年团等群众组织发挥领导作用。1956年9月,中共八大报告明确指出,国有企业应当建立以党为核心的集体领导和个人负责相结合的领导制度,凡是重大问题都应当经过集体讨论和共同决定。这是中国国有企业发展史上首次明确企业党委领导下的厂长负责制,与今天我们所实行的党委集体领导的体制一脉相承。1961年9月,中共中央发布了具有重要意义的《国营工业企业工作条例(草案)》,明确国家对国有工业企业实行统一领导和分级管理原则,明确党委领导下的行政管理上的厂长负责制等企业制度核心要素,以规范企业基础管理。在实行党委领导下厂长负责制的同时,实行职工代表大会制,吸收广大职工参加企业民主管理。图9-2为大连机床附件厂厂长王林同技术人员一起研究滚轮轴的质量。劳动工资制度主要是建立全国统一的企业工资制度;经济核算制主要是构建全国统一的会计核算制度,并将其嵌入企业制度中。

图9-2　大连机床附件厂厂长王林(左三)同技术人员一起研究滚轮轴的质量

图片来源:大连机床集团

9.1.2　社会主义计划经济时期对国有企业制度作出的调整和探索

由于没有现成模式可供参考,新中国成立至改革开放的近30年时间里,中国国有企业制度探索过程中也出现过曲折。但党和政府能从中汲取教训,努力纠偏纠错,作出了以权限下放和上收为特征的两次国有企业制度调整。

1957年,中共八届三中全会通过的《关于改进工业管理体制的规定(草案)》明确将部分国有企业管理权、物资分配权、利润分配(使用)权等下放给地方和企业,在减少指令性计划、简化计划编制程序、实行国家与企业利润分成、改进企业财务管理和人事管理等方面作出了制度性调整。

权限下放使得国有企业获得了一定的经营自主权,国有资产运营效率有所提高。图9-3为当年《人民日报》发表的有关权力下放的文章。但是当时推行过于急促,过度下放权力,导致经济生活出现混乱局面,加上地方政府管理大企业的经验和能力不足,很多制度落实不下去,一些企业管理比较混乱,企业生产效率低下,而中央对国民经济管理的控制力也在下降,因此后来又促使中央再次上收管理权限。1961年1月,中共中央作出《中共中央关于调整管

图 9-3　1958 年 3 月 23 日《人民日报》发表的有关权力下放的文章

理体制的若干暂行规定》，提出把经济管理权力集中到中央、中央局和省（市、自治区）委三级，并提出在两三年内更多地集中到中央和中央局。同年 9 月 15 日，中共中央下发《中共中央关于当前工业问题的指示》，强调要改变过去一段时间内权力下放过多、分得过散的现象，要把权力更多地集中到中央（包括中央局），对全国人力、财力和物力进行统一安排。实际上，整个经济管理体制就又回到了中央高度计划和高度集中的"大一统"体制。权限上收的主要体现为：第一，集中统一上收一批下放不当的企业；第二，计划管理权限再度集中统一，改变"大跃进"期间"两本账"的做法，克服计划失控现象，高度集中的计划体制又回来了；第三，集中统一上收基本建设管理权限，压缩基本建设规模，上收基本建设审批权，收回投资计划管理权限，严格基本建设程序，加强对基本建设拨款的监督；第四，取消企业利润留成制度，上收财政信贷管理权，保障中央财力；第五，统一上收物资管理权限。

9.1.3　社会主义计划经济体制下国有企业制度的成就和局限性

高度计划的社会主义经济体制是以国民经济中居于主导地位的社会主义国家所有制工业为基础的，这是符合工业水平低和工业结构简单的历史情况的体制选择。这种国有企业制度对社会主义工业化的迅猛推进、对中华人民共和国成立初期市场的稳定和经济的恢复发展、对迅速赶超工业化国家，起到历史性作用。必须承认这一国有企业制度在中国工业化和经济增长中所发挥的重要作用。这一制度的优势是便于集中生产资源和提升要素调配效率，但也出现管得过多过死、影响企业活力等问题。国有企业经营自主权的缺失和激励体系的缺失，是这一制度的主要缺陷。国有企业成为国家计划的附属物和执行国家计划的工具，成为国家执行赶超战略的工具。

总之,至 20 世纪 70 年代末改革开放之前,新中国建立的是高度集中的计划经济体制,包含其中的"国有国营"企业制度存在动力与活力不足等问题。但站在历史视角审视,当时的制度选择并非偶然。"国有国营"企业制度其实是实现国家工业化发展战略所提出的内生性制度,是整个计划经济体制的基础部分。至 1978 年,全国工业总产值达到 4 231 亿元,其中国有企业部分占 77.6%,国有企业制度所作出的贡献显而易见。

9.2 改革开放初期国有企业改革探索:放权让利和承包经营责任制改革

在高度集中的计划经济体制下,国有企业面临的效率不高、大面积亏损和激励不足等问题亟待解决。企业生产经营自主权缺失导致企业组织结构僵化和活力不足。于是,为了建立起适合国有企业的激励制度,1978 年改革开放之初,中共中央决策层便迅速确定了以"放权让利"为中心的国有企业改革方向,承包经营责任制即承包制成为这一时期所采用的主要形式。

9.2.1 放权让利改革的特征和内容

与权限下放有所不同,放权让利的着重点在于扩大企业自主权改革,意在通过让渡一部分收益支配权给企业来激励管理者和职工,最终达到管理者、职工和国家利益共同增加的目的。1979 年 7 月,中国国务院印发了《关于扩大国营工业企业经营管理自主权的若干规定》及《关于国营企业实行利润留成的规定》等配套文件,提出改企业基金制为利润留成制,试图以实施利润留成制度赋予企业一定的分配权为切入点扩大企业自主权,努力解决"以政代企"问题。

四川省率先试点"放权让利",在四川省委的支持下,1978 年 10 月,四川省率先给予省内的宁江机床厂、重庆钢铁公司、成都无缝钢管厂、四川化工厂、新都县氮肥厂、南充丝绸厂等 6 家国有企业一定的经营自主权。图 9-4 为改革开放前的南充丝绸厂生产车间。

图 9-4 改革开放前的南充丝绸厂生产车间
图片来源:南充市政府

在放权让利的改革过程中,有两个配套措施是极其重要的,即"拨改贷"和"利改税"。在信贷方面,中国进行了"拨改贷"改革,即对基本建设的投资由拨款改为贷款。1979 年,"拨改贷"首先在北京、上海、广东三个省市及纺织、轻工、旅游等行业试点。1980年,中国又扩大范围,规定凡是实行独立核算、有还贷能力的建设项目,都要进行"拨改贷"改革。1985年,"拨改贷"在全国各行业全面推行。"拨改贷"对国有企业运行机制的变革起到重要的作用,财政部不再自上而下拨款了,也不再存在各个地区到财政部争取更多地方投资拨款的问题,预算软约束问题慢慢开始缓解。

"利改税"改革从1983年起实行,即以纳税代替上缴利润。图9-5为当年《人民日报》发表的相关文章。税代利有以下好处:第一,将税收形式固定下来,可以避免实行利润留成、盈亏包干办法存在的争基数、吵比例的扯皮现象;第二,企业实现利润后以税收形式作为第一笔扣除上缴国家,可以保证国家财政收入的稳定增长;第三,减少部门、地区对企业不必要的行政干预,企业在照章纳税后能够更加自主地安排生产经营活动;第四,国家根据宏观经济的需要,可以采取调整税率、减免税收负担等措施调节生产和分配,促进国民经济的协调发展。

图9-5 "利改税"改革消息登上了《人民日报》的头版头条

9.2.2 承包经营责任制的特征和内容

1984年10月,中共十二届三中全会通过的《中共中央关于经济体制改革的决定》把"在公有制基础上的有计划的商品经济"设定为当时制度改革的目标模式。早期以"利润留成"为主要形式的放权让利,因留成基数确定和市场价格体系不合理等在企业之间造成了不平等竞争,因而未能达到所设想的激励和约束效果。1986年开始大范围实施承包经营责任制,承包经营责任制其实是"放权让利"的一种深化形式,具有"两权分离"的含义。承包经营责任制作为改革之初全民所有制企业采用的主要经济责任制形式,是国有企业由单纯生产型企业向生产经营型企业转型的初始形态。企业通过承诺利润(税收)上缴、经济效益、资产增值、技术改造等义务,以及自负盈亏的经营责任获得部分经营自主权和剩余索取权。1988年2月,国务院发布《全民所有制工业企业承包经营责任制暂行条例》,对企业承包内容、内部承包方法、责任制落实和管理制度等作出详细规定,1988年4月发布的《中华人民共和国全民所有制工业企业法》进一步提升了承包经营责任制的合法地位。到1988年,全国预算内9 900多家工业企业中已有91%实行了承包经营责任制。图9-6为无锡试点实行国有企业承包经营责任制的签约现场。

图 9-6　无锡试点实行国有企业承包经营责任制——无锡油泵油咀集团全员劳动合同制签约现场

图片来源：无锡市政府

9.2.3　以放权让利为切入点的承包经营责任制改革的局限性

"放权让利"本质上是对作为国有企业股东的政企关系的调整，对国有企业内部治理产生直接影响，国有企业治理制度也发生了一些变化。一是企业领导体制的探索，主要是围绕企业内部党、政、工关系进行了探索。先是明确国有企业实行党委领导下的厂长负责制和党委领导下的职工代表大会制，1986 年大范围实施承包经营责任制之后，又开始强化厂长的生产经营和行政管理权。二是企业内部层层建立岗位责任制，尤其是开始关注如何探索建立适合中国国情的企业现代化管理体系。三是进行企业内部工资分配制度改革，实行了职务工资、岗位工资津贴、浮动工资、奖金提取与分配、承包工资等新的工资制度，使企业管理者和职工工资总额与企业经济效益挂钩。20 世纪 70 年代末到 90 年代初的国有企业改革，主要是有限利用经济利益原则，在原有计划经济制度框架下扩大企业自主权、给予企业和职工部分经济激励为特征的局部改革。放权让利因触及控制权和收益权，激发了企业和职工积极性，提升了企业效率。

承包经营责任制部分解决了企业严重亏损、经营不善、激励不足的问题。但是，承包经营责任制这个方法应该说是折中的、过渡性的、不彻底的方法，因为在这个激励制度当中，企业的治理结构和企业家的激励结构仍然是不完善的，企业独立决策权仍然是非常有限的，计划经济体制还没有被打破，企业还没有成为独立的法人实体。

以放权让利为切入点和以承包经营责任制为主要形式的国有企业制度改革，虽然未能动摇企业所有权制度，但毕竟使其控制权结构、收益分配结构和经营目标等发生了许多有积极意义的变化，具有重要制度试验意义。

9.3　20 世纪 90 年代初期国有企业改革：股份制改革和现代企业制度

进入到 20 世纪 90 年代，国有企业面临着资金与管理的困境，主要存在三个问题，即资金不足带来的长期亏损问题、激励问题和国有企业法人治理结构问题。资本市场的建立，是中国国有企业改革的一个必然产物。1992年,邓小平南方谈话以及召开的中共十四大及时调整了原有的经济体制改革目标,十四大报告明确提出,经济体制改革的目标,是在坚持公有制和按劳分配为主体、其他经济成分和分配方式为补充的基础上,建立和完善社会主义市场经济体制。

9.3.1 股份制改革下现代企业制度的建立

1993年11月11日至14日,中共十四届三中全会召开,审议通过《中共中央关于建立社会主义市场经济体制若干问题的决定》,对"转换国有企业经营机制,建立现代企业制度"等重大问题作出决定,提出建立"产权明晰、权责明确、政企分开、管理科学"的现代企业制度。1993年12月通过的《中华人民共和国公司法》(简称《公司法》),从法律上规范了包括国有企业在内的市场经济体制下企业组织形式的种类和基本组成。国有企业便开始以《公司法》为基本遵循,围绕市场主体的培育,以产权为突破口,进行了以公司制为主要实现形式的企业制度改革。从1994年开始,国务院选择了具有不同地区和不同类型的100家企业进行现代企业制度的试点工作,按照《公司法》要求组建及规范现有的股份制企业,成为当时国有企业改革的一项重要任务。图9-7为广州海运(集团)公司现代企业制度试点实施方案论证会。截至1994年底,据不完全统计,中国共有股份制企业3.3万家,比1993年增长1.52倍。其中有限责任公司约2.66万家;股份有限公司达到6 326家,股本总额约为2 867.56亿元。

图 9-7 广州海运(集团)公司现代企业制度试点实施方案论证会
图片来源:中远海运(广州)有限公司

1999年9月,中共十五届四中全会通过的《中共中央关于国有企业改革和发展若干重大问题的决定》明确指出,建立现代企业制度是发展社会化大生产和市场经济的必然要求,是公有制与市场经济相结合的有效途径,是国有企业改革的方向;公司制是现代企业制度的一种有效组织形式;公司法人治理结构是公司制的核心。同时还指出,坚持党的领导,发挥国有企业党组织的政治核心作用,是一个重大原则,任何时候都不能动摇;坚持国有企业党委负责人与董事会、监事会、经理层人员"双向进入"原则,以及党委书记和董事长可由一人担任等治理原则。

9.3.2　现代企业制度下的国有企业内部治理

这一时期的国有企业内部治理制度建设,主要按照中共中央关于国有企业改革尤其是国有大中型企业建立现代企业制度的精神建立健全有效的法人治理结构。《公司法》在有序推进国有企业法人治理结构建设方面起到了关键作用。《公司法》按照资本逻辑,确定了公司人事、经营、投资、财务管理、收益分配、薪酬等重大事项在股东、董事会、监事会、经理层等层级的权力配置,建立了公司治理的激励与制衡机制。根据《公司法》,公司制企业法人资格的取得克服了全民所有制企业下国家作为投资者要承担无限责任的弊端,也突破了筹资规模的限制,增强了产权的流动性,为国有资本的自由进退提供了便利。2003年10月,中共十六届三中全会通过的《中共中央关于完善社会主义市场经济体制若干问题的决定》提出,要"建立归属清晰、权责明确、保护严格、流转顺畅的现代产权制度",希望通过深化产权改革与政企关系调整、发展混合所有制经济等促进有效法人治理结构的建立健全。2005年,中共中央启动了股权分置改革,通过引入市场化激励约束机制、搭建利益平衡协商机制、构建有效的外部监督与自我约束机制,进一步完善了国有企业法人治理结构。

9.3.3　现代企业制度的贡献和局限

1992年之后的改革可以看作以所有权改革为突破口、以建立法人治理结构为中心、以国有资产监管体制改革为辅助、以培育市场主体为目标的企业制度革命性变革。截至2011年底,全国90%以上的国有企业完成了公司制股份制改革,中央企业的公司制股份制改制面由2003年的30.4%提高到2011年的72%。随着国有企业现代企业制度建设及国有资产监管体制改革的深入,国有企业的经济效益改善明显。2003—2011年,非金融类国有企业营业收入从10.73万亿元增加到39.25万亿元,年均增长率高达17.6%;净利润从3 202.3亿元增加到1.94万亿元,年均增长率高达25.2%;上缴税金从8 361.6亿元增加到3.45万亿元,年均增长率高达19.4%。2011年末,全国国有企业资产总额为85.37万亿元,所有者权益为29.17万亿元。

以股份制为代表的现代企业制度,对增强国有企业的独立性、规范性和完善国有企业的治理结构很有意义,但是,股份制改革也有弊端。当时在国有资本管理体制不完善的情况之下,国有企业的股份制改革导致了国有资产大量流失,其根源在于既得利益者和内部控制人可以以非常便宜的价格把国有资产卖掉,使大量国有资产瞬间成为个人财富,造成很大的社会不公。同时,股份制并没有彻底改变中国国有企业的所有制问题。

9.4　新时代中国特色现代国有企业制度全面完善:混合所有制改革

中共十八大之后,中国特色现代国有企业制度建设进入全面完善新时代。其主要特征是强化顶层设计,整体推进中国特色现代国有企业制度建设。2013年11月,中共十八届三中全会通过的《中共中央关于全面深化改革若干重大问题的决定》指出了新时代国有企业改革的方向为积极发展混合所有制经济,以管资本为主加强国有资产监管,推动国有企业完善现代企业制度;明确了健全协调运转、有效制衡的公司法人治理结构、建立职业经理人制度、更好发挥企业家作用,以及深化企业内部劳动、人事和分配制度改革等现代国有企业制度的具体要求。随后中共中央出台了《关于深化国有企业改革的指导意见》等系列文件,进一步对完善企业法人治理结构、加强党的领导、发展混合所有制经济、员工持股、分类改革与考核、国有资产管理体制改革等内容给出了指引。中共十九大和中共十九届四中全会更加明确地强调了发展混合所有制经济、完善中国特色现代国有企业制度、形成以管资本为主的国有资产监管体制等国有企业改革的核心内容。新时代对国有企业改革的顶层设计是对自1992年之后长达20年现代国有企业制度建设经验总结的升华,也是中国特色现代国有企业制度建设新阶段的基本遵循。

9.4.1 新时代中国特色现代国有企业制度建设的特点与主要内容

以混合所有制改革为切入点,提升公司法人治理结构的有效性是新时代中国特色现代国有企业制度建设的重要特点。中共十八大之后,混合所有制改革被提升到重要位置,2015年9月国务院发布《国务院关于国有企业发展混合所有制经济的意见》。

现阶段完善现代国有企业制度主要内容包括:推进公司制股份制改革、健全公司法人治理结构、建立企业领导人员分类分层管理制度、实行企业薪酬分配制度改革、深化企业内部用人制度改革、加强党的领导和党的建设等。其中,将企业党组织内嵌到公司治理结构中,并使其发挥领导核心和政治核心作用,是新时代现代企业制度建设的重要创新。习近平总书记指出,坚持党对国有企业的领导是重大政治原则,必须一以贯之;建立现代企业制度是国有企业改革的方向,也必须一以贯之。这两个"一以贯之",也是中国特色现代国有企业制度建设的根本遵循。

9.4.2 新时代中国特色现代国有企业制度建设的组成体制

分类改革与分类治理是推进国有企业现代企业制度建设的新方略。以因企施策推进改革为基本前提,按照国有资本的战略定位和发展目标,以及国有企业在经济社会发展中所起作用、发展现状和需要,将国有企业分为商业类和公益类,并进行功能界定和分类治理,明确不同的发展方向、监管方式、责任使命和考核内容,表9-1据此进行了分类。

表9-1 不同类型的国有企业采取不同的公司法人治理结构

国有企业分类	公司法人治理结构
主业处于充分竞争行业和领域的商业类国有企业	国有资本出资人代表或者投资运营公司只能按照以"管资本"为主的原则,实行严格意义上的"两权分离",出资人只能以股东身份承担责任和参与公司治理
主业处于关系国家安全、国民经济命脉的重要行业和关键领域与主要承担重大专项任务的商业类国有企业	国有资本出资人在"管资本"的同时,通过合法程序关注企业服务国家战略、保障国家安全和国民经济运行、发展前瞻性战略性产业及完成特殊任务的情况
处于自然垄断行业的商业类国有企业	治理结构主要围绕提升市场化程度进行优化,注重经济效益和社会效益的有机结合

续表

国有企业分类	公司法人治理结构
公益类国有企业	采取国有独资形式或投资主体多元化(非国有企业可以通过购买服务、特许经营、委托代理等方式参与经营,但不作为投资者持有股份和参与公司治理)的方式建立公司法人治理结构,通过加大信息公开力度,接受社会监督等手段来强化外部监督

契合完善法人治理结构需要,改革完善国有资产管理体制,是新时代中国特色现代国有企业制度建设的重要抓手。中共十八届三中全会通过的《中共中央关于全面深化改革若干重大问题的决定》、中共十九大报告及中共十九届四中全会通过的《中共中央关于坚持和完善中国特色社会主义制度、推进国家治理体系和治理能力现代化若干重大问题的决定》都强调完善国有资产管理体制、改革国有资本授权经营体制的重要性。国有资产监管体制和国有资本授权经营体制的改革,本质上是国有资本委托代理关系的改革,也是政企关系和政资关系的改革。推进国有资本投资运营公司的改组和组建,是以管资本为主改革国有资本管理体制并服务于本轮现代企业制度建设的重要举措。"政府—履行国有资本出资人职责的机构(部门)—国有资本投资运营公司—国有企业"将成为国有资本委托代理链条的普遍模式。从制度安排的角度看,国有资本投资运营公司在国有资本委托代理链条中起到了"承上启下"的关键作用,特别是能够有效隔离国有资本出资人与生产经营实体之间的直接联系,进一步分离所有权与经营权,建立以管资本为主线的国有资本治理新体系。

内部管理制度是中国特色现代国有企业制度的重要组成部分,"劳动、人事和分配"制度又是其中十分关键的内容。中共十八届三中全会通过的《中共中央关于全面深化改革若干重大问题的决定》和中共中央出台的《关于深化国有企业改革的指导意见》等政策文件对国有企业"劳动、人事和分配"制度改革提出了明确要求。近年来,国有企业围绕增强企业活力和竞争力,着力构建企业各类人员能上能下、员工能进能出、收入能增能减的市场化劳动用工、人事和收入分配机制。

9.4.3 新时代中国特色现代国有企业制度建设取得的成效

中共十八大之后,中国特色现代国有企业制度建设的全面完善和提升已经取得了良好制度绩效。到2018年底,中央企业公司化改制已经全面完成。随着混合所有制改革的有序推进,根据2019年发布的《中央企业高质量发展报告》,上市公司已经成为中央企业运营的主体,中央企业资产的65%、营业收入的61%、利润总额来源的88%都来自上市公司。企业制度的全面完善带来了国有企业绩效的提升。2021年,全国国有及国有控股企业实现营业总收入75.55万亿元,与上年度同比增长18.5%。其中,中央国有企业41.73万亿元,同比增长17.7%;地方国有企业33.83万亿元,同比增长19.5%。国有企业利润总额4.52万亿元,同比增长30.1%;其中中央国有企业2.86万亿元,同比增长27%;地方国有企业1.66万亿元,同比增长35.9%。

10 工业化进程与城市发展

工业化是工业驱动的一个国家或地区人均收入的提高和产业结构从农业主导向工业主导的演进过程,其实质是国民经济中一系列重要的生产要素组合方式连续发生由低级到高级的突破性变化,进而推动经济增长的过程。从现代化理论看,工业化可以认为就是经济现代化。现代化一个比较普遍的解释就是人类社会从传统社会向现代社会转变的历史过程,而社会变迁的动力是经济增长和结构变革,这也就是工业化。这意味着现代化的实质就是由工业化驱动的现代社会变迁过程,因此,一个国家要实现现代化,就需要开启并推动自己的工业化进程。

总结新中国成立以来中国特色工业化的历程,可以将其分为三个阶段:一是20世纪50年代到70年代,中国社会主义工业化道路的形成;二是改革开放之后到21世纪初的社会主义工业化模式;三是新时代中国特色社会主义工业化的建设。与工业化建设息息相关的则是中国的城镇化发展。

10.1 社会主义工业化道路的形成

新中国成立之后的社会主义工业化道路,用一句话来概括,就是"以国家高度集权为特征的、优先发展重工业的工业化道路"。受苏联模式和当时国际环境的影响,中国作为一个后发大国在短时期要实现工业化和经济赶超,选择这样的道路是有道理的。1949年9月29日,中国人民政治协商会议第一届全体会议通过的《中国人民政治协商会议共同纲领》也明确提出,应以有计划有步骤地恢复发展重工业为重点,创立国家工业化的基础,同时恢复和增加轻工业的生产,满足人民群众的消费需要。中华人民共和国成立后,中国开启了波澜壮阔的工业化,但是工业化的进程非常曲折。

10.1.1 国民经济恢复期:以重工业优先的发展战略

1949年10月到1952年的新民主主义社会时期,中国实施了没收官僚资本的经济政策,完成了国民经济恢复任务,建立起高度集中的经济管理体制雏形,为大规模的国家工业化建设奠定了基础。

首先,党和政府确立了国有工业的主体地位,并建立了工业经济高度集中的计划经济体制。1949年,国有工业产值占全国工业总产值的比重达到26.2%,占全国大型工业总产值的41.3%,成为国民经济的领导力量。1950年3月,政务院颁布《关于统一国家财政经济工作的决定》(见图10-1),标志着以集中统一为基础的财经管理体制初步形成。工业经济高度

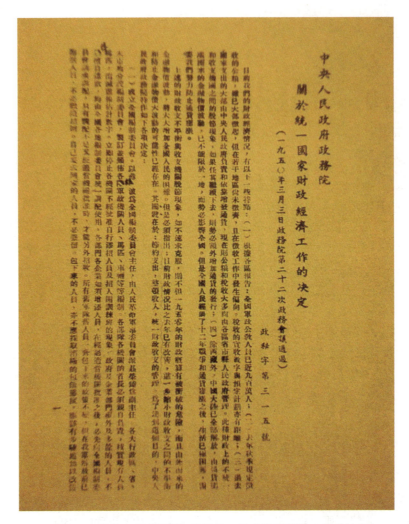

图 10-1　1950 年 3 月颁布的《关于统一国家财政经济工作的决定》

集中的计划经济体制有两个层次。第一个层次,对工业的管理权限在中央政府与地方政府之间,实行统一领导和分级管理;第二个层次,在国家和国有企业的关系方面,财政上实行统收统支,物资供应和产品销售实行以计划调拨为主的物资供应和产品收购体制,劳动力由全国各级编制委员会统一管理,对国有企业实行直接的指令性计划。

其次,党和政府以重工业优先作为当时工业的主要发展战略。作为一个大国,中国必须要建立独立的工业体系。建立在一穷二白基础上的中国重工业基础尤其薄弱,1949 年前后,中国仅能制造一些轻工业产品,"一辆汽车、一架飞机、一辆坦克、一辆拖拉机都不能造"。为了快速改变重工业基础薄弱的现状,增强综合国力特别是国防实力以应对严峻的国际形势,中国选择了优先发展重工业的战略。

10.1.2　向社会主义过渡的初期工业化:156 项重点工程

1953 年到 1956 年是从新民主主义社会向社会主义社会过渡的时期,围绕着"一化三改"的过渡时期总路线,中国在"一五"计划时期开始引进布局的 156 项重点工程,初步奠定了新中国工业化的基础。"一五"计划取得巨大成功,高度集中的计划经济体制在"一五"计划期间逐渐形成。

作为一个工业化后发国家,中国摆脱落后面貌的心态十分急迫。1951年2月,中共中央政治局扩大会议决定自1953年起实施"一五"计划,并要求政务院着手进行编制计划的各项准备工作。1952年下半年,"一五"计划的编制工作开始紧锣密鼓地进行。从着手编制新中国的第一个长期经济建设计划开始,优先发展重工业的指导思想就清晰地表现出来。经过国民经济的恢复和近一年的酝酿,1953年9月,过渡时期总路线正式出台。同年,"一五"计划启动。1953年底,《为动员一切力量把我国建设成为一个伟大的社会主义国家而斗争——关于党在过渡时期总路线的学习和宣传提纲》明确提出了"社会主义工业化",强调"发展国家的重工业,以建立国家工业化和国防现代化的基础"是实现"社会主义工业化的中心环节"。新中国选择了一条重工业优先的工业化路线,形成这一局面的原因很多,而其中最根本的原因是中国的重工业基础过于薄弱,这一事实所造成的不利影响又因为连年的战乱和外敌的入侵而被不断强化。

156项重点工程是中国"一五"计划时期苏联援助中国建设的一系列重大重工业项目的统称。156项重点工程中,实际实施的150项工程主要分布在能源、冶金、化学、机械、轻工、医药、军工七大行业,都属于重工业部门或生产资料部门。如图10-2是沈阳飞机研究所,图10-3是华北制药厂。以156项重点工程为主体的工业基本建设是"一五"计划的中心。

图10-2　在苏联专家指导下沈阳飞机研究所学习飞机制造

图片来源:中航工业

在"一五"计划中,工业部门获得的投资高达313.2亿元,占比40.9%,体现了工业建设在该计划中的中心地位。"一五"计划明确规定,在工业基本建设投资中,制造生产资料工业的投资占88.8%,制造消费资料工业的投资占11.2%。投资的比例关系必须根据生产资料

图 10-3 "一五"计划时期政府投资新建的华北制药厂

图片来源:国药集团

有限增长的原理来决定,而在每个发展时期中,这种比例关系的具体规定,又应该照顾到当时的具体条件。生产资料优先增长,也就是重工业优先。156 项重点工程不但使中国在较短的时间内基本形成了较为完整的工业体系,而且显著缩小了中国与世界工业生产力前沿的差距,在保障国家安全、促进经济增长方面具有重大的历史意义。

10.1.3 "大跃进"及国民经济调整时期的工业化

在"一五"计划取得辉煌成果和三大改造基本完成的基础上,中共中央决定实施第二个五年计划(简称"二五"计划),要求继续进行以重工业为中心的工业建设并建立中国社会主义工业化的巩固基础。"二五"计划期间,中国继续推进和扩大了冶金、机器制造、电力、煤炭和建筑材料等工业部门的建设,攻克了冶金、采矿、电站、石化等现代化大型设备的设计和制造技术。由于在钢铁工业发展中操之过急,中国在 1958 年至 1960 年甚至掀起了"大跃进"运动,意图加快钢铁工业发展,使钢铁和其他主要工业产品产量赶上或超过英美,造成钢产量不合格率较高和国民经济比例严重失调等问题。图 10-4 为这一时期大炼钢铁的情况。

图 10-4 "大跃进"时期大炼钢铁

图片来源:科学网

1964年12月,周恩来在中华人民共和国第三届全国人民代表大会第一次会议上作了政府工作报告,明确阐述了两步走战略:"今后发展国民经济的主要任务,总的说来,就是要在不太长的历史时期内,把我国建设成为一个具有现代农业、现代工业、现代国防和现代科学技术的社会主义强国,赶上和超过世界先进水平。"1975年1月,周恩来在第四届全国人民代表大会第一次会议上所作的政府工作报告中,重申了四个现代化的目标和两步走战略。

10.1.4 成就与总结

总体上看,在这个时期,工业化道路的核心是优先快速发展重工业,特点是政府作为投资主体、国家指令性计划作为资源配置手段。在这个前提下,党不断探索正确处理国民经济比例关系和农业、轻工业和重工业的关系,逐步建立起独立的、比较完整的工业体系和国民经济体系,为改革开放后快速的工业化进程积累了经验,打下了较好的物质基础和人才基础,特别是重工业基础,有力地突破了帝国主义封锁,保障了国家经济独立和国防安全,也为中国在改革开放时期发展成为世界制造业大国奠定了牢固的经济和技术基础。

新中国成立后近30年的社会主义工业化建设的重大成就可以概括为三点:一是巩固了国家政权。国防工业从无到有逐步建设起来,兴建了一批新的工业基地,特别是成功地发射了"两弹一星"。二是在较短时间内建立了独立的、比较完整的工业体系。1949—1978年,中国工业总产值从140亿元增加到4 237亿元;其中,轻工业产值从103亿元增加到1 826亿元,重工业产值从37亿元增加到2 411亿元;1978年工业总产值、轻工业产值和重工业产值分别是1949年的30.3倍、17.7倍、65.2倍;按照可比价格,1978年工业总产值是1949年的29.8倍,年均增速12.4%。三是国民经济逐步完善,经济发展有大幅增长。同完成经济恢复的1952年相比,1980年主要工业品增长明显:棉纱产量增长3.5倍,达到293万吨;原煤产量增长8.4倍,达到6.2亿吨;发电量增长40倍,达到3 000多亿千瓦时;原油产量达到1亿多吨;钢产量达到3 700多万吨;机械工业产值增长53倍,达到1 270多亿元。

10.2 改革开放后社会主义市场经济下的工业化

20世纪70年代中后期,面对趋于缓和的国际政治环境,中国开启了改革开放的宏伟历程。通过利用国际资金、市场和资源,充分发挥劳动力丰富、工资水平和制造成本低的优势并抓住全球产业分工格局重构的机遇,中国工业迎来高速增长期,中国迅速发展成为世界重要的制造基地。以改革开放为动力,这个时期的工业化经历了1978—1991年的社会主义市场经济方向探寻阶段和1992—2012年的社会主义市场经济构建完善阶段。

10.2.1 社会主义市场经济方向探寻阶段

在该阶段,以1984年为界,整个经济体制改革经历从农村到城市、从农业到工业和调整轻、重工业比例的重点转变过程。到改革开放之初,重工业优先发展战略由于不符合中国当时的比较优势已经难以为继,改变重工业优先发展战略势在必行。

1978年,中共十一届三中全会决定,从1979年1月起,把全党的工作中心转移到社会主义现代化建设上来,提出让地方和工农业企业在国家统一计划的指导下有更多的经营管理自主权,中国进入改革开放新时期。在这段时间内,中国经历了从"五五"计划向"七五"计划的工业化建设调整(见图 10-5)。1979 年 4 月,中央工作会议制定了用 3 年时间对国民经济实行"调整、改革、整顿、提高"的方针。20 年代 80 年代初期又出台轻纺工业优先发展政策,加快推动轻工业发展,调整轻、重工业比例关系和重工业内部结构。轻、重工业发展重点的转变符合改革开放之初中国资本稀缺、劳动力丰富的资源禀赋条件。工业部门普遍进行了结构调整和技术改造,工业发展迅速,工业产值占比稳步提升,同时,工业中的轻工业发展迅速,占比有大幅提升。而农业占比开始了持续下降,总体上中国产业结构更加合理。在对外开放带动下,经济区域分布也发生了巨大变化,制度要素、资金要素和技术要素在东部集聚,劳动力要素也开始向东部迁移,自此形成了持续多年的自西向东、自内地向沿海的"打工潮",东部沿海产业开始崛起。

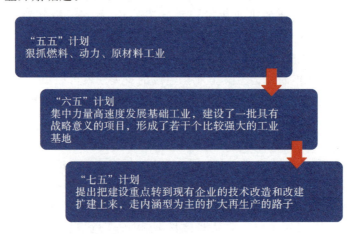

图 10-5 "五五"计划至"七五"计划期间工业化建设重点

10.2.2 社会主义市场经济构建完善阶段

以 1992 年邓小平南方谈话和中共十四大为标志,社会主义市场经济进入构建完善阶段。1993 年,中共十四届三中全会通过了《中共中央关于建立社会主义市场经济体制若干问题的决定》,提出建立市场在国家宏观调控下对资源配置起基础性作用的社会主义市场经济体制,坚持以公有制为主体、多种经济成分共同发展的方针,并提出将要素市场作为市场体系培育重点,从此进入了全面建设和不断完善社会主义市场经济的阶段。这个阶段的快速工业化进程呈现出以下几方面特征:

第一,伴随着居民消费重点转向耐用消费品,中国工业体现出了重化工主导的特征,促进了中国经济结构的快速升级,中国产业结构从劳动密集型主导转向资金密集型主导。1996 年,中国商品市场基本告别短缺状态;到 21 世纪初,中国拥有了巨大的工业生产能力和显著的价格竞争力,成为世界重要的加工制造基地。

第二,低成本出口导向的工业化战略取得巨大成效。尤其是 2001 年加入 WTO 后,中国充分利用自己的比较优势积极参与了全球价值链分工,深度融入经济全球化,通过"干中学"推进产业升级,快速地推进经济增长和工业化进程,迅速成为纺织服装、消费电子等劳动密集型产业和产业链环节的全球加工制造中心,对世界经济增长作出了巨大贡献。

第三,地方政府在推动工业化中发挥了重要的作用。在国家战略上,区域协调发展逐步成为中国工业化的区域布局主导战略,西部大开发、中部崛起和东北老工业基地振兴等重大战略举措开始实施和持续推进。同时,中央推进了放权让利的改革:实施中央与地方分税制改革;对市县政府下放土地出让权利。这使得地方政府拥有了两个重要的抓手,在扩大地方投资、加强招商引资等方面有了很大的用武之地。地方政府作为一个具有中国特色的新的市场主体,直接统领本地企业、运用本地资源、谋划战略布局,与其他地区展开加快工业化的市场竞争。地方政府推进工业化的工作主要有三个方面:制定和实施地区中长期发展战略规划;建立不同类型的工业开发区和产业园区;全方位开展各种形式的招商引资活动。在这种发展和竞争的实践中,各地创造了丰富多样的工业化模式,如"珠三角模式""苏南模式""晋江模式""温州模式"等,对中国工业化的快速推进起了独特作用。

第四,在解决规模问题后,中国工业发展战略和政策的重点开始转向提高创新能力、环境质量、经济效益等高质量发展方面。2002年,中共十六大提出"走出一条科技含量高、经济效益好、资源消耗低、环境污染少、人力资源优势得到充分发挥的新型工业化路子"。2007年召开的党的十七大将科学发展观写入党章,针对工业发展提出"加快转变经济发展方式,推动产业结构优化升级",要发展现代产业体系,大力推进信息化与工业化融合,促进工业由大变强。

10.2.3 成就与总结

改革开放后是中国工业化进程最快、工业国际地位提升最快的阶段,具有明显的"压缩型工业化"特征。我们用几十年时间走完了发达国家几百年走过的工业化历程,有力支撑了中国人民从站起来到富起来、强起来的伟大飞跃。中国工业生产能力在持续扩大,工业的国际竞争力在不断增强。

这个时期,中国积极探索并确立了中国特色社会主义市场经济体制下的工业化道路,工业化战略和政策的重心逐步转向市场在配置资源中发挥基础性作用、低成本出口导向、建设开放型经济、基于产业演进规律不断促进产业结构优化升级。中国工业化实现了前所未有的高速发展,创造了经济增长奇迹。

10.3 2012年以来中国特色社会主义工业化建设

中共十八大以来,中国特色社会主义进入新时代,中国在经济改革发展的理论和政策方面实现了一系列创新,工业化建设取得了重大成就。

2015年,中共十八届五中全会围绕适应、把握和引领经济发展新常态,明确提出了以人民为中心的发展思想,提出了创新、协调、绿色、开放、共享的新发展理念,中国工业化道路开始向创新驱动的、包容的、可持续的高质量工业化转型。尤其是坚持将创新作为引领发展的第一动力,加快创新型国家建设。通过不断优化创新生态,加大科研创新投入,使得新产业、新业态、新模式蓬勃发展,创新型国家建设取得新进展。2015年11月,供给侧结构性改革成为中国经济工作的主线,之后各年确立了"三去一降一补""破、降、立""巩固、增强、提升、畅通"等阶段性方针政策,这极大地促进了中国产业结构向高级化、绿色化、智能化方向转型升级,深化了中国工业化进程,提升了中国工业化质量。针对新时代中国工业化进程的区域不平衡问题,中共中央推出了一系列重大的区域发展战略,加快推进以人为核心的新型城镇化战略,促进了新型工业化、信息化、城镇化和农业现代化"四化"同步发展。

10.3.1　中国特色社会主义工业化建设的特色

这期间,中国工业化的突出特点是贯彻新发展理念,加快经济结构战略性调整,改造提升制造业,提高工业整体素质和国际竞争力。主要表现在三个方面:第一,党和政府将国民经济和社会信息化置于优先位置,大力开发电子信息产品和新型元器件等的制造能力;第二,依托基础设施和重大工程振兴装备制造业,提高重大技术装备研发设计、核心元器件配套、加工制造和系统集成的整体水平;第三,培育战略性新兴产业,加快高技术产业从加工装配等低端环节向研发和先进制造等中高端环节攀升。

10.3.2　新发展阶段的工业化进程和战略取向

中共十九大提出了全面建设社会主义现代化国家新征程,并作出分两个阶段实现第二个百年奋斗目标的战略部署,以推动我国社会主义现代化建设取得新进展。第一阶段是到2035年基本实现社会主义现代化和新型工业化,人均国内生产总值达到中等发达国家水平。第二阶段是到21世纪中叶将中国建成社会主义现代化强国。2020年10月,中共十九届五中全会通过的《中共中央关于制定国民经济和社会发展第十四个五年规划和二〇三五年远景目标的建议》提出,坚持创新在中国现代化建设全局中的核心地位,坚定不移建设制造强国、质量强国、网络强国、数字中国,推进产业基础高级化、产业链现代化,提高经济质量效益和核心竞争力。以上部署明确了中国工业化的历史方位以及实现新型工业化和建设世界工业强国这个新时代中国工业化的任务与目标。中国工业必须直面各种短板和挑战,全面贯彻新发展理念,以攻克核心技术、改善国际分工地位和提高绿色低碳发展能力为主攻方向,在继续做大总量的基础上,加快传统产业升级、新兴产业培育和先进制造业壮大,努力提高发展质量,目的在于如期完成基本实现新型工业化和建设世界工业强国的目标,为基本实现现代化和建设社会主义现代化强国提供有力支撑。新发展阶段工业化道路有以下三个战略取向:

首先,在创新和技术上下功夫,大力推进创新驱动战略,开展核心技术攻关,走创新驱动的工业化道路。中国工业创新发展要充分发挥中国工业体系完整、制造业规模世界第一和新型举国体制的优势,发展壮大以研发、设计为基础的先进制造业,体系化提升制造业的自主创新能力。特别地,从全球层面来看,要响应世界科技进步步伐,加快攻克集成电路、数控机床、机器人、智能装备、数字技术、工业软件等领域核心技术,突破关键基础材料、核心基础零部件、先进基础工艺、产业技术基础等瓶颈,促进物联网、大数据、机器人等新技术在工业中的应用,实现战略性新兴产业和前沿技术产业的突破,占领未来产业竞争的制高点,实现技术自立自强。因此,中国必须明确科技创新政策的目标指向,加强国家战略需求的长期支持能力,加强对关键核心技术攻关组织的指导和支持,完善以政府为主导、各创新主体紧密联系和有效互动的社会系统,更多采取公共部门长期采购、激励商业化需求等方式促进关键核心技术的持续改进和提升,在关键核心技术市场创造者和促进者方面发挥更积极的作用。

其次,在产业链分工上下功夫,积极应对国际产业分工新调整,提升国际分工地位,构建自主可控的产业链。当前国际分工体系因愈演愈烈的逆全球化和保护主义正在进行新的调整,研发、设计和先进制造环节的地位和附加值呈现提高趋势,工业仍然具有强大的按全球化方式组织生产的内在动力。作为世界第二大经济体和第一制造业大国,中国是国际产业分工体系不可或缺的重要组成部分。中国应积极响应国际产业分工带来的新的调整,妥善应对全球产业链区域化趋势,构筑向研发、设计、先进制造等价值链高端攀升的内生动力,强化产业链薄弱环节,推动信息化、智能化、网络化等新一代科技与先进制造业融合发展,加强中小型制造企业数字化和智能化改造,促进中小企业与大企业之间的专业分工与融通发展,增强产业链黏性,进而提升中国在全球生产网络中的地位。与此同时,政策方面也要跟上,中国应着力放宽市场准入,改善要素供给和协作配套条件,提高对美国等发达国家先进制造业领域的资本、技术和人才的吸引力。在高端装备和核心零部件、生物制药和下一代半导体材料等尖端领域,通过形成研发、设计和制造紧密交织、相互依赖的专业化协作体系,积极参与全球产业分工和技术合作,提升国际竞争力。

最后,建立低碳的发展理念,加快发展方式绿色转型,构建低碳工业体系,提高低碳发展能力。低碳发展成为全球普遍接受的理念,当前世界各国普遍积极推动低碳发展。大规模的工业经济使得中国资源能源消费和污染排放量多年处于高位,生态环境压力激增。2020年,中国宣布二氧化碳排放力争于2030年前达到峰值,努力争取2060年前实现碳中和。因此,中国应倡导绿色低碳发展理念,加快绿色低碳技术应用,提升绿色低碳发展能力,大力采用低碳技术和工艺装备,发展低碳产业,构建低碳工业体系,完善重点行业低碳发展政策,探索技术可行、经济可承受的低碳转型战略,走碳达峰及深度脱碳的绿色发展道路。

10.3.3　成就与总结

总之,这个时期的工业化道路是以创新、协调、绿色、开放、共享的新发展理念为指导,工业化战略和政策更加强调新型工业化、城镇化、信息化和农业现代化"四化"同步发展,更加强调满足创新驱动、包容和可持续的工业化要求。随着中国从高速增长逐步转向高质量发展,中国的工业化战略也从高速度工业化转向高质量工业化。以新发展理念为指导,加快构建新发展格局,成为新发展阶段中国共产党探索中国特色工业化道路的重大任务。

10.4　改革开放以来中国的城市发展:工业化与城镇化

改革开放以来中国工业化与城镇化的关系大体上经历三个阶段:第一个阶段是20世纪70年代末至90年代初期,农村工业化快速兴起,大量乡镇企业相继创立和扩张,整体上城镇化的发展与工业化的进程并行。第二个阶段是20世纪90年代初期到2012年左右,由于乡镇企业多数实行了产权改造和企业改制,农村工业化向城市工业化转移,东部沿海城市加快了工业化进程,工业化发展助推城镇化的进程。第三个阶段是中共十八大之后,坚持走中国特色新型城镇化道路,在加快推进城镇化的同时,更加注重城镇化质量的提升,工业化与城镇化趋于融合发展。

10.4.1　城市体制改革(1979—1991年)

改革开放开启了中国城镇化的新历程。1979年至1991年,渐进式的中国城镇化道路逐步形成。这一阶段的特点是,农村体制和城市体制改革相继推出。改革开放前,中国城镇化在计划体制的严控下,始终处于被压制的状态。改革开放之初,农村体制改革形成了城镇化的"推力",而城市体制改革为城镇化提供了"拉力"。

在1978年中共十一届三中全会拉开农村经济体制改革序幕的基础上,1984年,中共十二届三中全会通过的《中共中央关于经济体制改革的决定》开启了城市体制改革,经济改革工作的重心由农村转移到了城市。特别是乡镇企业异军突起,以小城镇为主导的农民就近城镇化成为主流。图10-6为当年的乡镇企业生产车间。城乡贸易市场繁荣,沿海港口的14个城市进一步开放,大批农民"离土又离乡、进厂又进城",形成了很多小城镇化模式。这一时期城镇化取得的效果有:城市数量由1979年的216座增长到1991年的479座;城镇人口由1979年的18 495万人上升到1991年的31 203万人;城镇化率由1979年的18.96%上升到1991年的26.94%。

图10-6　中国最早的乡镇企业——慈溪县宗汉乡黎明农庄粮棉加工厂

图片来源:凤凰网

总体来看,这一阶段经济体制改革成为中国城镇化的主导力量,整体上城镇化和工业化仍然处于并行状态。非公有制经济快速发展,市场体制不断发育,基于经济、法律和行政手段的国家宏观调控体系逐渐形成。这一系列的以城市为中心的经济体制改革成果,为城镇化的进一步发展创造了良好的经济环境。但是户籍制度、住房制度、城市就业和社会福利制度的限制仍然存在,城乡二元结构没有根本发生改变,具有鲜明的"离土不离乡"特点,农村剩余劳动力大多数只能就近流入小城镇,出现常住人口城镇化率高于户籍人口城镇化率的现象,并呈现逐渐扩大的趋势。城市的大门仍然没有完全向农民打开,城镇化的快速发展期还没真正到来。

10.4.2　社会主义市场经济体制下的城镇化进程(1992—2012年)

在改革开放前的沉积和改革开放之初的探索基础上,1992—2012年,伴随着社会主义市场经济体制框架逐步建立和完善,中国城镇化迎来了快速发展时期。这一阶段的特点是,社会主义市场经济体制确立,一系列促进大中小城市和小城镇协调发展、鼓励和支持农民进城务工的新政策出台,城市体制改革进一步深化,城镇化进程进入快速推进、快速发展轨道。

社会主义市场经济体制改革是一项规模宏大的系统工程,从城镇化的角度来看,主要有户籍制度改革、住房市场化改革、农村土地制度改革、人力资源市场改革等。户籍制度改革方面,《小城镇户籍管理制度改革试点方案》(1997年)和《关于推进小城镇户籍管理制度改革的意见》(2001年)的发布,标志着户籍制度改革从小城镇开始全面展开,并逐步向中小城市扩展。城镇住房市场化改革方面,通过《国务院关于深化城镇住房制度改革的决定》(1994年)、《国务院关于进一步深化城镇住房制度改革加快住房建设的通知》(1998年)、《国务院关于促进房地产市场持续健康发展的通知》(2003年)等文件,中国逐步建立多数家庭购买或承租的普通商品住房市场,同时不断完善保障房制度。农村土地制度改革方面,在长期稳定土地承包经营的基础上,国家加快推进农村集体土地确权登记发证工作,建立健全土地承包经营权流转市场。人力资源市场改革方面,《中华人民共和国国民经济和社会发展第十个五年计划纲要》(2001年),明确提出取消对农村劳动力进入城镇就业的不合理限制,引导农村富余劳动力在城乡、地区间的有序流动。随后各部门又密集出台了鼓励农村富余劳动力进城务工的政策,全面取消了各项不合理收费,并逐步建立了就业服务体系。

这一阶段工业化率和城镇化率的差距越来越小,2003年,中国城镇化率为40.53%,工业化率为40.29%,这表明工业化为快速城镇化提供了强劲动力。到2012年,城镇化率已增至53.1%。从城镇化规模来看,1992—2012年城镇常住人口由32 175万人增加至72 175万人,平均每年有2 000万农村人口转移到城镇。从城镇化形式来看,户籍人口城镇化和以农民工为主的非户籍人口城镇化并存,且二者呈现逐步扩大趋势。到2012年全国农民工总量为26 261万人,其中外出农民工16 336万人,本地农民工9 925万人。由此可见,随着市场经济体制的逐渐完善,中国由偏向就地城镇化向偏向异地城镇化转变,特别是东部经济发达地区和中西部的大城市对异地流动人口的吸引力迅速增强。

不可否认,中国在快速城镇化的过程中也出现了很多突出问题,比如土地利用效率低、"半城镇化"问题突出、城乡不平等和社会矛盾加剧、城市分布和规模结构不合理、"城市病"问题普遍、生态环境问题严重等,这些问题必然要求转变城镇化方式。

10.4.3 中国特色新型城镇化(2013年至今)

2012年,中共十八大明确提出了"新型城镇化"的概念。2013年11月,中共十八届三中全会通过的《中共中央关于全面深化改革若干重大问题的决定》明确提出坚持走中国特色新型城镇化道路,这标志着中国城镇化又进入了一个崭新的发展阶段。这一阶段是以人为核心的新型城镇化阶段,其特点是在加快推进城镇化的同时,更加注重城镇化质量的提升。

改革开放以来,中国城镇化水平大幅提升,但"重物轻人"的城镇化发展模式已经难以为继,转变城镇化方式势在必行。如同中国经济面临转型升级的战略重任,城镇化同时走到了新的路口。新型城镇化阶段是通过全面深化各领域的改革,不断完善城镇化科学发展体制机制和政策体系的发展新阶段。在户籍制度改革方面,中国国务院2014年公布的《国务院关于进一步推进户籍制度改革的意见》明确提出,要建立城乡统一的户口登记制度;2016年印发的《国务院关于深入推进新型城镇化建设的若干意见》进一步提出,全面实行居住证制度,且将居住证与基本公共服务统一起来。2019年4月,中国国家发展和改革委员会在《2019年新型城镇化建设重点任务》提出,城区常住人口100万~300万的Ⅱ型大城市要全面取消落户限制。在住房市场改革方面,坚持"房子是用来住的、不是用来炒的"的定位,逐步建立起多主体供给、多渠道保障、租购并举的住房制度。在农村土地制度改革方面,建立并完善农村承包地"三权分置"制度,为引导土地有序流转、保护农民权益、形成城乡统一的建设用地市场建立了基本制度框架和政策依据。

这一阶段城镇化取得了较好的效果:2013—2021年常住人口城镇化率由54.49%增至64.72%,年均增长率为2.17%。新型城镇化阶段的城镇化质量显著提高。比如,户籍人口城镇化率与常住人口城镇化率的差距自"十三五"规划以来首次缩小,2021年户籍人口城镇化率为46.7%,比上一年提高了1.3个百分点,高于常住人口城镇化率0.83个百分点的提高幅度。同时,随着中国对外出务工人员返乡创业就业的鼓励和支持,外出务工人口增长规模开始相对下降,见表10-1。

表10-1 2013—2021年外出和本地农民工统计

指标	2013年	2014年	2015年	2016年	2017年	2018年	2019年	2020年	2021年
外出农民工/万人	16 610	16 821	16 884	16 934	17 185	17 266	17 425	16 959	17 172
外出农民工增长率/(%)	1.7	1.3	0.4	0.3	1.5	0.5	0.9	−2.7	1.3
本地农民工/万人	10 284	10 574	10 863	11 237	11 467	11 570	11 652	11 601	12 079
本地农民工增长率/(%)	3.6	2.8	2.7	3.4	2.0	0.9	0.7	−0.4	4.1

数据来源:《国民经济和社会发展统计公报》(2013—2021)

由此可见,就地城镇化的比例相对在提高,中国城镇化向着就地和异地并重的趋势发展。在城镇化布局上,新型城镇化强调合理布局、以大带小、协同发展,以城市群为主体,构建大中小城市和小城镇协调发展的城镇格局。

11 中国的宏观经济政策和财税体制

1978年12月召开的中共十一届三中全会开创了中国改革开放和现代化建设的历史进程。贯穿这个历史进程的有两条基本线索：首先是经济体制改革，也即通过改革开放，建立能够有效提高资源配置效率、推动经济发展的体制机制；其次是探索适合中国国情的发展模式，找到一条实现工业化、现代化的道路。在这个历史进程中，宏观经济政策的演进大体可分为三个重要阶段：第一个阶段为1978—1991年，以经济体制转型为背景、以抑制经济过热为主线；第二个阶段为1992—2011年，以确立和完善社会主义市场经济体制为背景、以有效扩大内需和应对外部冲击为主线；第三个阶段为2012年至今，以全面深化改革为背景、以适应经济发展新常态和推进供给侧结构性改革为主线。经过40多年的艰辛探索，中国宏观经济政策在实践中发展和完善，宏观经济管理能力不断提高，并逐步形成了具有中国特色的宏观经济管理体系。

11.1 中国宏观经济政策的演变

11.1.1 经济体制转型时期的宏观调控（1978—1991年）

1978年12月，中共十一届三中全会召开，中国开启了改革开放的新航程。1978年的政府工作报告指出："计划经济是社会主义经济的一个基本特征。我们必须……把经济活动纳入有计划按比例发展的轨道。制订计划要走群众路线，中央部门和地方都要加强调查研究，切实搞好综合平衡，把计划建立在既积极又可靠的基础上，把人力、物力和财力用到最必需的地方去，使国民经济各部门协调发展。"可见，在20世纪70年代末到80年代初，"有计划按比例"和"综合平衡"是指导中国宏观调控的主要理念。

由于传统计划体制的弊端逐步暴露，如何正确处理计划经济和市场调节的关系成为关键，市场调节和价值规律开始受到重视。1982年召开的中共十二大正式提出，要"正确贯彻计划经济为主、市场调节为辅的原则"，这是党的重要文献中首次使用"市场"提法，相当于在计划经济的壁垒中打开了一个突破口，成为中国经济体制改革的重大事件。1984年10月，中共十二届三中全会通过的《中共中央关于经济体制改革的决定》提出，要突破把计划经济同商品经济对立起来的传统观念，明确认识社会主义计划经济必须自觉依据和运用价值规律，是在公有制基础上的有计划的商品经济。这一文件把社会主义商品经济作为改革目标，市场的作用得到了一定程度的认可。中国市场化改革的起步阶段也是间接调控思想的萌芽时期，政府也开始注重在调控中引入经济手段。

11.1.2 市场经济体制建立时期的宏观调控(1992—2011年)

11.1.2.1 三位一体宏观调控体系的初步建立(1992—1996年)

1992年邓小平的南方谈话后,社会主义市场经济体制得以确立,宏观调控目标逐步聚焦保持经济总量基本平衡,同时强调结构优化、经济发展和社会进步。通过建立计划、货币和财政分工明确、协调配合的具有中国特色的三位一体宏观调控体系,实施积极的财政政策和稳健的货币政策,中国实现了经济的平稳发展。许多研究表明,20世纪90年代中期以后,中国经济一改之前大起大落的运行态势,总体上实现了在适度高位的平滑波动。

1993年11月,中共十四届三中全会通过的《中共中央关于建立社会主义市场经济体制若干问题的决定》,详细阐述了宏观调控的主要任务、政策手段和机构体系。文件指出,"宏观调控的主要任务是:保持经济总量的基本平衡,促进经济结构的优化,引导国民经济持续、快速、健康发展,推动社会全面进步。宏观调控主要采取经济办法,近期要在财税、金融、投资和计划体制的改革方面迈出重大步伐,建立计划、金融、财政之间相互配合和制约的机制,加强对经济运行的综合协调。"至此,中国特色宏观调控体系初步成型。在调控目标方面,除了总量平衡之外,还强调结构优化、经济发展和社会进步。在调控手段方面,强调市场化手段的主导作用,并注重运用体制改革的办法推动宏观调控质量的改善。在调控体系方面,明确要求建立计划、货币和财政分工明确、协调配合的三位一体宏观调控体系。这一体系中既有常规的财政与货币政策,还包括主攻中长期发展的战略规划,体现出鲜明的中国特色。在具有中国特色的宏观调控体系下,1996年,中国经济成功实现了"软着陆",国内生产总值增长9.7%,通货膨胀得以控制。在1997年居民消费价格指数回落至102.8,美元对人民币汇率稳定在1∶8.3,年末国家外汇储备达到1 399亿美元,并实现了人民币经常项目可兑换。

11.1.2.2 总需求管理框架的形成(1997—2002年)

1997年,亚洲金融危机爆发,中国宏观经济形势发生了前所未有的根本性转变,出现了信贷萎缩、通货紧缩和需求不足等新现象。这表明中国经济体制改革推动宏观经济体系发生了某些阶段性、根本性的变化,经济从供给约束转为需求约束。在该时期,如何应对外部冲击、有效扩大内需,进而稳定经济增长并保障就业是宏观调控的首要目标。相应地,从1998年开始,宏观经济政策由长期实施的紧缩性政策转变为扩张性政策,中国开始实施"积极的财政政策"和"稳健的货币政策",总需求管理框架逐步形成。主要表现在以下几个方面:

第一,中国经济发展阶段发生了根本性转变,扩大内需和总需求管理成为宏观调控的主要抓手。1998年中央经济工作会议明确指出,扩大国内需求、开拓国内市场,是中国经济发展的基本立足点和长期战略方针。2002年的中共十六大报告继续强调,扩大内需是中国经济发展长期的、基本的立足点。坚持扩大国内需求的方针,根据形势需要实施相应的宏观经济政策。

第二,积极的财政政策在总需求管理中起着至关重要的作用。在货币政策无法充分发挥作用的情况下,积极的财政政策在扩大内需中发挥着关键作用。加强财政政策和货币政策的协调配合,能够发挥财政政策时滞较短的优势,盘活闲置资源以增加产出;而货币政策则能提供必要的流动性,防止出现经济恐慌,并配合财政政策。

第三,密切关注和防范政策风险。中国在宏观经济管理活动中一直比较注重贯彻综合平衡的思想,从"七五"计划开始,保持财政、信贷、物资和外汇的各自平衡和综合平衡就成为宏观经济管理活动中的重要原则。另外,中央政府还出台了金融机构分业经营、贷款五级分类等一系列措施,积极防范金融风险。

总体而言,该时期政府坚定地实施了积极的财政政策,用推动经济增长的办法避免了政府负债率的快速增长。中国经济在这一时期的财政支出乘数很高,财政政策有效发挥了推动经济增长的积极作用。当然,这几年的积极财政政策都是在特殊环境下实施的,一旦经济走出低谷,积极财政政策就要适时退出,否则将偏离综合平衡原则,导致结构失衡和经济扭曲。相关研究显示,中国从2003年起,已通过实施增加财政收入为主、削减财政支出为辅的财政稳固措施,成功地实现了财政政策从积极向稳健的转型。

11.1.2.3 宏观调控体系的完善(2003—2011年)

2002年中共十六大提出,"我们要在本世纪头二十年,集中力量,全面建设惠及十几亿人口的更高水平的小康社会"。2003年中共十六届三中全会通过的《中共中央关于完善社会主义市场经济体制若干问题的决定》明确了深化改革的目标,激发了地方政府加快发展的热情。一些地方固定资产投资开始升温,尤以房地产投资为甚,中国在加入WTO后外贸出口迅速增长,出现了经常账户和资本账户"双顺差"(见图11-1),外汇储备不断增长,央行被动购汇并不断释放基础货币,人民币流动性迅速增强,为扩大投资创造了条件。2004年,中国经济走出此前的通货紧缩阴影,出现了投资膨胀、能源供应紧张等新现象。于是,"积极的财政政策"淡出,政府转而实行"稳健的财政政策"。同时,央行反复强调继续执行"稳健的货币政策",并先后出台了一些紧缩措施。相关决策部门采取了"有保有压、区别对待"的方针,采取点刹车的方式来调控经济运行。

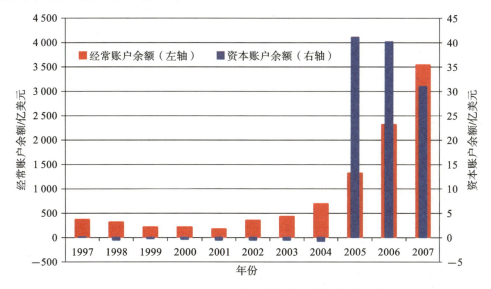

图11-1 1997—2007年中国外贸净出口额变化(亿美元)

图片来源:此图转载自"改革开放以来我国宏观经济政策的演进与创新"一文,该文于2018年发表在《管理世界》上,作者为王一鸣

2008年第四季度,全球金融危机进一步加剧,针对经济增速明显回落但物价涨幅仍在高位的情况,同年11月,中国政府提出要实行积极的财政政策和适度宽松的货币政策,并陆续出台了一系列刺激措施。一是推出了进一步扩大内需、促进经济平稳较快增长的十项措

施,计划两年增加约 4 万亿元投资,重点投向"三农"、交通等基础设施、节能减排等五个领域;二是启动轻工、汽车、钢铁、电子信息等十大产业振兴规划,遏制和扭转工业增速下滑;三是加大金融对经济发展的支持力度,中国人民银行自 2008 年 9 月以来先后五次下调基准利率,四次下调存款准备金率,促进货币信贷稳定增长;四是着力促进就业,加大支农惠农力度,扩大居民消费需求。通过实施一揽子经济计划,中国政府迅速扭转了经济快速下行的态势,中国在全球主要经济体中率先实现复苏。

中央政府进行宏观调控的经验日益丰富,技巧日趋成熟,特别注重在繁荣期实施紧缩性的适度预调微调。在实践中,在经济出现过热苗头时,中央政府往往会通过适时适度、有节奏地多次小步微调,使每次调控都有一定的消化吸收过程。在繁荣时期的适度调控抑制了大泡沫的产生,从而避免了中国经济的剧烈波动。可见,"管理繁荣"是中国宏观调控的一大特色。

11.1.3 供给侧结构性改革(2012 年至今)

2013 年以来,中国经济发展进入新常态,经济增速换挡、结构调整阵痛和前期政策消化"三期叠加"的挑战,促进了经济的持续健康发展。在新常态的背景下,中国宏观调控思想有了重大突破,在适度扩大总需求的同时,供给侧结构性改革成为宏观调控的主线。在实践中,"稳中求进"成为新时代宏观调控的基本原则和总基调。

11.1.3.1 新常态下的宏观调控

2012 年底,中国从全面反危机的政策轨道逐步退出。宏观经济失衡逐步由总量性失衡为主转向结构性失衡为主,经济发展进入新常态。其一是经济增长速度开始由高速增长转为中高速,进入换挡期;其二是长期累积的结构性矛盾逐步显现,表现为供需结构性失衡,进入结构调整阵痛期;其三是自 2008 年下半年后反危机的刺激政策导致了超量的 M2(广义货币)供应,并由此带来货币化比率(即广义货币与国内生产总值的比值)的迅速攀升(见图 11-2),金融风险不断积累,进入前期政策消化期。经济运行进入"三期叠加"的新轨道。

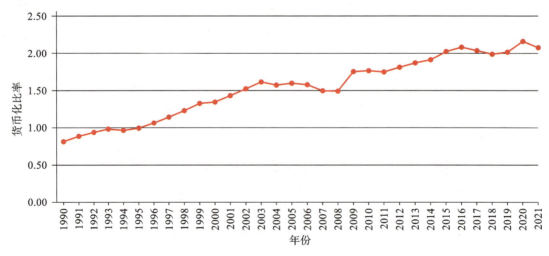

图 11-2　1990—2021 年中国货币化比率的变化情况

数据来源:中华人民共和国国家统计局

2014 年的中央经济工作会议进一步明确:"认识新常态,适应新常态,引领新常态,是当前和今后一个时期我国经济发展的大逻辑。"可见,新常态是对中国经济发展新阶段的战略判断和精当概括。新常态蕴藏着新的发展动力,发现、挖掘和运用好这些新动力,就必须对惯用的发展方式进行彻底变革,必须对扭曲的经济结构进行壮士断腕式改革,同时也需要对调控体系中不适应新常态要求的部分进行及时调整。

这一时期,面对国内外发展的新形势新挑战,特别是经济下行压力,中国在宏观调控方面有所创新。2013年,中央政府提出"区间调控"的概念,要求把握好宏观调控的方向、力度、节奏,使经济运行处于合理区间,守住稳增长、保就业的"下限",把握好防通货膨胀的"上限",在这样一个合理区间内,推动经济转型升级。2014年,中央政府提出"定向调控",也就是在调控上不采取短期强刺激措施,而是抓住重点领域和关键环节,更多运用市场力量,先后实行向小微企业等定向减税和普遍性降费、扩大"营改增"试点等政策,同时积极采取定向降准、定向再贷款等措施,加大对经济发展薄弱环节的支持力度。2015年,中央政府又提出要更加精准地实施"相机调控",强调做好政策储备和应对预案,把握好调控措施出台的时机和力度,不断提高相机抉择的水平。从"区间调控"到"定向调控"再到"相机调控",体现了中央政府创新和完善宏观调控的新探索和新实践。

11.1.3.2 供给侧结构性改革

2013年11月召开的中共十八届三中全会是在中国改革进入关键时期和攻坚阶段具有重要意义的一次会议,会议通过的《中共中央关于全面深化改革若干重大问题的决定》强调,"使市场在资源配置中起决定性作用和更好发挥政府作用"。这是具有里程碑意义的重大理论创新,是对市场经济规律认识的重大突破,为推进供给侧结构性改革做了理论上的准备。

2015年末,中共中央作出推进供给侧结构性改革的重大决策,在适度扩大总需求的同时,着力加强供给侧结构性改革,这是对中国经济发展思路和工作着力点的重大部署,是新时代中国宏观调控的工作主线,这同时意味着,宏观调控首先要发挥好供给侧结构性改革在提升效率、优化结构方面的主导作用,重点推进"三去一降一补",即去产能、去库存、去杠杆、降成本、补短板。

在供给侧结构性改革的推动下,中国过剩行业的价格水平逐步恢复平衡,供求状况得到明显改善。但由于政府的过多干预和市场机制作用发挥不够,还存在各种结构性矛盾。因此,2018年中央经济工作会议强调,必须坚持以供给侧结构性改革为主线不动摇,更多采取改革的办法,更多运用市场化、法治化手段,在"巩固、增强、提升、畅通"八个字上下功夫。即在巩固"三去一降一补"成果的基础上,通过增强微观主体活力、提高产业链水平、畅通国民经济循环,促进经济高质量发展。

以供给侧结构性改革为主线不意味着放弃总需求管理,决策者认为不应把供给与需求对立起来,也不应把短期宏观稳定与中长期增长对立起来,适度有效的总需求管理是中国经济持续健康发展的重要政策保障。2018年,政府还特别强调要强化逆周期调节,继续实施积极的财政政策和稳健的货币政策,适时预调微调,稳定总需求。

11.2 中国的公共财政体制

财政是政府为满足社会公共需要,对一部分社会产品进行分配和再分配所形成的分配关系。财政分配与市场分配不同,财政分配是以国家为主体的分配,是政府参与国民收入分配的活动。以下从公共财政出发,介绍公共财政的职能以及中国财政体制的特点和建设进展,阐述中国的财政收支构成和财政能力,分析改革开放以来中国财税体制改革的进程。

11.2.1 中国公共财政的职能

根据市场经济的一般规定,中国政府的财政职能包括资源配置职能、收入分配职能、调控经济职能和监督管理职能四个方面。

11.2.1.1 资源配置职能

财政的资源配置职能,是把一定数量的社会资源集中,构成财政收入,在此基础上,通过财政支出的分配渠道,由政府提供公共物品或服务。在市场经济中,财政不仅是一部分社会资源的直接分配者,而且也是全社会资源配置的调节者。这种特性决定了其资源配置职能不仅包括对资源的直接分配,而且涉及对全社会资源的间接调控。财政调节社会资源在政府部门和非政府部门之间的配置,使之符合优化资源配置的要求。

11.2.1.2 收入分配职能

财政的收入分配职能,是指政府财政收支活动对各个社会成员收入在社会财富中所占份额施加影响,以实现收入公平分配的目标。如果政府不进行干预,市场一般会按照生产要素对生产的贡献多少等因素,初次分配社会财富。这种分配的结果可能会造成极大的收入差距,但市场却无能为力,因此,只有依靠政府的力量来调节过大的收入差距。这种调节分配主要有以下两种方式:通过税收调节收入差距、通过转移支付给低收入群体以补贴。

11.2.1.3 调控经济职能

财政的调控经济职能,是指通过实施特定的财政政策,促进较高的就业水平、物价稳定和经济增长等目标的实现。在不同的经济发展阶段,政府会实施不同的财政政策,以达到社会总供给和总需求的基本平衡。在经济萧条时,社会总需求不足,失业率上升,政府应采取扩张性的财政政策,增加财政支出,同时降低税收,从而刺激总需求的增长,降低失业率;在经济繁荣时,社会总需求过剩,会引起通货膨胀,政府应采取紧缩性的财政政策,减少财政支出,同时增加税收,以便抑制总需求,缓解通货膨胀。

以 2020 年新冠肺炎疫情冲击为例,疫情使世界经济严重衰退,产业链供应链循环严重受阻,国际贸易投资萎缩,大宗商品市场动荡。中国的财政政策在这个时候真正发挥了稳定经济的关键作用:一是加大减税降费力度,重点减轻中小微企业、个体工商户和困难行业企业税费负担,预计全年减负超 2.5 万亿元;二是多渠道筹集资金,比 2019 年增加 1 万亿元财政赤字,同时发行 1 万亿元抗疫特别国债,加大对新冠肺炎疫苗和药物科研攻关的支持力度,切实保障资金需求;三是缓解地方财政困难,新增加的财政赤字和抗疫特别国债全部安排给地方,同时建立特殊转移支付机制,资金直达市县基层,直接惠企利民;四是扩大政府投资规模,比 2019 年增加地方政府专项债券 1.6 万亿元,以疫情防控为切入点,加强农村人居环境整治和公共卫生体系建设。中国通过实施一系列财税政策,补短板、惠民生、促消费、扩内需,促进经济社会全面恢复、财政平稳运行。

11.2.1.4 监督管理职能

在宏观调控中,财政部门通过建立健全的财政、税政的法规制度,为市场竞争提供基本的规则。跟踪、监测宏观经济运行指标并及时反馈,为国家宏观调控提供决策依据。对于微观企业的管理,财政部门通过规范经济秩序,严格执行财政、税政、会计法规,保证国家财政收入。对于国有资产的管理,财政部门通过编制国有资本经营预算来保证实现国有资产的保值和增值,增强国家财力,提高财政配置效率和财政管理水平。

11.2.2 现代财政体制的建立

11.2.2.1 现代预算管理制度的基本建立

"全口径""全过程"预算管理制度初步确立。通过出台《中华人民共和国预算法》并对之进行修订,中国已形成了由"四本账"构成的具有中国特色的复式预算体系,基本实现了对预算收入的全口径管理。引入权责发生制的政府会计制度、深化部门预算改革、大力推行绩效预算、加强财政审计、加大预算公开力度、试行跨周期预算等改革,加强了中国预算管理的科学性、规范性和透明度,优化了支出结构,提高了资金使用效率。一个与国家治理体系和治理能力现代化相适应的现代预算管理制度已经基本建立起来。

11.2.2.2 现代税收制度建设的主要进展

(1) 实行增值税制度改革

"营改增"试点的全面推进,实现了增值税对货物和服务的全覆盖,营业税退出历史舞台。在此基础上,将四档税率的增值税简化至三档,降低了增值税税率水平。"营改增"改革贯通了服务业内部和二、三产业之间的抵扣链条,促进了社会分工协作,有效减轻了企业税负。

(2) 消费税制度不断完善

调整消费税征收范围,优化税率结构,改进征税环节,先后三次提高成品油消费税单位税额,取消对小排量摩托车、汽车轮胎等产品征收消费税,将电池、涂料纳入消费税征收范围,较大幅度提高卷烟消费税税率,对超豪华小汽车加征消费税等,进一步增强了消费税的调节功能。

(3) 实行资源税和环境保护税改革

全面推行矿产资源税从价计征改革,开展水资源税改革试点,根据"清费立税"原则取消或停征了相关收费基金,颁布施行环境保护税法,有力促进了资源节约和环境保护。

(4) 逐步建立综合与分类相结合的个人所得税制度

对部分劳动性所得实行综合征税,提高综合所得基本减除费用标准,优化调整税率结构,设立子女教育、继续教育、大病医疗、住房贷款利息、住房租金、赡养老人等六项专项附加扣除项目,标志着中国个人所得税制向综合方向迈出了重要一步。

11.2.2.3 中央与地方财政体制改革的推进

收入划分方面,"营改增"之后,中央和地方的增值税分享比例由75∶25调整为50∶50,同时后移消费税的征收环节,逐渐将其改造为中央地方共享税,保障了地方政府正常履职的需要。转移支付制度方面,早在2014年,一般性转移支付占比就达到58.2%,接近60%的改革目标,在2019年设立共同事权后,这一比例已接近90%。专项转移支付项目个数也大幅减少。不过总体而言,由于改革的难度和涉及面大,这方面的改革亟须进一步深化。

11.3 财政收入和财政支出

11.3.1 公共财政收入

公共财政收入是政府为了供应政府公共活动支出的需要,履行政府的公共管理、公共服务以及国民经济的市场化管理等职能,利用税收等各种财政手段从企业、家庭等社会目标群体中所获得的一切货币收入的总和。

11.3.1.1 中国公共财政收入的形式

中国公共财政收入主要有税收收入和非税收入两大部分。

税收收入包括国内增值税、国内消费税、进出口货物增值税、进出口消费品消费税、个人所得税、关税、耕地占用税、烟叶税等其他税收收入。

非税收入主要包括专项收入、行政事业性收费收入、罚没收入、国有资本经营收入、国有资源(资产)有偿使用收入和其他收入。

我们以2019年、2020年的财政数据为例进行说明,如表11-1所示。

表11-1　2019年和2020年中国公共财政收入主要项目

项目	中国公共财政收入/亿元		占比/(%)	
年份	2019	2020	2019	2020
总计	190 390.08	182 913.88	100.00	100.00
税收收入	158 000.46	154 312.29	82.99	84.36
非税收入	32 389.62	28 601.59	17.01	15.64
专项收入	7 134.16	7 123.36	3.75	3.89
行政事业性收费收入	3 888.07	3 838.65	2.04	2.10
罚没收入	3 062.09	3 113.87	1.61	1.70
国有资本经营收入	7 720.52	1 938.95	4.06	1.06
国有资源(资产)有偿使用收入	8 061.01	9 934.33	4.23	5.43
其他收入	2 523.77	2 652.43	1.33	1.45

数据来源:《中国统计年鉴》(2020年、2021年)

(1) 税收收入

税收是政府凭借国家权力,为满足社会公共需要,依法强制地、无偿地取得财政收入的一种方式。税收在各国的财政收入中都占主体地位。

2021年,中国公共财政收入共计202 554.64亿元,比上年增长10.7%,其中税收收入达到172 735.67亿元,占比85.3%。中国年人均税负已经超过1万元,以三口之家计算,就是户均3万元的税收负担。所以税收制度变革对每个人、每个家庭都有重大的切身利益关联。

(2) 非税收入

非税收入是由各级人民政府及其所属部门和单位,依法利用行政权力、政府信誉、国家资源、国有资产或提供特定公共服务而征收、收取、提取、募集的除税收和政府债务收入以外的财政收入。非税收入包括行政事业性收费、国有资源(资产)有偿使用收入等。

各类非税收入的取得依据有所不同,行政事业性收费、罚没收入和主管部门集中收入是利用行政权力征收的,具有强制性;国有资源(资产)有偿使用收入、国有资本经营收入是利用国家资源和国有资产所有权取得的,体现了国家作为所有者或出资人的权益;彩票公益金、以政府名义接受的捐赠收入是依托政府信誉募集的,遵循自愿原则。

11.3.1.2 中国的主要税收项目

税收在各国都是最主要的一种财政收入形式,它对经济运行、资源配置和收入分配都具有重要作用。目前,中国现行税种有18个,其中关税和船舶吨税由海关征收,进口环节的增值税、消费税由海关代征,其他税种由税务部门负责征收,表 11-2 为 2017—2020 年中国财政各项税收情况。

表 11-2 2017—2020 年中国财政各项税收 （单位:亿元）

项目	年份			
	2017	2018	2019	2020
合计	144 369.87	156 402.86	158 000.46	154 312.29
国内增值税	56 378.18	61 530.77	62 347.36	56 791.29
国内消费税	10 255.09	10 631.75	12 564.44	12 028.10
进口货物增值税、消费税	15 970.67	16 878.97	15 812.34	14 535.50
出口货物增值税、消费税	−13 870.37	−15 913.93	−16 503.19	−13 628.98
企业所得税	32 177.29	35 323.71	37 303.77	36 425.81
个人所得税	11 966.37	13 871.97	10 388.53	11 568.26
资源税	1 353.32	1 629.90	1 821.64	1 754.76
城市维护建设税	4 362.15	4 839.98	4 820.57	4 607.58
房产税	2 604.33	2 888.56	2 988.43	2 841.76
印花税	2 206.39	2 199.36	2 462.96	3 087.45
城镇土地使用税	2 360.55	2 387.60	2 195.41	2 058.22
土地增值税	4 911.28	5 641.38	6 465.14	6 468.51
车船税	773.59	831.19	880.95	945.41
船舶吨税	50.40	49.78	50.26	53.72
车辆购置税	3 280.67	3 452.53	3 498.26	3 530.88
关税	2 997.85	2 847.78	2 889.13	2 564.25
耕地占用税	1 651.89	1 318.85	1 389.84	1 257.57
契税	4 910.42	5 729.94	6 212.86	7 061.02
烟草税	115.72	111.35	111.03	108.67
环境保护税	—	151.38	221.16	207.06
其他税收收入	4.08	0.04	79.57	45.50

数据来源:《中国统计年鉴》(2018 年、2019 年、2020 年、2021 年)
注:"—"表示由于税目调整造成的缺失数据

11.3.2 公共财政支出

11.3.2.1 公共财政支出的定义

公共财政支出是指政府为提供公共产品和服务,满足社会共同需要而进行的财政资金的支付。主要有保证国家机器正常运转、维护国家安全、巩固各级政府政权建设的支出,维护社会稳定、提高全民族素质、提升人民生活水平的社会公共事业支出,有利于经济环境和生态环境改善、具有巨大外部经济效应的公益性基础设施建设的支出,对宏观经济运行进行必要调控的支出,等等。

11.3.2.2 中国财政支出的分类

财政支出分类是将政府支出的内容进行合理的归纳，以便准确反映和科学分析支出活动的性质、结构、规模以及支出的效益。财政收支分类改革后，中国现行支出分类采用了国际通行做法，即同时使用支出功能分类和支出经济分类两种方法对财政支出进行分类。

支出功能分类就是按政府主要职能活动分类。支出功能分类类级科目包括一般公共服务、外交、国防、公共安全、教育、科学技术、文化旅游体育与传媒、社会保障和就业、卫生健康、节能环保、城乡社区、农林水、交通运输等支出。表 11-3 是以支出功能分类表示的财政支出项目。

表 11-3 2019 年和 2020 年中国公共财政支出项目

项目	2019 年 金额/亿元	2019 年 占比/(%)	2020 年 金额/亿元	2020 年 占比/(%)
一般公共服务支出	20 344.66	8.52	20 061.10	8.17
外交支出	617.50	0.26	515.44	0.21
国防支出	12 122.10	5.08	12 918.77	5.26
公共安全支出	13 901.93	5.82	13 862.90	5.64
教育支出	34 796.94	14.57	36 359.94	14.80
科学技术支出	9 470.79	3.97	9 018.34	3.67
文化旅游体育与传媒支出	4 086.31	1.71	4 245.58	1.73
社会保障和就业支出	29 379.08	12.30	32 568.51	13.26
卫生健康支出	16 665.34	6.98	19 216.19	7.82
节能环保支出	7 390.20	3.09	6 333.40	2.58
城乡社区支出	24 895.24	10.42	19 945.91	8.12
农林水支出	22 862.80	9.57	23 948.46	9.75
交通运输支出	11 817.55	4.95	12 197.88	4.96
资源勘探工业信息等支出	4 914.40	2.06	6 066.88	2.47
商业服务业等支出	1 239.70	0.52	1 568.92	0.64
金融支出	1 615.36	0.68	1 277.39	0.52
援助其他地区支出	471.31	0.20	448.59	0.18
自然资源海洋气象等支出	2 182.70	0.91	2 333.94	0.95
住房保障支出	6 401.19	2.68	7 106.08	2.89
粮油物资储备支出	1 897.11	0.79	2 117.30	0.86
灾害防治及应急管理支出	1 529.20	0.64	1 940.66	0.79
债务付息支出	8 442.53	3.53	9 812.62	3.99
债务发行费用支出	65.64	0.03	77.05	0.03
其他支出	1 748.79	0.73	1 737.18	0.71

数据来源：《中国统计年鉴》(2020 年、2021 年)

从表 11-3 中可以看出,2019 年全国公共财政支出最大的三项是教育支出(14.57%)、社会保障和就业支出(12.30%)、城乡社区支出(10.42%)。2020 年全国公共财政支出最大的三项是教育支出(14.80%)、社会保障和就业支出(13.26%)、农林水支出(9.75%)。

11.3.3 财政自给能力

政府的财政自给能力可以用财政自给能力系数来衡量,具体是用本级财政收入占财政总支出的比值。显然,财政自给能力系数是一个大于零的正数,如果系数为 1,表明政府刚好财政自给自足,既没有能力向其他层级政府提供转移支付,也不需要其他层级政府向其提供转移支付;如果系数大于 1,说明该层级政府具有充分的财政自给能力,除了满足本级支出之外,还能向其他层级政府进行转移支付;如果系数小于 1,说明该层级政府的财政自给能力不足,需要依赖其他层级政府的转移支付。

近几年来,中国的财政自给能力维持在较高的水平,但财政自给能力系数有所下降。从表 11-4 来看,2017—2020 年全国的财政自给能力系数在 0.74 和 0.85 之间。

表 11-4 2017—2020 年中国财政自给能力系数

项目	年份			
	2017	2018	2019	2020
公共财政收入/亿元	172 592.77	183 359.84	190 390.08	182 913.88
公共财政支出/亿元	203 085.49	220 904.13	238 858.37	245 679.03
财政自给能力系数	0.85	0.83	0.80	0.74

数据来源:《中国财政年鉴》(2018 年、2019 年、2020 年、2021 年)

11.4 财政体制改革

11.4.1 市场经济探索时期:包干制财政体制

在 1978 年的中共十一届三中全会后,中国开始了改革开放的进程,逐步由计划经济转向市场经济。与市场化经济体制改革相适应,中国财政体制改革也体现中央放权让利,调动地方政府积极性的宗旨,实行了财政包干体制,具体措施有对企业"减税让利",推出企业基金制、利润留成制、第一步利改税、第二步利改税、各种形式的盈亏包干制和多种形式的承包经营责任制等;实行"复税制",建立起以流转税、所得税为主体,其他税种相配合的多税种、多环节、多层次征收的复税制体系;以财政支出支撑价格、工资、科教等领域改革。

这一时期财政改革措施推动了社会主义市场经济体制的建立。财政改革赋予了企业和地方政府一些自主权,促使企业和地方政府在市场经济发展中发挥了重要作用;推动政府职能由原来的直接组织社会再生产转变为制定市场经济规则,为企业生产经营服务和开展国民经济和社会宏观管理;促进有利于市场经济运行的良好法治环境的建立;推动社会主义市场体系和运营机制的完善,推动消费品市场、生产要素市场、劳动力市场、金融市场、技术市场繁荣发展。

11.4.2　市场经济确立时期：分税制财政体制

1992年社会主义市场经济体制目标确立，市场化程度的加深使财政包干制弊端显现：一是各种"放权""让利"的举措使"诸侯经济"和地方保护主义盛行，一定程度上助长了地方经济的封锁和盲目建设；二是"两个比重"降低，稀释了中央对地方的宏观调控能力。为此，国务院决定从1994年1月1日起对各省、自治区、直辖市以及计划单列市实行分税制改革。

分税制的主要内容是在划分事权的基础上，划分中央与地方的财政支出范围；按税种划分收入，明确中央与地方各自的收入范围；分设中央和地方两套税务机构；建立中央对地方的税收返还制度。其意义体现在：第一，初步构建了与市场经济相适应的现代财政管理体制；第二，提高了"两个比重"，即财政收入占国内生产总值的比重和中央财政收入占全国财政收入的比重；第三，全面改革税收制度，搭建了一个新型的税收制度体系，实现了统一税法、公平税负、简化税制和合理分权，为社会主义市场经济的运行提供了制度保障。

11.4.3　市场基础性地位巩固时期：构建公共财政体制

随着市场经济的不断成熟，1998年到2012年中国逐步构建了公共财政体制。2007年1月，中国按照"公开透明、符合国情、便于操作"的原则，全面实施政府收支分类改革。财政收入方面，税收收入占财政收入的比重下降，政府性基金收入规范增长，房地产相关行业在营业税收入中所占的比重逐渐上升。财政支出方面，中国财政支出的绝对规模和相对规模增长，缩减了经济事务支出和一般公共服务支出的比例，对"三农"和涉及民生的教育、医疗、社会保障和就业支出逐步增大。民生财政的改善、财政透明度的增强以及财政激励机制的发挥，对于这一阶段的经济发展和福利提升起到了重要作用。

这一阶段财政改革的成果主要体现在：第一，实行了全口径预算管理。通过积极推行部门预算，加强预算外资金管理，形成了四类预算体系和两类预算权力划分，促进了公共资源的透明高效配置，加重了自收自支、自求平衡的责任，促进了经济建设和财源建设向依靠科技进步、低投入、高效益的方向转变。第二，民生财政改善。主要体现在农业基础进一步巩固和加强，教育公平进一步推进，基本医疗保险覆盖范围继续扩大，社会保障体系建设取得突破性进展，节能减排和生态环境保护大力推进。第三，市场待遇更加平等，内外资企业所得税统一。自2008年1月1日起施行的《中华人民共和国企业所得税法》实现了"四个统一"，对维护良好的市场竞争环境具有重要意义。

11.4.4　国家治理现代化时期：建设现代财政体制

2014年出台的《深化财税体制改革总体方案》对现代财政制度作出具体描述，并且提出预算、税制、事权与支出责任划分三大改革任务。现代财政体制的建设，通过更加稳健集约的预算支持、公平赋能的税收制度和均衡有效的政府间财政关系，能有效推动新兴经济业态的增长，并妥善解决政府运行和地方发展的财政资金问题。如前文所述，现代财政体制建设已取得一定进展，但现状和目标之间还存在差距，改革仍需持续发力。

财政收入方面，直接税比重还需提高，税制结构仍待优化，地方税体系需加快建立。其中，房地产税能提高直接税比重，同时也能成为地方主体税种，推动房地产税还是税制改革的重要突破口。同时,遗产税和赠与税也应纳入规划和论证。

财政支出方面,优化财政支出结构需进一步转变政府职能。当前中国既要解决发展问题,还要解决发展不平衡不充分的问题。中国政府需要参与经济建设,推动经济发展,但其中更重要的是提升政府支出效率,加大医疗卫生、文化旅游体育与传媒、教育、社会保障和就业等方面的支出,提高社会福利性支出比重。

预算制度方面,需加快建立现代预算制度。包括完善全口径预算管理体系;扎实推进预算公开,并以公开透明约束政府行为规范;发挥人大与审计的监督优势,健全预算问责体系,增强预算约束力;研究和制定科学的预算标准;健全绩效管理体系,完善绩效支出评价体系,促进绩效与预算管理一体化。

财政体制方面,财政体制是否合理的关键在于能否调动中央与地方政府的积极性,其改革重点是明确地方政府的收入来源和支出去向,将地方政府的关注点聚焦于推动经济发展和公共物品的有效提供。

构建现代财政制度、推动财政现代化是实现国家治理现代化的基础,也是建设现代化国家、实现第二个百年奋斗目标和应对未来各种可能冲击的关键。因此,构建现代财政制度的目标不能动摇,进程仍需提速。

12 中国现代金融体系的改革与建立

改革开放以来,中国金融从原来唯一的一家中国人民银行,发展成为一个符合中国国情、制度较为完善、机制较为灵活、门类较为齐全、结构较为合理、功能较为充分和监管较为有效的金融体系,在支持国民经济快速健康可持续发展的同时,积极推进市场化、法治化、国际化和现代化建设,取得了举世公认的巨大成就,给发展中国家的金融改革和发展提供了可供借鉴的宝贵经验。

12.1 中国金融体系改革的阶段性回顾

12.1.1 社会主义市场经济金融体系基本框架的构建及其规范化

中共十一届三中全会确立改革开放的基本国策,标志着中国开始进入由计划经济向市场经济、由传统经济向现代经济的过渡时期。国民经济分配格局中,居民与企业部门在财政收入结构中占比越来越大,银行信用的作用越来越突出,又加上1985年国家全面实行"拨改贷"政策,原有的计划金融体系已经不适应新时期经济发展的需要,必须审时度势对传统"大一统"模式的计划金融体系进行改革,由此开始了由传统社会主义的计划金融体系向社会主义市场经济金融体系的过渡。该进程分为三个阶段。

12.1.1.1 市场经济金融体系基本结构的引进

1978年1月,中国人民银行从财政部分离出来。原有的"大一统"中国人民银行逐渐被拆分,中国银行、中国农业银行、中国建设银行、中国工商银行相继成立,成为专业银行。这些银行不仅进行商业化经营,也承担国家政策性业务。专业银行从中国人民银行拆分与分设,为后者从单一国家银行转变为市场经济条件下的中央银行创造了条件。1983年9月,国务院发布《关于中国人民银行专门行使中央银行职能的决定》,标志着中央银行制度的建立。

除专业银行外,中国还建立了全国性股份制银行[如交通银行、中信实业银行(现更名为中信银行)]、地方性银行、非银行金融机构(如中国平安保险公司),这些机构开始尝试按照市场经济的要求来开展金融活动。此时,金融市场也开始建立起来。随着中国经济体制改革的全面展开与深入进行,各种形式的市场融资活动开始出现,上海飞乐音响股份有限公司就在这一时期发行了股票(见图12-1)。中国在1990年、1991年分别成立了上海证券交易所、深圳证券交易所。这样,包括票据承兑贴现市场、同业拆借市场、外汇市场和资本市场在内的金融市场就初步形成了。

图 12-1 中国上海飞乐音响股份有限公司股票

图片来源:证券时报

12.1.1.2 社会主义市场经济金融体系的建立

为落实 1993 年中共十四届三中全会通过的《中共中央关于建立社会主义市场经济体制若干问题的决定》精神,国务院作出了关于金融体制改革的决定,就金融体制改革进行了新的部署,中国金融体系开始进入与社会主义市场经济相契合的改革探索时期。

按照中共十四大的精神,市场在社会主义国家宏观调控下对资源配置起基础性作用,原有的专业银行开始向独立经营的商业银行转变,其政策性业务由新成立的国家开发银行、中国进出口银行和中国农业发展银行三家政策性银行承担,中国人民银行原有的政策性与商业性金融业务也被剥离,只承担中央银行的职能,即负责制定货币政策、加强金融监管、实施金融业的宏观调控等。1995 年,《中华人民共和国中国人民银行法》《中华人民共和国商业银行法》的颁布和实施,从根本上理顺了中央银行与商业银行、政策性银行之间的关系,为中国人民银行行使中央银行职能与商业银行独立开展经营活动提供了法律保障。

金融市场改革取得了重要进展。在货币市场方面,1996 年基本建立起全国统一的银行间拆借市场;在票据市场方面,1993 年中国人民银行发布《商业汇票办法》,1997 年又实行《支付结算办法》,对加强汇票管理、促进商业汇票健康发展起到重要作用;在资本市场方面,中国人民银行颁布一系列政策法规整顿和规范证券市场,积极稳妥地发展债券和股票融资,规范股票的发行与上市;在外汇市场方面,1994 年建立银行间外汇市场,实行有管理的浮动汇率制度,1996 年人民币实现了国际收支经常项目下的可兑换。

在金融机构与金融市场改革发展的基础上,金融制度也不断完善。第一,建立新的金融宏观调控体系,商业银行由分业经营向混业经营发展,宏观调控由直接调控转向间接调控。第二,在建立和完善金融监管制度方面取得重要进展。对金融业实行分业监管,1998 年成立的中国保险监督管理委员会(于 2018 年撤销)与 1992 年成立的中国证券监督管理委员会分别负责保险业和证券业的监管,中国人民银行专门负责银行业、信托业的监管。

这一时期,中国基本建立起由国有银行主导的、与社会主义市场经济相适应的金融体系框架。但是在支持国有企业改革中,由于原有制度惯性与金融法制不健全、监管制度不完善,国有银行聚集了大量的不良资产,大概在 25%～45%,又加上 1997 年爆发了亚洲金融危机,中国经济、金融都面临巨大的考验。1997年,第一次全国金融工作会议召开,国家决定成立四大资产管理公司,专门管理国有四大行剥离的1.39万亿元不良资产。实际上,中国国有银行主导的金融体系为战胜亚洲金融危机和国有企业脱困起到重要作用。

12.1.1.3 金融体系的治理及规范化改革

中共十六大以来,中国经济体制改革进入新的阶段,经济发展方式发生转变,工业化、城市化加速发展。同时,中国加入WTO后对外开放迈入了新的台阶,这些变化对金融体系的改革提出新的要求,中国金融体制进入治理整顿与规范化改革时期。

金融机构改革的重点在于落实2002年第二次全国金融工作会议精神,中国采取一系列措施对国有金融机构进行整顿与规范化改革,包括改革会计准则、实行贷款五级分类、继续剥离国有银行不良资产、充实国有金融机构资本金等政策,对大型国有金融机构的财务进行重组,并完成股份化改造,积极鼓励国有大型金融机构在境内外上市融资。

2003年以后,四大国有商业银行完成财务重组和股份制改造,并成功上市,中国人寿、中国人保等国有保险公司也完成重组改制并成功上市。上市以后的国有金融机构能够按照现代企业制度的要求去改善治理结构,更加注重财务风险管理,并接受中小投资者的监督,提高了国有金融机构的资产质量与整体实力。

2003年,中国成立了中国银行业监督管理委员会(于2018年撤销),形成了"一行三会"的分业监管格局,厘清了中国人民银行宏观调控与金融监管的职能,使中央银行制度更加完善。

在各项改革措施推动下,银行、证券、保险等方面的金融制度不断完善,国有银行主导的金融体系得到规范化发展。其中,银行类金融机构发展最快,截至2008年底,各类金融机构达到5 600多家,银行业金融机构总资产达到62.39万亿元;金融市场也得到较快发展,债券市场发行量、存量稳步增加。根据2008年国民经济和社会发展统计公报,中国国内生产总值为30.07万亿元,而截至2008年底,债券存量15.1万亿元、股票总市值12.1万亿元、保险总资产3.34万亿元,分别占中国国内生产总值的50.3%、40.4%、11.1%,资本市场的筹资功能不断完善。正是对金融体系的规范化改革,才使中国金融业具有成功抗击2008年全球金融危机的初步基础。

12.1.2 金融体系的市场化、国际化、多元化发展

随着2008年全球金融危机的爆发,世界各国都在想方设法减轻金融危机对经济社会的冲击。其中,中国政府在经济领域提出了刺激经济的一揽子计划,特别需要金融配合国家宏观经济决策,这对中国金融体系提出了新的要求与挑战,金融体系的规范化改革还没有完成,就开始向市场化、国际化与多元化方向发展。

金融危机后,特别是中共十八届三中全会提出"使市场在资源配置中起决定性作用"后,中国政府就加快了金融市场化改革的步伐。金融领域的市场化主要是指资金的价格市场化,包括利率和汇率的市场化,以降低资金配置的低效与扭曲度,从而更好地服务实体经济。

随着2010年中国国内生产总值超过日本,中国成为全球第二大经济体,中国经济日益迈向世界舞台的中心,金融业的对外开放步伐加快,金融体系国际化进程也快速发展,并表现在以下方面。首先,人民币的国际化。2008年全球金融危机后,美元、欧元等世界主要货币的汇率波动很大,全球跨境贸易结算风险很大。为降低风险,2009年中国开始快速发展跨境贸易人民币结算业务,并发挥人民币互换协议的作用。同时,2016年10月,人民币正式

被纳入国际货币基金组织的特别提款权货币篮子,人民币国际化的速度大大加快。截至 2018 年底,中国与 38 个国家和地区的央行或货币当局签署了人民币互换协议,扩大了人民币的国际使用范围。其次,资本市场的国际化。2014 年 11 月 17 日"沪港通"开始启动,2016 年 12 月 5 日"深港通"正式运行,至此实现了上海证券交易所、深圳证券交易所和香港联合交易所有限公司(简称"香港联交所")的互联互通,中国内地资本市场通过与香港联交所的联通走向国际。最后,金融体系支持企业"走出去"。2013 年,习近平主席提出了"一带一路"倡议,加大了中国与欧亚各国的互联互通;2014 年丝路基金有限责任公司成立,2015 年亚洲基础设施投资银行成立,金融体系支持企业在"一带一路"建设中寻找投资机会并提供相应的投融资服务。

2021 年 9 月 2 日晚,国家主席习近平在 2021 年中国国际服务贸易交易会全球服务贸易峰会上宣布,深化新三板改革,设立北京证券交易所,打造服务创新型中小企业主阵地。北京证券交易所设立之后,京、沪、深三地交易所功能互补、各具特色、各显优势,不仅可以承载更大的融资规模,畅通资本流通机制,还可以为中小企业构建更为有力的信用增长通道。从定位上来讲,它进一步畅通了中小企业直接融资的路径。

12.2 中国的金融体系

12.2.1 中国的货币制度和货币政策

12.2.1.1 中国货币制度演进

70 多年来,随着经济发展和体制机制转变,中国的货币制度也在不断完善中发展着。这一演进历程,大致上可分为两个时期。

(1) 货币制度的建立(1949—1978 年)

新中国成立初期的人民币制度,是以商品物资为准备的、发行和流通都是计划好的、完全为计划性生产服务的纸币制度,与"全部生产资料公有化"的计划经济体制相协调。1948 年 12 月成立的中国人民银行,最初为了协调各个解放区的金融政策和货币发行,它的成立为货币的统一奠定了基础。

新中国成立之后,中国人民银行服务于高度集中的计划经济体制,人民币制度安排是以商品物资为准备的、完全为计划性生产服务的纸币制度。人民币的发行管理权统一于中央人民政府,在当时的背景下有利于人民币市场的统一、有利于国家有计划地调节人民币的流通、有利于国家支配人民币发行带来的铸币税收益,并且便于群众识别,与当时特殊的计划经济背景是相互协调的。

(2) 货币制度的发展(1978 年至今)

1978 年改革开放以后,与商品自由交易的社会主义市场经济体制相协调,中国逐步实现了由中央银行垄断发行的法定银行券制度,人民币制度演变至今,可以分为以下三个阶段:

① 计划性特征的延续(1978—1992 年)

从人民币发行制度安排的角度而言,伴随着商品统购统销模式的改革,1978 年 1 月,中国人民银行与财政部分设,开始负责吸收和分配资金、监督工商企业和一般信贷业务。1981年,中国着手建立真正意义上的中央银行体制。这一阶段,人民币发行的数目基本遵循计划经济时代的计划式发行标准,主要表现为一种"还账式"的发行方式,难免出现赤字型的通货膨胀。

在这一阶段,市场经济体制还处于摸索时期,当时的宏观经济体制依然保留计划的特征,因此,这一时期的人民币制度是由财政部和中国人民银行共同决定的,人民币制度的转型还处于探索之中。

②从计划向市场的过渡(1992—1994年)

经过经济、金融领域十几年的改革,中国基本建立了具有利益激励机制的社会主义市场经济新秩序。为了配合社会主义市场经济体制的改革、降低交易成本,人民币发行制度由财政经济时代的还账式发行改为银行经济时代的银行主导型发行,形成了短暂的银行经济。从人民币流通的角度而言,1994年中国的信贷管理体制变为贷款限额控制下的资产负债比例管理,并成立三家政策性银行,将商业银行的政策性业务和经营性业务分离,促进专业银行向商业银行转变。

③市场化改革的持续深化(1994年至今)

1994年之后,中国着力发展外向型经济并制定了汇率管理制度。这一制度发展至今,目前中国实施的是以市场供求为基础、参考一篮子货币进行调节、有管理的浮动汇率制度。市场经济的发展和市场交换方式的改革,导致人民币制度开始大刀阔斧地改革。这一阶段的改革依然是以人民币发行制度安排作为突破口。1995年颁布的《中华人民共和国中国人民银行法》,从法律的高度明确了中国人民银行的独立性,其中明令禁止财政向中央银行透支以弥补赤字的行为。

同时,中国还开展了人民币流通制度安排的一系列的关键改革。为了加强中央银行的权威性,提高其管理人民币的实力,省级分行的贷款规模调剂权和向非金融部门发放的专项贷款均被取消。1999年,《中华人民共和国人民币管理条例》颁布,该条例明确了当前中国实施的人民币制度,其内容涉及人民币制度的多个方面,包括人民币的法律偿付性质、用途、票面的单位、种类,人民币发行组织、程序和更新办法,对伪造人民币的惩罚办法,以及人民币的汇兑办法等。把人民币制度用法律形式确定下来对深化人民币制度的改革具有重大意义。

12.2.1.2　中国的货币政策工具

1993年12月25日,国务院在《关于金融体制改革的决定》中提出,中国金融体制改革的目标之一就是建立在国务院领导下独立执行货币政策的中央银行宏观调控体系。中央银行按照规范化、法治化的目标,以完善宏观调控为目标,试行市场化调控为主的模式。存款准备金、再贴现业务和公开市场业务是主要的三大货币政策工具,而市场化调控就是充分利用市场机制,相机抉择地进行政策调控,以达到中央银行的宏观调控目标。

（1）存款准备金

1983年国务院发布的《关于中国人民银行专门行使中央银行职能的决定》专门规定,银行吸收的存款要按比例存入中国人民银行。1998年3月,中国人民银行改革存款准备金制度,将准备金账户与备付金账户合并,同时设立单一的准备金账户。2015年9月,中国人民银行改革存款准备金的考核制度,由时点法改为平均法考核。这样就避免了临近考核期的非正常变动,使得存款准备金更加平稳长效地发挥货币管理与宏观调控的功能。

(2) 再贴现业务

再贴现业务用来进行货币管理也是这一时期的新进展。早在 20 世纪 80 年代初,中国就在票据承兑中开办贴现业务,而再贴现业务是商业银行以未到期的合格票据再向中央银行贴现。再贴现业务的开办有利于加快货币流通速度,从而影响到货币供给量。中国人民银行于 1986 年 4 月 16 日发布《中国人民银行再贴现试行办法》来规范再贴现业务的具体操作。中央银行可以运用再贴现政策调节信贷规模和市场供应量,通过票据市场运作实现中央银行的货币政策目标。

(3) 公开市场业务

社会主义市场经济的建立也开启了中国公开市场业务作为货币政策的先河。中国人民银行从 1998 年开始建立公开市场业务一级交易商制度,选择一批能够承担大额债券交易的商业银行作为公开市场业务的交易对象。1999 年以来,公开市场业务发展较快,目前已成为中国人民银行货币政策日常操作的主要工具之一,其主要交易品种包括回购交易、现券交易和发行中央银行票据。2002 年 9 月,由于国债数额小且期限结构不合理,不足以满足公开市场业务的需求,中国人民银行开始发行央行票据。

除常规货币政策工具的发展之外,中央银行从 2014 年起出台常备借贷便利、中期借贷便利、抵押补充贷款等新型货币工具。这对于调节银行体系流动性水平、引导货币市场利率走势、促进货币供应量合理增长发挥了积极作用。

12.2.2 中国当前的金融机构

12.2.2.1 中国当前的银行体系

改革开放 40 多年来,中国的银行业体系结构发生了巨大变化,长期实行的"大一统"银行体制逐步发展成为多元化金融体制,建立了以中国人民银行为中央银行、国有商业银行为主体、多种形式金融机构并存与分立合作的具有中国特色的金融体制。这一体制在中国的宏观经济调控与社会主义现代化建设中发挥着越来越重要的作用。

随着改革开放以来经济的高速发展,中国现代银行业体系也进一步形成且快速发展。根据《中国金融年鉴(1987)》和《中国金融年鉴(2010)》的数据,如果按照名义值进行估算,1986 年中国金融机构总资产为 13 784.84 亿元,2009 年增至 787 690.54 亿元,提高了 56 倍之多。从 1986 年到 2009 年,金融机构总资产的名义年均增长率为 19.23%,其中银行业金融资产增长率为 19.20%,非银行业金融资产增长率高达 21.07%,而根据《中国统计年鉴(2010)》的数据,同期国内生产总值的年均名义增长率则为 16.44%。

目前,中国的金融结构和金融体系正沿着适应市场经济需要的方向进行调整和优化,股份制商业银行、城市商业银行、政策性银行、证券、保险、信托和各种基金等相继产生并快速发展。从总体来看,中国的金融深度和总规模与实际经济的发展相适应,这些金融资源很好地满足了现阶段经济增长的需求。据《中国金融年鉴(2020)》的统计,截至 2019 年 12 月底,中国银行业金融机构达到 4 595 家,其中:大型商业银行 6 家,即中国工商银行、中国农业银行、中国银行、中国建设银行、交通银行和 2018 年底被列入大型国有商业银行的中国邮政储蓄银行;开发性金融机构和政策性银行 3 家,分别是国家开发银行、中国进出口银行及中国农业发展银行;此外,股份制商业银行 12 家,城市商业银行达到 134 家,另外还有 18 家民营银行;在农村银行业金融机构方面,有农村信用社 722 家,农村商业银行 1 478 家,农村合作银行 28 家,外资金融机构 41 家。为了满足经济发展的需要,多家企业集团财务公司、信托公司、金融租赁公司、汽车金融公司、资产管理公司、货币经纪公司等多种金融机构也在改革开放后快速发展起来,这些金融机构与银行一起构成了多元化的银行业金融结构。

中国加入 WTO 之后,银行业改革进一步深化,利率逐步放开,大型商业银行在所有银行机构总资产中所占的比例有所下降。但与此同时,从 2003 年到 2019 年,中国银行业金融机构资产总额增长 7 倍以上,截至 2019 年底,中国境内银行业金融机构总资产为 282.51 万亿元,银行业金融机构总负债为 258.24 万亿元;分机构类型看,资产规模较大的为大型商业银行、股份制商业银行、农村金融机构和城市商业银行,占银行业金融机构资产的份额分别为 39.1%、18.0%、13.2% 和 13.2%。

回顾新中国成立以来银行体系的改革与发展历程,可以说现代银行体系的建立是社会主义市场经济建设、改革开放的胜利成果,中国多层次、现代化的银行体系紧密结合中国实际情况,在实践中不断改革,在发展中持续创新,中国银行体系的改革与发展对中国经济社会建设贡献巨大。总的来看,新中国成立后的 70 多年,中国银行业既有效支持了中国经济的快速发展,又探索出了一条中国特色银行业发展之路。

12.2.2.2 中国当前的非银行金融机构

非银行金融机构是随着金融资产多元化、金融业务专业化而产生的,是一国金融体系的重要组成部分。非银行金融机构主要包括保险、信托、证券、金融公司等,在金融体系和经济发展中发挥着重要作用。

(1) 保险公司

中共十一届三中会议以后,恢复保险事业势在必行。1979 年 2 月,中国人民银行召开全国分行行长会议,提出要逐步恢复国内保险业务,同年 4 月国务院作出"逐步恢复国内保险业务"的决定。2001 年,中国正式加入 WTO,承诺在 5 年内取消外资保险公司的地域限制,并开放大部分业务,中国保险市场主体日趋多元化,中资保险企业的体制改革步伐加快,外资保险机构凭借优质的服务、完善的产品和先进的管理经验,对中国保险业起到示范和标杆作用,推动中国保险业经营和监管方式与国际保险业并轨。

自 2003 年起,中国内地主要大型保险公司开始实行股份制改革。2008 年全球金融危机以后,中国保险业发展表现出明显的综合化经营趋势,银行、证券、保险、信托、租赁和基金等金融业务交融发展。目前中国保险机构的混业经营主要体现在两个方面:一方面是保险公司开始积极向其他非保险金融业务延伸;另一方面是以非保险起家的其他机构不同程度地参与保险市场,金融综合经营的发展趋势越来越明显。

经过改革开放后 40 多年的发展,中国保险业与保险机构得到了长足的发展,产业规模和机构数量都在不断增长,经营管理水平也有了显著的提高,目前保险业已成为中国金融体系中的重要部分,在促进中国经济发展和社会稳定中正发挥着越来越重要的作用。

近年来,中国保险市场基础制度建设和保险监管体系不断发展完善,在继续进行深化改革的同时,更注重改革的科学性和协调性,不断丰富和发展保险功能,拓宽保险业务的服务领域,逐渐向着标准化、多样化、国际化的方向迈进。

(2) 信托公司

改革开放后,国家决定恢复信托业。1979 年 10 月,经国务院批准,中国国际信托投资公司在北京成立,这是改革开放后成立的第一家金融信托投资公司。其任务是引导、吸收和运用外国资金引进先进技术和先进设备,对国内进行建设投资。随后中国金融信托业迅速发展,中央各部委和各级地方政府纷纷设立多种形式的信托投资公司,银行系统也纷纷设立附属的信托投资机构,停滞了近30年的中国信托业得到迅速恢复。

截至1982年底,全国各类信托机构发展到620多家,其中中国人民银行的信托部有186家,建设银行的有266家,农业银行的有20多家,中国银行的有96家。信托机构构成中以地方政府和国有银行为主。然而,由于信托公司投资种类丰富和风险偏好较高,行业多次出现无序发展现象。因此,从1982年到2007年,监管层对信托业先后进行六次大规模清理整顿,引导信托业务发展逐步迈向规范。

2010年8月24日,中国银行业监督管理委员会公布实施《信托公司净资本管理办法》,将信托公司的信托资产规模与净资本挂钩,并对信托公司实施以净资本为核心的风险控制指标体系。《中华人民共和国信托法》和《信托公司净资本管理办法》共同构成中国信托业监管的主要政策依据,中国信托机构的经营走上更加规范的道路。根据《中国信托行业研究报告(2018)》相关数据,截至2017年末,全行业68家信托公司注册资本合计2 474.63亿元,净资产规模合计5 250.67亿元,营业总收入合计1 190.69亿元。

(3) 证券公司

证券公司是专门从事有价证券买卖的法人企业,分为证券经营公司和证券登记公司。狭义的证券公司是指证券经营公司,是经主管机关批准并到有关工商行政管理局领取营业执照后专门经营证券业务的机构。它具有证券交易所的会员资格,可以承销发行、自营买卖或自营兼代理买卖证券。普通投资人的证券投资都要通过证券商来进行。

2011—2021年,中国证券公司蓬勃发展,证券公司从2011年的109家增加到2021年的140家,增幅为28.44%。证券行业营业收入也同样水涨船高,从2011年的1 359.50亿元增长到2021年的5 024.10亿元,增长了3 664.60亿元。

随着中国证券业务的持续发展,中国证券行业呈现多元化发展,其中投行业务和资产管理业务收入占比逐渐增多。

证券公司作为中国金融市场重要组成部分,通过提高直接融资比重,改善资源配给,为中国金融市场持续发展奠定基础。

(4) 金融公司

①财务公司

财务公司是为企业技术改造、新产品开发及产品销售提供金融服务,以中长期金融业务为主的非银行金融机构。中国第一家企业集团财务公司为东风汽车工业财务公司(后更名为东风汽车财务有限公司),成立于1987年5月,同年9月经中国人民银行总行批准,中山集团财务公司在南京成立,标志着中国产业资本和金融资本开始结合。到目前为止,全国能源电力、航天航空、石油、化工、钢铁、冶金、机械制造等关系国计民生的基础产业和各个重要领域的大型企业集团,几乎都拥有了自己的财务公司。

②金融租赁公司

根据2007年中国银行业监督管理委员会颁布的《金融租赁公司管理办法》,金融租赁公司是指经中国银行业监督管理委员会批准,以经营融资租赁业务为主的非银行金融机构。融资租赁是指出租人根据承租人对租赁物和供货人的选择或认可,将其从供货人处取得的租赁物按合同约定出租给承租人占有、使用,向承租人收取租金的交易活动。

截至2018年9月,中国金融租赁公司有69家,它们主要从事公交、城建、医疗、航空、信息技术等产业。同时,金融租赁公司在小微企业业务的资金来源和服务模式方面积极创新。截至2018年底,全国融资租赁公司总数为11 777家,注册资金约合32 763亿元,融资租赁合同余额约为66 500亿元人民币。

③金融资产管理公司

金融资产管理公司是经国务院决定设立的收购国有银行不良贷款,管理和处置因收购国有银行不良贷款形成的资产的国有独资非银行金融机构。中国四大金融资产管理公司,即中国华融资产管理公司、中国长城资产管理公司、中国东方资产管理公司、中国信达资产管理公司,分别接收从中国工商银行、中国农业银行、中国银行、中国建设银行剥离出来的不良资产。2004年后,财政部规定,金融资产管理公司在2006年底完成向商业化转型,业务发展趋于多元化。

2017年7月,习近平主席在全国金融工作会议上强调:"遵循金融发展规律,紧紧围绕服务实体经济、防控金融风险、深化金融改革这三项任务……促进经济和金融良性循环、健康发展。"为更好地服务金融供给侧结构性改革,金融资产管理公司应围绕"三去一降一补"核心任务,以金融不良资产收购处置为重点助力提升金融供给质量,以非金融不良资产收购业务为重点服务实体经济转型升级,以实质性重组手段为重点纾困救助问题项目和危机企业。

④其他金融公司

随着市场经济发展以及消费多元化,汽车金融公司、消费金融公司和货币经纪公司等金融公司相继出现。

总之,非银行金融机构是金融制度发展到一定程度的产物。随着市场经济的发展,信用关系的深化,人们对于金融服务的需求越来越趋向于多元化。非银行金融机构资产在金融资产中的比重逐渐增大。非银行金融机构作为银行业的主要补充,是一个国家金融体系中不可分割的组成部分。

12.2.3 中国当前的金融市场

从1949年中华人民共和国成立至改革开放前,在传统计划经济体制下,中国金融市场仅仅在短时间内有所发展。改革开放初期,人们普遍认为,金融市场是资本主义社会经济和金融的产物,与社会主义制度是不相容的。从20世纪80年代中期开始,随着思想解放以及社会主义经济逐步繁荣,原来遭遇压制的金融市场又逐渐恢复了生机,不但丰富了货币市场,而且发展了资本市场,拓展了金融市场空间,促进了金融市场体系的完善。21世纪以来,各类金融市场飞速发展,市场规模不断扩大,基础建设扎实推进,市场交易制度和监管机制不断成熟完善,市场参与主体越来越丰富,至今已经形成一个由票据市场、同业拆借市场、股票市场、债券市场、外汇市场等若干子市场组成的完整的金融市场体系。

商业票据市场是商业票据承兑、贴现和再贴现的市场,是货币市场发展中历史最悠久的市场之一。商业票据是企业为筹措资金在公开市场上签发的,承诺在指定日期按票面金额向持票人兑现的一种无抵押担保的信用凭证。在商业票据市场上,由于缺乏担保,票据发行者大多是一些信用卓著、资金实力雄厚、经过评级的大型公司或企业。

2000年11月9日,中国第一家票据专营机构——中国工商银行票据营业部在上海成立,标志着票据业务经营模式迈入了集约化和专业化的发展轨道。

进入21世纪以来,中国票据市场规模迅速扩大,票据业务不断拓展,市场参与主体更趋多元化,制度与法规建设逐步完善,票据风险得到有效控制,票据利率市场化水平不断提高,创新产品不断涌现,票据市场得到进一步发展。

同业拆借市场是各类金融机构之间进行短期资金拆借活动所形成的市场,主要满足金融机构日常经营活动中经常发生的头寸盈缺调剂的需要,也是中央银行执行货币政策操作的窗口和传导渠道。

1996年1月,中国人民银行建立了全国统一的银行间同业拆借市场,该市场由一级网络和二级网络组成。同年5月17日,中国人民银行下发《关于取消同业拆借利率上限管理的通知》,决定从6月1日起,取消同业拆借利率上限管理,拆借利率由拆借双方根据市场资金供求情况自行决定。全国统一同业拆借市场架构的确立和试运行,标志着中国同业拆借市场发展进入了一个新时代。

1998年,中国人民银行先后批准符合规定的外资银行、商业银行、保险公司成为全国同业拆借市场的成员,从事同业拆借业务。1999年,批准部分农村信用社联社和证券公司成为全国同业拆借市场成员,从事同业拆借业务。2007年7月,中国人民银行颁布《同业拆借管理办法》,将保险公司、保险资产管理公司、金融资产管理公司、信托公司、汽车金融公司、金融租赁公司等非银行金融机构均纳入拆借市场参与者的范围。近年来,同业拆借市场不仅已经形成了全国性的网络,而且凭借先进的通信手段,逐渐开始向国际化方向发展。同业拆借市场稳定、有序地发展,不仅完善了中国的货币市场体系,也推进了中国货币调控机制的改革。

股票是企业进行直接融资的重要形式。股票市场是股票发行与交易的市场,在中国经济转轨和企业转制过程中,股票市场已成为中国经济市场化的引擎和助推器,成为企业融资、资源配置和企业转制的重要途径和手段。

进入21世纪以来,中国资本市场特别是股票市场进入一个新的发展阶段,中国股票市场在经历了10余年的摸索后进入了一个重要的发展转折期,迎来历史上最为深刻的制度性变革。2019年底,沪深两市上市公司3 777家,主板、中小企业板、创业板、科创板分别为1 973家、943家、791家和70家。沪深两市总市值59.29万亿元,流通市值48.35万亿元,较2018年末分别增加36.33%和36.65%;流通市值占总市值的81.54%,较2018年末上升0.19个百分点。沪深两市总市值占2019年国内生产总值的59.84%,总市值位居全球第二位,仅次于美国。

随着中国股权分置改革的不断推进,股票市场的规章制度更加规范,市场监管水平和市场治理结构日益完善。股权激励等措施的实施进一步提高了上市公司的竞争力,同时也提高了上市公司的质量。

1981年,为了集中各方面的财力进行社会主义现代化建设,缓解国家财政赤字问题,国务院决定恢复国库券的发行。自恢复发行国债以来,中国一直在摸索和改革国债的发行方式。1991年,中国首次试验以承购包销的方式发行国债,初步实现了市场化。这标志着中国国债一级市场即发行市场机制开始形成。

进入21世纪以来,中国国债一级市场基本形成,市场化程度不断提高。国债发行的品种进一步多样化。财政部相继推出贴现国债、附息国债等新品种,并完成券面无纸化记账式改革。在期限上,既有 3 个月、6 个月期的短期国债,也有 7 年、9 年、10 年期的长期国债,初步形成了合理的国债期限体系。同时,国债发行的频率也大大提高。国债市场不仅为投资者提供了多样化的、多选择的投资工具,也有利于财政部门调整债务结构、均衡债务负担、缓解偿债高峰压力。

进入 21 世纪以来,中国金融衍生品市场开始繁衍、发展,产品数量不断增加,品种不断丰富,金融衍生工具日益成为规避金融风险、降低交易成本的有效手段。但和发达国家相比,中国目前的金融衍生品市场仍然处于起步阶段,金融衍生工具的品种和规模仍然较少。

12.2.4　中国当前的金融监管体系

1978 年以来,中国通过以国有银行为主体的金融制度安排,保持着对金融资源和经济领域的强大控制能力,为中国的经济体制变革提供了宽广的制度空间和巨额的成本补偿。

1998 年 12 月召开的中央经济工作会议指出:"保持币值稳定,支持经济发展,防范和化解金融风险,是金融工作的主要任务。"会议就推进金融改革、加强金融监管、加快法制建设以及建立和完善防范与化解金融风险的有效机制等方面提出明确要求,表明了中国建立与国际接轨的审慎金融监管制度的决心。

1998 年以来,中国为审慎金融监管制度的构建采取了一系列措施,如推行以风险为基础的贷款五级分类制度、强化资本充足率监管、化解国有银行巨额不良资产、建立健全专业监管结构、制定和完善监管法律法规等,逐步强化了审慎金融监管制度,取得了明显成效。

同时,在构建和强化审慎监管制度的过程中,中国通过不断深化国有企业和财政体制改革、持续推进金融开放和金融体系结构优化,为中国审慎金融监管制度的完善创造了良好的外部环境。

2017 年,中共十九大报告明确提出要"健全货币政策和宏观审慎政策双支柱调控框架",2020 年《中华人民共和国中国人民银行法》迎来 17 年来首次大修,从法规上明确了"货币政策和宏观审慎政策"的双支柱框架。至此,中国货币政策"双支柱"框架已经正式明确,双支柱是理解当前以及未来几年的宏观调控思路的核心。2021 年 12 月 31 日,央行发布了《宏观审慎政策指引(试行)》,标志着中国双支柱框架从制度上又迈出一大步。《宏观审慎政策指引(试行)》的核心内容可以归结为四大要素:其一,宏观审慎政策的目标是防范系统性金融风险;其二,宏观审慎管理牵头部门会同相关部门对系统性金融风险进行监测、识别和评估;其三,宏观审慎政策工具具有"宏观、逆周期、防传染"的基本属性和"时变"特征;其四,宏观审慎政策与货币政策、微观审慎监管及其他政策的协调。

12.3　中国金融体系改革的基本经验

70 多年的发展历程中,中国金融体系为本国经济发展和改革开放作出了关键贡献,且成功抗击了两次全球性金融危机的冲击,形成了中国特色的金融发展道路,必须总结金融体系演变的经验来指导金融业的进一步改革开放与金融业的高质量发展。中国金融体系 70 多年发展演变的基本经验主要包括以下几个方面。

12.3.1 坚持金融改革走中国道路

新中国金融体系 70 多年发展历程取得了光辉的成就,最重要的一条经验就是坚持走中国特色的发展道路。中国政府在金融改革中坚持走自己的道路,引进市场经济金融体系的基本结构,针对国内缺乏资本市场发展环境有步骤地培育金融市场,并根据自己的国情建立起国有专业银行主导的金融体系。

1992 年,中共十四大确立了社会主义市场经济体制,金融体制开始围绕建立社会主义市场经济的金融体系框架而进行改革,构建起以国有商业银行为主导的金融体系,资本市场开始发展壮大,大型国有金融机构承担着金融资源配置的功能。2004 年后,国有金融机构股份制改革中主要坚持"国有控股",并积极引进国外战略投资者,推动金融体系的健康化、规范化发展,保证了中国央行不受外资银行的约束而采取独立自主的货币政策,不仅形成了中国特色金融发展之路,也为发展中国家金融改革发展树立典范。

12.3.2 坚持金融服务实体经济

中国金融体系自建立起就围绕实体经济开展业务运作,并在为实体经济服务中发展。改革开放以来,中国经济建设取得巨大成就,这与金融服务于实体经济分不开,金融改革发展始终与经济体制改革发展相伴而生。1985 年,随着中国投融资体制由财政拨款改为银行贷款的全面实行,金融开始代替财政成为经济资源配置的核心。国有银行由专业银行向商业银行、股份制商业银行发展,这种变化代表着金融在支持实体企业发展过程中随着实体企业组织形式与市场环境的变化而变化。20 世纪 90 年代末中国政府开始实施的剥离国有商业银行不良资产的举措、对证券市场和保险市场进行治理整顿以及 2008 年后开展的利率汇率市场化改革、人民币国际化、非银行金融机构的兴起等,这些措施是为了协调金融体系与实体经济的关系而在金融机构、金融市场和金融产品等方面作出的制度安排,是为适应中国经济体制的进一步改革以及实体企业市场化、国际化发展而作出相配套的金融改革支持政策。

正是因为中国建立起了国有银行主导的金融体系,把低成本吸收的储蓄转为对实体企业(国有企业、民营企业等)的投资,其高储蓄、高投资的特点保证了劳动人口与资本的结合,推动着中国"投资驱动型"经济模式的发展。2008 年以后,随着中国人口红利的消失,中国经济进入了新常态,投资驱动开始向创新驱动发展,金融体系对实体经济的支持重点转向高新技术产业、绿色产业等领域;而且中国政府逐渐开放资本市场,大力发展非银行金融机构,为实体企业提供多样化融资渠道。同时,针对农村地区和中小企业融资难、融资贵情况,中国政府提出"金融扶贫""金融服务中小企业"等政策引导金融服务实体经济。近年来,随着对外开放的深入,中国企业"走出去"成为一种新趋势。与此相适应,中国金融业也加大了对外开放的步伐,"人民币国际化""资本项目可兑换"以及金融国际化过程中建立的"丝路基金""亚洲基础设施投资银行"等都是金融体系支持实体企业走出去的基本策略。可见,为实体经济服务是中国金融业的根本宗旨,正是牢牢抓住"金融服务实体经济"这个"牛鼻子",才保证了中国金融业的健康发展与不断壮大。

12.3.3 坚持金融改革的稳定有序发展

金融是经济的核心,金融稳则经济稳。新中国金融体系 70 多年的发展历程,有一条重要经验就是坚持金融改革的稳定有序发展。

就金融机构来说,中国政府通过设立准入门槛支持国有金融机构发展。国有银行从20世纪80年代的专业银行、90年代的商业银行发展到21世纪的股份制银行,都是在中央政府的主导下稳定有序进行的。中国金融机构不仅为国有企业提供低成本资金支持,促进了国民经济稳定发展,而且在为国有企业改革服务中自身组织也不断优化。

就金融市场来说,中国政府一直对各类金融市场开放持谨慎态度,然而,金融市场发展的核心是要让市场在金融资源的配置中发挥关键作用,也就是金融市场化。金融市场化的关键是利率市场化和汇率市场化,虽然在20世纪90年代利率市场化、汇率市场化试点已经启动,但真正的利率市场化、汇率市场化是在2008年全球金融危机后随着金融体系的市场化、国际化和多元化发展逐渐形成并稳定发展的,且利率市场化还没有完全实施。

综上,在中国国有银行主导的金融体系中,国有金融机构在金融市场上垄断了金融业务,金融机构改革、金融市场化改革都采取渐进性的、滞后经济发展的"被动"改革策略,保证了金融业的稳定有序发展,也有利于国民经济的稳定发展。

12.3.4　坚持党对金融工作的领导

70多年来,新中国金融体系由无到有、由无序到有序、由弱到强、由封闭到开放,还有一条重要经验就是坚持党对金融工作的领导。在党的领导下,金融改革始终坚持以国有银行、国有资本为主导的渐进性改革,能正确处理金融改革、经济发展与社会稳定的关系,既保证了金融业的健康发展,又保证了金融改革的政治方向。同时,金融业是高风险行业,金融稳定关系到千家万户的利益。中共非常重视金融的稳定发展,始终坚持金融为实体经济服务,为人民群众服务,并在金融实践中重视金融改革与金融创新的自主性、安全性和可控性,注重防范系统性金融风险,成功抵御了全球金融危机对中国经济和金融市场的冲击。

12.4　中国金融体系发展的趋势和未来展望

12.4.1　当前中国金融发展趋势

目前中国仍然是银行主导型的金融结构,银行在社会融资中发挥着主要作用。随着中国金融市场化改革持续推进以及金融创新不断发展,近年来中国金融结构呈现出一些新的特征,主要表现在下述的四个方面。

一是金融市场在中国金融体系中的作用和地位在不断提升。首先从政策支持角度看,中国一直把发展资本市场作为实施国家战略的重要组成部分。中共十八大以来,以习近平同志为核心的党中央高度重视资本市场工作,加强对资本市场的集中统一领导,作出一系列重大决策部署,明确提出要通过深化改革,打造一个规范、透明、开放、有活力、有韧性的资本市场。

二是传统金融机构的业务边界在逐步模糊。首先,金融控股集团的出现打破了金融分业经营的限制,对于金融控股集团而言,传统的金融分业限制已经不复存在。其次,金融产品创新模糊了金融机构的边界。最后,金融机构业务交叉和融合不断加强。这些行为加强了金融机构之间以及金融机构与金融市场之间的联系。

三是新型金融媒介和类金融机构快速发展。近年来,随着金融创新发展以及互联网技术在金融领域的广泛应用,包括第三方理财销售、互联网众筹等各种新型金融媒介快速发展。这些金融媒介与传统金融机构相结合,能够更加便捷地提供新的金融功能和服务,弱化了传统金融机构之间的边界,强化了金融机构与金融市场的联系。

四是金融机构与金融市场之间的联系更加紧密。随着金融市场的发展,金融机构在资金来源和资金运用方面对金融市场的依赖程度不断上升。随着新型金融机构和金融工具的发展,资金在金融市场与金融机构之间的流动更加便捷和隐蔽。

12.4.2 当前中国金融改革

与中国经济一样,中国金融面临着转型升级的挑战,即由要素驱动型向创新驱动型发展模式转变。然而,创新也意味着风险,当前中国的金融体系不能有效支撑创新活动,仍需进一步改革,主要在下述的三个方面。

第一,大力发展资本市场。以银行为主体的间接融资金融体系并不利于创新活动的发展,只有通过直接融资,才能为企业的创新行为,尤其为中小企业的创新行为提供资金支持。大力发展资本市场,可以增加企业融资渠道,扩大直接融资规模,提高资源配置效率,有力支撑中国企业的创新行为。

第二,大力推动金融创新。经济结构的改变需要金融结构作出相应调整,需要适应经济发展的创新金融工具。随着中国金融综合经营趋势的发展,新兴的金融工具也在不断发展,新一轮的金融产业布局与竞争已经展开,中国应当结合自身资源禀赋优势和产业结构,构筑金融全产业链,推动金融更好地服务实体经济。

第三,大力增强金融监管。以人工智能、区块链、云计算和大数据为代表的新一代信息技术与金融深度融合发展,催生了科技金融。一方面,科技金融扩大了融资渠道,降低了融资成本,加速了金融业综合经营趋势。另一方面,科技金融加大了各类金融风险。同时,随着金融业对外开放的逐步推进,中国金融风险监控的复杂性加剧,金融监管体制需要转型,从而增强金融监管。尤其需要加强金融法治建设,加强金融市场交易的全过程"穿透式"监管,提高识别金融风险的能力,坚决守住不发生系统性金融风险的底线,为中国经济发展保驾护航。

13 中国特色的经济发展模式

中国的经济发展模式是中国改革开放政策的产物。因为改革开放包括对内改革和对外开放这两个互相依存的方面,讨论中国模式就应把改革开放置于中国和国际发展这两个维度中去探讨其意义。

基本上,中国模式对于西方发达国家和其他发展中国家具有不同的意义。对很多第三世界发展中国家来说,中国模式的意义在于其是否能够成为有别于从前其他所有现代化模式的一个替代模式。第二次世界大战后,世界的发展模式基本上分为苏联模式和西方模式,苏联模式解体后只剩下西方模式,西方模式主要指的是美国、欧洲的资本主义模式。美国在冷战结束后成为唯一的超级大国,推行其以"自由放任"为特征的市场经济模式,即"华盛顿共识"。但不管是欧洲还是美国,在推行其模式方面并没有取得很大的成功,很多采用西方模式的发展中国家并没有因此而得到社会经济的发展和民主政治的稳定运作。在这种情形下,中国模式对发展中国家具有非常重要的借鉴意义。

中国模式对中国本身发展的意义更不容忽视。从宏观的角度来看,改革开放最深刻的意义在于对国家发展道路,包括经济、社会和政治道路的探索。中国在近代之前尽管历史漫长,但多为历史的简单重复,农业社会和王朝更替是数千年历史最持续的特色。只有到了近代和西方强国接触之后,中国在各方面才发生了根本性的变化。中国模式是一种发展中的模式,是世界经验和中国本身经验的累积。

13.1 中国特色社会主义市场经济模式

13.1.1 有为政府与有效市场的统一

政府本身是一个国家发展过程中最重要的制度条件。有效市场和有为政府相互依存共生、相互协调促进的状态,是中国特色社会主义市场与社会主义基本经济制度相结合的伟大实践成果。

中国在改革开放前实行的是计划经济,政府的经济作用是极端的,市场被视为资本主义制度的一部分,从而其功能也被否定。改革开放后,中国对市场有了不同的看法。邓小平认为资本主义可以利用市场,社会主义也可以利用市场,这就将市场中立化了。同时中国政府大力推进市场建设,各种所有制经济都是在同一个市场平台上互动竞争的。以市场和政府之间关系探索为主线,不断向经济主体释放改革红利和制度红利,是改革取得巨大发展成就的关键因素。不同于西方主流经济学理论所界定的那样,中国政府并非局限于一般性市场经济所要求的功能,而是还承担着培育市场体系、实施产业政策等广泛职责。这些更加多样和复杂的政府功能,是在以社会主义基本经济制度为依托、以社会主义现代化国家建设根本目标为驱动的背景下,才最终得以充分而高效地实现。中国政府在整个改革开放过程中所发挥的职能作用,具有极其重要的主导和引领意义,具体而言包括下述几个方面。

13.1.1.1 培育市场体系

改革开放初期至21世纪初,中国政府培育市场体系的重点在产品市场和物价管理方面。1983年,国务院发布了《关于加强市场和物价管理的通知》,对国营、集体和个体商业的经营范围、价格权限进行了规定,该文件有效扩大了商品生产规模,扩展了市场流通渠道。1994年,国内贸易部(于1998年改组为国家国内贸易局,于2000年撤销)发布了《全国商品市场规划纲要》,确立了发展商品市场的基本思路、原则、目标和建设程序,同时指出商品市场是市场体系的重要基础,统筹规划商品市场体系的重点是统筹好全国性、区域性重要商品市场的建设和管理。2004年,商务部发布了《全国商品市场体系建设纲要》,倡导各级政府着眼于建立统一开放、竞争有序、布局合理、结构优化的现代商品市场体系,提高商品市场在国民经济中的地位。2005年以后,伴随着一系列政策文件与培育措施的推动,中国商品市场建设日趋完善。2020年,中国97%以上的商品和服务已由市场定价。

除了商品市场,中国土地、劳动力、资本等生产要素市场的培育也取得了巨大成就。对于土地市场而言,20世纪80年代开始,通过土地所有权与使用权的分离,中国创造了优化配置土地要素的先决条件。之后中国政府陆续发布了《中华人民共和国城镇国有土地使用权出让和转让暂行条例》等多个文件,有效地规范了地方政府土地出让行为,提高了土地资源配置效率。对于劳动力市场而言,《进一步做好城镇劳动就业工作》和《关于广开门路,搞活经济,解决城镇就业问题的若干决定》两个文件提出的"三结合就业方针",成为刺激城镇劳动力市场发育的重要推动力。与此同时,农民变成了自营劳动者,农村劳动力开始流动,限制城乡之间劳动力流动的政策也开始松动。1992年,中共十四大明确中国经济体制改革方向是建立社会主义市场经济之后,国有企业改革和民营经济发展推动了劳动力市场迅速发育,创造了大量的非农就业机会。《中华人民共和国劳动法》和《中华人民共和国劳动合同法》的先后出台,保证了劳动者权益,规范了劳动力市场秩序。对于资本市场而言,1992年以来发布了《国务院关于进一步加强证券市场宏观管理的通知》等文件,2014年进一步发布了促进资本市场健康发展的《国务院关于进一步促进资本市场健康发展的若干意见》。这些文件通过构建多层次资本市场体系,不断拓宽了中国企业和居民的投融资渠道,积极促进了实体经济发展。

13.1.1.2 促进微观市场主体发展

企业是最基本的市场活动主体,是市场机制运行的微观基础。增强微观主体活力的关键是要增强企业发展的内生动力,让企业走入具有自生能力的良性发展轨道。中国以公有制为主体、多种所有制经济共同发展的基本经济制度框架,决定了公有制企业和非公有制企业都是中国特色社会主义市场经济的重要组成部分,通过改革措施不断释放二者的经营活力,可以构成经济社会发展的重要驱动力。

在公有制企业改革方面,中国政府通过内部层面的制度创新和整体层面的战略重组,使国有经济布局和结构得到了有效升级。该历程可以概括为:第一,1978—1984年以"放权让利"为重点,积极扩大国有企业自主权,实施了两步利改税、拨改贷等措施;第二,1985—1992年以所有权与经营权相分离为特征,目标是使国有企业真正成为相对独立的经济实体,采用了承包经营责任制、利税分流制度、股份制试点等具体形式;第三,1993—2002年以推动国有企业建立现代企业制度目标,实行"抓大放小"、战略重组;第四,2003—2013年以国有资产监管体制改革为主线,成立国务院国有资产监督管理委员会,实行股权分置改革和董事会制度;第五,2014年以来强调坚持政企分开和政资分开,发展混合所有制企业,并对国有企业进行分类,提出了公益性国有企业与竞争性国有企业的区分。

在支持非公有制企业发展方面,2005年发布了《国务院关于鼓励支持和引导个体私营等非公有制经济发展的若干意见》,这是第一次以中央政府名义颁发的促进非公有制经济发展的专门文件。2020年发布的《中共中央 国务院关于新时代加快完善社会主义市场经济体制的意见》,也对非公有制企业发展的相关政策支持作了系统性论述。概括而言,中国政府始终努力消除影响非公有制企业发展的体制性因素,在要素获取、审批许可、准入许可、经营运行、政府采购和招投标等方面,大幅度破除了制约其参与市场竞争的各类障碍和隐性壁垒,包括支持引导非公有制企业进入电力、油气等领域,并参与国家重大战略实施和重大项目建设。同时,中国政府也从减轻非公有制企业负担入手,通过"营改增"改革、降低增值税税率、提高个税减除费用标准等方式逐步减税降费。特别是对小微企业、科技型初创企业,还实施了普惠性税收免除政策。

13.1.1.3 完善宏观治理

宏观经济稳定运行是经济增长的必要条件。政府进行宏观治理的目标,在于修正市场经济自发调节经济活动的偏误,稳定社会经济主体预期,最终实现可持续的经济增长。

在2015年末供给侧结构性改革战略提出之前,中国政府很长一段时间采取了西方主流经济学所倡导的政府干预及调控政策,并依据具体国情发展出了更加丰富的调控组合方式。1984年,中国政府提出"越是搞活经济,越要重视宏观调节",尝试通过价格、税收、信贷等途径调节社会供需总量,以及积累和消费、三次产业结构等重大比例关系。1992年,社会主义市场经济体制改革目标确立以后,中国政府进行宏观调控的工具更加多样化,同时也注重税收、价格、产业、汇率、利率等不同调控方式之间的综合协调。1998年,为了应对亚洲金融危机可能导致的通货紧缩,中国政府采取了以积极增加投资、扩大内需为核心的宏观调控政策,国债和信贷发行明显放宽。2007年,中国政府对于宏观调控体系的定位中,虽然仍保留着国家计划与财政政策和货币政策的配合作用,但是着重强调了国家发展规划的指导作用。2008年,美国次贷危机引起的全球金融危机发生之后,中国经济增长速度放缓,对外出口甚至出现了负增长,因此,中国政府实施了以"4万亿投资"为代表的经济刺激计划。

中国政府往往从凯恩斯主义视角制定宏观调控政策,以削弱经济波动,维持物价水平稳定。这种干预行为基于凯恩斯主义总需求管理理论,一定程度上使得中国经济不时地出现投资和消费过热、通货膨胀和经济结构失衡等问题。鉴于此,2015年末,中国政府在继续重视扩大内需的前提下,提出了供给侧结构性改革。这也将中国政府调控经济的理念和水平系统性地提高到了一个新的高度。中国政府意识到,制约经济获得长期稳定增长的产能过剩、结构重复,以及与人民生活休戚相关的住房、教育、医疗和养老等问题,不仅涉及需求层面,而且也与高质量产品或服务供给的相对不足紧密相关。

改革开放进程中,中国政府采取多种手段进行经济调控,总体上有效保持了经济平稳健康发展。在不断摸索和调整过程中,中国政府的调节手段逐步稳健,行政干预方式更多地过渡到了经济和法律调节方式,从注重规模性的总量指标向注重结构性的比例类指标转变。同时,中国政府也常常将具体的经济干预与所需的制度变革二者协调、配套地进行,很好地符合了中国特色社会主义市场经济的运行规律。

13.1.2 混合所有制经济

混合所有制经济是财产权分属不同性质所有者的经济形式,是一种主体多元化的财产制度。在中国特定的经济环境中,混合所有制具有宏观和微观两个层面的含义。对于宏观层面而言,混合所有制是指中国经济体中所有制成分的非单一性,即在以公有制经济为主体的前提下,形成公有制经济与私有制经济并存的基本格局;对于微观层面而言,混合所有制是指企业投资主体所有权性质的非单一性,即产权结构呈现国有资本、民营资本、外资资本相互交融的态势。

混合所有制改革在国有企业中形成了一种更具兼容性的所有权运行制度安排,一方面混合所有制改革借助非公有制活力促使市场机制在国有企业中发挥积极作用;另一方面混合所有制改革在打开国有企业改革突破口的同时推动了优化非公有制经济发展环境的增量改革,对于充分发挥多元经济成分比较优势进而合理配置社会资源具有重要意义。作为中国社会主义基本经济制度的重要实现形式,混合所有制改革是国有企业改革的重要组成部分,是公有制多种实现形式的积极探索,更是国有经济与市场经济交融模式的重大突破。

在混合所有制改革逐步深化的基础上,中共十八届三中全会确立了全面深化改革的总体精神,经济体制改革进入攻坚期,国有企业亦进入"全面深化改革"的纵深推进期,民营企业发展也在经济体制全面改革的背景下进入"跨越期"。国家鼓励民营企业积极融入国家战略,积极与国有资本结合。随着混合所有制作为"社会主义基本经济制度的重要实现形式"的战略地位得以确立,一系列针对性改革方案标志着混合所有制改革进入深化加速的新周期,开始注重引入高匹配度、高协调性、高认同感的战略投资者参与治理,落实劳动、人事、分配制度改革并深度转化市场化经营机制,实施薪酬激励与股权激励相结合的差异化员工激励分配机制等。

13.1.3 开放型经济

20世纪60年代,来自发达经济体的劳动密集型加工环节开始流入亚洲地区,中国香港、中国台湾、新加坡、韩国通过承接劳动密集型加工工序参与经济全球化实现了经济的快速发展,被称为"亚洲四小龙"。20世纪80年代,发达国家主导的全球价值链逐步发展,但"亚洲四小龙"的生产成本已高居不下,因此迫切需要一个新的市场承接劳动密集型产业。中国的对外开放在时间点上正好契合了以全球价值链发展为主要推动力的第三次全球化浪潮。以渐进式为主要特点的对外开放和以市场化为主要特征的国内改革相辅相成,使得中国逐步融入全球经贸体系。

中国自1978年开始的对外开放是一个不断拓展和深化的历史进程。在改革开放之初,打开国门的中国是国际经济体系的适应者和融入者,之后变为参与者和完善者,再后来又努力成为国际体系改革的倡导者和引领者,并在实践中形成了一系列层层递进、一脉相承的中国特色开放经济政策与理论。

13.2 经济增长和社会发展的"中国奇迹"

13.2.1 中国经济的增长

1978年改革开放以来,中国经济经历了40多年的持续高速增长,国内生产总值从1978年的3 678.7亿元扩大到2021年的1 149 237亿元,如图13-1所示,在扣除价格因素后年均增速在9%以上。按美元计算,中国国内生产总值在2010年超过日本,中国成为仅次于美国的全球第二大经济体,如图13-2所示。人均国内生产总值从1978年的385元提高到2021年的81 370元,中国也从改革开放初期人均收入仅相当于低收入国家人均国内生产总值的62%的低收入国,进入中等偏上收入国家行列。

图 13-1 中国、美国和日本 1978—2021 年的国内生产总值增长率

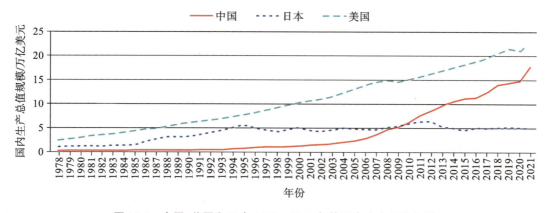

图 13-2 中国、美国和日本 1978—2021 年的国内生产总值规模

经过40多年的高速发展,中国已发展为全球最大制造业国家、最大商品出口国、仅次于美国的第二大商品进口国。根据中国国家统计局数据,2013年至2021年,中国对世界经济增长的平均贡献率达到38.6%,超过七国集团国家贡献率的总和。2021年,中国国内生产总值达17.7万亿美元,占世界比重达到18.5%,比2012年提高7.2个百分点。2021年,中国

国内生产总值相当于美国的77.1%,比2012年提高24.6个百分点,是日本的3.6倍、印度的5.6倍。同时,中国人均国民总收入实现飞跃,2021年中国人均国民总收入达11 890美元,较2012年增长1倍。中国主要工农业产品产量稳居世界前列。其中,2012年以来,谷物、肉类、花生和茶叶等农产品产量,粗钢、煤、发电量、水泥、化肥、汽车、微型计算机和手机等工业产品产量均保持在世界第一位。

改革开放以来,中国的对外经贸作为连接国内经济和世界经济的纽带,发生了翻天覆地的变化,取得了举世瞩目的成就。中国对外贸易实现历史性跨越,"引进来"和"走出去"齐头并进,区域经贸合作持续推进,成功实现从封闭半封闭到全方位开放的伟大转折,形成了全方位、多层次、宽领域的全面开放新格局。中共十八大以来,国家稳步推进贸易强国建设,着力优化营商环境,加快实施自由贸易区战略,积极促进"一带一路"国际合作。

1950年,中国货物进出口额为11.3亿美元,1977年为148亿美元,28年间货物进出口累计1 487亿美元,在低基数基础上年均增长不足10%。2004年货物进出口规模突破1万亿美元;2007年和2011年分别突破2万亿美元和3万亿美元;2013和2021年中国货物进出口规模分别突破4万亿美元和6万亿美元。从2001年中国加入WTO到2021年,20年来,中国货物进出口规模年均增长12.2%。

2001年加入WTO加速了中国融入全球贸易体系的步伐,成为中国开放型经济发展的关键节点。中国逐步健全了贸易促进、贸易救济法律体系、保护知识产权法律法规体系等,推动了对外经济贸易法制化建设。这些制度性红利极大地促进了中国对外贸易的发展,推动了中国经济与世界经济在更高层次上的融合。中国在2013年成为世界第一大货物贸易国,实现了由"贸易小国"向"贸易大国"的转变。2020年,中国对外贸易总额由2012年的4.4万亿美元升至5.3万亿美元,首超美国成为全球第一大贸易国。2021年,中国对外贸易总额达到6.9万亿美元。

中共十八大以来,中国大力实施创新驱动发展战略,创新型国家建设取得明显成效,创新能力大大增强,国际竞争力显著增强。2021年,中国创新指数居全球第12位,比2012年上升22位,在中等收入国家中排名首位。2012年以来,世界500强上榜的中国企业数量持续增长,并在2018年首次超越美国,连续4年居世界首位。2021年,中国上榜企业数量再创新高,达145家,比2012年增加50家,实现了上榜企业数量连续19年增长。

13.2.2 消除贫困的中国经验

2021年2月25日,习近平总书记在全国脱贫攻坚总结表彰大会上庄严宣告,我国脱贫攻坚战取得了全面胜利,现行标准下9 899万农村贫困人口全部脱贫,832个贫困县全部摘帽,12.8万个贫困村全部出列,区域性整体贫困得到解决,完成了消除绝对贫困的艰巨任务,创造了又一个彪炳史册的人间奇迹。以2010年的贫困线标准估计,中国40多年的扶贫工作累计使得7亿多人脱贫,贫困发生率下降了93个百分点以上。这一伟大奇迹揭示了中国制度和国家治理体系的巨大优越性,证明了精准扶贫理念及其指导下的具体行动的科学性与有效性,为当今世界反贫困提供了范例。

区域性整体贫困现象是中国几千年来贫困问题的最集中表现。根据2014年国务院扶贫办公布的名单,全国832个贫困县涉及22个省区市,其中贫困县覆盖率最高的西藏,其全区74个县都是贫困县。

中共十八大以来,中国将彻底解决区域性整体贫困与绝对贫困问题作为全面建成小康社会决胜期的三大攻坚战之一。进入"十三五"时期后,中国更明确规定脱贫攻坚的核心考核指标是到2020年稳定实现农村贫困人口"两不愁三保障",同时实现人均可支配收入增幅必须高于全国平均水平,基本公共服务的主要指标接近全国平均水平,为此,中国充分发挥了集中力量办大事的制度优势。据统计,在脱贫攻坚期间,政府财政投入专项扶贫资金累计达近1.6万亿元,再加上地区之间的对口支援和社会各界的扶贫投入,贫困地区的面貌在短期内获得了翻天覆地的变化。道路交通、水电、居住环境等基础设施建设和义务教育、医疗卫生等公共设施建设取得长足进展,教育文化医疗条件明显改善。长期制约贫困地区的行路难、吃水难、住房难、就医难等问题得到了全面解决。

改革开放以来,中国自身持续快速发展、社会保障制度日益健全,这使得中国的贫困人口快速减少。2015年,中国作出了坚决打赢脱贫攻坚战的决定,中央政府调整了以往以区域开发为主的扶贫开发模式,将精准扶贫和精准脱贫作为基本方略。2015年召开的中共十八届五中全会明确作出了实施脱贫攻坚工程的具体部署,即通过产业扶持、易地搬迁和社会保障兜底等多措并举,从2015年到2020年实现了现行标准下的5 575万建档立卡贫困人口全部脱贫。

13.2.3 社会保障事业的成就

社会保障作为保障和改善民生、增进人民福祉的基本保障制度,对社会经济发展与民生保障起到至关重要的促进作用。2012年以来,中国从社会保险、社会救助等多个方面对社会保障体系进行一体化、全方位的调整与改革,实现了保障人群和待遇水平的稳步提升,社会保障在脱贫攻坚中兜底扶贫效果显著,服务保障功能日益完备。目前主要有下述几项社会保障制度。

第一,养老保险制度。2014年,中国正式建立城乡居民基本养老保险制度,实现了基本养老保险层面的城乡统筹。2015年,中国实施机关事业单位工作人员的基本养老保险制度全面改革,使其与城镇企业职工基本养老保险的制度设计与运作机制相统一,提升社会保险的公平性。2018年,中国正式建立基本养老保险基金中央调剂金制度,旨在缓解各区域间城镇企业职工基本养老保险基金给付压力。2022年,中国提出个人养老金应实行完全积累的个人账户制度,促进了第三支柱养老金制度的完善。

第二,医疗保险制度与生育保险制度。2015年,中国在全国实施城乡居民大病保险,作为基本医疗保险制度的有益补充,缓解了城乡居民因大病返贫、致贫的可能。2016年,中国建立了统一的城乡居民基本医疗保险制度,实现了基本医疗保险层面的城乡统筹。2018年,国务院提出建立国家医疗保障局,将基本医疗保险、医疗救助等职能统一纳入该机构并实行规范化管理。2019年,中国正式将生育保险与职工基本医疗保险合并。

第三,长期护理保险制度。为满足由人口老龄化、高龄化所带来的长期护理需求,缓解基本医疗保险的支付压力,中国从2016年起在多个城市开展了长期护理保险制度的试点工作。

第四,中国社会救助制度。该制度主要包含最低生活保障、特困人员供养、专项救助制度以及临时救助制度。2014年,中国在顶层设计层面首次将上述社会救助内容进行统筹化管理,社会救助制度得以统一化与规范化,步入从分散向统一的体系化发展阶段。2016年,中国将农村设立的"五保户"制度与城市设立的"三无"人员救助制度进行合并,形成了城乡统一的特困人员救助供养制度。2021年,《最低生活保障审核确认办法》将涉及区分城乡低保的概念删除,统一规范为"最低生活保障"。至此社会救助制度从城乡分割走向城乡统筹。

与此同时,社会保障事业取得长足发展。社会保障普惠项目持续增加、保障人群覆盖范围不断扩大。一是基本保险扩围与增量同步提升。截至2021年底,中国基本养老保险参保人数为10.3亿人。基本医疗保险参保人数为13.6亿人,参保率稳定在95%以上,全民医保基本实现。二是社会救助与社会福利覆盖人群逐步增长。城乡低保、城乡特困人员救助待遇享有人数达4 682.4万人,做到应救尽救;儿童福利覆盖面有所延伸,扩展到所有困境儿童,且保障水平逐渐提升;残疾人"两项补贴"基本落实,享有残疾人待遇人数为2 697.3万人,约占残疾人总数的31.6%。

此外,社会保障待遇水平不断提高。一是养老待遇水平逐年上调。中国从2005年开始持续上调企业职工养老金,且自居民养老保险实施以来周期性上调居民基础养老金。二是医保费用负担减轻力度显著。基本医疗保险、大病保险、医疗救助三重制度累计惠及农村低收入人口就医1.23亿人次。三是医保财政补贴待遇稳步提升。2012年居民医疗保险补助标准为240元,而到2021年补贴标准提高到580元。四是城乡最低生活保障标准差距逐渐缩小。

中国社会保障已然从补缺型向普惠型特征发展,社会福利覆盖对象更加普遍化,福利项目围绕老年人、残疾人、儿童及妇女群体建立了相应服务内容,各个服务内容也构成福利体系,国家主导型社会福利制度在促进全民共享经济发展成果发挥正向作用。

14 新时代的发展理念与发展格局

根据中共十九届五中全会精神,2021年起中国进入新发展阶段。这是在全面建成小康社会、实现第一个百年奋斗目标之后,全面建设社会主义现代化国家、向第二个百年奋斗目标进军的新发展阶段。

进入这样的新发展阶段,实现新发展阶段的目标任务,对于实现中华民族伟大复兴具有决定性意义。中华民族有着5000多年的历史,创造了灿烂的中华文明,为全人类作出了杰出贡献。鸦片战争之后,中国人民遭受了空前的灾难,陷入积贫积弱、任人宰割的悲惨境地。从那以后,中华民族的复兴就成为一代代中华儿女的伟大梦想和不懈追求。这个复兴,是经济、政治、文化、科技、军事和国际地位等的全面复兴,其根本目标就是实现国家富强、民族振兴、人民幸福。

"十四五"时期是新发展阶段的新起点,是中国实现更大发展的重要时期。立足新发展阶段、贯彻新发展理念、构建新发展格局事关中国经济社会持续健康发展、事关全面实现社会主义现代化大局,具有重要的历史与现实意义。

14.1 新发展理念的提出及其内涵

14.1.1 新发展理念的内涵

中共十八届五中全会首次提出了创新、协调、绿色、开放、共享的新发展理念,经过"十三五"时期的发展,全党全社会对新发展理念的认识和实践不断丰富、提高。"十四五"期间,面对新的发展形势和任务,更需要坚定不移贯彻新发展理念。

新发展理念中,创新发展的重点在于解决发展动力问题,协调发展的重点在于解决发展不平衡问题,绿色发展的重点在于解决人与自然和谐问题,开放发展的重点在于解决发展内外联动问题,共享发展的重点在于解决社会公平正义问题。

从内在结构看,五个方面的发展理论各成体系,相对独立。创新发展是指把创新作为发展的根本,通过建立一个以创新为支撑的体制框架来形成以创新驱动为主导的发展,通过创新为发展增添新的动能、释放新的需求、创造新的供应以及为新技术和新业态的蓬勃发展提供新的动力。协调发展的重点是城乡之间的协调、经济和社会的协调以及新工业化和信息化的协调、农业现代化和城镇化的协调等。绿色发展包括可持续发展和建设资源节约和环境友好型社会,为绿色生态生产和消费建立法律框架和政策指导,并为发展低碳节约绿色循环建立健全的经济制度。开放发展包括需要进行内部和外部协调,平衡进出口,结合引进和输出,吸引资本和吸引技术,发展高水平的开放经济,积极参与经济治理等。共享发展包括更有效的制度安排,更多地提供公共服务,实施脱贫项目,更公平和更持久的社会保障制度以及提高老百姓对共同发展的幸福程度,切实提升人民的获得感、参与感、幸福感,不断促进全体人民共同富裕、实现人的全面发展。

新发展理念深刻揭示了实现更高质量、更有效率、更加公平、更可持续发展的必由之路,是关系中国发展全局的一场深刻变革;是针对中国经济发展进入新常态、世界经济复苏低迷形势所提出的治本之策;是针对当前中国发展面临的突出问题和挑战所提出来的战略指引。新发展理念反映了我们党对经济社会发展规律认识的深化,更指明了中国长时期的发展思路、发展方向和发展着力点,具有战略性、纲领性、引领性。

14.1.2 以创新驱动为核心的发展

中国人民是具有伟大创造精神的人民,在很早之前就提出了"天行健,君子以自强不息"的思想。中国推进高质量发展,而创新则是引领发展的第一动力。目前中国经济发展正处于三期叠加时期:增长速度换挡期、结构调整阵痛期、前期刺激政策消化期。高质量发展符合中国现在的发展新形势。中国目前经济总量跃居世界第二,中国发展的后劲需要用创新来激发,尤其在世界关注的重点、难点领域更需要听到更多的中国"新声音",只有抓住了创新这个"牛鼻子",才能让高质量发展之路行稳致远。

同时,"五大发展理念"是内在关系紧密联系的集合体,创新作为第一动力,对其他四个发展理念也起引领作用:创新为协调发展拓展新空间,为绿色发展提供新路径,为开放发展创造新优势,还为共享发展筑建了新的支撑。

新时代中国特色创新发展理念是对"科学技术是第一生产力""创新是一个民族进步的灵魂,是一个国家兴旺发达的不竭动力""建设创新型国家"等重要思想在新时代条件下的坚持与创造性的发展。要实现发展动力转换,就必须坚持创新发展,把创新摆在核心位置。惟创新者进,惟创新者强,惟创新者胜。中国是世界上最大的发展中国家,发展是解决中国一切问题的基础和关键,创新是"五大发展理念"之首,解决的正是发展动力的关键所在。

14.1.3 以绿色发展推进经济转型

目前,人类社会发展面临着气候变化、环境恶化和资源危机等诸多问题。从新世纪开始,联合国就先后多次通过召集会议、发出倡议、举办论坛等形式,宣传绿色发展理念,世界各国也予以积极的响应,并根据本国实际情况采取了诸多有效的措施。中国作为在世界上有着重要影响力的大国,也及时响应,将绿色发展列入新时代的"五大发展理念",体现出一个大国的责任与担当。

中共十八大以来,中国高度重视生态文明建设,提出了一系列新理念新思想新战略。中共十九届五中全会将"生态文明建设实现新进步"确立为中国"十四五"时期经济社会发展主要目标之一,强调"推动绿色发展,促进人与自然和谐共生"。这体现了以习近平同志为核心的党中央在生态文明建设上的战略定力和长远谋划,也为"十四五"时期生态文明建设提供了重要遵循。

绿色发展是永续发展的必要条件,也是人民对美好生活追求的重要体现,绿色发展注重的是解决人与自然和谐问题。实现碳达峰碳中和,是贯彻新发展理念、构建新发展格局、推动高质量发展的内在要求,是党中央统筹国内国际两个大局作出的重大战略决策。推进经济社会发展全面绿色转型,加快形成绿色生产生活方式,是实现碳达峰碳中和的重大举措。

2020年,中国正式宣布力争2030年前实现碳达峰,2060年前实现碳中和,这也是中国基于推动构建人类命运共同体的责任担当和实现可持续发展的内在要求作出的重大战略决策。而为了实现这一目标,就需要在新能源、新材料、环保等领域做加法,在钢铁、化工、建筑等行业做减法,推动经济结构转型,逐步实现碳中和。

14.2 新发展格局的内涵和特点

近10年来,全球经济发展的环境发生很大变化,中国进入新发展阶段,原来的发展模式与新阶段已经不相适应,难以为继。构建新发展格局,是以习近平同志为核心的党中央根据中国发展阶段、环境、条件变化审时度势作出的重大决策,是把握未来发展主动权的战略性布局和先手棋,是新发展阶段必须努力推动完成的重大历史任务,是习近平经济思想的重要内容。

新发展格局具有丰富的理论内涵,概括起来主要包括以下五个方面:一是以国内大循环为主体,确保把经济发展的主动权、控制权牢牢掌握在自己手里,这是构建新发展格局的核心;二是以扩大内需为战略基点,不断巩固和增强中国超大规模市场优势,这是构建新发展格局的基础;三是以供给侧结构性改革为主线,穿透循环堵点,消除瓶颈制约,增加就业和收入,创造需求能力,这是构建新发展格局的关键;四是实现高水平自立自强,这是构建新发展格局最本质的特征;五是实行高水平对外开放,以国际循环提升国内大循环效率和水平,这是构建新发展格局的基本要求。这五大要素相互联系、相互依存、相互促进,构成了有机的内在逻辑体系。

14.2.1 国内大循环是主体

构建新发展格局,必须以国内大循环为主体。这既是经济强国建设的一般规律,也是中国经济发展的必然选择。

纵观世界经济发展史,立足国内大循环发展经济,是建设经济强国的一般规律。作为世界上最大的发展中国家,中国已实现全面建成小康社会目标。在今后的发展道路上,中国必须坚持以国内大循环为主体。中国人口超过14亿,中等收入人群超过4亿,这些是中国形成超大规模市场优势的重要支柱。同时,城市化进程的快速发展以及农民收入的增加,也加快了中国超大规模市场优势的形成。2021年,内需对中国经济增长贡献率达到79.1%,较2020年增加4.4个百分点。可以说,从2008年全球金融危机开始,中国经济就已经在向以国内大循环为主体转变。并且在未来的一段时间里,国内需求潜力将持续释放,国民经济循环由内需主导的特点将更加显著。总体上看,在当前严峻的国际形势下,以国内大循环为主体,充分发挥国内超大规模市场优势,可以使我们更好地防风险、稳增长,把握发展的主动权,为中国经济的持续稳定发展提供有力保障。

14.2.2 扩大内需是战略基点

坚持以国内大循环为主体构建新发展格局,内需的持续稳定增长是基础。特别是在逆全球化趋势加剧和新冠肺炎疫情对经济发展造成严重影响的情况下,巨大规模的市场资源显得尤为重要。扩大内需并非只用于短期内解决金融风险和外部冲击,而应将其转变为一个可持续的历史进程。

中国将扩大内需作为战略基点,不断巩固和增强中国超大规模市场优势,具有现实可能性。第一,稳定的经济增长会带来更大的市场需求总量。随着共同富裕目标的推进,中等收入群体的大量增长将释放出巨大的消费需求,进而促进国内市场需求总量持续稳定增长。第二,居民消费结构的不断升级也将带来新的市场需求。根据世界经济发展经验,人均国内生产总值达到5000美元之后,居民消费结构进入升级轨道,并由此不断产生大量的市场新需求。第三,产业结构的不断升级创造出巨大的市场新需求。新一轮科技革命带来的产业变革,使原有的生产方式和生活方式发生了变化,创造出大量的居民消费市场新需求。最后,投资仍有巨大增长空间,原因有以下四点:一是中国工业化水平不均衡,加速发展中西部地区新兴工业势必会带来大量的投资;二是随着中国居民消费水平的提高,传统产业的转型升级与服务业的快速发展必然会吸引大量的投资;三是新一轮科技革命快速发展,将引发对新基建、新产业、新技术的大规模投资;四是推进公共服务均等化仍需要大规模投资。

14.2.3　供给侧结构性改革是主线

随着中国超大规模市场优势的不断巩固,要想构建新发展格局就必须畅通国内大循环,将中国超大规模市场需求由潜在需求转变为现实需求,从而推动经济持续稳定增长。而畅通国内大循环,就必须以供给侧结构性改革为主线。

供需错配不是供求总量的问题,而是结构性问题,其最明显的特征就是产能过剩和需求过剩并存。造成供需错配的主要原因是供给结构升级滞后于居民消费结构升级。由于供需错配的根源在于供给侧,因此,加快供给侧结构性改革,畅通国内大循环,打通生产、分配、流通、消费的堵点、断点,就成为解决社会主要矛盾的关键。构建新发展格局,必须以深化供给侧结构性改革为主线,加强供给体系的弹性,以达到高水平的经济动态平衡。

14.2.4　科技创新是强大动力

实现高水平的自立自强,是构建新发展格局最本质的特征。各国之间的竞争,说到底是科技的竞争,是关键核心技术的竞争。只有自主掌握关键核心技术,才能从根本上实现国内大循环畅通,确立国内大循环主体地位。

首先,要实现国内大循环,必须依靠科技的创新。习近平总书记明确指出,畅通国内国际双循环,也需要科技实力,保障产业链供应链安全稳定。其次,科技创新是扩大国内需求的关键。在居民消费升级的新形势下,扩大内需不仅要对需求进行控制,更要依靠供给侧结构性改革。只有加快科技创新,运用新技术形成新产业、新业态、新模式、新产品,才可以创造出更多新产品和新服务,从而不断推进内需的扩大。最后,科技创新是推进供给侧结构性改革的关键。一方面,改造传统产业,通过提升产品和服务的品种丰富度、品质满意度和品牌认可度来满足人民对美好生活的需要,需要加快传统产业数字化转型;另一方面,加快发展服务业,推动生活性服务业向高品质和多样化升级,有赖于加快推进服务业数字化、智能化,亦需要技术的自主创新。

14.2.5　高水平对外开放是基本要求

构建新发展格局,在确立以国内大循环为主体的同时,还必须实施更大范围、更宽领域、更深层次的对外开放,推动国内国际双循环相互促进。中国发展要赢得优势、赢得主动、赢得未来,就需要在全球范围内,依托自身超大规模市场优势,实施更为主动的对外开放战略。

国内大循环离不开更加开放的国际循环。从有效发挥国内外两种力量推动经济高质量发展的角度来看,中国必须通过国内大循环来吸引全球资源要素,弥补自身要素短板,这就需要积极促进国内循环和国际循环的协调发展。同时,国际循环必须以国内大循环为基本盘。为顺利推进高水平对外开放,克服经济全球化遇到的逆流和险滩,就需要以国内大循环为基本盘,充分发挥国内超大规模市场优势,更好把握参与国际经济循环的主动权和规则制定权。此外,国际循环对提高国内大循环的效率和水平也起到了促进作用。为加快建设制造强国、科技强国、人才强国、贸易强国、数字强国,就必须统筹好国内国际两个大局,用好国内国际两个市场两种资源,堵漏洞、补短板、强弱项、锻长板,不断提升对外开放的层次,不断提升国内大循环的效率和水平,打造中国发展新优势。

总而言之,构建新发展格局,是根据中国发展阶段、环境、条件变化作出的重大战略决策,是与时俱进提升中国经济发展水平的战略抉择,是塑造中国国际经济合作和竞争新优势的战略抉择。构建新发展格局是习近平经济思想的重要内容。准确、科学理解新发展格局的理论逻辑,对于全面阐释习近平经济思想的科学理论体系具有重要意义。构建新发展格局有助于中国通过可控的国内大循环来实现国内外发展的平衡以及应对外部环境所带来的风险,从而促进中国自身发展与全球经济的发展,并为解决中国与世界的经济关系提供了一个新的思路。

1　Natural Conditions and Foundation of the Chinese Economy

China is located in the east of the Eurasia Plate, the world's largest land, and on the west shore of the Pacific Ocean, the world's largest ocean. China has a vast territory. With a total land area of about 9.6 million sq km, China is the third largest country in the world, next only to Russia and Canada. With a land boundary of around 22 000 km. China is bordered by 14 countries. The coastline of China's mainland measures around 18 000 km and the total area of maritime zone is approximately 4.73 million sq km. The seas surrounding the continental margin from north to south are the Bohai Sea, the Yellow Sea, the East China Sea, and the South China Sea. Along the coast, there are more than 7 600 islands of various sizes, such as Taiwan Island, Hainan Island, Chongming Island, Zhoushan Archipelago, and South China Sea islands. China shares maritime boundaries with 8 countries.

Most of China's territory extends around 5 500 km from north to south and about 5 200 km from east to west, and lies in the middle latitude, among which the temperate zone, warm temperate zone, and subtropical zone have the widest range, with good water and heat conditions. China has numerous natural resources and species, and strong monsoon, which are conducive to the development of agricultural production. The vast sea area and rich marine resources are conducive to China's foreign economic and trade exchanges. With complex natural conditions, a wide variety of biological species and rich types of resources, China is one of the few countries in the world that have a relatively complete range of minerals and abundant mineral resources. However, China has a population of more than 1.4 billion, which results in a small number of per capita resources. Also, the resources are unevenly distributed across regions, and renewable resources tend to be overloaded.

Based on the above background, this chapter introduces the natural conditions and foundation of the Chinese economy from five aspects: terrain, climate and environment, administrative division, natural resources, and infrastructure.

1.1　Terrain

China's terrain is high in the west and low in the east, gradually descending from west to east like a staircase. It has a wide variety of terrain, with mountainous areas occupying about 33% of the total land area. Since tens of millions of years ago, the Qinghai-Tibet Plateau, which is the youngest plateau in the world, has been gradually uplifted and formed as the Indian Plate continued to advance northward and thrust under the Eurasia Plate. Due to the continuous outward spread of the power generated by the collision of plates, the formation of the Qinghai-Tibet Plateau also drives the changes in its surrounding topography. The uplift of the Qinghai-Tibet Plateau has greatly influenced the overall distribution of plateaus, mountain systems and basins in China, thus directly contributing to the topography of higher in the west and lower in the east, forming a three-step staircase. The first step is mainly composed of the Qinghai-Tibet Plateau, with an average elevation of over 4 000 meters, including the Himalayas and Qaidam Basin. The second step is mainly composed of a series of plateaus and basins, with an average elevation of 1 000 meters to 2 000 meters. This area covers one-third of China's land area, and its boundary with the first step is the Kunlun Mountains-Altun Mountains-Qilian Mountains-Hengduan Mountains. Most of the area is deep inland, which is drought and little rain, and with extensive desert in the basin, including the Inner Mongolian Plateau and Loess Plateau in northern China, the Yunnan-Guizhou Plateau and the Sichuan Basin in southwestern China, and the Tarim Basin and Junggar Basin in northwestern China. The boundary between the third step and the second step is the Greater Khingan Mountains-Taihang Mountains-Wushan Mountains-Xuefeng Mountains. The area in the third step is dominated by plains and hills, with an average elevation of less than 500 meters, and mainly includes the Northeast Plain, the North China Plain, the Plain in the Middle-Lower Yangtze Plain, and the Liaodong Hills, Shandong Hills and Jiangnan Hills. The eastern plains of China are generally connected. Most of them are alluvial plains with fertile soil and low and flat terrain, which is conducive to the development of agricultural production. This area has also become a highly developed, economically and culturally advanced, and densely populated urban area in China.

The diversity of terrain and the complexity of geological structure contribute to rich types of drainage patterns in China, mainly including dendritic drainage (e. g., Minjiang River system), fan-shaped drainage (e. g., Haihe River system), and pennate drainage (e. g., Qiantangjiang River system), etc. The topography of higher in the west and lower in the east makes most rivers in China flow from west to east. Three important rivers in China, the Yangtze River, the Yellow River and the Pearl River, all flow from west to east along with the terrain. The topography of China affects the distribution of rivers and, consequently, the distribution of population. Among the many geographical patterns of China, there is a famous dividing line, the Heihe-Tengchong Line, which stretches from Heihe City of Heilongjiang Province on the northeast border, to Tengchong City of Yunnan Province on the southwest border, at an angle of around 45 degrees. This dividing line is also known as the geographical dividing line of China's population and also reflects the contrasting population densities in the southeast and northwest areas. In the northwest region of this line, around 6% of the country's total population shares 57% of China's land area, which is concentrated in a few basins and scattered oases, with a low population density of fewer than 10 people per sq km. One of the main reasons for this is the shortage of water resources, which greatly limits the population development of the region. In contrast, in the southeast region of this line, 43% of China's land area houses around 94% of the country's total population; the main terrain of this area is hills, which is called the Southeast Hills, including Jiangnan Hills, Zhejiang-Fujian Hills and Guangdong-Guangxi Hills, where plains and mountains are scattered wherein. The abundant precipitation of the monsoon climate provides the region with abundant water resources and promotes the population development of the region. China's eastern coastal areas are densely populated, with an average of more than 400 people per sq km. China's population density is higher than the world average but much lower than that of the top-ranked countries in population density, such as South Korea, India, the Netherlands, Japan, and the United Kingdom.

China possesses all five basic landform types on the global land mass, which provides a variety of options and conditions for the development of China's agriculture and industry. However, mountains and hills cover about 43% of China's total land area, which brings difficulties to the development of transportation and agriculture. According to geological surveys, less than 20% of China's land is "suitable for human habitation", about half of which is arable land, and China's per capita arable land area is small. Most of the good agricultural land is found in fertile plains and river valleys divided by hills and mountains. Data from the third national land survey shows that by the end of 2019, China had 1.918 billion mu① of arable land, ranking third in the world, but only 1.36 mu of per capita arable land, less than 40% of the world average. However, China's total grain output in 2021 ranked first in the world, and it feeds about 22% of the world's population with about 7% of the world's total arable land.

1.2 Climate and Environment

China has a vast territory, a wide latitude span, a large difference in distance from the sea, and a distinctive topography of a three-step staircase, resulting in a complex and diverse climate in China, with a prominent monsoon climate and a strong continental climate. China is affected by the alternation of winter and summer monsoons over a wide area and is the region with the most typical monsoon and the most significant monsoon climate in the world, so it is humid, hot, and rainy in summer while dry, cold, and with little rain in winter. In winter, the prevailing northerly wind, which is generated by the formation of a high-pressure belt over the interior of Asia, brings cold, dry air, so there is generally little

---

① 1 mu equals to 666.67 square meters

rainfall in China and the temperature is low, especially in the north. In summer, an opposite low-pressure belt is formed over the interior of Asia, which sends warm, moist air from the Pacific Ocean in the southeast and the Indian Ocean in the southwest. The warm air entering southeastern China is blocked by the mountains and collides with cold air, resulting in abundant rainfall and a season of simultaneous rain and high temperature. Therefore, when the inland basin areas and the western desert areas are extremely hot in summer, the coastal areas are relatively cool.

After the summer monsoon makes landfall from the southeast coast, it continues to weaken in the process of advancing to the northwest, and thus the precipitation also tends to decrease significantly. This has created an extremely characteristic difference between the north and the south of China, where the north is dry with little rain while the south is rich in rivers. In ancient Chinese wars, the climate difference between the north and the south also formed the stereotype that "the south is good at warfare in water, and the north is good at warfare on horses". This long-standing north-south difference has also become more and more prominent due to global warming. The monsoon brings moderate summer rainfall to northern China as it passes through the mountains between the Yangtze River and Yellow River. It is worth noting that if the monsoon is too weak to reach the Yellow River valley and lingers in the central mountainous areas, China's mainland is about to face drought in the north and flooding in the south. Thus, the Qinling Mountains-Huaihe River line becomes another dividing line between the south, where rainfall is abundant, and the north, where water is chronically scarce.

China is a country with severe drought and water scarcity, judging from the aspect of water resources situation. The Yellow River basin in northern China is almost all arid and semi-arid areas. The Yellow River is the second largest river in China, with a total length of about 5 464 km and a total basin area of 795 000 sq km (including 42 000 sq km of the endorheic region). However, the water volume of the Yellow River is only moderate, and its natural annual runoff accounts for only 2.1% of the national river runoff. Its annual runoff ranks fourth among the seven major rivers in China, smaller than the Yangtze River, the Pearl River, and the Songhua River. About 70% of the Yellow River basin is the Loess Plateau, which is covered with a loess layer of tens to hundreds of meters, with loose soil and low resistance to erosion, and thus, it is highly susceptible to disintegration when exposed to water. In contrast, the Yangtze River in the south is the largest in China by volume, with an annual runoff of 960 billion cu m, accounting for about 36% of the country's total river runoff and 20 times that of the Yellow River. Even though the Pearl River is less than half the length of the Yellow River, its water volume is as much as 7 times that of the Yellow River. It is for this reason that the South-to-North Water Diversion Project is carried out in China to facilitate the rational allocation of water resources between north and south, and between east and west.

The hydrological characteristics of outflow rivers in China are strongly influenced by the monsoon climate. With the arrival of the summer monsoon, the rain belt moves from south to north, the water flow of rivers increases rapidly and the water level rises, resulting in a flood season. With the strengthening of the winter monsoon, the rain belt withdraws southward and the rivers enter the withered water period. The withered water period in China generally starts from autumn and lasts to the next spring, with a shorter duration in the southern regions and a longer duration in the northern regions.

Compared with the vast majority of countries in the world, China's economic development faces harsher resource constraints. In the future, the frequency of extreme weather and climate events in China is still likely to increase, which will also have a great impact on China's economic and social development, and people's production and life.

The rapid development of China's economy in recent decades has caused varying degrees of pollution to the environment, especially urban-centered environmental pollution, which has been intensifying and gradually spreading to rural areas. Particularly, in economically developed and densely populated areas, environmental pollution is more prominent. Through a series of measures, such as afforestation, prevention and control of sandy desertification, soil and water conservation, territorial management, grassland construction, and protection of natural forest resources, the ecological environment in some areas of China has been significantly improved. However, the speed of protection is far behind the speed of destruction, and the ecological deficit is gradually expanding, mainly in the form of increasing soil and water loss, expanding sandy desertification, serious grassland degradation, and growing atmospheric pollution, etc. Among them, atmospheric pollution is the first environmental pollution problem in China. The situation is still very severe, and the total emission of atmospheric pollutants remains high. The main causes of air pollution are industrial pollution, traffic pollution and domestic pollution, among which industrial pollution and traffic pollution account for the main factors. China is one of the countries with the most serious soil and water loss in the world. Due to the special natural geography and socio-economic conditions, soil and water loss exists in most provinces and regions of China to varying degrees. Soil and water loss is not only the main form of land degradation and ecological deterioration, but also the concentrated reflection of the degree of land degradation and ecological deterioration. Its impact on economic and social development is multi-faceted, overall and far-reaching, and even irreversible. The main problem in northern China is serious desertification, where more than 1.49 million sq km are desert, gobi, and desertified land, occupying 15.5% of the national land area. At present, in the natural grasslands of China, about 90% of the available grassland in China has been degraded to varying degrees, and the areas with coverage of 5%-20% have been significantly reduced. The situation of grassland degradation, desertification, and salinization is worrying. Compared with the 1950s, the current forage yield of grassland in China has dropped by 30%-50%.

In the face of severe ecological damage and environmental pollution, China has to embark on the road of green development, and vigorously advocate green development with sustainable development as its core. Within the framework of the green economy, China will promote the development of various fields including circular economy, low-carbon economy, ecological economy, and rational consumption, etc. At the same time, China will adjust its industrial structure, transform the mode of economic development, eliminate backward industries, and develop emerging energy-saving and green industries.

1.3 Administrative Division

To facilitate the management of China's vast land area, the administrative regions are divided into four levels: province, prefecture, county, and township. China has 23 provinces, 5 autonomous regions, 4 municipalities directly under the central government, and 2 special administrative regions, making a total of 34 provincial-level administrative regions. According to the data of 2022, among the administrative regions, Macao Special Administrative Region has the smallest resident population of 0.68 million, while Guangdong Province has the largest resident population of 126.57 million. Figure 1-1 shows the administrative divisions of the People's Republic of China.

Figure 1-1 Administrative divisions of the People's Republic of China
Photo from Ministry of Natural Resources of the People's Republic of China

China's provincial administrative division can be traced back to the provincial system of the Yuan Dynasty, but it has not always been the most natural way to divide China's economic space. According to the method of anthropologist William Skinner, the regional land of China as a whole is first divided into several large regions according to its characteristics, each consisting of more than one province, so as to facilitate regional study and management of geography, climate, economy, military, communication, transportation and administration. Based on the characteristics of geographical location, physical geography and human geography, China can be divided into four geographical regions, namely, the northern region, the southern region, the northwestern region and the Qinghai-Tibet region. In terms of administrative division, six administrative regions have been established: North China, Northeast China, Northwest China, East China, Central South China, and Southwest China. Another method is also known as the administrative geographic division, which is carried out under relevant regionalization principles based on science and takes into consideration of various dimensions such as history and nationality. In this way, China is divided into seven regions, namely Central China, South China, Southwest China, Northwest China, North China, Northeast China, and East China. The Beijing-Tianjin-Hebei region in North China has the largest and most dynamic economy in northern China. The North China Plain is one of the three major plains of China, which has the largest population density as well as the largest population. Beijing, the capital of the People's Republic of China, and its sister city Tianjin, with a residential population of about 13.87 million(data from the Seventh National Population Census), form the urban center of North China. However, the level of urbanization in North China is generally slightly lower than the national average. North China mainly has a temperate monsoon climate, which is hot and rainy in summer and cold and dry in winter. The annual average temperature is about 8-13 ℃ and the annual precipitation is about 400-1 000 mm. The Inner Mongolia Autonomous Region in this area is a semi-arid region with precipitation of less than 400 mm. But this does not have any impact on agriculture becoming an important industry in North China. North China develops comprehensive agriculture, mainly with traditional crops such as wheat and cotton, and is an important national commodity grain base. At the same time, North China is also vigorously developing suburban agriculture, water-saving agriculture, mechanized production and so on. In 2019, North China contributed 25.4% of the GDP (gross domestic product) with 24.2% of China's total population.

The most developed region in China is the middle and lower reaches of the Yangtze River. With an area of 50 000 sq km, the Yangtze River Delta is the largest estuary delta in China. The agriculture in Yangtze River Delta is based on grain production with wheat, rice, soybean and corn. Superior farming conditions, a long history of agriculture and a high level of agricultural production make it a world-famous land of fish and rice and the home of silk. The middle and lower reaches of the Yangtze River have a long history of development because of its fertile land, suitable water and heat conditions in the plain.

Large-scale development began as early as the Sui and Tang Dynasties. From the Jin Dynasty to the Song Dynasty, the northern population, culture and economy moved southward, and this region soon became the center of China's economic development. In modern times, with its superior location and convenient waterway transportation along the Yangtze River, the region has become the cradle of China's modern industry. Shanghai is the birthplace of China's modern industry and the center of China's economy, finance, trade and shipping. In 2020, the GDP of the Yangtze River Delta region was 24.5 trillion yuan; the urbanization rate of the resident population exceeded 60%. This region creates nearly 1/4 of China's economic aggregate and 1/3 of the total export-import volume with less than 4% of the national land area. The Yangtze River Delta includes Shanghai city, as well as Jiangsu, Zhejiang and Anhui provinces, totaling 41 cities. As of the end of 2021, the Yangtze River Delta region has a population of 236.478 million, a regional area of 358 000 sq km. This region's GDP in 2021 is 27.6 trillion yuan, accounting for 24.1% of China's GDP in the same year. In 2019, the density of the railway network in the Yangtze River Delta reached 325 km per 10 000 sq km, 2.2 times the national average, and it is planned to reach 507 km per 10 000 sq km by 2025.

A counterpart to the Yangtze River Delta is the Pearl River Delta, located in South China, which is a pioneering region of China's reform and opening-up, and an important economic center of China. It is also an important engine of China's economic development, a gateway to the opening up of the South, and the leader in driving the development of South China, Central China, and Southwest China. Moreover, it is one of the three major city clusters with the largest population agglomeration degree, the strongest innovation capacity, and the strongest comprehensive strength in China, and is known as the "Pearl of the South China Sea". The Pearl River Delta have a total area of 55 368.7 sq km and a total residential population of more than 78.6 million. In 2021, the total GDP of the Pearl River Delta region exceeded 10 trillion yuan, accounting for 8.8% of China's GDP. Although there are only 9 cities in the region, they created more than 80% of the Guangdong Province's total output value, among which Shenzhen and Guangzhou accounted for a higher proportion. With the increasing maturity of the region, a new development pattern in China has gradually formed, i.e., establishing the Guangdong-Hong Kong-Macao Greater Bay Area(hereinafter referred to as Greater Bay Area), which comprises the nine cities in the Pearl River Delta and the two Special Administrative Regions of Hong Kong and Macao. Greater Bay Area has a superior geographical condition of "mountains on three sides and convergence of three rivers" with a long coastline, a good port group and a wide sea area.

The region boasts an extensive economic hinterland with a broad radiation range, engaging in cooperative efforts with adjacent areas such as Jiangxi, Hunan, Guangxi, Hainan, Sichuan, Guizhou, Yunnan, and others. Referred to as the "Pan-Pearl River Delta Regional Cooperation", this area has about 1/5 of the national land area, 1/3 of the population and 1/3 of the economic aggregate. As of December 2020, the resident population of the Greater Bay Area reached 86 171 900. As of February 2022, the GDP of the 11 cities in the Greater Bay Area reached 12.63 trillion yuan. Hong Kong, Macao, Guangzhou and Shenzhen are taken as the core engines of regional development. Furthermore, the construction of the Greater Bay Area, a world-class city cluster, is also a way to help enrich the practical connotation of "one country, two systems".

Western China, comprising the five northwestern provinces (Shaanxi, Gansu, Ningxia, Qinghai and Xinjiang), five southwestern provinces, regions and municipalities (Tibet, Yunnan, Guizhou, Sichuan and Chongqing), Inner Mongolia and Guangxi, has a total land area of 6.87 million sq km, occupying about 72% of the national land area. However, due to the relatively poor terrain and climate conditions, according to the Seventh National Population Census, the region has a total population of only about 380 million, accounting for about 27.12% of the total population in China. Among its land resources, 42% are plains, less than 10% are basins, and the remaining 48% are deserts, gobi, rocky hills, and alpine areas with an elevation of above 3 000 meters, which makes the average population density in this region less than 60 people per sq km, much lower than the national average. However, the western region has two major natural advantages, one is the rich natural resources, and the other is that the western region borders more than 10 countries with a land border of about 18 thousand km. Such a long land border undoubtedly presents an attractive prospect for the development of border trade in the western region. In the past, the "Silk Road" that passed through the western region was the first channel for China's foreign exchange. Today, the western region will certainly regain its glory with the process of the development of the region.

1.4 Natural Resources

China has only 6.44% of the world's land area, while its population accounts for about 18% of the world's total population. As a result, though the natural resources are rich in total amount and variety and show great potential, the resources per capita are insufficient. According to the data of the third national land survey, China's arable land area is 127.862 million hectares, of which Heilongjiang, Inner Mongolia, Henan, Jilin, and Xinjiang contribute large areas that account for 40% of the country's total. The total area of gardens is 20.172 million hectares, mainly distributed in the regions south to the Qinling Mountains-Huaihe River Line, accounting for 66% of the total area of gardens in China. The total area of forest land is 284.126 million hectares, of which Sichuan, Yunnan, Inner Mongolia, and Heilongjiang contribute large areas that account for 34% of the total. Grassland covers a total area of 264.53 million hectares, mainly distributed in six regions of Tibet, Inner Mongolia, Xinjiang, Qinghai, Gansu, and Sichuan, accounting for 94% of the total. Although the absolute amount of land resources in China is large, the per capita possession is small. China's per capita land area is only about 10 mu, less than 1/3 of the world's average. And, the distribution of land resources is unbalanced, with more than 90% distributed in the humid and semi-humid areas in the southeast. Also, about 2/3 of the total arable land is low- and medium-yield. The reserve land resources suitable for development as arable land have little potential.

By the end of 2021, 173 kinds of minerals had been discovered in China, including 13 kinds of energy minerals, 59 kinds of metallic minerals, 95 kinds of non-metallic minerals and 6 kinds of water and gas minerals. In terms of the reserves of major energy minerals in China, coal reserves are about 207.89 billion tons, petroleum reserves are about 3.69 billion tons, and natural gas reserves are about 6 339.27 billion cu m. Reserves of petroleum and natural gas account for only 1.4% and 4.5% of the world's total proven reserves, respectively. China's energy resources are distinctively characterized as "rich in coal, poor in petroleum, and little in natural gas". China has favorable geological conditions as a shale gas-rich area, with huge resource prospects and development potential with about 544.06 billion cu m of shale gas reserves. However, the investigation, exploration and development of shale gas resources in China is still in the initial stage, and no comprehensive estimate of the potential has been made so far. Table 1-1 shows the reserves of major energy minerals in China in 2021.

Table 1-1　Major energy minerals and their reserves in China in 2021

No.	Mineral	Unit	Reserves
1	Coal	Billion tons	207.89
2	Petroleum	Billion tons	3.69
3	Natural gas	Billion cu m	6 339.27
4	Coalbed methane	Billion cu m	365.97
5	Shale gas	Billion cu m	544.06

Source: China Mineral Resources Report 2022

China is rich in non-ferrous metal resources with relatively complete varieties. The reserves of seven metals, including tungsten and rare earth, rank first in the world, and the reserves of five metals, including lead, nickel, mercury, molybdenum and niobium, are also quite abundant. Although the total amount of non-ferrous metal resources is large, the per capita possession is small, which is the same as China's land resources, so China can also be called a country with relatively poor non-ferrous metal mineral resources. In the second place, there are many lean ores and few rich ores, which makes the development and utilization more difficult, and there are many symbiotic and associated deposits, but few single deposits. In addition, the distribution of mineral resources is wide and geographically uneven.

The hydropower and mineral resources in China are distributed in a highly uneven manner. In general, they are widely distributed with a relative concentration in central and western China. Western China has 82.5% of the hydropower reserves nationwide and 77% of the developed hydropower resources, but less than 1% is developed and utilized. Mineral resources are even more considerable. According to the "2022 Annual Development Report on the Coal Industry", the proportion of raw coal output in the western region increased from 54.4% to 60.7%, the proportion of the central region stabilized at 33.7%, while the proportion of the eastern region dropped from 7.2% to 3.2%, and the proportion of the northeast region dropped from 4.7% to 2.4%. In the ten years since 2011, the newly proved geological reserves and production of oil in western China accounted for 62% and 34% of the national total, respectively, and that of natural gas accounted for 85% and 84%. The accumulative proved geological reserves of oil and natural gas in Ordos were nearly 7 billion tons and over 5 trillion cu m. Among the 159 kinds of proven mineral resources in China, 143 are found in the western region, and the reserves of some rare metals are among the top in China and even in the world. In contrast to the energy minerals, which are mainly distributed in the north, non-ferrous metals are mainly distributed in the south. At the same time, the rich water resources in the south and the large topographic difference between the east and west contribute to the huge potential for hydropower in southwestern China. However, the southern coastal areas with extremely fast economic growth have nearly no energy reserves. There is an urgent need to strengthen the construction of transportation to efficiently allocate unevenly distributed resources across the country. A resource- and land-intensive industry based development strategy is not feasible, and China can only develop labor-intensive industries and will eventually embark on a knowledge-intensive development path. Environmental constraints make the trade-offs in China's economic development more difficult and complex.

1.5 Infrastructure

As an important support for economic and social development, infrastructure plays a strategic, fundamental and leading role. Infrastructure construction can be divided into four parts: transportation, energy and power, digital communication, and livelihood projects.

From 2012 to 2022, China has built the world's largest high-speed railroad network, highway network and world-class port cluster. China has not only achieved rapid development in traditional infrastructure construction but also has made breakthroughs in new infrastructure construction. This section introduces China's infrastructure construction in four parts: transportation, energy and power, digital communication and livelihood projects.

1.5.1 Transportation

By the end of 2021, the operating mileage of China's national railways has reached

150 000 km, ranking second in the world, among which the high-speed railway mileage has reached 40 000 km, ranking first in the world; the double-track rate is 59.5%; the electrification rate is as high as 73.3%; the operating mileage in the western region has reached 60 000 km. The density of the national railway network is as high as 156.7 km per 10 000 sq km. China's railway and highway mileage has increased by about 1.1 million km in 10 years, which is equivalent to traveling 27.5 times around the earth's equator. The accumulated investment in railway fixed assets has exceeded 7 trillion yuan, and the production mileage has increased by 52 000 km.

According to the administrative classification, China's highways are divided into three levels: national highways, provincial highways, and rural highways. The national highway network, including the national expressway network and the ordinary national road network, is the highest level in the highway network. According to the National Highway Network Plan(2013-2030) released in 2013, the total scale of China's national highway network will reach 400 000 km by 2030, including 136 000 km of national expressways and 265 000 km of ordinary national roads, of which 85% and 96.5% have been completed respectively by the end of 2021. By the end of 2021, China's total highway mileage has reached 5.28 million km, with a highway network density of 55 km per 100 sq km, ranking top in the world, among which the total mileage of expressways ranks first in the world. At present, the expressway network, mainly national expressways, has covered 98.8% of the urban cities and prefecture-level administrative centers with a population of 200 000 or more, connecting approximately 88% of county-level administrative regions and 95% of the population nationwide. Ordinary national roads basically cover administrative regions at or above the county level and border ports open all year round. In addition, by the end of 2021, the total number of transport airports in China has reached 248, with a total designed capacity of more than 1.4 billion passengers.

The construction of transportation also plays an important role in winning the battle against poverty and supporting rural revitalization. Statistics show that from 2011 to 2021, the total mileage of rural highways increases from 3.564 million km to 4.466 million km, and 1 040 townships and 105 000 administrative villages have been equipped with tarmac roads. The construction of transportation makes the flow of people, goods, and capital between urban and rural areas interact in an accelerated manner, leading to higher incomes for villages as well as farmers.

Chinese infrastructure has also gone abroad. The opening and operation of the China-Laos Railway, the Addis Ababa-Djibouti Railway, and the Mombasa-Nairobi Standard Gauge Railway, along with the official launch of the Jakarta-Bandung High-Speed Railway have strongly promoted the construction and development of the Belt and Road Initiative.

1.5.2 Energy and Power

Contemporary China has built a number of world-class energy infrastructure projects.

Focusing on ensuring energy security, China has accelerated the implementation of a new energy security strategy, focused on building a clean, low-carbon, safe and efficient energy system, and significantly improved its energy supply capacity. Today, China's installed capacity of renewable energy power has exceeded 1 billion kW, and China ranks first in the world in total installed capacity of green power. By the end of 2021, grid-connected wind power and photovoltaic installations totaled 635 million kW, nearly 90 times that of 2012. In October 2021, all 59 wind turbines in Xinghua Bay, Fuqing were connected to the grid, and they can generate 1.4 billion kWh of electricity annually, which can meet the normal electricity demand of 700 000 families of three. In January 2021, the Hualong One nuclear power plant, Fujian Fuqing Nuclear Power Plant No. 5, was put into commercial operation, marking that China ranks among the world's leaders in the field of third-generation nuclear power technology.

By the end of 2021, China's total installed capacity of power generation has reached 2.38 billion kW, double that of 2012, with an average annual growth rate of 8.4%; China had 843 000 km of 220 kV or above power transmission lines, and the capacity of power transformation equipment has reached 4.94 billion kVA, 1.7 times and 2.2 times of 2012, respectively. At the lower reaches of the Jinsha River bordering Sichuan and Yunnan, Baihetan Hydropower Station, with a total installed capacity of 16 million kW, is the largest hydropower project under construction in the world and the most technologically difficult one. When fully completed and put into operation, the annual average power generation will reach 62.443 billion kWh. In addition, the construction of inter-provincial and inter-regional energy transmission channels in China has been continuously strengthened. By the end of 2021, the length of oil and gas pipelines in China has reached 180 000 km.

1.5.3 Digital Communication

With the rapid development of China's communication technology, China's information and communication industry has leapfrogged and China has built the world's largest and leading-edge network infrastructure. Among them, the access bandwidth of the optical fiber network has achieved an exponential growth from 10M(megabit) to 100M and then to gigabit, and the mobile network has achieved a leap from "breaking through in 3G" to "paralleling in 4G" and then to "leading in 5G".

In 2012, the number of mobile phone base stations in China just exceeded 2 million, and by the end of 2021, this number has reached 9.96 million. At the end of April 2022, China has historically extended broadband access to all administrative villages nationwide. The average download rate of broadband networks has increased by nearly 40 times. Furthermore, the scale of 4G base stations accounts for more than half of the world's total, and 1.615 million 5G base stations have been built.

The nationwide information infrastructure provides strong support for China's efforts to build a digital society and a digital government. It has also greatly increased the administrative efficiency, and has promoted process transparency and data sharing of public services, greatly saving residents' time and energy.

The developed information infrastructure network has completely changed people's living habits. Led by new telecommunication technologies, internet applications such as e-commerce, e-government and remote office have gained widespread popularity, and the annual transaction volume of mobile payment has reached 527 trillion yuan.

As the core productivity of digital economy development, computing power infrastructure has become an important infrastructure for national economic development. In February 2022, the "East Number and West Calculation" project was officially launched, which not only alleviates the energy shortage in the east, but also opens up a new path for the development in the west by transferring data from developed regions in the east to regions rich in computing resources in the west for calculation and storage.

In the future, China will also comprehensively strengthen the construction of information infrastructure, expand the coverage of 5G networks, and accelerate the large-scale application of 5G and other emerging technologies to promote the development of the digital economy.

1.5.4 Livelihood Projects

Before 2012, in some places such as Handan and Xingtai in Hebei Province of China, the problem of excessive fluoride in drinking water in rural China was very serious, and brackish and high fluoride water threatened the health of residents' drinking water. At the end of 2014, the first phase of the middle route of China's South-to-North Water Diversion Project entered into full operation. From the Danjiangkou Reservoir in the upper and middle reaches of the Han River, the clear water flows for thousands of kilometers to the north, bringing water to northern China that is desperately short of water. Now, families in the water-receiving areas of the project can drink water from the Hanjiang River thousands of miles away as soon as they turn on the tap.

As one of the world's largest water diversion projects, the South-to-North Water Diversion Project has built the world's largest water transfer aqueduct and the world's largest group of modern pumping stations by using various techniques such as open channels, aqueducts, and tunnels. Since its operation, the "southern water" has become the main source of water for more than 140 million people in more than 280 counties (cities and districts) of more than 40 large and medium-sized cities in Beijing, Tianjin, Hebei, Henan and other places.

Till May 13, 2022, 53.1 billion cu m of water had been transferred through the eastern and middle routes of the South-to-North Water Diversion Project, 8.5 billion cu m of water had been replenished to more than 50 rivers along the route, and groundwater overexploitation in water-receiving areas had been reduced by more than 5 billion cu m. Other livelihood infrastructure projects, though not as large as the South-to-North Water

Diversion Project, have also brought a lot of convenience to people's lives. Since the action to improve rural living environment launched by Chinese government in 2018, the "toilet revolution" in rural areas has been promoted to improve rural living facilities. By the end of 2021, the rate of access to sanitary toilets reached more than 70% in China's rural areas, and more than 90% in areas with foundations and conditions, such as eastern regions and urban suburbs in central and western regions.

2 Historical Development of the Chinese Economy (Before 1949)

2.1 The "Small-Scale Farming" in Ancient and Modern China

Since ancient times, China has advocated the concept of "the Great Unity" in the community. The ideas of "similar customs and consistent administration across the country" and "the harmonization of the world" are both its reflections. Behind this macro-level ideology of "the Great Unity" is the traditional rural society formed since ancient times based on numerous scattered small-scale peasants. "Feeling attached to the land and unwilling to move" has been a widespread way of thinking and sentiment among Chinese people. This kind of stability of traditional rural society actually guarantees the stability of the country as well as the stability of culture.

Traditional China was based on a rural society, with over 90% of the population living in rural areas. People "get up at sunrise and work until sunset". They employed a sophisticated agricultural method to cultivate the land and multiply. The land harvest was almost the whole source of their livelihood. However, the traditional agricultural system, where large-scale mechanized production was not possible, depended highly on massive human labor, so high productivity per unit of land coexisted with low productivity per farmer.

Such a mode of production has given birth to the industrious and intelligent nature of the Chinese people. Day in and day out, year in and year out, almost all the land has undergone different degree of human modification. At the same time, people continued to explore the experience of farmland work and passed it on from generation to generation. Gradually, an efficient traditional agricultural production system was developed. It was first formed in the middle and lower reaches of the Yellow River and the middle and lower reaches of the Yangtze River, and then gradually spread to low-lying and hilly areas where irrigation was possible. The suitable living environment also promoted population growth, so that the existing cultivated land area could no longer meet the actual needs. To solve this problem, farmers began to build terraces on the hillside (Figure 2-1) as early as in the Qin and Han dynasties.

2 Historical Development of the Chinese Economy (Before 1949)

Figure 2-1 Scene of terraces
Photo from Xinhuanet

In the vast territory of China, natural resources and climatic conditions vary from place to place, and crop yields and types vary greatly. As the saying in *Yanzi Chunqiu* goes, "orange born in Huainan is orange, and orange born in Huaibei is trifoliate orange". With the needs of production and life, people began to exchange and buy and sell, and a market with trade gradually took shape. Land transport and water transport were the most important ways to transport goods. During the Sui Dynasty, to strengthen the connection between the northern region and the affluent regions in the south, the imperial court completed the Beijing-Hangzhou Grand Canal, which ran from north to south, and strengthened the economic exchanges. Such densely populated city and relatively developed transportation network, in effect, formed a highly commercialized socio-economic system based on agriculture, with competitive markets and a mature trading system.

Chinese traditional agriculture was based on individual, small-scale households. There were no large farms or large landowners. Other non-agricultural production was also small-scale and carried out by farmers themselves. For example, some farmers, in addition to cultivating their farmlands, also opened small village workshops to produce textiles, iron tools, tea, sugar, and noodles for sale in the market. Therefore, the basic pattern of the traditional Chinese economy is small-scale farming, which is based on the dynamic household economy and individual economy.

From the Southern Song Dynasty until the 1860s, China was world-renowned for its exports, the most important export products were silk, porcelain, and tea. Exports represented by silk and porcelain formed the land Silk Road and the Maritime Silk Road respectively, which were the main channels of China's foreign trade in ancient times. For centuries, China had maintained an export surplus in the world trade market, and a large amount of silver flowed into China. The high-quality tea produced by tea farmers and processed by small tea workshops had won wide acclaim in the world market. However, this small-scale, decentralized production was unable to provide standardized, high-quality products, so after the early 20th century, Chinese exporters were forced to withdraw from the world tea market.

This reflects the fact that the small-scale farming is a kind of economy with low stability but high flexibility in resource allocation. On the positive side, both resources and labor flow very efficiently to where they have the highest rate of return, and exit as soon as the return falls, which is conducive to the effective allocation of resources. However, on the negative side, economic activities are subdivided into countless small businesses with only small capital participation, preventing the formation of large-scale standardized production modes and economies of scale.

The naturalistic production and lifestyle of China's traditional small-scale farming, which can be described as "the mountain dweller lives off the mountain, while the shore dweller lives off the sea", is obviously incompatible with the industrialization process since modern times. Rich labor and relatively scarce land resources have led to the preference for labor-intensive techniques by Chinese farmers and craftsmen at the expense of productivity progress and technological innovation. The decentralized, selfish and conservative nature of the small-scale farming has gradually become the most serious obstacle and resistance to China's modernization and industrialization.

By the 1870s, China's foreign trade surplus had turned into a deficit due to cheap manufactured goods and opium. The influx of opium brought serious harm to China's society and economy. Lin Zexu presided over the destruction of opium at Humen and it became the fuse of the Opium War. The Opium War ended in China's defeat, and in 1842 the *Treaty of Nanking* was signed, forcing China to "cede" Hong Kong Island to the United Kingdom and open five treaty ports. The Opium War contributed to the disintegration of the small-scale farming. Since then, China began to gradually become a semi-colonial and semi-feudal society.

From the 1860s to the 1890s, the Westernization faction of the late Qing Dynasty started the self-rescue movement aimed at "self-strengthening" and "pursuing wealth", known as the "Westernization Movement" in history. During the Westernization Movement, western science and technology, military equipment, and machine production were introduced on a large scale, which stimulated the development of Chinese capitalism and promoted China's exploration road to modernization. The Westernization Movement promoted the establishment of several enterprises, representatives of which were the Anqing Internal Ordnance Station founded by Zeng Guofan, the Jiangnan Manufacturing Bureau and China Merchants Steam Navigation Company (see Figure 2-2) founded by Li Hongzhang, and Hanyang Iron Works (see Figure 2-3) founded by Zhang Zhidong.

From the late 17th century to the early 19th century, China excelled in population

Figure 2-2 China Merchants Steam Navigation Company

Figure 2-3 Hanyang Iron Works

growth, economic development, and territorial expansion. Until 1820, just before the Opium War, China was still the world's largest economy, with its GDP accounting for almost a third of the world's GDP, while the United States of American(USA) accounting for only 1.8% and Europe as a whole accounting for only 26.6%. However, for more than a century, China's economic share of the world's GDP declined dramatically. By 1949, China's GDP accounted for less than 5% of the world's GDP and ranked 13th in the world.

2.2 The Beginning of Modernization(1912-1937)

The Revolution of 1911 ended China's thousands of years of absolute feudal monarchy, since then, China's institutional development and economic changes accelerated and entered a completely new stage. With the rise of modern transportation and communication, other sectors also flourished and China's modern industries gradually developed and perfected. In the late Qing Dynasty and early Republic of China, China was in a period of warlords and political division, which had a certain negative impact on the economy. From the establishment of the Nanjing National Government in 1927 to the full-scale Japanese invasion of China in 1937, China enjoyed a relatively peaceful and stable decade, with certain space for economic development and continuous promotion of investment in education and agricultural extension.

On the whole, from 1912 to 1936, China experienced rapid industrialization. Despite a relatively weak foundation, modern factory production was able to achieve growth at a rate about 9% per year. Statistics show that by 1933, modern industrial production accounted for 2% of China's GDP and employed nearly a million workers.

In the early 20th century, the initial stage of industrial development, China's industrialization was mainly concentrated in the treaty ports and the northeast region. Among them, the modern industry at treaty ports was the leading mode of industrialization in China. Foreign businessmen set up factories there, mainly in light industry. Statistics show that in 1933, textiles accounted for 42% of the total industrial output, and Shanghai, Tianjin, and Qingdao were the main production sites. 70% of the textile industry was concentrated in these three cities, among which Shanghai alone accounted for 40% of the total industrial output. In contrast, the industrialization in the northeast region, whose initial investors were the Japanese government and its semi-official agencies, focused on heavy industry and railways. Taking advantage of the rich coal and iron resources there, Japan vigorously promoted heavy industries such as steel, metallurgy and machinery, and built a dense railway network to meet its own economic and development needs.

In the 1920s and 1930s, China's modern industry, although still small in overall scale, was of great significance and influence. From 1914 to 1936, agriculture, handicrafts, and traditional transportation all grew considerably. Modern small businesses increased rapidly, and per capita GDP growth was slow but significant. It is obvious that, although the industry in this period did not fundamentally change the overall economic structure in China, industrialization had already started and provided the foundation and precondition for the development of the Chinese economy in the future.

This period also saw an increase in the number of literate people in society. As a result of the opening-up, nearly 100 000 Chinese students went overseas for long-term study. The number of foreigners coming to live in China also increased. In 1936, the number of foreigners living in China reached as many as 370 000. The exchange of people between China and foreign countries also promoted technological, ideological, and cultural exchanges. Although the Chinese society is divided by political and social fragmentations, it also seems to be moving forward rapidly.

2.3　The Economy under the State of War(1937-1949)

The Lugou Bridge Incident in 1937 marked the beginning of Japan's full-scale invasion war of China. After the War of Resistance against Japanese Aggression, China entered the War of Liberation, which lasts until the founding of the People's Republic of China in 1949.

During the War of Resistance against Japanese Aggression, the Nanjing National Government moved to Chongqing. As always, wartime pressures would lead to increasing state intervention in the economy. To relocate industry from Shanghai to the inland regions and rebuild military industry there, the Nanjing National Government established the National Resources Commission(NRC) to implement government-led industrial development. By the early 1940s, the NRC operated many factories with a total of 160 000 people. Of all enterprises on unoccupied land in China, capital and labor in state-owned enterprises accounts for 70% and 32% respectively.

In the late 1940s, with the expropriation of Japanese factories by companies already owned and run by the NRC, the Nanjing National Government had huge assets in a short time and controlled about 2/3 of the industrial capital. According to statistics, by 1947, the government controlled 90% of steel production, 66% of electricity production, and 45% of cement production. Most big banks and transportation companies were also under the government's control.

To pay for the war, the Nanjing National Government began printing money to keep its finances afloat. However, the effect of this action was to accelerate inflation and eventually lead to hyperinflation. Worsening inflation and severe macroeconomic imbalances, which brought the economy almost to its knees, contributed significantly to the rapid collapse of the Nanjing National Government.

2.4　The Economic Foundation at the Establishment of New China

The war severely damaged the economic infrastructure, especially industrial capital and agricultural infrastructure (especially irrigation systems), which greatly undermined economic development. At this point, short-term real output was far below output capacity. At the same time, hyperinflation reflected the extreme chaos in the financial sector. Overall, many years of war have undermined the extremely fragile economic growth that began in the 1920s and 1930s, so China in this period was still very poor.

Statistics show that in 1949, China had a population of 540 million with people's average life expectancy of only 35 years. There were 180.82 million employed people in both urban and rural areas, among which only 15.33 million were in urban areas. The urban unemployment rate was as high as 23.6%. In agriculture, the total area of arable land was 1.468 billion mu, and the total grain output was 113.2 million tons; in industry, steel output was 150 000 tons, coal output was 32 million tons, oil output was 120 000 tons, and cement output was 660 000 tons. The gross national product was 12.3 billion USD, with a per capita of 23 USD and a per capita national income of 27 USD. The broad masses of the people were living in poor conditions, and the whole society was in a very poor and backward state.

However, the fragile and even near-collapsed economy may have contributed to China's relatively smooth adoption of a socialist planned economy and socialist industrialization strategy after 1949. Although China was still very poor by 1949, economic development had already begun. China had a relatively good endowment of human capital, and the literacy rate of its population was growing. The university system, though small, had been established, and technicians had been trained abroad. Certain modern industrial and transport capital that can meet the needs of further economic development had also been created.

3 Development and Exploration of the Chinese Economy (1949-1978)

3.1 The Period of National Economic Recovery (1949-1952)

In the early days of People's Republic of China, the Chinese people faced severe tests. In terms of economy, domestically, years of war had devastated agriculture and industry, and hyperinflation was still rampant; internationally, due to the political isolation and economic blockade of the imperialist countries led by the United States, China was subjected to increasing trade restrictions. In the face of domestic turmoil and foreign aggression, the Chinese government acted quickly to revive the domestic economy, strictly controlled the currency, and adopted a positive yet prudent attitude to promote economic construction.

In rural areas, the land reform movement was in full swing. In the land reform movement, land was uniformly and evenly distributed, and was privately owned by farmers, which greatly stimulated the production enthusiasm of farmers. By the end of 1952, land reform had been basically completed nationwide. In the cities, the government took over most factories, including the Japanese factories which were confiscated after the War of Resistance against Japanese Aggression and those of the Kuomintang. Government investment during this period was mainly concentrated in the northeast region which was of great significance to the industrialization development strategy. By the end of 1952, China's economic recovery and construction had achieved great success, with both industrial and agricultural development surpassing the highs before 1949. According to statistics, by the end of 1952, the total output value of industry and agriculture had reached 81 billion yuan, an increase of more than 70% over 1949. The comprehensive recovery and initial development of the national economy also mean that the time was relatively ripe for the full-scale construction of socialist industrialization throughout the country. China was about to usher in a completely new stage of development.

3.2 The "First Five-Year Plan" and "Three Socialist Transformations" (1953-1957)

After the founding of New China, its economic development focused on two main areas, one is industrialization, the other is the establishment of socialist planned economy system. Under the leadership of the Communist Party of China(CPC) Central Committee with Comrade Mao Zedong at its core, China had moved away from the traditional household-based small-scale farming and had, through direct government planning, vigorously developed a large-scale socialist industrial complex. During this period, China's resources and energy were concentrated in capital-intensive enterprises producing metals, machinery and chemical products.

In May 1953, China and the Soviet Union signed in Moscow "the Agreement on the Assistance of the Government of the Union of Soviet Socialist Republics to the Central People's Government of the People's Republic of China for the Development of China's National Economy", which stipulated that the Soviet Union would help China build 91 industrial projects, plus 50 projects that had been confirmed in 1950 and 15 projects added to the agreement in 1954, a total of 156 projects. In this way, the First Five-Year Plan of New China was officially launched with the support of the Soviet Union.

The basic task of the First Five-Year Plan was to "focus on the development of the heavy industry and build the foundation for the country's industrialization and national defense modernization". During the First Five-Year Plan, China's industrial production capacity was greatly developed, especially in the heavy industry sector. Figure 3-1 shows

Figure 3-1 Successful trial production of the first batch of Jiefang brand heavy-duty cars during the "First Five-Year Plan" period

Photo from Xinhuanet

successful trial production of the first batch of Jiefang brand cars. On the one hand, the output of many industrial products increased substantially and the level of technology improved significantly; on the other hand, the internal structure of the industrial sector was gradually improved and some industries achieved breakthroughs and leaps from nothing to something, from something to something excellent, laying a solid foundation for the all-round development of China's industrial system. In terms of output, compared with 1952, the output value of China's heavy industry in 1957 increased by 210.7% and that of the light industry by 83.3%. In terms of structure, in 1952, the heavy industry and light industry accounted for 37.3% and 62.7% of all industries respectively. In 1957, the proportion of the heavy industries rose to 45% and the light industry dropped to 55%. At the same time, the internal structure of light and heavy industries also tends to be reasonable. In addition to industry, the development of agricultural production and the construction of agricultural infrastructure had also made remarkable progress. In general, the First Five-Year Plan saw a significant increase in China's industrialization, which enhanced China's national defense security and comprehensive competitiveness.

Almost simultaneously with the First Five-Year Plan was the socialist transformation of agriculture, handicraft industry, and capitalist industry and commerce. From 1953 to 1956, China completed the "Three Socialist Transformations" in just four years, transforming private ownership of the means of production into socialist public ownership, and initially establishing the basic socialist system.

To be specific, in the "Three Socialist Transformations", agriculture and handicraft industries were implemented through a cooperative path, and capitalist industry and commerce were implemented through public-private partnership. The socialist transformation of agriculture was also known as the agricultural cooperative movement. In 1953, the CPC Central Committee successively issued "Resolution of the CPC Central Committee on Mutual Assistance and Cooperation in Agricultural Production" and the "Resolution of the CPC Central Committee on the Development of Agricultural Production Cooperatives". China's rural areas began to follow the socialist road of collectivization and common prosperity, and the individual peasant economy gradually transformed into the socialist collective economy. By the end of 1956, 96.3% of peasant households had joined cooperatives. The socialist transformation of handicraft industry was to transform the individual handicraft industry into a socialist economy under collective ownership by the working mass through a cooperative path. By the end of 1956, 91.7% of the handicraftsmen nationwide had joined handicraft cooperatives.

Public-private partnership was an advanced form of state capitalism adopted by China for the socialist transformation of national capitalist industry and commerce. It is broadly divided into two stages: the public-private partnership of individual enterprises and the public-private partnership of the whole industry. The characteristics of public-private partnership are the state invests and sends management personnel to private enterprises, the cooperation between the two parties goes deeper into the enterprise, i. e., the production field, where the means of production are shared by the state and the capitalists, and the socialist economic component is in a leading position. The profits of the enterprises are distributed according to the principle of "dividing the fertilizer among four horses". About 34. 5% are turned into the state in the name of income tax, 30% are used as the enterprise's accumulation fund, 15% as workers' welfare, and 20. 5% as dividends of the capital. By the end of 1956, industrial enterprises implementing public-private partnership had accounted for 99% of the total number of households and employees in the original capitalist industrial and accounted for 99. 6% of the total output value. With the completion of the transformation of capitalist industry and commerce, China established the basic system of socialism and entered the primary stage of socialism.

3.3 The "Great Leap Forward" and the People's Commune Movement(1958-1960)

The Great Leap Forward was serious setback in the process of exploring the path of building socialism. They overstate the role of subjective will and efforts, ignore the objective laws of economic development, and cause mistakes like overambitious targets, misdirection, exaggeration and "communist wind" to run rampant, all of which caused great damage to industrial and agricultural production, serious imbalance in the proportion of the national economy and severe difficulties in the people's livelihood.

In May 1958, the Second Session of the Eighth National Congress of the CPC approved the general line of "work hard, strive for the top, and build socialism as better, faster and more economically as possible." The Session called on the whole Party and the entire nation to earnestly implement the general line of socialist construction and strive to catch up with United Kingdom in terms of the output of major industrial products within 15 years or even shorter and to complete the national program for agricultural development five years ahead of schedule. After the Session, on every front in the country, the "Great Leap Forward" climax was triggered overnight. In August 1958, the Political Bureau of the CPC Central Committee held an expanded session in Beidaihe to discuss the 1959 national economic plan. The Session set several overambitious targets for industrial and agricultural production, and discussed and approved the "Resolution of the CPC Central Committee on the Establishment of People's Communes in Rural Areas". After the Session, the whole country set off the "steel movement of the whole people" and the rural areas of the country appeared the climax of the People's Commune Movement.

In 1958, there were a growing number of "good news" on the economic front, as depicted in Figure 3-2, which corresponds to relevant reports in that year's Shaanxi Daily. In the autumn of 1958, grain harvests exceeded those of the previous two years, and steel production also rose sharply. However, almost all reports were exaggerated. Statistical reports became increasingly overstated, and these problems eventually almost led to an economic meltdown. The reckless progress that does not follow the objective laws of economic development has also caused many problems. For example, the inferior quality of most products making them unable to use, the massive loss of labor from the agricultural sector, and the unsustainable consumption of resources, etc. In 1960, local food shortage has developed into regional shortage. And the relatively harsh climate environment made the situation worse. China's food supply was in serious difficulty and the national economy fell into an unprecedented depression and downturn.

Figure 3-2 Newspaper during the "Great Leap Forward" period

The idea and specific institutional arrangement of rural people's communes are to integrate agriculture (including crop farming, forestry, animal husbandry, side-line production and fishery), industry, commerce, culture and education, military and national defense into rural grass-roots social organizations. "Integration of government administration with commune management" is a basic characteristic of people's communes. Objectively, people's communes have both negative and positive sides. On the negative side, the People's Commune Movement showed the problems of being over drastic and disrespecting the objective laws of economic development. Moreover, during this movement the "communist wind" was widely spread in the form of "promoting egalitarianism, allocating materials free of charge, and recovering loans by banks"; on the positive side, the People's Commune Movement harnessed collective strength and greatly changed the appearance of China's rural areas, objectively promoting the growth of agricultural economy and the improvement of rural production conditions.

3.4 Adjustment of the National Economy (1961-1965)

In November 1960, the CPC Central Committee issued an "Urgent Letter of Instruction on Current Policy Issues Concerning the Rural People's Communes", urging the whole Party to do its utmost to resolutely rectify the "communist wind". Soon after, in January 1961, the Ninth Plenary Session of the Eighth CPC Central Committee formally decided to implement the policy of "adjustment, consolidation, enrichment and improvement" for the national economy. Marked by these two events, the "Great Leap Forward" movement had actually been stopped, and the national economy had begun to shift to a new track of adjustment.

At the same time, then Chairman Mao Zedong called on the whole Party to restore the style of seeking truth from facts and conducting investigation and research, as a result, 1961 became the year of such title. This laid a solid ideological foundation for adjustment in all areas. In the industrial sector, the adjustment focused on reducing steel output and other indicators and rectifying enterprise orders. In September 1961, the CPC Central Committee issued the "Instructions on Current Industrial Problems", which clearly pointed out that the targets of industrial production and capital construction must be brought down to a reliable level with room for improvement. In addition, the trial implementation of the "Regulations on the Work of State-Owned Industrial Enterprises" (Draft), also known as "Seventy Articles on Industrial Work", also played a positive role in restoring and rebuilding the normal production order of enterprises. In the rural areas, although the people's communes were preserved, all of them had been rectified to thoroughly check and correct the "communist wind" and exaggeration, etc. At the same time, the original provisions on the public canteen and the supply system were abolished, requiring the reduction of urban population and grain sales.

The formulation and implementation of a series of national economic adjustment policies made China's economy gradually move to the normal track. From the end of 1962, the national economic situation began to recover, industrial and agricultural production was restored, state finance achieved a balance between income and expenditure, the supply of commodities in the market was eased, and the living standards of urban and rural residents were improved. Statistics show that compared with the beginning of 1961, in June 1963, the total number of employees in the country decreased by 18.87 million, the urban population decreased by 26 million, and the population consuming commodity grain decreased by 28 million. By 1965, the task of national economic adjustment had been basically completed. By 1966, the whole country had basically fulfilled the tasks set for adjusting the national economy, and China's economy had gained recovery and development.

3.5 The "Cultural Revolution" Period (1966-1976)

When China completed the task of national economic adjustment, the "Cultural Revolution" began. The "Cultural Revolution" brought serious disasters to the Party, the nation and the people of all ethnic groups, and left an extremely painful lesson. The purpose of the "Cultural Revolution" was actually to prevent the restoration of capitalism and seek for China's path of building socialism. However, due to the lack of clear understanding of the law of construction and development of socialist society, the "left wing" policy occupied the dominant position, which finally led to 10 years of civil unrest. From a political point of view, the impact of the "Cultural Revolution" was huge, but from an economic point of view, the economic impact during the "Cultural Revolution" was relatively small. This phenomenon occured because of the rare coincidence of the political radical phase with the economic retrenchment phase. Unlike the "Great Leap Forward", the economic operation during the "Cultural Revolution" was relatively efficient: investment was shrinking, but it was a relatively orderly process, and agricultural production was relatively unaffected; industrial production declined, but only to a limited extent; moreover, the projects of important necessities and prioritized development were not interrupted. Similar to 1965 and 1966, the focus of economic development is still on the "third line", that is, the economically underdeveloped areas in western China except for Xinjiang and Tibet.

3.6 The Decisive Turning Point (1977-1978)

The two or three years from the end of the Cultural Revolution in 1976 to the Third Plenary Session of the 11th CPC Central Committee in 1978 were a momentous and critical historical stage for China's economy. During this period, China began the great emancipation of the field of economic thought and the initial reflection on the planned economic system. How to establish the priorities and central tasks of the Party and the nation became an important issue at this stage.

In these two or three years, great changes had been observed in both economic and ideological fields. The whole Party launched a great discussion on the standard of truth, which laid the ideological foundation for the successful Third Plenary Session of the 11th CPC Central Committee. The Third Plenary Session of the 11th CPC Central Committee is a far-reaching turning point in the history of the Party since the founding of the People's Republic of China. The Plenary Session made the historic decision to shift the work focus of the Party and the nation to economic construction and carry out reform and opening up. Some of the main themes of the Plenary Session, such as proposal to respect for objective economic laws, distribution according to work, opening up to the outside world and importing foreign capital and technology, respecting for knowledge and talents, and reform of the unreasonable production system. Figure 3-3 shows the relevant report at that time.

Figure 3-3 *People's Daily* published the communique of the Third Plenary Session of the 11th CPC Central Committee

From the founding of the People's Republic of China to the reform and opening up, after nearly 30 years of accumulation and development, China's economy also showed some growth. In terms of economic aggregate, China's GDP in 1978 was 367.9 billion yuan, accounting for 1.8% of the world economy. However, due to the rapid growth of the population and the unreasonable relationship between accumulation and consumption, the per capita disposable income of the national residents in 1978 was only 171 yuan, and the per capita consumption expenditure was 151 yuan. Meanwhile, fiscal revenue increased to 113.2 billion yuan. But foreign exchange reserves remained rather tight, of just 167 million USD at the end of 1978, ranking the 38th largest in the world. In addition, the total import and export of goods in 1978 was 20.6 billion USD, ranking 29th in the world. From the perspective of industrial structure, the proportion of agriculture decreased, while that of industry increased. In 1978, the share of the primary, secondary and tertiary industries was 27.7%, 47.7% and 24.6%, respectively. From the perspective of society and people's livelihood, compared with the early days of the founding of New China, the situation at this time had improved. In 1978, primary education was universal, and the enrollment rate of school-age children reached 94%; meanwhile, the number of medical and health institutions reached 170 000 and the number of medical and health professionals reached 2.46 million, but the overall level of medical and health services remained low. At this time, there were still a large number of rural people living in poverty. By the end of 1978, if according to 2010 rural poverty standards, 770 million people were living in poverty in rural areas, and the incidence of rural poverty was 97.5%.

3.7 Summary of Economic Development and Exploration from 1949 to 1978

3.7.1 Economic Construction Achievements of China from 1949 to 1978

From the founding of the People's Republic of China in 1949 to the beginning of the reform and opening up in 1978, this period of nearly 30 years is a momentous historical stage for China. During this stage, China carried out the transition of the socialist economic system, made profound exploration and accumulated rich experience in economic construction.

From the perspective of social nature and economic system, we can roughly divide the nearly 30 years from 1949 to 1978 into three important stages: the first one is the period of the new democratic society(1949-1952); the second one is the transition period from the new democratic society to the socialist society(1953-1956); the third one is the period of unitary public ownership and planned economic system(1957-1978). Specifically, in the period of the new democratic society, the main task was to restore and rebuild the national economy. Through a series of economic measures such as confiscation of bureaucratic capital and land reform, a highly centralized economic management system was initially established, which laid a solid foundation for the subsequent large-scale industrialization. During the transition period from the new democratic society to the socialist society, the focus was on the general line of the transition period of "one industrialization and three transformation". The highly centralized planned economic system was gradually formed, and the First Five-Year Plan achieved great and far-reaching success. During the period of unitary public ownership and planned economic system, China went through a highly tortuous road of economic construction, with intertwined political and economic factors, extremely unstable policies, and an industrialization process that was blocked multiple times.

After nearly 30 years of socialist industrialization, significant achievements had been made in New China. A number of new industrial bases had been gradually established in China's inland, and the national defense industry had achieved a breakthrough from scratch. In particular, the successful launch of "Two Bombs and One Satellite" had greatly safeguarded Chinese national security. Figure 3-4 shows the relevant reports of successful launch of "Two Bombs and One Satellite" by *Guangming Daily*. Furthermore, resource exploration and development together with infrastructure construction had made great progress and development, and an independent and relatively complete industrial system and national economic system had taken shape.

In general, during this period, China's industrialization path focused on the development

Figure 3-4　The relevant reports of successful launch of "Two Bombs and One Satellite" *by Guangming Daily*

of heavy industry, characterized by the government as the main investor and the state's mandatory planning as a means of allocating resources. Against this background, China had continuously explored how to correctly handle a series of important issues such as the relationship between the national economic structure and the industrial relations between coastal areas and inland areas. China had gradually established an independent and relatively complete industrial system and national economic system, which accumulated precious experience and laid a good material and talent foundation, especially heavy industrial foundation, for further accelerating the socialist industrialization process after the reform and opening up.

3.7.2　Characteristics and Evaluation of Planned Economy

Implementing socialist planned economy is an important event since the founding of New China, and the socialist planned economy system is also an important turning point in China's industrialization and modernization since modern times. In its essence, a planned economy is a positive attempt by human beings to explore and try to master the law of economic operation, which many countries are constantly exploring and practicing. In a broader sense, the planned economy has gone beyond the economic category. It is not only a system for resource allocation, enterprise operation and income distribution, but also a comprehensive system for the nation to mobilize all resources. For relatively backward large countries, the planned economic system with a high resource mobilization capability helps to achieve rapid industrialization and economic catch-up and surpass.

The famous statement made during Deng Xiaoping's South China tour in 1992 is of great significance to our understanding of planned economy and socialism. He believed that the planned economy and the market economy are not the criteria for distinguish socialism from capitalism. The planned economy is not equal to socialism, and the market economy is not equal to capitalism. Either socialism or capitalism can adopt the system or mechanism of a planned economy or market economy.

From the concrete practice of China, it only took about 30 years to leap from a poor country to a country with a relatively strong industrial base and a relatively complete modern industrial system. The speed and effect of Chinese development are astonishing. Therefore, judging only from this point of view, those who argue that the planned economy is a completely inefficient backward economy are not convincing. Today, we have realized that the planned economy is not equal to a single system of national ownership, nor is it completely equal to absolute national control, and its role in the economic development of New China shall be fully recognized and correctly evaluated.

4 Reform and Transformation of the Chinese Economy (after 1978)

The reform of China's economic system after 1978 greatly unleashed productive forces, increased the vitality of economic growth and development, and created the "Chinese miracle". This market-oriented economic reform gradually lifted up control over economic activities and individual lifestyles and went through roughly four stages. The first stage was the reform initiation and experiment stage (1978-1984). At this time, the small-scale individual and collective commodity exchange market appeared, and the country took the cultivation of individual and collective economies as a supplement to the socialist planned economy at the policy level. The second stage was the comprehensive exploration stage of reform (1984-1992), when various reform policies and programs related to the market system were introduced. During this stage, the system and components of the planned economy were weakened, while those of the market economy were strengthened, and market rules such as equivalent exchange, supply and demand relations, and competition began to play an important role in economic life. The third stage was the stage of establishing the framework of the socialist market economic system (1992-2000), in which the market economy as a whole began to dominate the development pattern of Chinese economy. In this stage, with the eventual integration of state-owned enterprises into the market economic system and the deepening of the marketization of labor, capital and land resources, market rules penetrated the whole economic field, public utilities and social life. The fourth stage was to improve the socialist market economy (from 2000 to the present). In this stage, a perfect socialist market economy and a more dynamic and open economic system were gradually built. While emphasizing the continued deepening of economic reform, China began to pay attention to the formulation of policies and investment in social development.

4.1 The Great Historical Turning Point of 1978

No matter in the history of the development of the CPC, or in the history of the development of the People's Republic of China, or even in the history of the development of the Chinese nation, 1978 is a year that shall always be remembered. This year, Deng

Xiaoping promoted the realization of a great historical turnaround with far-reaching significance. In this year, through the great discussion on the standard of truth, people broke through the bondage of "Two Whatevers" and emancipated their minds. The Party and the nation, responding to the people's eagerness to change the backwardness of the productive forces, boldly put forward proposals to reform the relations of production and the superstructure. Moreover, China improved its relations with Japan, USA and other countries, established the policy of reform and opening up to the outside world. Finally, through the Third Plenary Session of the 11th CPC Central Committee, the Party re-established the ideological line of seeking truth from facts and realized the shift of the focus of the whole Party's work.

To reform, first of all, the correct ideological line shall be established. Specifically, we shall promote the realization of the focus shift of the Party and the nation's work, and deeply understand the necessity and significance of the reform and opening up. In other words, the process of China's economic system reform is a process of ideological emancipation, theoretical breakthrough and practical exploration.

On May 11, 1978, *Guangming Daily* published an article by a special commentator entitled *Practice Is the Sole Criterion for Testing Truth*, which triggered a nationwide discussion on the issue of the criterion of truth, creating conditions for bringing order out of chaos, resolving issues inherited from the past, and making ideological preparations for the Third Plenary Session of the 11th CPC Central Committee.

During this period, China also fully learned from the experience of Western countries, being eager to break through the shackles, put down the burden, and learn all advanced things from all advanced countries, including Western capitalist countries with different political systems. At the decision-making level of the CPC Central Committee, the decision on opening up had already been made. What they pondered and considered was not whether to open up or not, but how to open up.

The State Council Theory-Discussing Meeting held from July to September 1978 was an important meeting to prepare for the reform and opening up. The theme of this meeting was to study the speed of Four Modernizations in China. The general tone of the State Council Theory-Discussing Meeting, which lasted for more than two months, was "reform and opening up". The discussions, solutions and policies produced on this meeting laid the foundation for the final determination of the general principle and policy of the reform and opening up at the Third Plenary Session of the 11th CPC Central Committee.

From December 18 to 22, 1978, the Third Plenary Session of the 11th CPC Central Committee was held in Beijing. The meeting completely rejected the wrong theory and practice based on class struggle and made the historic decision to shift the work focus of the Party and the country to economic construction and implement the reform and opening up. It opened the door to China's reform and opening up and marked that China had entered a new period of socialist development. Since then, the Party had led the people of all ethnic groups in China to start a great new revolution under new historical conditions. This great historical turn showed that the exploration of the road of socialist construction in China, which started in the 1950s, had finally gotten on the right track.

4.2 The Stage of Reform Initiation and Experiment (1978-1984)

After the Third Plenary Session of the 11th CPC Central Committee, the theory of "setting planned economy as the main, market regulation as the auxiliary" was put forward, which made market regulation in the economic system for the first time. The reform in this period was mainly to introduce market mechanisms into the planned economic system, to improve the planned economic system. In practice, this period mainly included the reform of the household contract responsibility system in rural areas and the reform of expanding the autonomy of some industrial enterprises.

4.2.1 The Rise of Rural Economic Reform

The most significant changes of the reform process occurred in the weakest link of the national economy, which is agriculture. The household contract responsibility system, and the two-tier management system, which combined the control and division, replaced the "three-level ownership and team-based" people's commune system, and began to be widely implemented in rural areas throughout the nation.

The decollectivization of agriculture and the reform of the household contract responsibility system were carried out from the bottom up. The pioneer of the household contract responsibility system came from a small mountain village in Anhui Province, Xiaogang Village in Fengyang County, Anhui Province. It was once a famous "beggar village" in the local area. In December 1978, 18 local farmers, taking a great political risk, privately signed an agreement to contract the collective land to their households, and started to try "an all-round contract". Figure 4-1 is the group photo of people taking the lead in practicing the all-around responsibility system. Their practice was that the production team makes an agreement with each farmer regarding the determination of how much grain shall be turned into the state and how much grain shall be left to the collective, the remaining grain after the harvest, no matter more or less, belongs to the farmer him/herself. By harvest time, these farmers had more grain than their neighbor villages, so more farmers soon joined in. The great feat of these 18 farmers in Xiaogang Village played the prelude to China's reform.

However, the agricultural reform was not smooth. In some places, "Learning from Dazhai in Agriculture" and "Taking Grain as the Key Link" was still the guiding ideology of agriculture at that time, and the practice of farm output quotas fixed by each household

Figure 4-1 Group photo of people taking the lead in practicing the all-round responsibility system
Photo from *People's Daily*

triggered huge debates. At the critical moment when the implementation of fixing farm output quotas for each household encountered heavy resistance, Deng Xiaoping stood out and gave his unequivocal support. Not only did he express great support for the rural reform in Anhui Province, but also pointed out the direction for the national rural reform, which had a significant impact on the development of the package to the household in the whole country. In September 1980, the CPC Central Committee issued a notice, for the first time affirming the "household-based contract system" reform action, thus rural reform rolled out in an all-round way. Subsequently, a new type of agricultural production relationship, mainly in the form of the household contract responsibility system, was generally established in rural areas all over the country.

In 1980, natural disasters occurred frequently in China. According to statistics, more than 47.33 million hectares of farmland were affected nationwide, accounting for about 30% of the sowing area. The disaster was so severe that the masses as well as the state leaders were concerned about it. However, due to the favorable rural policy in this year, the national grain output in the year of such disaster reached 318 million tons, and this year became the second year of high yield since the founding of the People's Republic of China. The advantages of household sideline work were also particularly obvious, and the per capita net income increased by 42.2% over the previous year. Many areas that had long been poor and backward had enjoyed bumper agricultural harvests. Those places that implemented the policy of fixing farm output quotas for each household early, such as Anhui, Sichuan and Gansu, had seen more cheerful results. The production practice of the year with great disaster made a good summary for the big debate of farm output quotas fixed by household. "Farm output quotas fixed by household lead to wealth" had become the consensus of most people.

On New Year's Day of 1982, the first "Central Document No. 1" on rural work in the history of the CPC— "the National Rural Work Meeting Minutes" was officially issued. It clearly points out that: "The various responsibility systems currently in practice including fixed remuneration for small-scale labor contracts, professional contract remuneration for joint production, joint production to labor, joint production to household and group, etc., are the production responsibility system of the socialist collective economy." This unequivocally rectified the name of "farm output quotas fixed by household" and "household-based contract system". Not only did it unify people's understanding of fixing farm output quotas for each household, but also brought the countryside, farmers and agricultural issues to a highly important position. It greatly encouraged the momentum of rural cadres and improved the enthusiasm of farmers in production. In 1982, China's total agricultural output, grain production, and farmers' income increased by 11%, 8.7%, and 15% respectively, compared with the previous year. The practice once again proved that the policy of farm output quotas fixed by household is reasonable, the central documents are in line with the people's wishes, and the rural economy is full of hope.

In general, the implementation of the household contract responsibility system exerted a profound influence and greatly promoted the enthusiasm of hundreds of millions of farmers, broke the difficult situation of long-term stagnation in agriculture, accelerated agricultural development and changed the face of rural areas.

4.2.2 Expansion of the Enterprises' decision-making powers

Outside the countryside, experiments with other kinds of reform were about to begin. In the period after 1979, the central link of economic reform was the expansion of corporate autonomy. China carried out a pilot project to expand the autonomy of enterprises, carried out the two-step financial restructuring of "substitution of tax payment for profit delivery", and gradually promoted the restructuring of the fiscal system with "division of revenue and expenditure between the central and local governments and contracts at different levels". This allowed the gradual recovery and development of the shrinking collective economy and the almost extinct individual economy.

Pilot projects to expand corporate autonomy were initially initiated in Sichuan Province. In the fourth quarte of 1978, Sichuan Province first carried out the pilot projects in six local state industrial enterprises, and received good results. In January 1979, Sichuan Provincial Party Committee and Provincial Government summarized the experience of six enterprises in the pilot projects to expand corporate autonomy, formulated the "Pilot Project Opinions on Expanding the Autonomy of Local Industrial Enterprises and Accelerating the Pace of Production and Construction", and decided to expand the range of this pilot projects to 100 industrial enterprises from 1979 onwards. These reform measures brought unprecedented vitality to the industrial enterprises of Sichuan Province and achieved remarkable economic results. In the first year of the pilot projects, the total industrial output value of 84 local industrial enterprises in Sichuan Province increased by 14.9% over the previous year, while the profits and profits turned into the state increased by 33% and 24.2% respectively, all of which were higher than those of non-pilot enterprises.

In May 1984, the State Council issued the "Interim Provisions on Further Expanding the Autonomy of State-owned Industrial Enterprises", granting enterprises their due authorities in 10 aspects, including production and operation plans, product sales, etc. In September 1985, The State Council approved and transferred the notice of "Interim Provisions on Several Issues Concerning the Vitality Enhancement of Large and Medium-sized State-owned Industrial Enterprises" formulated by National Economic Commission (which was renamed as National Economic and Trade Commission in 1993 and withdrawn in 2003) and National Economic System Reform Commission (which was renamed as the Office of Economic Restructuring of the State Council in 1998 and reorganized as National Development and Reform Commission in 2003), which made 14 provisions requiring the continued expansion of enterprise autonomy.

At this time, the reform focused on adjusting the relationship between the state and enterprises, focusing on mobilizing the enthusiasm and initiative of enterprises and employees. Through the reform at this stage, enterprises had certain production autonomy and began to become independent interest subjects, which improved the enthusiasm of enterprises and employees and opened a gap to the traditional planned economy system. However, the reform idea of expanding the autonomy of enterprises was carried out under the framework of the planned economy, and the reform of state-owned enterprises at this stage still did not shake the foundation of the planned economy system.

4.2.3 Establishing Special Economic Zones and Gradually Opening Up to the Outside World

The establishment of special economic zones in China is based on the requirements of opening up to the outside world and with reference to foreign experience. The initial planning of the establishment of the special economic zones can be roughly traced back to the proposal of designating Baoan and Zhuhai counties in Guangdong Province as foreign trade bases made in the "Economic Investigation Report of Hong Kong and Macao" in May 1978, and the report of the Ministry of Transport and Guangdong Province on the site selection of Baoan Shekou Commune to establish an industrial zone in January 1979.

On May 31, 1978, the Central Committee investigation delegation submitted the "Economic Investigation Report of Hong Kong and Macao". For the first time, this report put forward the idea of setting up special economic zones in Shenzhen and Zhuhai, and creatively proposed special policies conducive to speeding up the pace of opening up in the two cities and these policies were called on as the focus of work. In other words, this was China's first attempt to establish special economic zones.

On January 6, 1979, Guangdong Province and the Ministry of Transport jointly submitted to the State Council the report "On Establishment of Industrial Zone in Baoan District, Guangdong Province by China Merchants (Hong Kong)". This report indicated that, "It is unanimously agreed that China Merchants Group shall establish an industrial zone in Baoan, Guangdong Province, near Hong Kong." In this way, "China Merchants Shekou Industrial Zone" was established in early 1979 before the establishment of Shenzhen Special Zone. Figure 4-2 shows the Shekou Industrial Zone under construction. Amid the skepticism, Shekou Industrial Zone, with 2% of Shenzhen's population, generated 16% of the city's total profit. From breaking the practice of "eating from the same big pot" to attracting investment, from the commercialization of housing to national talent recruitment, during year 1979-1984, Shekou created "24 national No.1 records". The successful experience of Shekou was praised by the media as the "Shekou model" and became the pioneer of the special economic zones.

Figure 4-2　In April 1984, Shekou Industrial Zone in Shenzhen under construction, standing the slogan "Time is money, efficiency is life"

Photo from China Reform Information Base

On March 24, 1980, the CPC Central Committee held a meeting in Guangzhou with the participation of Guangdong and Fujian provinces, and officially named the "export special zones" as the "special economic zones". On August 26, 1980, the "Regulations on Special Economic Zones in Guangdong Province" were approved, marking that the establishment of special economic zones had a legal basis. On November 26, 1981, the Standing Committee of the National People's Congress granted Guangdong and Fujian Provinces the power to enact individual economic laws and regulations for their special economic zones, and thus China formally unveiled the prelude to running special economic zones on a trial basis.

From the perspective of regional space, China's opening up has experienced a transformation from coastal special economic zones to coastal open cities and coastal economic open zones, and then to inland central cities, border ports and the all-around opening and development of the western region. In the process of spatial expansion, from the Shekou Industrial Zone established in 1979 to Guangdong and Fujian provinces implemented special policies and flexible measures, China's reform and opening up started off gradually. In 1984, China opened 14 coastal cities, including Beihai, Zhanjiang, Guangzhou, Fuzhou, Wenzhou, Ningbo, Qinhuangdao, Shanghai, Nantong, Lianyungang, Qingdao, Yantai, Tianjin and Dalian, and successively approved the establishment of 14 national economic and technological development zones.

In summary, the "specialty" of special economic zones can be summarized into four points. First, the economic development of special economic zones mainly depends on the use of foreign capital. Second, under the guidance of the socialist planned economy, the economic activities of the special economic zones give full play to the role of market regulation, or take market regulation as the main factor. Third, special preferential treatment and convenience are given to investors in terms of taxation, land use fees and entry and exit management. For example, for foreign-invested enterprises, the enterprise income tax is levied at a reduced rate of 15%. Finally, the state gives the special economic zones more autonomy in economic activities. For example, for construction projects less than 50 million yuan in heavy industry and less than 30 million yuan in light industry, which do not require the state to balance production and construction conditions, the special economic zones can examine and approve by itself; infrastructure indicators can be counted in addition to state-controlled ones, etc.

4.3   The Stage of Comprehensive Exploration of Reform(1984-1992)

The reform at this stage was mainly to enrich the ownership structure, respect the law of value, further decentralize power and yield profits, and stimulate the vitality of the market. By doing so, China started restructuring the system and operation mechanism to promote the planned economy to turn to the commodity economy, laying the institutional foundation for the implementation of the socialist market operation mechanism. The main characteristics of the reform in this period include the pattern of public ownership as the main body, and the common development of various forms of ownership further revealed, the state-owned economy practiced the contract management responsibility system. The cultivation of modern market system, the adjustment of macro-economic management system and the opening up to the outside world had all gained further development.

4.3.1   Developing a Planned Commodity Economy and Expanding Reform and Opening Up

After the Third Plenary Session of the 11th CPC Central Committee, China's economic system reform made great achievements first in rural areas. Township enterprises became the fastest-growing part of China's economy throughout the 1980s. In contrast to the rapid development of the rural economy, the Chinese government's reform plan to revive state-owned enterprises since 1978 had not been smoothly implemented. The original intention of reform was to give state-owned enterprises more operational autonomy while allowing them to set aside a portion of their earnings for discretionary use, thereby increasing the motivation of management and workers, but the enterprises themselves must negotiate with the authorities about their rights and the profits they can keep. However, in this bargaining process, political and other non-economic factors tend to ignore economic laws. This led many high-earning enterprises to hand over much of their earnings to the state, while loss-making companies continued to receive government subsidies. Over time, the profits of enterprises with good efficiency did not continue to grow, and enterprises with poor efficiency did not go bankrupt. In addition, these reforms implemented a decentralized management structure, which led local governments could create trade barriers to protect local enterprises in exchange for the right to control the operation of enterprises. Across the country, local protectionism had almost pushed economic operations into a fiefdom economy of fragmentation. If there is no price system for all enterprises to follow the same market norms, the reform of state-owned enterprises will not be successful.

In October 1984, the Third Plenary Session of the 12th CPC Central Committee discussed and approved the "CPC Central Committee's Decision on Economic Restructuring", which expounded the necessity and urgency of accelerating the restructuring of the whole economic system with emphasis on cities, and stipulated the direction, nature, tasks and various principles and policies of the restructuring. The Decision pointed out that to restructure the planned system, the first step is to break through the traditional concept of opposing planned economy to commodity economy, and clearly understand that the socialist planned economy must consciously abide by and apply the law of value, and is a planned commodity economy based on public ownership. The full development of the commodity economy is an insurmountable stage of socio-economic development and a necessary condition for realizing China's economic modernization. The Third Plenary Session of the 12th CPC Central Committee marked that the focus of China's economic system reform shifted from rural to urban areas, and the reform entered a period of comprehensive exploration.

Around the 13th National Congress of the CPC in 1987, dramatic progress has been made in the reform of the urban economic system and the opening up to the outside world, which was mainly reflected in the following six aspects. First, on the premise of adhering to the dominant position of the public ownership economy, adjust the ownership structure, forming a situation with the public ownership as the main body, the individual economy, the private economy, the foreign economy and other economies as the supplement, and the multiple economic sectors develop together. Second, draw on the successful experience of rural reform to properly separate the ownership of the means of production from the right to manage the business, and further expand the autonomy of enterprises around the experience of enhancing the vitality of enterprises. Third, gradually restructure the government macro management system such as planning, fiscal taxation and finance. Fourth, trial implement of shareholding system reform. Fifth, restructure the circulation system, develop the commodity market and the unreasonable price system. Sixth, restructure the wage and labor system.

The comprehensive development of economic system restructuring has made China's economy emerge an unprecedented positive situation. In 1987, China's gross national product reached 1 092 billion yuan, representing an average annual growth rate of 11.1% at comparable prices since 1982; while in the same period, national income reached 915.3 billion yuan, with an average annual growth rate of 10.7% at comparable prices. After five years of development since the 12th National Congress of the CPC, China's overall economic strength reached a new level.

4.3.2 Reform and Opening Up Advancing Amid Twists and Turns

By the end of the 1980s, China has accelerated reform and opening up and socialist modernization, and achieved remarkable results. China's economic together with scientific and technological strengths have been significantly enhanced. In 1987, China's mainland had more than 1 billion people and the vast majority of its population had been able to live a subsistence lifestyle, meanwhile, some areas had begun to live a moderately prosperous life. However, after nearly 10 years of rapid economic growth, with the deepening of reform and opening up, some deep-rooted contradictions in economic development began to rise, and the restructuring of China's economic system faced its first crisis and challenges.

After the Third Plenary Session of the 12th CPC Central Committee in 1984, while the economic restructuring was bringing economic growth, it also sowed hidden dangers of inflation. Increase in money supply in 1984 was 50% higher than in 1983 and 45% higher than the amount set in the economic plan. Inflation remained high in 1986 and 1987 and finally reached double digits in 1988. The main reasons for inflation occurred were as follows. First, the total social demand far exceeded the total social supply, and the national power and social production capacity were unable to support the huge construction scale and the social consumption demand with serious inflation. Second, the proportion of industries was unbalanced. Agricultural production could not support the oversize industrial production, and the supply capacity of energy, transportation and raw materials failed to support the oversize processing industry. Third, in the production, construction and circulation fields, the phenomenon of high consumption, low benefit and high input and low output was ubiquitous. Fourth, the process of industrial production and sales might involve a long series of economic activities and the participation of many enterprises, which made it more complicated for government's industrial management and price control, and the efficiency of policy implementation was also lower.

In this context, China embarked on price reform, hoping to help state-owned enterprises get rid of the dilemma faced by the double-track price system. Previously, China had developed a "double-track price system", in which the state set prices for goods produced on a planned order, while market supply and demand determined prices for goods produced beyond the planned increase. While significantly stimulating production, this transitional system also created distributional confusion. In August 1988, a meeting of the Political Bureau of the CPC Central Committee approved the "Preliminary Plan on Price and Wage Reform". After the formal announcement was made, there was a trend of people rushing to buy food and other daily necessities and withdraw their deposits from banks all over the nation. Ten days later, the State Council made an announcement to strengthen price control, no longer introduce price adjustment items, raise bank deposit interest, and comprehensively rectify the market order. Since September, China entered a three-year period of "governance and rectification". The main task was to substantially compress demand, drastically overhaul the circulation sector, and quickly curb and reduce price increases. Since then, the excessive social demand had been effectively controlled, and the market had begun to cool down. However, this also made a significant negative impact on economic growth, creating great resistance for economic reform during this period.

4.4 The Stage of Establishing the Socialist Market Economy (1992-2000)

At the time when the economic reform was faced with many obstacles, Deng Xiaoping made great efforts to promote China's reform again in the spring of 1992. In 1992, Deng Xiaoping started his South China tour and put forward the reform goal of establishing the socialist market economic system, which was established by the 14th National Congress of the CPC. Since then, China's economic system restructuring has entered a new stage with institutional innovation as the main content. The "Decision of the CPC Central Committee on Several Issues Concerning the Establishment of a Socialist Market Economic System" approved at the Third Plenary Session of the 14th CPC Central Committee pointed out that the establishment of a socialist market economic system means that the market shall play a fundamental role in the allocation of resources under the macro-control of the state and put forward the basic framework of a socialist market economic system. In 1997, the 15th National Congress of the CPC established the basic economic system with public ownership as the main body and various forms of ownership developing together, achieving a series of breakthroughs in thoughts and theories. This promoted the further development of the reform to establish a socialist market economic system.

4.4.1　New Stage of Accelerated Development of Reform and Opening Up

In the early 1990s, China and even the world were undergoing important social and economic changes. At that time, the world economy had a major turning point and entered a period of differentiation and reorganization. After the end of the Cold War, the competition for comprehensive national strength based on economy and science and technology has increasingly become the main content of international competition. It is a major turning point in the history of international relations to put economic security in the first place of national security and to replace military affairs as the focus of exchanges and concerns among countries around the world. At that time, China was also in a critical period of reform, opening up and modernization. On the one hand, the CPC and the government successfully resisted the pressure brought by the upheaval in Eastern Europe, thus further stabilizing the domestic political situation. While on the other hand, some deep-rooted contradictions and problems in the course of reform and opening up had gradually been exposed. In the reflection on the domestic development situation and the upheaval in Eastern Europe, there has emerged a tendency to deny the pivotal role of reform and opening up and economic development, causing troubles for China's reform and development.

At the critical moment when "the cause of reform and opening up faced the hardest challenge", Deng Xiaoping went to southern China for inspection and gave the South Tour Speeches which shocked the whole world. From January 18 to February 21 in 1992, Deng Xiaoping visited Wuchang, Shenzhen, Zhuhai, Shanghai and other places, and made important speeches along the way. Usually people call these speeches "South Tour Speeches". The essence of the "South Tour Speeches" can be summarized as follows.

First, these speeches pointed out that the key to adhering to the CPC's line since the Third Plenary Session of the 11th CPC Central Committee is to adhere to the "one center and two basic points". If we do not adhere to socialism, reform and opening up, develop the economy or improve people's lives, we will reach a dead end in our party's development. The party and the nation must follow the basic line for a hundred years and must not waver.

Second, these speeches focused on refining the problem of re-understanding socialism, highlighting the emancipation and development of the productive forces and progress towards common prosperity. Deng Xiaoping pointed out that revolution is the emancipation of productive forces, and so is reform. The essence of socialism is to emancipate and develop the productive forces, eliminate exploitation and polarization, to ultimately achieve common prosperity.

Third, these speeches put forward the concepts of the nature of socialism, the relationship between planning and market, the "three benefits" standard, and science and technology as the primary productive force, and finally concluded that "development is the absolute principle". Deng Xiaoping pointed out that attention shall be paid to stable and coordinated economic development, but stability and coordination are not absolute. Development is the absolute principle. To develop faster, we must rely on science and technology, as well as education. Science and technology constitute a primary productive force.

Fourth, these speeches emphasized the importance of seizing opportunities for self-development and never losing the opportunities. Deng Xiaoping pointed out that, the key to seizing the opportunity for self-development is to develop the economy. To seize the opportunity, now is a good time.

Fifth, adhere to the basic view that socialism is bound to replace capitalism. Deng Xiaoping unswervingly adhered to the view that socialism is bound to replace capitalism. He emphasized the need to have confidence in the future of socialism and the conviction that socialism is bound to replace capitalism. He put forward the great strategic goal of "building our country into a moderately developed country in a hundred years" and pointed out that the realization of this goal requires dedicated hard work.

In essence, the main message of Deng Xiaoping's South China tour was to encourage the second revolution to further deepen reform. As the spirit of Deng Xiaoping's South Tour Speeches spread throughout the country, the prevalent negative attitudes and opposition to reform began to recede, and the social atmosphere was changed once again. As a result, 1992 is also known as the year of reform and opening up.

The 14th National Congress of the CPC was held on October 12, 1992, and Deng Xiaoping's instructions to further deepen reform were fully embraced. The congress established Deng Xiaoping's theory of building socialism with Chinese characteristics as the guiding principle for the whole Party and made it clear that the goal of China's economic system restructuring was to establish a socialist market economic system. It called on the whole Party to seize opportunities, speed up development and concentrate on improving economic construction.

For the first time, the 14th National Congress of the CPC formally established the construction of a socialist market economic system as the ultimate goal of China's economic system restructuring. At this point, people's understanding of socialism was completely enhanced from the idea of traditional planned economy, and the market economy began to be combined with the basic system of socialism, becoming the basic goal of China's economic reform.

4.4.2 The Initial Establishment of the Socialist Market Economic System

The 14th National Congress of the CPC clearly stated that "the goal of China's economic restructuring is to establish a socialist market economic system." After the 14th National Congress, the CPC Central Committee and the State Council successively made a series of major arrangements to accelerate the development of reform and opening up, as well as modernization, and promptly customized the overall plan for a socialist market economic system. In November 1993, the Third Plenary Session of the 14th CPC Central Committee approved the "Decision of the CPC Central Committee on Several Issues Concerning the Establishment of a Socialist Market Economic System", which specified and further developed the objectives and principles of economic restructuring that put forward at the 14th National Congress of the CPC, thus establishing the basic framework of a socialist market economic system. This document became the action plan for China to establish a socialist market economic system in the 1990s.

In accordance with the arrangements of the 14th National Congress of the CPC and the Third Plenary Session of the 14th CPC Central Committee, since January 1994, reforms in fiscal and taxation, finance, foreign exchange, investment, housing and social security systems have been carried out in full swing, and important progress has been made in the reform of prices and state-owned enterprises, enabling China to take a big step towards establishing the basic framework of a socialist market economic system. After the 15th National Congress of the CPC, various reforms centering on the reform of state-owned enterprises have been further deepened. By the end of 2000, China's socialist market economic system had been preliminarily established.

Specifically, in terms of price reform, the government has made a series of decisions to completely lift price control. The number of items involved in price management of raw materials, means of production and transportation services was reduced from 737 to 89 (further reduced to 13 in 2001). By the end of 1992, the national grain market had been fully liberalized. In addition, the State Planning Commission (which was renamed as the National Development Planning Commission in 1988 and reorganized as National Development and Reform Commission in 2003) reduced the 1993 mandatory production plan by half, greatly increasing the scope for market forces to play. In 1994, price control was abolished on a large scale, the prices of major means of production were "integrated" inside and outside the plan, and all prices of unified coal were liberalized and regulated by the market. The prices of refined oil and fertilizer have also been "integrated". Furthermore, the price structure was appropriately adjusted, significantly raising the ex-factory price of crude oil, the purchase and sale price of grain, etc. The prices of the vast majority of commodities have been lifted, and the share of market regulation has been expanding. The state has used a combination of economic and legal means and necessary administrative means to strengthen macro-control and market management.

In the reform of state-owned enterprises, it is clear that through the establishment of a modern enterprise system, enterprises can become independent commodity producers and operators, fully participate in market competition, and become real market entities. The central and local governments have selected a number of representative state-owned enterprises to carry out the pilot projects of establishing a modern enterprise system, strategically adjusting the layout of the state-owned economy, so that state-owned capital is gradually concentrated in important industries and key areas related to the lifeline of the national economy. The exploration of various forms of state-owned assets supervision and administration system has been actively carried out in some places to meet the needs of the restructuring of state-owned enterprises and the adjustment of the distribution and structure of the state-owned economy, and has achieved good results.

In terms of fiscal and taxation, a turnover tax system with value-added tax as the main body together with a new fiscal institutional framework with a tax distribution system as the core was established. In December 1993, The State Council issued the "Decision on Implementing the Tax Distribution Financial Management System", which decided to implement the tax distribution system reform and the industrial and commercial tax system reform starting from January 1, 1994. Tax distribution system refers to a financial management system that divides all national taxes between the central and local governments, to determine the income scope of the central finance and local finance. The new tax distribution policy has played a key role in eliminating the previous market distortions, allowing enterprises no longer controlled by the direct and rapid impact of the central fiscal policy, and at the same time separating the microeconomic environment from the government's macroeconomic policy, creating a competitive microeconomic environment for them.

In the reform of supporting systems such as finance, foreign exchange and investment, the central bank strengthened its ability to regulate and control the money supply and its functions in financial supervision and began to separate policy-based finance from commercial finance. A single and managed floating exchange rate system based on market supply and demand has been established, realizing the convertibility of RMB under the current account; meanwhile, the management of the national plan has changed from the overall mandatory plan to the overall guiding plan; and the project legal person system, capital system and bidding system were implemented to strengthen constraints on investment risks.

Important steps have been taken in the reform of the social security system, and the establishment of a multi-level social security system has been explored. Based on pilot projects, the pension and medical insurance systems that combine social pooling with individual accounts would be gradually established. To meet the needs of deepening enterprise reform, unemployment insurance, social relief system and the system of subsistence allowances for urban residents have been established.

In addition, important progress was made in the restructuring of science and technology, education and health systems. In accordance with the principle of "stabilizing one end and opening up an area", promoting restructuring of the scientific and technological system; accelerating the restructuring of the educational system with emphasis on adjusting the distribution and structure of schools and restructuring the enrollment and distribution systems of colleges and universities; implementing a hierarchical and classified management system for medical institutions and expand their autonomy in operation and management. At the same time, new progress had been made in the reform of the rural economy, foreign trade and urban housing. Through the joint efforts of the entire nation, the socialist market economic system was initially established.

4.5 The Stage of Improving the Socialist Market Economic System (2000 to Present)

Judging from the development stages of the economic system reform, by 2000, China's socialist market economic system had been preliminarily established, and since then, China has entered a new stage in which improving the socialist market economic system is the basic task.

This period theoretically further affirmed the necessity in establishing and improving the socialist market economic system. The 16th National Congress of the CPC in 2002 set out that the main task of reform in the first 20 years of 21st century was to improve the socialist market economic system. That is, a complete socialist market economic system and a more dynamic and open economic system would be established by 2020. The third Plenary Session of the 16th CPC Central Committee in 2003 adopted "Decision of the CPC Central Committee on Several Issues Concerning the Improvement of the Socialist Market Economic System", making an overall arrangement for establishing a complete market economic system. Since then, the principal thought of "Scientific Outlook on Development" has been formed centering on the reform of the market economic system and other issues. Under the guidance of the Scientific Outlook on Development, a series of new development philosophy such as "Five Overall Plans", "building a socialist harmonious society" and "building a new socialist countryside" were put forward, which greatly deepen the reform practice and provided theoretical guidance for improving the socialist market economic system.

Since the 18th National Congress of the CPC, under the leadership of the CPC Central Committee with President Xi Jinping at its core, China has made all-round and groundbreaking achievements and undergone profound and fundamental changes based on the development over the past 30 years and more. The report of the 19th National Congress of the CPC pointed out that China's economy has shifted from a stage of rapid growth to a stage of high-quality development. This is a pivotal stage for transforming our growth pattern, improving our economic structure, and fostering new drivers of growth. Building a modernized economic system is an urgent requirement for the country to make breakthroughs and a strategic goal of China's economic development. This means that the new stage of economic development requires the support of a new economic system and a modernized economic system guided by new development philosophy. A modernized economic system highlights the characteristics of modernity. The requirement for modernity in current era is to adapt to the high-quality development stage in the modernization process and build a modernized economic system that is compatible with that stage.

The goal of internal reform of this stage was to deepen the reform of state-owned enterprises and reshape the relationship between the government and these enterprises. The reform of state-owned enterprises entered a pivotal stage. The 16th National Congress of the CPC for the first time put forward the policy that "We must unswervingly consolidate and develop the public ownership economy" and "We also must unswervingly encourage, support and guide the development of the non-public economy". The Third Plenary Session of the 16th CPC Central Committee put forward to "vigorously develop the mixed-ownership economy with the participation of state-owned capital, collective capital and non-public capital, realizing the diversification of investment subjects, and making the shareholding system become the main form of public ownership" and "establish a modern property rights system with clear ownership, manifest rights and responsibilities, strict protection and smooth circulation", promoting the reform of state-owned enterprises from the contracting out system to the property rights system. The target of this round of reform of state-owned enterprise was small and medium-sized state-owned enterprises without comparative advantages. The reform mode was the reform of the enterprise property rights system and employee status replacement compensation, which had a profound impact on China's economy. On the one hand, it prompted the state-owned enterprises to withdraw from small and medium-sized enterprises in a short time, which promoted the development of non-public economy, and fundamentally changed the ownership structure of the national economy. On the other hand, the large and medium-sized state-owned enterprises established a modern enterprise system with the support of the nation and revitalized the economy.

The goal of opening up is to join the WTO and enter the global market. In 2001, China formally joined the WTO. China has since joined the large world trading market. Figure 4-3 is a photo of China officially signed the agreement to join the WTO. China's accession to the WTO first solved the problem of USA granting China the most-favored-nation treatment and created a favorable international environment. Under the WTO framework, international grain prices have been low for a long time, thus some grain prices at home and abroad have been inverted. These posed certain challenges to vulnerable industries such as agriculture and pushed China to reform the domestic grain collection and storage system. That was a transfer of the nation holding the market to the "market-oriented acquisition" with a "targeted subsidies" mechanism. Accession to WTO also indicated further participation in international economic cooperation and division of labor. A large influx of international capital, especially foreign direct investment, continuously improved the technical level and organizational efficiency of China's economy through the spillover effect and learning effect, thus enhancing the level of total factor productivity.

Figure 4-3 China officially signed the agreement to join the WTO in 2001
Photo from *China Daily*

At the same time, the system environment for the development of the non-public economy has further improved. Market access for the non-public economy has been gradually relaxed, and non-public capital has been allowed to enter industries and fields not prohibited by laws and regulations. Regulations, rules and policy provisions restricting the development of the non-public economy were reviewed and revised, so the private property rights and the development of the non-public economy obtained legal protection and system guarantee.

In addition, the socialist market economy system has been further improved, and reform of the fiscal and taxation, financial and investment systems has been deepened. The public finance system has been continuously improved, and steady progress was made in the trial transformation of the value-added tax and the reform of the export tax rebate mechanism. Reform of the financial system was intensified, and the joint-stock system reform of state-owned commercial banks was accelerated. Major steps were taken to reform the exchange rate formation mechanism. The scope of government investment has been further narrowed, enterprises had more investment autonomy, and the investment approval system has been standardized. The development of the market system was further accelerated. The variety and quantity of commodity markets have increased year by year. The factor markets of land, labor, technology, property rights, capital and other factors have further developed. The development of market-based pricing of water, electricity, oil, natural gas and other important resources has accelerated.

The magnificent reform and opening up launched in 1978 broke the traditional planned economy system and laid the foundation for the new socialist market economy system. After more than 40 years of painstaking exploration of the socialist market economic system with

Chinese characteristics, from the goal to the framework and from the construction to the improvement, China has successfully embarked on a path of gradual reform and development of socialism with Chinese characteristics. The nation has also made great achievements in economic growth that have been acknowledged throughout the world. China's economy has shifted from rapid growth to high-quality development since 2017. Based on the experience of reform and opening up, further improving the socialist market economic system and promoting a new pattern of all-round opening up are the inevitable choices to promote a transition to high-quality development in China.

5 Economic and Social Development in China since the Reform and Opening Up

For more than 40 years since 1978, the economic development in China has achieved fruitful results, which can be called a "miracle" of economic development. This miracle is reflected in the scale and quality of the economic development in China. The development over the past 40 years has not only brought tremendous changes to Chinese society, but also has a profound impact on the growth and development of the world economy.

The achievements of the reform and opening up are all-round. Over the past 40 years and more, China has made significant achievements in the reform of its economic system. For example, it has achieved leaps and bounds in economic development, deepened opening up and significantly increased the comprehensive national power. Chinese economy has been transformed from backwardness and imbalance into coordinated development, and the economic structure has been continuously improved. People's lives have made a historic leap from inadequate food and clothing to a moderately prosperous life in all respects. This does not mean that China has explored a completely new economic development path. China needs to put its achievements over the past 40 years and more of reform and opening up in perspective and accelerate the transformation and upgrading of its economic development in the new era, so as to make greater contributions to the sustainable development of the world economy.

5.1 Achievements of Economic Development in China since the Reform and Opening Up

Over the past 40 years and more of reform and opening up, China has achieved sustained and rapid economic growth which can be rarely seen in the world. China's economic development has been significantly accelerated; the quality of economic development has been continuously promoted; the comprehensive national power has been increasingly enhanced; China has made brilliant achievements in socialist economic construction.

First of all, the economic strength of China has jumped dramatically, from "all start from scratch" to the world's second largest economy. Since modern times, its economic development has lagged behind the world for a long time, so the CPC has consciously shouldered the historic mission of strengthening the country and enriching its people since its founding. In the early days of the founding of New China, its people's livelihood was impoverished and a full-scale reconstruction is under way. Under the leadership of the CPC, the Chinese people realized the full recovery of the national economy in three years, which created a prerequisite for the start of large-scale economic construction. China's economic growth entered a fast lane after the reform and opening up. In 1986, China's economic aggregate exceeded 1 trillion yuan for the first time in history. In 2000, the economic aggregate exceeded 10 trillion yuan, overtaking Italy to become the world's sixth largest economy. After the accession to the WTO in 2001, Chinese economy joined the wave of global development and entered a new round of rapid development. By 2010, its economic aggregate surpassed Japan and became the second largest in the world. In 2020, despite the impact of the COVID-19 pandemic, China's GDP reached 101.4 trillion yuan, surpassing 100 trillion yuan for the first time in history (see Figure 5-1). Since the 18th National Congress of the CPC, China's economy has maintained a relatively fast growth, and the acceleration of which was far higher than the world's average. From 2013 to 2021, Chinese economy grew at an average annual rate of 6.6%, much higher than the world average of 2.6% for the same period, and higher than the average of 3.7% for developing economies. Its economic growth rate is one of the highest among major economies in the world. According to the National Bureau of Statistics of the People's Republic of China, from 2013 to 2021, the average contribution of China to world economic growth reached 38.6%, exceeding the total contribution of G7. China has become an important engine driving world economic growth. China has created a miracle of rapid economic development rarely seen in the world.

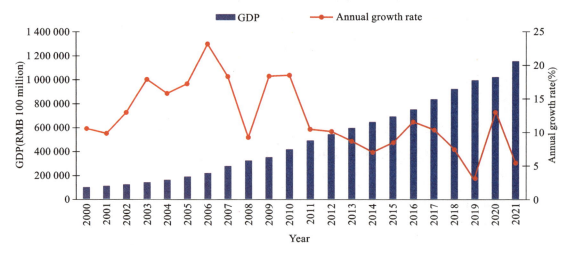

Figure 5-1 Changes in China's GDP from 2000 to 2021
Data from National Bureau of Statistics of the People's Republic of China

Second, the quality of China's economic development has been improving, shifting from extensive growth driven by factors to intensive development driven by innovation. China has achieved rapid economic growth based on its advantages in capital, labor and land since the reform and opening up. However, the extensive mode of growth relying on factor expansion cannot be sustained with the gradual disappearance of demographic dividends, the weakening of the investment effect and the strengthening of land constraints. At the 18th National Congress of the CPC, a major plan was made to "implement the strategy of innovation-driven development", and the economic growth engine accelerated from "factor-driven" to "innovation-driven". With the guiding principle of promoting high-quality development, China has integrated the strategy of expanding domestic demand with deepening supply-side structural reform, strengthened the internal driving force and reliability of the domestic circulation, upgraded the quality and level of the international circulation, and accelerated the building of a modernized economy. Against this backdrop, China has made great efforts to raise the total factor productivity, improve the resilience and safety of industrial and supply chains, promote urban-rural integration and coordinated development among regions, and promote qualitative and quantitative economic growth.

Third, a modern market system featuring unified, open and orderly competition has taken shape, and the basic role of market mechanisms in allocating resources has been significantly enhanced. A multi-level, multi-category and multi-form commodity market pattern has taken shape, so modern circulation modes represented by chain operation, logistics distribution and e-commerce developed rapidly. Capital, land, labor and other factors have been far more market-oriented, and a multi-tiered capital market system, such as stocks and bonds, has been developed. A system has been established for workers to choose their own jobs and for the market to regulate employment. The market for transfer with compensation of land use rights has developed rapidly, and the scale of intellectual property transactions has also expanded rapidly. According to the new version of "Central Pricing Catalogue" issued in 2020, commodity prices were basically determined by the market. China has formed a price mechanism mainly regulated by the market, which accounted for more than 97% among all.

Fourth, remarkable progress has been made in developing market entities. Before the reform and opening up, the state-owned economy played a dominating role in the nation's economic development and the non-public economy were not allowed to develop under the planned economy system. State-owned enterprises were responsible for all aspects of manufacturing and people's livelihood during this period. Since the reform and opening up, China's non-public economy has emerged and developed simultaneously with the reform of the market economic system. With the deepening of the economic system reform, especially the adjustment of the ownership pattern and the strategic adjustment of state-owned enterprises, the self-employed, private and other non-public economy in China has developed from scratch to rich and from small to large. Non-public enterprises have achieved great development in terms of quantity, scale, entry fields and competitiveness. They have become the main driving force for national economic development. At present, the non-public economy plays a fundamental role in stabilizing growth, promoting innovation, increasing employment and improving people's livelihood. From the perspective of its position in the national economy, it contributes more than 50% of tax revenue, more than 60% of GDP, more than 70% of technological innovation, more than 80% of urban employment and more than 90% of the number of market entities. Hence, it is clear that the non-public economy is a fundamental force for achieving sustainable development and enhancing international competitiveness.

Fifth, China has opened up at a deeper level to the outside world, and its export-oriented economy has continued to develop. China has achieved a historic turn from a closed and semi-closed nation to an all-round opening up nation. With the deepening of China's economic system reform, China has made connections between domestic and foreign markets, promoted the development of the export-oriented economy, accelerated its participation in the process of economic globalization, so the scale of foreign trade was expanded, the absorption of foreign investment steadily increased, and foreign economic cooperation maintained a favorable development trend. After reform and opening up, especially after China's accession to the WTO in 2001, China's foreign trade has developed rapidly. In 2009, China became the largest exporter and the 2nd largest importer of global trade in goods. In 2013, it surpassed USA to become the largest nation in global trade in goods. At the same time, China's overseas investment cooperation developed rapidly, and its global resource allocation capacity has been significantly enhanced. In 2002, the 16th National Congress of CPC put forward the strategy of "going global", and China's outward foreign direct investment (OFDI) entered a stage of rapid development. Since the 18th National Congress of CPC, China has implemented a new round of all-round opening up strategy, vigorously promoted the construction of the "Belt and Road Initiative", and the stock of the OFDI has repeatedly hit a record high. According to the "World Investment Report" 2020 released by the United Nations Conference on Trade and Development (UNCTAD), China ranked second and third in the world in terms of OFDI flows and stocks in 2019. Moreover, since October 1, 2016, the RMB has been officially included in the new currency basket of the International Monetary Fund (IMF) Special Drawing Rights (SDR), thus gaining the status of a major international currency. With the gradual enhancement of China's economic strength and the continuous improvement of its right of speech in the global market, its import and export trade and foreign investment will have an increasing impact on the growth of global trade, and gradually become an important force for global economic re-balancing.

5.2 Adjustment of Economic Structure and Transformation of Growth Pattern

The economic structure is the proportion and relationship that reflect the characteristics of an economy as a whole in time and space. The rapid growth of one or more new production departments is a powerful and core engine for economic structural transformation, since these production sectors with new production functions emit various diffusion effects that lead to a leap in economic growth. In this process, new production departments are born as old ones recede. Economic structure and economic growth are reciprocal causation with interaction effect and close connection. Different forms of the economic structure reflect different patterns of economic growth, and the transformation of economic growth pattern is largely determined by the adjustment of economic structure.

In terms of overall development, the industrial structure in China continues to optimize and upgrade, and the development of the three industries is more coordinated. The old China was a backward agricultural nation with a very weak industrial base and mainly light industry. When China completed the task of national economic recovery in 1952, the added-value of the primary industry accounted for 50.5% of GDP, while that of the secondary and tertiary industries accounted for only 20.8% and 28.7% of GDP respectively. Since the reform and opening up, the socialist market economy system has been gradually established, industrial restructuring has continued to be deepened, the foundation of agriculture has been consolidated and strengthened, and the development level of the industrial and service sectors has been continuously improved. In 2011, the proportion of employment in the tertiary industry increased to 35.7%, surpassing the primary industry for the first time to become the industry with the largest proportion of employment. In 2012, the added-value of the tertiary industry accounted for 45.5%, surpassing the secondary industry for the first time to become the largest industry driving national economic growth. Since the 18th National Congress of the CPC, China has accelerated economic restructuring, transformation and upgrading, deepened supply-side structural reform, steadily improved agricultural modernization, and improved its industrial system. At 2019, China became the only nation in the world with all the industrial categories listed in the UN Industrial Classification Catalogue. The service sector is on the ascendant, and the three industries are more coordinated. In 2020, the proportion of added-value of the primary, secondary and tertiary industries were 7.7%, 37.8% and 54.5%, respectively. The structure of the three industries is becoming increasingly improved, and the tertiary industry is gradually taking the dominant position.

Since 1949, the economic structure in China has undergone two important upgrades. The first is the structural transformation and upgrading of the agricultural economy to the industrial economy, and the second is the industrial economy to the service economy. The first economic structural transformation and upgrading was characterized by a decline in the proportion of agriculture and an increase in industrial and service sectors, and the industrial economy gradually became the leading industry of the economy. The main feature of this stage is that the economic growth and the rapid structural changes interact and reinforce each other. The economy in the process of industrialization transformation was in the stage of rapid growth. Economic growth was not only manifested by the input growth effect of production factors such as labor and capital, but also by the growth effect of the change in demand and supply structures. Since the First Five-Year Plan, China has promoted industrialization under the condition of a highly centralized planned economy, giving priority to the development of heavy industry in its development strategy. This industrialization has changed the backward situation of China in a relatively short period of time and achieved a rapid upgrading of the industrialization level. In 1978, the proportion structure of the three industries in China changed to 27.7%, 47.7% and 24.6%, respectively. China has formed a modernized industrial system with a sound structure and a full package of categories after more than 70 years of industrialization since 1949. In terms of the industrialization process, the industrialization level in China has entered a post-industrialism era. Its industrialization composite index was 84 in 2015 and 93 in 2020. In other words, China has completed the process of industrialization, and the development pattern that relies on industrial transformation to release "industrialization dividends" and promote economic growth was difficult to maintain. After entering the post-industrialism era, technological progress becomes the main form of labor productivity and total factor productivity improvement, since the marginal effect of the "technology dividend" brought by the introduction and absorption of technology has reduced.

The second economic structural transformation and upgrading was characterized by a decline in the proportion of both agriculture and industry, a continuous increase in the service industry, and the service industry becoming the leading industry of the economy. From the perspective of power transformation, with the disappearance of "demographic dividends" and the decline of return on investment, the driving force of economic growth relies more on technological innovation and promotes economic growth by improving total factor productivity. At this stage, China's industry development must shift from capital-driven to knowledge-driven. According to international experiences, when becoming a middle and high-income country, the high-speed growth economies must have experienced a significant slowdown and shift of economic development gear. After experiencing a period of high-speed growth, the economic development in China will also appear temporary new characteristics, from high-speed growth into a new normal of medium-high growth. Chinese economy has undergone structural deceleration since 2009. From the perspective of the industrialization process, the operation characteristics and upgrading tasks of Chinese economy at this stage were consistent with that of entering the post-industrialism era. In fact, China's industrialization process entered the post-industrialism era around 2011.

Against the backdrop of the economic new normal, the focus of industrial growth in China changed from the pursuit of rapid growth to the pursuit of quality improvement, which was embodied in improving the supply quality of the real economy through supply-side structural reform, actively adapting to the new round of scientific and technological revolution and industrial change trend, vigorously cultivating emerging industries and using new technologies to transforming traditional industries. First, in terms of agricultural development, the distribution of agricultural production was further optimized, the establishment of a modern agricultural industrial, production and management system was accelerated, the grain output was maintained and increased in major grain-producing areas, and new types of agricultural production and management entities and service entities emerged rapidly. Second, in terms of industrial development, the industrial structure continued to optimize and upgrade, and the overall industrial structure presented a trend of transformation and upgrading from resource- and capital-intensive oriented to technology-intensive oriented. In the internal structure of the manufacturing industry, positive progress was made in supply-side structural reform. On the one hand, the work of actively phasing out outdated production capacity was being comprehensively and deeply promoted. On the other hand, the equipment and high-tech manufacturing industries were developing rapidly. Third, in terms of the development in the service industry, the integration of the traditional service industry and the Internet accelerated, the modern service industry developed vigorously, new business forms emerged constantly, and the service industry developed rapidly.

Despite the above achievements in the industrial development of China at this stage, as mentioned above, the economic development in China has entered a completely new stage, which is both the new normal of the economy and post-industrialism era. At a crucial stage of transforming the growth pattern and replacing old growth drivers with new ones, Chinese economy still faces new features in its development, such as an unreasonable supply-side industrial structure, insufficient innovation capacity, weak consumer demand from demand-side, insufficient investment impetus, and grim foreign trade. Changing the pattern of economic development is the basic law to adapt to the succession of development stage and is a long-term mechanism to promote sustainable economic development. By injecting new vitality into traditional industries and new momentum into economic growth, promoting total factor productivity, unleash future economic growth potential and expanding economic development space.

5.3 Social Development in China since Reform and Opening Up

Economic development does not only include indicators of economic growth. We also need to look at China's economic development from the perspective of social welfare. Chinese-style modernization is following a path of civilized development featuring increased production, a prosperous life and a sound ecological environment.

First of all, the living standards and quality of people's have been greatly improved, and a historic leap has been made from inadequate food and clothing to a well-off society in an all-round way. The nation was weak and its people were poor when the CPC was born.

After the founding of New China, the CPC led its people to quickly restore production in the face of the devastation by the war. After more than 40 years of economic system reform since the reform and opening up, the social economy has achieved rapid and stable development, people's income has steadily increased, and people's living standards have been greatly improved. From the perspective of per capita GDP, the Chinese per capita GDP was 381 yuan in 1978, and China was a typical low-income nation in the world at that time. By 2021, China's per capita GDP has reached 81 000 yuan (over 11 000 USD), making China one of the upper middle-income countries. The per capita disposable income of urban and rural residents in China has been on the rise with the continuous economic growth, increasing from 171 yuan in 1978 to 32 189 yuan in 2020. That of urban residents has increased even more dramatically, from 343 yuan in 1978 to 43 834 yuan in 2020.

Second, rising incomes drive further growth in consumption. Residents' consumption level has been continuously raised, and the quality of people's lives has been greatly improved. Before the founding of New China, the nation was plagued by wars and social turmoil for a long time. People were displaced and it was difficult to meet their basic needs of food and clothing. Since the founding of New China, the income of Chinese residents has steadily increased, and consumption has also constantly improved along with the rapid development of the economy. After the reform and opening up, Chinese residents' consumption level has further improved, the scale of consumption continues to expand, and the basic role of consumption in economic development has been strengthened. China is now the second largest consumer market in the world, and the final consumption expenditure has been the primary driving force for Chinese economic growth for six consecutive years since 2013. In 2020, the final consumption expenditure reached 55.8 trillion yuan, of which the national consumption expenditure was 38.4 trillion yuan. At the same time, the consumption structure of Chinese residents was also constantly upgrading. In terms of the proportion of residents' food consumption in total consumption, the Engel's coefficient has been declining. From 1978 to 1992, the Engel's coefficient was above 50% for Chinese urban residents and above 54% for rural residents. By 2020, it had dropped to 29.2% for urban residents and 32.7% for rural residents (see Table 5-1).

Table 5-1　Per capita disposable income and Engel's coefficient of urban and rural residents in China of partial years from 1978 to 2020

Year	The per capita disposable income of urban residents (yuan)	The per capita disposable income of rural residents (yuan)	Engel's coefficient for urban residents (%)	Engel's coefficient for rural residents (%)
1978	343	134	57.5	67.7
1985	739	398	53.3	57.8
1989	1 374	602	54.5	54.8
1992	2 027	784	52.9	57.5

Continued

Year	The per capita disposable income of urban residents(yuan)	The per capita disposable income of rural residents(yuan)	Engel's coefficient for urban residents(%)	Engel's coefficient for rural residents(%)
1995	4 283	1 578	49.9	58.6
1998	5 418	2 171	44.2	53.2
2001	6 824	2 407	37.0	46.7
2004	9 335	3 027	35.8	45.3
2014	28 844	10 489	30.0	33.6
2015	31 195	11 422	29.7	33.0
2016	33 616	12 363	29.3	32.2
2017	36 396	13 432	28.6	31.2
2018	39 251	14 617	27.7	30.1
2019	42 359	16 021	27.6	30
2020	43 834	17 131	29.2	32.7

Source: National Bureau of Statistics of the People's Republic of China

Third, the income gap between urban and rural areas has narrowed significantly, and major achievements have been made in the battle against poverty. Since the founding of New China, the CPC has led its people in continuously waging a battle against poverty. Based on the efforts since the reform and opening up, the nation has successfully blazed a path of poverty alleviation and development with Chinese characteristics, lifting over 700 million rural people out of poverty and laying a solid foundation for building a moderately prosperous society in all respects. Athar Hussain, a British scholar, once pointed out that hundreds of millions of people in rural China have lifted themselves out of poverty and become self-sufficient in food. This is a marvelous event in the history of human development and a great achievement in improving human rights. The Political Bureau of the Central Committee of the CPC deliberated and issued the "Decision on Winning the Battle Against Poverty" in 2015. Policies for rural revitalization and targeted poverty alleviation have been introduced since the 18th National Congress of the CPC. The real per capita disposable income of rural residents has grown faster than that of urban residents for consecutive years, and poverty alleviation has been significantly accelerated. On November 23, 2020, Guizhou announced that the last 9 deeply impoverished counties would withdraw from the impoverished county sequence. This not only marks the completion of poverty alleviation in the 66 impoverished counties in Guizhou, but also marks an overall victory in the tough battle against poverty in China. By the current standard, 98.99 million rural people and 832 impoverished counties have been lifted out of poverty, and 128 000 impoverished villages have been withdrawn from the sequence. China has completed the arduous task of eliminating absolute poverty with region-wide poverty alleviation and created another miracle that will be remembered in history.

Fourth, the quality of employment improves significantly. In 2020, over 11.86 million new urban jobs were created annually, the average surveyed urban unemployment rate nationwide was 5.6%, and the employment structure continued to improve. Education develops vigorously. According to the main results of National Education Statistics in 2021, the average length of schooling for the working-age population reaches 10.9 years, making China move forward from a big nation in human resources to a strong nation in human resources.

Fifth, equal access to basic medical and public services has been improved in both urban and rural areas. Chinese average life expectancy ranks among the highest among middle- and high-income countries, and a public service system for sports and fitness has been established. Social security benefits the entire people. China has established the world's largest social security system, with basic medical insurance covering more than 1.3 billion people and basic old-age insurance covering nearly 1 billion people during the 13th Five-Year plan period.

Sixth, significant achievements have been made in science and technology. The science and technology in China have undergone historic, holistic and structural changes, with the successful development of the deep submersible vehicle "Deep-Sea Warrior" and Mars probe "Tianwen 1", and breakthroughs in quantum computing capabilities. World-class scientific and technological achievements in basic research and strategic high-tech fields continue to emerge, and innovation capacity continues to improve. Scientific and technological innovation becomes the primary driving force behind high-quality economic development and improvement of people's lives. China has continuously increased investment in science and technology and stepped up the reform of scientific and technological systems since the reform and opening up. In 2020, the total research and development expenditure reached 2.44 trillion yuan, accounting for 2.4% of GDP. According to the World Intellectual Property Organization(WIPO), China ranked 14th in the Global Innovation Index in 2020, a decisive achievement in constructing an innovative country. In recent years, China has made major achievements in manned space flight, lunar exploration programs, quantum science, deep-sea exploration, supercomputing, satellite navigation and other fields. High-tech industries such as high-speed railways, 5G mobile communications and new energy have entered the forefront of the world.

Seventh, great progress has been made in public cultural undertakings. Over the past 40 years and more of the reform and opening up, under the firm leadership of the CPC Central Committee, all regions and sectors have adhered to the direction of advanced socialist culture, deepened reform of the cultural system, and established and improved a modern cultural market system and a public cultural service system. The cultural industry developed rapidly, cultural undertakings benefit the people, and steady progress was made in building China into a strong cultural nation. Remarkable achievements were made in cultural reform and development. Grassroots public cultural facilities were constantly improved, the distribution of cultural investment became more rational, the proportion of added-value of the cultural industry to GDP increased year by year, people's cultural consumption level continued to rise, and foreign cultural trade grew strongly, so China's international cultural influences have been increasingly strengthened. The construction of the modern public cultural service system in China has entered a fast lane since the 18th National Congress of the CPC, with the standardization and equalization characteristics continuously highlighted. According to data released by the National Bureau of Statistics of the People's Republic of China, by the end of 2021, 99.5% of the population was covered by radio programs and 99.7% by TV programs; 3 217 public libraries, 3 317 cultural centers and 3 671 museums were distributed across the country, more than 90% of museums are now free of charge, making them "barrier-free and no threshold".

5.4 Main Experience and Enlightenment of China's Economic and Social Development since the Reform and Opening Up

It is of great significance to sum up the experience of economic system reform in the past 40 more years and conclude the key factors of creating the "China Miracle" for better promoting economic system reform and the sound and rapid development of national economy. The reform and opening up in China is unprecedented. With bold explorations and steady progress, we have not only achieved major changes in the economic system and tremendous development in the economic society, but also formed a rich understanding of the socialist market economy and accumulated important experience in constructing a socialist market economy. Mainly includes follows.

The first one is to adhere to the basic state policy of reform and opening up. First of all, the reform and opening up is a powerful driving force for the economic system reform. In the course of establishing and improving the market economic system, we can easily encounter contradictions and problems, and we rely on deepening reform to provide a strong driving force for solving both development and institutional problems. Secondly, opening up to the outside world has provided an external impetus for the establishment of China's economic system. Highly developed international market economic relations and fierce international market competition have become the external driving force for domestic reform of economic system and strengthening competition mechanism, and promoted the development of China's market economy. After an open economy connected to the international market, it provided international standards for the cultivation and improvement of all kinds of markets, and supplied an external impetus for accelerating the establishment of corresponding markets in China. In addition, opening up to the outside world has opened up the international market, provided a platform for introducing foreign investment, learning advanced technology and management experience, and laid a foundation for further deepening the economic system reform.

The second one is to adhere to the basic policy of taking economic development as the central task. China has adhered to that basic policy over the past 40 more years of reform and opening up, which has laid the foundation for the establishment of the market economic system. First of all, adhering to the economic development as the central task for the implementation of economic system reform provided the ideological basis. Taking economic development as the central task requires that China must reform the backward productive relations which have constrained the development of productive forces, and constantly emancipate and develop productivity. Thus, this requires that China must reform the backward economic system so that it can adapt to the development of the productivity. Secondly, adhering to the economic development as the central task for the implementation of economic system reform provided an environmental basis. Taking economic development as the central task requires the government to provide all-round services and constantly explore new ways and models for economic reform and development. All these can provide a favorable environment for economic system reform.

The third one is to constantly innovate reform theories and guide reform practice with scientific theories. Reform is, first of all, a revolution in traditional thoughts and theories. We must emancipate people's minds through theoretical innovation and unify their understanding, so as to provide an ideological guarantee for the practice of the reform and opening up. The practice of reform has proved that each important practice of reform is guided by the constant development and innovation of thoughts and theories. Each innovation of thoughts and theories has brought about a breakthrough in the practice of reform. The practice of reform cannot be successful without correct reform theories.

The fourth one is easy at first and difficult later, with a step-by-step approach and the organic combination of key breakthroughs and overall progress. Due to the complexity of reform and the special difficulty of reform undertaken in China, the government adopted the overall strategy of gradual reform, which is based on the reality, easy at first and difficult later, from the shallower to the deeper, and a step-by-step approach, so as to make key breakthroughs in some key links to drive the comprehensive reform. The strategy of progressive reform and the reform mode of promoting on the whole and making breakthroughs in key areas have not only ensured the necessary intensity, speed and continuity of reform, but also enabled the reform to gradually adapt to the social bearing capacity and prevented major social unrest. In other words, China's progressive reform is characterized by minimizing the cost of policy implementation rather than maximizing economic efficiency, minimizing the political resistance to market economic reform, gradually adapting to the changing economic environment, and gradually promoting reform in a pilot method in the order of reform from easy to difficult.

The fifth one is to adhere to the principle of combining the reform, development and stability. China established the basic principle that reform is the driving force, development is the goal and stability is the prerequisite at the very beginning of reform. In the process of reform, the nation has always combined the intensity of reform, the speed of development and the affordability of society, taken continuous improvement of the people's lives as an important link in addressing the relationship between reform, development and stability, promoted reform and development in the midst of social stability, and promoted social stability through reform and development. The practice of China's successful reform proved the importance of adhering to the principle of combining reform, development and stability, which are mutually reinforcing to promote the implementation of China's economic system reform.

In addition, China have adopted other effective measures in economic system reform. For example, China fully respected the pioneering spirits of the people and always safeguarded their interests; kept abreast of changes in the social and economic environment and conditions and adjusted reform measures flexibly; treated the previous system based on science, and strove to enhance the advantages of the new system; combined economic system reform with political, scientific, technological, educational and cultural system reforms to achieve substantive breakthroughs; paid attention to the overall support and coordination of the economic system reform in the focus on some new individual reforms, etc.

6 Opening Up to the Outside World and International Trade of China

The theory of opening up to the outside world is an important part of Deng Xiaoping Theory. Opening up to the outside world is China's historical choice under economic globalization and is an objective requirement for the socialization of production and the internationalization of economic life. It is the inevitable result of the international division of production process and the development of international market economy. The world economy is more integrated, and more and more countries are interdependent on each other more closely when they participate in the international division of production process and integrate into the world economic system. Production factors of any country cannot meet all the needs of its own economic development under economic globalization, so they must actively participate in the international division of labor and trade to meet their needs.

China's productivity was low with a severe capital shortage at the beginning of the opening up to the outside world. To achieve this transformation requires a large number of capital, relying on domestic capital accumulation and investment is far from enough. Therefore, China must open up to the outside world, and actively introduce foreign capital to make up the capital factor shortage. Throughout history, countries with backward economies and technology can quickly catch up with or even surpass developed countries in a relatively short time, all of which are the result of actively introducing foreign advanced technology and daring and being good at innovation. Foreign advanced management experience can be better drawn and learned through opening up to the outside world. Learning from and introducing foreign advanced economic management methods and business modes is also an important part of opening up to the outside world.

Market economy is an open economy, which is opposite to closed economy. If a nation wants to enjoy the benefits brought by international collaboration, it must participate in international exchange and cooperation. During the construction of the socialist market economy, China shall also open up to the outside world, develop economic and trade relations with other countries, and become an important part of the world market economy. Opening up to the outside world to make full use of domestic and foreign resources through the international market is the inherent requirement of the way of resource allocation in market economy and the inevitable choice to build a socialist market economy.

6.1 Basic Connotation for the Policy of Opening Up to the Outside World

6.1.1 Interpretations of Opening Up to the Outside World

"Opening up to the outside world" is a basic state policy of China. This state policy has two interpretations. One is that China takes the initiative to expand economic exchanges with other countries and regions. The other is that China shall relax its internal policies, lift restrictions, stop adopting protective policies to block the domestic market, and develop an open economy. On the basis of adhering to the socialist system, China is actively developing economic and trade exchanges with other countries or regions, as well as cooperation and exchanges of science, technology, culture and education to promote the development of socialist material civilization and spiritual civilization with the policy of opening up to the outside world in accordance with the principles of independence and self-reliance, equality and mutual benefit, and the objective requirements of production internationalization, capital internationalization, and further deepening of the international division of labor and the development of the socialist market economy. China's opening up to the outside world is all-dimensional and for the whole world. It presents an all-round cooperation with other countries and regions in the fields of trade, technology, economy and science on the principle of equality and mutual benefit.

6.1.2 Contents of Opening Up to the Outside World

China has adopted various policies with various aspects related to opening up to the outside world over the past 40 more years. The contents of opening up to the outside world also presented dynamic changes. The main contents of China's opening up to the outside world at present can be summarized in the following 6 aspects.

First, promoting system reform and supporting opening up to the outside world. Promoting opening up cannot stay out of the sound system guarantee. The system reform involved in opening up covers the rural economy, financial system, ownership structure and foreign trade system. Reform of system and mechanism can make the system more effective, reduce transaction costs, deepen opening up and contribute to the formation of a unified market.

Second, actively introducing advanced technology and equipments, especially those that are conducive to technological transformation for enterprises. Attracting advanced science and technology is one of the original intentions of China's opening up and a key factor fueling its rapid economic growth.

Third, promoting opening up in all areas by drawing upon the experience gained on key points. China follows the concept of "crossing the river by feeling the stones" and "prior to carry and try" at home to summarize the relevant experience and then gradually promote to the whole region, so as to fully expand the domestic and foreign markets. From the establishment of special economic zones to the opening up of coastal cities, border cities, cities along rivers, provincial capitals, and establishment of economic and technological development zones, high-tech industrial parks and bonded areas, China promotes the opening up of the inland through the beforehand development of coastal cities and regions, thus realizing the breadth and depth of China's opening up.

Fourth, actively participating in regional trade and financial cooperation. China's opening up on the international stage is mainly reflected in 3 aspects: participated in Asia-Pacific regional cooperation actively; established the ASEAN-China Free Trade Area; actively promoted the construction of the "Belt and Road".

Fifth, vigorously developing foreign trade. Foreign trade is the exchange of goods and services between countries or regions. Foreign trade has been in an important strategic position in China's national economy since its opening up to the outside world in 1978. It is the foundation of other forms of opening up and the central link in carrying out foreign economic exchanges. The effects of foreign trade on China's national economy are as follows: making up for the shortage of domestic resources and optimizing resource allocation; making use of international division of labor to obtain relative benefits; increasing foreign exchange earnings, the income of domestic residents and employment opportunities.

Sixth, adhering to opening up and steadily promoting the internationalization of RMB. China first realized the convertibility of RMB under the current account in 1996. Then in 2014, RMB internationalization project was officially started, and the convertibility of the capital account was gradually lifted. With the officially inclusion of RMB in the IMF's SDR basket in 2016 and its increasing weight, the internationalization of RMB has reached a new level on its way to becoming an international currency.

6.1.3 The Principles of Opening Up to the Outside World

6.1.3.1 Independence and Self-Reliance

China always adheres to the principle of independence and self-reliance in opening up and developing economic relations with other countries. Independence does not mean self-seclusion, nor does self-reliance mean blind rejection of foreign things. Science and technology are the wealth jointly created by mankind. On the basis of self-reliance, boldly implementing opening up and making free use of all the advanced science and technology available to China from abroad, and rapidly raising China's scientific and technological level are essential to accelerating China's modernization. As Deng Xiaoping said: "Technical problems are science, production management is science. They are useful in any society for any country. We learn advanced technology, science, and management in the service of socialism, but these things themselves have no class character." It is China's unswerving policy to achieve opening up based on self-reliance as a mainstay and seeking foreign aid as a supplement.

6.1.3.2 Equality and Mutual Benefit

The meaning of the principle of equality and mutual benefit is as below. The so-called equality means that countries, regardless of their size or strength, political system or level of economic development, shall respect each other's sovereignty and aspirations in trade relations and do not claim any special privilege. The so-called mutual benefit means that both sides shall exchange based on what they need and the possibilities in trade to promote each other's economic development. Foreign trade shall not be used as a tool to control and plunder other countries.

6.2 The Process of China's Opening Up to the Outside World

The State Council and the CPC Central Committee have confirmed the opening up strategy by region, stage and level according to Deng Xiaoping's opening up thoughts. China's opening up can be divided into 4 stages throughout the 40 more year's history of China's reform and opening up.

6.2.1 Stage of Broad Opening Up(1978-1992)

In the early days of opening up to the outside world, the CPC Central Committee and the State Council decided on the economic development strategy of "focusing on opening up the coastal areas and gradually moving to the inland". According to this strategy, China's opening up can be divided into 4 levels: special economic zones, coastal port cities, coastal economic zones and cities along the river, inland cities and border cities.

6.2.1.1 Establishment of Special Economic Zones

The establishment of special economic zones is a breakthrough and pioneering measure for China's opening up. The special economic zones, as the first pilot of China's opening up, paved the way for the opening up and prepared for a more comprehensive and deeper opening up. In May 1980, the CPC Central Committee decided to set aside certain areas in Shenzhen, Zhuhai, Shantou and Xiamen to pilot the special economic zones. In April 1983, the CPC Central Committee and the State Council approved the "Summary of Discussion on Accelerating the Development and Construction of Hainan Island", and decided to apply the preferential policy of special economic zones to Hainan. The First Session of the Seventh National People's Congress in April 1988 formally approved the establishment of Hainan Province and Hainan Special Economic Zone, and since then Hainan Island has become the largest special economic zone in China. The establishment of special economic zones was the first step in China's opening up. Deng Xiaoping described the special economic zones as "a window, a window of technology, a window of management, a window of knowledge, and a window of the opening up policy."

6.2.1.2 Opening Up of Coastal Port Cities

Opening up coastal port cities is the second step of China's opening up. In May 1984, the CPC Central Committee and the State Council approved the "Minutes of the Symposium on Some Coastal Cities", and decided to further open coastal port cities in China, from north to south, including Dalian, Qinhuangdao, Tianjin, Yantai, Qingdao, Lianyungang, Nantong, Shanghai, Ningbo, Wenzhou, Fuzhou, Guangzhou, Zhanjiang and Beihai, a total of 14 coastal port cities.

6.2.1.3 Establishment of Coastal Economic Open Zones

In February 1985, the CPC Central Committee and the State Council approved the "Minutes of the Symposium on the Yangtze River Delta, the Pearl River Delta and the Xiamen-Zhangzhou-Quanzhou Triangle in Southern Fujian", which designated the Yangtze River Delta, the Pearl River Delta, the Xiamen-Zhangzhou-Quanzhou Triangle as coastal economic open zones, and pointed out that this was a strategically important layout for China to revitalize the economy at home and opening up to the outside world. At the beginning of 1988, the CPC Central Committee decided to open up the Liaodong Peninsula and the Shandong Peninsula to the outside world, joining Dalian, Qinhuangdao, Tianjin, Yantai and Qingdao, which had already opened up to the outside world, to form the Circum-Bohai Sea Open Zone. The CPC Central Committee also proposed to form an integrated production structure of trade-industry-agriculture in these open economic zones.

6.2.1.4 Gradual Opening Up of the Cities Along the River, Inland Cities and Border Cities

Since the 1990s, China's opening up has gradually extended from the coastal areas to the cities along the river, inland cities and border cities. In June 1992, the CPC Central Committee and the State Council decided to open 5 cities along the Yangtze River: Wuhu, Jiujiang, Yueyang, Wuhan and Chongqing. Opening up along the Yangtze River has greatly promoted the rapid economic development of the whole Yangtze River basin region and the formation of a new pattern of all-round opening up in China. Soon after, the CPC Central Committee and the State Council approved a total of 17 provincial capitals as inland open cities. Meanwhile, China also gradually opened a large number of border cities. The opening up of cities along the river, inland cities and border cities was the fourth step in China's opening up.

By 1992, after years of practice in opening up, continuous summing up of experience and improving policies, China's opening up advanced from the south to the north and from the east to the west. It has formed a pattern of opening up to the outside world of "special economic zones—coastal open cities—coastal economic open zones—open cities along river, inland cities and border cities". At that time, China's opening up to the outside world gradually entered the deep stage.

6.2.2 Stage of Deep Opening Up(1992-2001)

Under the background of Deng Xiaoping's South Tour Speeches and the 14th National Congress of the CPC, which established the reform goal of socialist market economy system, the reform and opening up deepened comprehensively, the degree of China's opening up continued to improve, the influence of export-oriented economy on the national economy increasingly enhanced, the opening up was carried out throughout the nation, and an all-round pattern of opening up was formed. Table 6-1 shows the process of China's opening up. At the same time, China actively integrated with the rest of the world, actively deepened the reform of its domestic and foreign trading systems, and accelerated the opening up of its domestic market and related industries. Bonded areas, export processing zones and other special customs supervision areas have been established successively. Throughout the 1990s, China made the adjustment of the international industry, especially the information technology industry. China took the development of Pudong as a new measure, vigorously introduced overseas direct investment, actively participated in the restructuring of global industrial chain, and promoted the upgrading of the domestic industrial structure.

Table 6-1 Process of China's opening up

Level of Opening Up	Time of Opening Up	Territorial Scope
Special economic zone	1980 1988	Shenzhen, Zhuhai, Xiamen, Shantou Hainan Province
Coastal port opening cities	1984	Dalian, Qinhuangdao, Tianjin, Yantai, Qingdao, Lianyungang, Nantong, Shanghai, Ningbo, Wenzhou, Fuzhou, Guangzhou, Zhanjiang, Beihai
Coastal economic open zones	1985 1988	Yangtze River Delta, Pearl River Delta, the Xiamen-Zhangzhou-Quanzhou Triangle in Southern Fujian Shandong Peninsula, Liaodong Peninsula
Economic and technological development zone	1990	Pudong, Shanghai
Cities and towns of land border	1992	Hunchun, Suifenhe, Manzhouli, Heihe, Erenhot, Yining, Tacheng, Bole, Ruili, Wanding, Hekou, Pingxiang, Dongxing
Open cities along the Yangtze River	1992	Chongqing, Yueyang, Wuhan, Jiujiang, Wuhu and other port cities along the Yangtze River

Continued

Level of Opening Up	Time of Opening Up	Territorial Scope
Inland provincial cities	1992	Taiyuan, Hefei, Nanchang, Zhengzhou, Changsha, Chengdu, Guizhou, Xi'an, Lanzhou, Xining, and Yinchuan, Kunming, Urumqi, Nanning, Harbin, Changchun, Hohhot, and Shijiazhuang
Further opening up the western region to the outside world	1999	Sichuan, Guizhou, Yunnan, Tibet, Shaanxi, Gansu, Ningxia, Qinghai, Xinjiang, Inner Mongolia, Guangxi, Chongqing

6.2.3 Stage of an All-Round Opening Up(2001-2012)

China officially joined the WTO in 2001, marking a new stage in its opening up. Since then, China has made full use of the complete legal rules and open market system under the WTO framework, vigorously promoted the reform of its external economic system, and formed an external economic system in line with international practices, laying the foundation for China to become a world manufacturing power and the world's second largest economy.

Against the backdrop of an increasing trend of world economic integration, not only will Chinese market be fully opened up, enabling international capital and commodities to enter Chinese market on a larger scale, but also Chinese capital will enter the international market at a faster speed, and more enterprises will engage in transnational production and operation. "Bringing in" and "going global" will become the two wheels of China's opening up, vigorously promoting a further deepened development of China's opening up.

6.2.4 The Formation of a New Pattern for All-Round Opening Up (After 2012)

The 18th National Congress of the CPC ushered in a new historical stage of China's opening up. In response to the needs of domestic economic transformation and institutional upgrading, a series of major strategic thoughts on economic diplomacy and international cooperation have been put forward. China's open economy entered a new stage, with a new layout taking shape and a new system being improved. In 2017, the report of the 19th National Congress of the CPC clearly pointed out that socialism with Chinese characteristics had entered a new era, made it clear that "promoting the formation of a new pattern of all-round opening up", and stressed once again that "China will not close its door to the world", marking the advent of a new era of China's opening up.

A key change during this period is that the investment focus in China has changed from "bringing in" to the combination of "bringing in" and "going global". In fact, it is the only way to upgrade an open economy from a trading power to an investment power, from commodity export to capital export, and from one-way use of foreign investment to two-way use of investment. When the economy develops to a certain extent, it is necessary to integrate global resources through foreign investment and realize the most reasonable allocation of resources. The Belt and Road Initiative put forward in 2013 has brought new opportunities for China's opening up and foreign investment. Another key change is China's more active participation in global governance and efforts to improve the global governance system. From the Boao Forum for Asia, the Conference on Interaction and Confidence Building Measures in Asia(CICA) and the Summit of the Shanghai Cooperation Organization to the Belt and Road Forum for International Cooperation, China has been sparing no effort to provide Chinese governance and trade ideas and promote economic and cultural exchanges among countries around the world. From the Belt and Road Initiative to the establishment of the Asian Infrastructure Investment Bank and the Silk Road Fund, and to building "a community with a shared future for mankind", various kinds of Chinese governance ideas have provided new ideas and directions for further improvement of the global governance system.

China has formed an all-dimensional, multi-level and wide-ranging pattern of opening up after more than 40 years of opening up. By March 2023, China has established diplomatic relations with 182 countries and signed 19 free trade zone agreements, involving 26 countries and regions. On November 15, 2020, all the 10 countries of Association of Southeast Asian Nations(ASEAN) and China, Japan, South Korea, Australia and New Zealand, 15 Asia-Pacific countries officially signed the "Regional Comprehensive Economic Partnership" (RCEP) agreement, marking the launch of a free trade area with the largest population, the largest trade scale and the greatest potential for development in the world. On June 2, 2023, the RCEP agreement took effect for the 15 member countries, the world's largest free trade zone will enter a new stage of full implementation. On December 30, 2020, the "China-EU Comprehensive Agreement on Investment" (CAI) was successfully signed after 7 years of negotiations. The signing of the CAI is a demonstration of China's commitment to deepening and high-quality opening up.

At the level of opening up, China has focused on the construction of pilot free trade zones and pilot free trade ports in recent years. In 2013, China established the China (Shanghai) Pilot Free Trade Zone for the first time, marking the beginning of the construction of free trade zones. As of October 2022, China has approved the construction of 21 pilot free trade zones. On April 13, 2018, China supported the construction of a pilot free trade zone across the island of Hainan and explored the establishment of a Hainan Free Trade Port. Figure 6-1 is a photo of Hainan Free Trade Port. The development of free trade ports is extremely beneficial to China's foreign trade. Implementing a more proactive

Figure 6-1　Hainan Free Trade Port

opening up strategy in Hainan and making Hainan an important gateway to the outside world facing the Pacific and Indian Oceans demonstrates China's determination and confidence in opening up.

A broad pattern of opening up means opening up not only in the economic field, but also in services and trade such as insurance, post and telecommunications, as well as in environmental protection, science and technology, medical and health care, sports, culture and education. In terms of economy, China is actively developing foreign trade and strengthening infrastructure construction with countries along the Belt and Road. In strengthening the concrete construction of the Belt and Road, China has contributed many constructive measures to promoting the economic exchanges between China and other countries, such as the construction of the China-Europe freight train and the holding of the China International Import Expo. As an important support to promote the construction of the Belt and Road, China-Europe freight train has become an important means of land transport connecting many countries. The China-Europe freight train is of great significance for promoting cooperation between countries and enhancing economic development and daily exchanges. Figure 6-2 shows the China-Europe freight train from Zhengzhou, China to Helsinki, Finland.

On November 4, 2022, the opening ceremony of the fifth China International Import Expo and the Hongqiao International Economic Forum was held in Shanghai. Figure 6-3 is a photo of the opening ceremony. The China International Import Expo is the world's first import-themed national expo and has been successfully held for six consecutive years. The China International Import Expo transforms exhibits into commodities, exhibitors into investors, and exchange ideas and concepts, and connects China and the world, so it becomes the four major platforms for international procurement, investment promotion, cultural and people-to-people exchanges, and openness and cooperation, and becomes international public goods shared by the whole world.

Figure 6-2   The China-Europe freight train
Photo from Xinhuanet

Figure 6-3   The opening ceremony of the fifth China International Import Expo and the Hongqiao International Economic Forum
Photo from Xinhua News Agency

6.3   Development of China's International Trade

Since the reform and opening up in 1978, China's foreign trade system has been continuously reformed and upgraded, and the degree of opening up to the outside world has been continuously expanded. Since 1978, China's foreign trade, which is the most important part of China's opening up, has experienced qualitative growth and achieved leapfrog development. By the end of 2021, China's foreign trade development made remarkable achievements, with the export volume of goods ranking first in the world, the import volume ranking second in the world, and the service trade ranking second in the world for eight consecutive years. China has realized the foreign trade strategy of attaching equal importance to imports and exports. China has gradually built up its own foreign trade network, radiating to neighboring countries along the Belt and Road and establishing foreign free trade zones with many countries. Even in the context of the global financial crisis of 2008, China's foreign trade import and export performance still outperformed other economies.

At the beginning of the reform and opening up in 1978, the total import and export volume of China's trade in goods was only 35.5 billion yuan, which can be converted to 20.6 billion USD during the same period. In 1978, the exports were significantly lower than the imports, China was in a state of trade deficit, and the total import and export volume was less than 1% of that of the world trade in that year. By 2021, the total import and export volume of China's trade in goods was 6 043.87 billion USD, with exports of 3 357.14 billion USD and imports of 2 686.73 billion USD, showing a trade surplus.

With the deepening of the opening up, China's foreign trade has undergone qualitative changes on the whole. China's foreign trade has made considerable progress in terms of trade in goods, trade in services, and cross-border e-commerce.

6.3.1 The Development of China's Trade in Goods

Since the reform and opening up, China has been emphasizing the strategy of "going global", constantly pushing forward the reform and innovation of the trade system, achieving leap-forward development of trade in goods, continuous optimization of trade structure, and continuous expansion of the international market. In 1981, the total import and export volume of China's trade in goods was only 44.02 billion USD, with exports of 22.01 billion USD and imports of 22.02 billion USD. In 2021, the total import and export volume of China's trade in goods amounted to 6 043.87 billion USD, 137 times that of 1981, with exports reaching 3 357.14 billion USD and imports reaching 2 686.73 billion USD. China's trade in goods has grown rapidly and China has now become the world's largest trading nation. As can be seen from Table 6-2, China's trade in goods has been in surplus for a long time. Despite the severe COVID-19 pandemic and international tensions in 2020, China's foreign trade in goods still achieved growth and remained the world's largest.

Table 6-2 Situation of China's imports and exports of goods from 1981 to 2021

Year	Total Imports and Exports of China		Exports of China		Imports of China		Balance (100 million USD)
	Amount (100 million USD)	Year-on-Year rate (%)	Amount (100 million USD)	Year-on-Year rate (%)	Amount (100 million USD)	Year-on-Year rate (%)	
2021	60 438.7	29.8	33 571.4	29.6	26 867.3	30	6 704.1
2020	46 559.13	1.7	25 899.52	3.6	20 659.62	−0.6	5 239.9

Continued

Year	Total Imports and Exports of China		Exports of China		Imports of China		Balance (100 million USD)
	Amount (100 million USD)	Year-on-Year rate (%)	Amount (100 million USD)	Year-on-Year rate (%)	Amount (100 million USD)	Year-on-Year rate (%)	
2019	45 778.91	−1	24 994.82	0.5	20 784.09	−2.7	4 210.73
2018	46 224.44	12.5	24 866.96	9.9	21 357.48	15.8	3 509.48
2017	41 071.38	11.4	22 633.45	7.9	18 437.93	16.1	4 195.52
2016	36 855.57	−6.8	20 976.31	−7.7	15 879.26	−5.5	5 097.05
2015	39 530.33	−8	22 734.68	−2.9	16 795.64	−14.1	5 939.04
2014	43 015.27	3.4	23 422.93	6	19 592.35	0.4	3 830.58
2013	41 589.93	7.5	22 090.04	7.8	19 499.89	7.2	2 590.15
2012	38 671.19	6.2	20 487.14	7.9	18 184.05	4.3	2 303.09
2011	36 418.64	22.5	18 983.81	20.3	17 434.84	24.9	1 548.97
2010	29 740.01	34.7	15 777.54	31.3	13 962.47	38.8	1 815.07
2009	22 075.35	−13.9	12 016.12	−16	10 059.23	−11.2	1 956.89
2008	25 632.55	17.8	14 306.93	17.3	11 325.62	18.5	2 981.31
2007	21 761.75	23.6	12 200.6	25.9	9 561.15	20.8	2 639.45
2006	17 604.38	23.8	9 689.78	27.2	7 914.61	19.9	1 775.17
2005	14 219.06	23.2	7 619.53	28.4	6 599.53	17.6	1 020
2004	11 545.54	35.7	5 933.26	35.4	5 612.29	36	320.97
2003	8 509.88	37.1	4 382.28	34.6	4 127.6	39.8	254.68
2002	6 207.66	21.8	3 255.96	22.4	2 951.7	21.2	304.26
2001	5 096.51	7.5	2 660.98	6.8	2 435.53	8.2	225.45
2000	4 742.97	31.5	2 492.03	27.8	2 250.94	35.8	241.09
1999	3 606.3	11.3	1 949.31	6.1	1 656.99	18.2	292.32
1998	3 239.49	−0.4	1 837.12	0.5	1 402.37	−1.5	434.75
1997	3 251.62	12.2	1 827.92	21	1 423.7	2.5	404.22
1996	2 898.81	3.2	1 510.48	1.5	1 388.33	5.1	122.15
1995	2 808.64	18.7	1 487.8	23	1 320.84	14.2	166.96
1994	2 366.21	20.9	1 210.06	31.9	1 156.15	11.2	53.91
1993	1 957.03	18.2	917.44	8	1 039.59	29	−122.15
1992	1 655.25	22	849.4	18.2	805.85	26.3	43.55
1991	1 356.34	17.5	718.43	15.7	637.91	19.6	80.52
1990	1 154.36	3.4	620.91	18.2	533.45	−9.8	87.46
1989	1 116.78	8.7	525.38	10.6	591.4	7	−66.02
1988	1 027.84	24.4	475.16	20.5	552.68	27.9	−77.52

Continued

Year	Total Imports and Exports of China		Exports of China		Imports of China		Balance (100 million USD)
	Amount (100 million USD)	Year-on-Year rate (%)	Amount (100 million USD)	Year-on-Year rate (%)	Amount (100 million USD)	Year-on-Year rate (%)	
1987	826.53	11.9	394.37	27.5	432.16	0.7	−37.79
1986	738.46	6.1	309.42	13.1	429.04	1.5	−119.62
1985	696.02	30	273.5	4.6	422.52	54.1	−149.02
1984	535.49	22.8	261.39	17.6	274.1	28.1	−12.71
1983	436.16	4.8	222.26	−0.4	213.9	10.9	8.36
1982	416.06	−5.5	223.21	1.4	192.85	−12.4	30.36
1981	440.22	—	220.07	—	220.15	—	−0.08

Source: Ministry of Commerce of the People's Republic of China

Note: The data in this table is from the website of the Ministry of Commerce of the People's Republic of China. The value in the "Balance" column may differ slightly from the value of "Imports of China" minus "Export of China" due to rounding or other reasons. This is to clarify. Similar tables in the following text will not be annotated.

While the scale of China's foreign trade in goods is expanding, the commodity structure is also being optimized. According to the Standard International Trade Class (SITC), import and export products are divided into primary products and industrial products based on the source of the industry sector. In terms of China's total import and export volume, the total import and export volume of primary products is smaller than that of industrial products. Since 1995, China's total import and export volume of industrial products has accounted for more than 80% of its total imports and exports as shown in Figure 6-4.

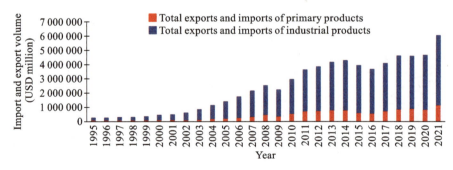

Figure 6-4 Composition of total imports and exports of primary and industrial products from 1995 to 2021
Data from National Bureau of Statistics of the People's Republic of China

Since 1995, with the development of the economy, China's primary products have largely been more imported than exported. As shown in Figure 6-5, in 1995, exports of primary products accounted for 46.8% of the total import and export volume of primary products. By 2015, the proportion dropped to 18%. In 2021, exports of primary products

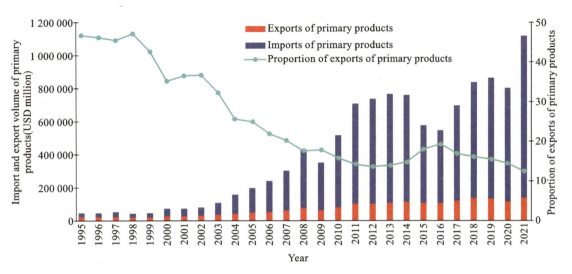

Figure 6-5 Imports and exports of primary products from 1995 to 2021
Data from National Bureau of Statistics of the People's Republic of China

accounted for only 12.5%. The proportion of China's exports of primary products has generally shown a downward trend.

Unlike primary products, the trade of industrial products has always been in a pattern in which exports are more than imports. As shown in Figure 6-6, since 1995, the exports of industrial products have accounted for more than 50% of the total import and export volume of industrial products. In 1995, the exports of industrial products accounted for 54.18% and has basically maintained a slow growth trend. In 2021, the exports of industrial products reached 65.34%.

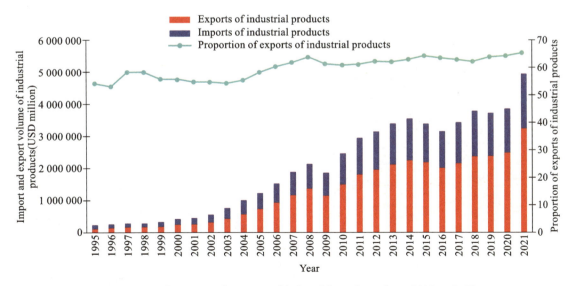

Figure 6-6 Imports and exports of industrial products from 1995 to 2021
Data from National Bureau of Statistics of the People's Republic of China

6.3.2　The Development of China's Trade in Services

Since opening up, China has been actively participating in international trade in services, and the scale of its imports and exports of services has expanded rapidly. China has been the world's second-largest importer and exporter of services for many years. During the period from 1982 to 2001, China's total imports and exports of services increased from 4.7 billion USD to 78.4 billion USD, an increase of more than 15 times, with an average annual growth rate of 16%. Exports rose from 2.7 billion USD to 39.2 billion USD, while imports rose from 2 billion USD to 39.3 billion USD. The scale of China's trade in services has already achieved stepwise growth before joining the WTO. After China's accession to the WTO, all aspects of China's foreign trade have shown rapid growth, and the scale of trade in services has continued to expand. During the period from 2002 to 2021, China's total trade in services increased from 92.8 billion USD to 821.2 billion USD. The overall scale has expanded by more than 7 times, with an average annual growth rate of 12%. Compared with 1982, the total trade in services in 2021 has increased by about 173 times. Table 6-3 shows the imports and exports of China's service trade from 1982 to 2021.

Table 6-3　Situation of China's imports and exports of services from 1982 to 2021

Year	Imports and exports of China		Imports of China		Exports of China		Balance (100 million USD)
	Amount (100 million USD)	Year-on-Year rate (%)	Amount (100 million USD)	Year-on-Year rate (%)	Amount (100 million USD)	Year-on-Year rate (%)	
2021	8 212	24.1	3 942	40.5	4 270	12.0	−327
2020	6 617	−15.7	2 806	−1.0	3 811	−24.0	−1 005
2019	7 850	−1.4	2 836	4.5	5 014	−4.5	−2 178
2018	7 965	14.5	2 715	19.0	5 250	12.3	−2 536
2017	6 957	5.1	2 281	8.9	4 676	3.4	−2 395
2016	6 616	1.1	2 095	−4.2	4 521	3.8	−2 426
2015	6 542	0.3	2 186	−0.2	4 355	0.6	−2 169
2014	6 520	21.3	2 191	5.9	4 329	30.9	−2 137
2013	5 376	11.3	2 070	2.7	3 306	17.5	−1 236
2012	4 829	7.6	2 016	0.3	2 813	13.5	−797
2011	4 489	20.8	2 010	12.7	2 478	28.2	−468
2010	3 717	22.9	1 783	24.2	1 934	21.7	−151
2009	3 025	−6.1	1 436	−12.1	1 589	0.0	−153
2008	3 223	21.4	1 633	20.7	1 589	22.1	44
2007	2 654	30.2	1 353	31.4	1 301	29.0	52
2006	2 038	21.1	1 030	22.1	1 008	20.1	21
2005	1 683	15.9	843	16.3	840	15.5	3

Continued

Year	Imports and exports of China		Imports of China		Exports of China		Balance (100 million USD)
	Amount (100 million USD)	Year-on-Year rate (%)	Amount (100 million USD)	Year-on-Year rate (%)	Amount (100 million USD)	Year-on-Year rate (%)	
2004	1 452	36.2	725	41.3	727	31.5	−2
2003	1 066	15.0	513	11.0	553	18.9	−40
2002	928	18.2	462	18.0	465	18.5	−3
2001	784	10.2	392	11.8	393	8.6	−1
2000	712	16.7	350	19.3	362	14.3	−11
1999	610	17.6	294	17.2	317	17.9	−23
1998	519	−16.6	251	−26.8	268	−4.0	−18
1997	622	23.0	342	22.4	280	23.8	63
1996	506	1.9	280	14.6	226	−10.5	54
1995	496	36.0	244	20.9	252	54.7	−8
1994	365	37.1	202	38.5	163	35.4	39
1993	266	20.9	146	15.9	120	27.6	25
1992	220	61.0	126	31.7	94	128.9	31
1991	137	10.1	95	18.4	41	−5.3	54
1990	124	22.8	81	30.0	44	11.3	37
1989	101	16.2	62	21.6	39	8.5	23
1988	87	32.5	51	24.9	36	45.0	15
1987	66	7.0	41	5.7	25	9.2	16
1986	61	9.2	39	24.6	23	−9.8	16
1985	56	−5.5	31	0.3	25	−11.7	6
1984	59	24.9	31	11.7	29	43.3	2
1983	48	1.4	28	3.6	20	−1.5	8
1982	47	—	27	—	20	—	6

Source: Ministry of Commerce of the People's Republic of China

In addition to maintaining rapid growth in the overall scale of China's service trade, the proportion of China's total import and export volume of service trade in the world's total service trade(see Figure 6-7) and the proportion of China's total import and export volume of service trade in China's total foreign trade also show an upward trend. Since 1992, China's trade in services began to grow rapidly, and the proportion of trade in services began to increase. In 2014, China's trade in services accounted for 6.79% of the world's trade in services, an increase of more than 10 times compared with 1982. China has gradually become a major trading country in services in the world. At present, China has

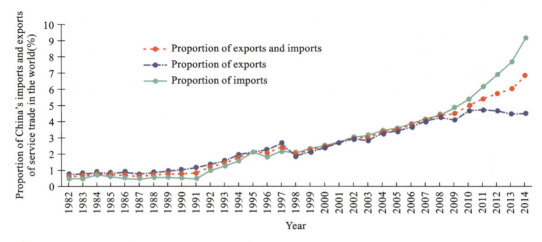

Figure 6-7 Proportion of China's imports and exports of service trade in the world from 1982 to 2014
Data from Ministry of Commerce of the People's Republic of China

become the world's second-largest trading country in services. In 2021, the total imports and exports of service trade reached 821.2 billion USD, with a growth of 24.1% year on year.

With the deepening of the opening up and the constant changes in the international situation, the composition of China's foreign trade in services has also undergone tremendous changes. China's foreign trade in services has changed from a focus on transport services to a development situation that places equal emphasis on transport, tourism, telecommunication, computer and information services. As shown in Figure 6-8, in 2021, transport services, travel services, and telecommunications, computer and information services accounted for 31.75%, 14.91% and 14.56% of foreign service trade, respectively.

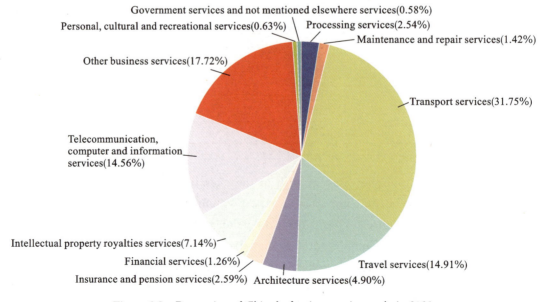

Figure 6-8 Proportion of China's foreign service trade in 2021
Data from Ministry of Commerce of the People's Republic of China

6.3.3 China's Foreign Trade Partners

Since the reform and opening up, China has actively developed its foreign trade and established trade relations with most countries and regions in the world. China's foreign trade partners have grown from dozens of countries and regions in 1978 to 182 countries in 2023 with which it has established diplomatic relations and conducted economic exchanges, covering almost all regions of the world. The EU, USA, ASEAN, Japan, and the BRICS countries have become China's major trade partners. Since the 21st century, especially after China's accession to the WTO, China's trade with emerging market economies and developing countries have continued to grow rapidly.

China's trade partners are mainly USA, Japan, the EU, ASEAN, South Korea, Brazil, and other countries. The proportion of different trade partners in China's foreign trade has undergone tremendous changes in the past decade. Figure 6-9 shows the import and export volume of each trading partner from 2000 to 2020.

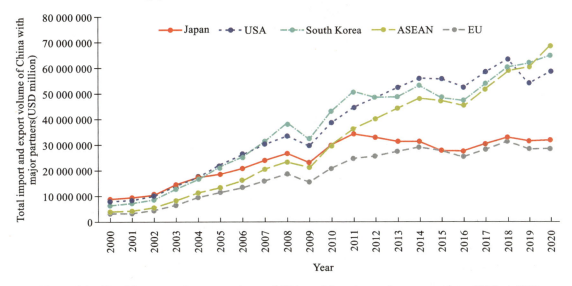

Figure 6-9 Total import and export volume of China with major trade partners from 2000 to 2020
Data from National Bureau of Statistics of the People's Republic of China

Figure 6-10 shows the proportion of total import and export volume of China's major trade partners in 2000, 2010 and 2020. In 2000, Japan was the most important country in China's foreign trade, with a total import and export volume of 83.164 billion USD, accounting for as high as 17.53%. However, since then, China's trade with the EU and USA has become closer. The total trade volume and trade growth rate have far surpassed Japan. From 2004 to 2019, they had alternately been China's largest trade partner. After 2011, the growth rate of China's trade with Japan and South Korea slowed down. Meanwhile, China's trade with ASEAN, the EU, and USA still maintained rapid growth. ASEAN have gradually become China's third-largest trade partner. In 2018, due to the trade friction initiated by USA against China, the import and export trade with the USA

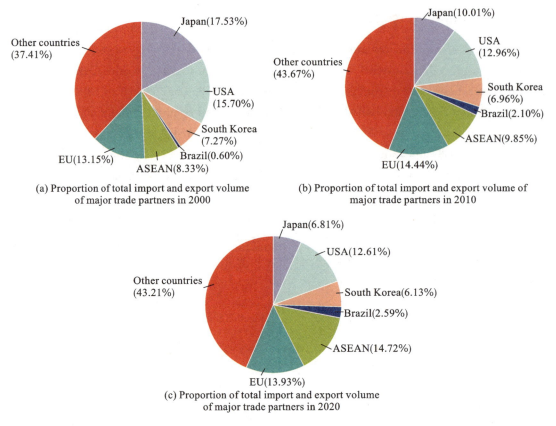

Figure 6-10 Proportion of total import and export volume of China's major trade partners in 2000, 2010 and 2020

Data from National Bureau of Statistics of the People's Republic of China

was greatly affected. From 2019 to 2022, the USA changed from China's largest trade partner to the third-largest. Since China proposed the Belt and Road Initiative in 2013, trade with countries along the Belt and Road has become closer, and the total foreign trade with ASEAN countries has maintained rapid growth. In 2020, ASEAN historically became China's largest trade partner. In 2021, China's top five trade partners were ASEAN, the EU, USA, Japan and South Korea, in that order. As of 2022, ASEAN became China's largest trade partner for three consecutive years, followed by the EU and the USA. China is now the largest trade partner of more than 120 countries and regions in the world.

6.4 The Evolution of China's Foreign Trade Policies

Foreign trade plays an important role in every stage of China's economic development. The foreign trade policies at each stage must fully reflect the objective needs of foreign trade development and conform to the international trade business environment at that time. Since China's reform and opening up in 1978, China's foreign trade policies can be roughly divided into two periods.

6.4.1　Foreign Trade Policies from 1978 to 2000

After the reform and opening up, China's foreign trade began to implement the strategy of combining import substitution with export orientation, introducing the view of comparative advantage in the market economy, adopting policies of encouraging export in the labor-intensive industries with comparative advantage, and introducing foreign investment to enhance competitiveness. In capital-intensive and technology-intensive industries that do not have competitive advantages, China adopted a strategy of import substitution to meet the needs of technology and capital for domestic industrial development. Accordingly, the foreign trade policies in this period was adjusted.

The general policy objective of foreign trade during this period was to promote export, restrict import, protect and promote national economic development and ensure national tariff revenue through foreign trade policies. The main characteristics of the foreign trade policies in this period were mainly manifested from three aspects. First, The foreign trade policies had changed from pure protection to "encouraging export and limiting import". Before the reform and opening up, China implemented the policy of "independence and self-reliance". After the reform and opening up, China realized the role of foreign trade in promoting economic growth and began to encourage export, utilize foreign resources to develop the economy, and pursue a trade surplus. The trade policies changed to "encouraging export and limiting import". Second, adjustments of foreign policies had shifted from micro fields to macro fields. China's foreign trade policies had changed from decentralizing management rights to encourage enterprises to engage in foreign trade at the beginning, to reforming the foreign exchange resource allocation system to achieve a dual-track exchange rate system, and then to realizing a market-based and managed floating exchange rate system. Third, the policy of expanding export had been implemented. Every policy adjustment in this period was carried out when the previous policy had factors that were not conducive to expanding export, so the expansion of export has become the basic policy of foreign trade policies adjustment.

6.4.2　Foreign Trade Policies from 2001 to the Present

In 2001, China officially joined the WTO. At this stage, the general direction of China's foreign trade policies formulation and adjustment was to integrate into the world trade system and fully participate in international competition. At the same time, China's foreign trade policies should strictly follow the requirements of the WTO. The purpose of this is to gain a fairer trading position and avoid unfair and unjust treatment by other countries. After accession to the WTO, China signed the "Protocol on the Accession of the People's Republic of China", in which China promised to open the market, reform its foreign economic and trade system in accordance with world trade rules, and establish a foreign-related economic and trade system in line with international practices. In the first year of the accession to the WTO system, China cleared up a large number of old laws and regulations in accordance with the requirements of the WTO, and formulated new regulations to adapt to the WTO. The general direction of China's foreign trade policies is to move towards trade liberalization. In order to ensure the interests of China's economic development and economic operation under the background of opening up, China has always adopted an attitude of actively participating in foreign trade. At the same time, China has adopted an active intervention trade policies to stabilize its economic development system in the context of its development. The foreign trade policies of active intervention is a selective trade protection policy, that is, to protect the industries that are not yet internationally competitive to a certain extent and for a certain period of time, to implement a strategic trade protection policy for enterprises or industries with certain international market share, and to implement a free trade policy for internationally competitive industries or enterprises.

After China's accession to the WTO, its market access management policies and measures have been adjusted. In terms of imports, the WTO has imposed a strict ban on high tariffs, requiring member countries to gradually reduce tariff levels and move towards trade liberalization. China's current tariff levels are already lower than those of developing countries, which greatly improves China's market access. Although China reduced its tariff levels after joining the WTO, China can still learn from the theory of effective tariff protection, implement a stepped tariff structure, and set the tariff level at the best position that is conducive to China's industrial development and welfare. In terms of non-tariff barriers to imports, after China's accession to the WTO, most of the traditional non-tariff barrier trade protection policies are no longer applicable, otherwise they would violate the constraints of the WTO. After accession to the WTO, China can use the following five non-tariff barrier trade measures: first, impose quantitative restrictions on the import of restricted products; second, conduct government procurement in a form recognized by the WTO; third, implement anti-dumping measures against imported products; fourth, request relevant countries to adopt "voluntary exports" for their product exports; fifth, utilize technical trade barriers.

7　Rural Reform in China

In the mid and late 20th century, due to the long-term shackles of "Left" ideology, China's rural areas implemented the people's commune system of "integration of government administration with commune management". Its rigid system of centralized management and unified distribution seriously dampened farmers' enthusiasm for labor and hindered the development of rural productivity, failed to solve the problem of food and clothing for the farmers, and the rural economy was in a state of stagnation. Therefore, adjusting rural production relations and changing rural policies have become the urgent needs of the vast number of farmers. For this reason, China started the rural economic system reform, which can be divided into four stages.

The first stage (1978-1984) is the initiation stage of reform. The people's communes were abolished, and the household contract responsibility system with remuneration linked to output was implemented instead. The land was contracted to rural households for long-term use based on public ownership of land, and collective agricultural production was transformed into independent management by individual households with full responsibility for their profits and losses. Through the combination of the active attempts of the grassroots and the policy promotion of the central government, the practice of farm output quotas fixed by household was rapidly expanded throughout the country, leading to the rapid development of the rural economy, increase in production and incomes, and significant improvement of economic conditions and living standards of farmers.

The second stage (1984-1992) is the exploration stage of market-oriented reform. The circulation system of agricultural products was reformed. In response to the difficulties in selling grain during the bumper agricultural harvest, the form of unified purchasing by the state according to fixed quotas, which was no longer suitable for the development of the rural economy, had to be canceled. Agricultural products began to be distributed to the market, and the price of products was implemented under a "double-track system".

The third stage (1992-1998) is the comprehensive transition to the market economy. Driven by the reform goal of the socialist market economic system established by the 14th National Congress of the CPC, a new rural system that meets the requirements of the development of a socialist market economy was established. At this stage, the rural economy entered a period of transition, and the agricultural economy began to fully connect with the market and developed rapidly.

The fourth stage (1998-present) is a new period of construction of a new socialist countryside. Rural reform has transitioned from economic reform to the comprehensive reform of the new socialist countryside. The central government has also increased its emphasis on the issues relating to agriculture, rural areas and the well-being of farmers, gradually changed the urban-rural dual economic structure, closely linked urban development and rural economic development, built the long-term mechanism of rural economic development, and strived to realize the comprehensive development of rural areas.

7.1 Household Contract Responsibility System

Rural reform, especially the implementation of the household contract responsibility system, is the first movement of reform and opening up. After the Third Plenary Session of the 11th CPC Central Committee, China's economic restructuring took the lead in making breakthroughs in rural areas. The household contract responsibility system, mainly in the forms of "farm output quotas fixed by household" and "work contracted to households", broke the egalitarianism of the rural distribution system and changed the system drawbacks of "eating from the same big pot" in people's communes, and gradually became an important cornerstone of the Party's and state's rural policies.

7.1.1 The Rise and Change of the Household Contract Responsibility System

China is a big agricultural country, and agricultural production and farmers' livelihood have always been the top priority of the Party and the government. From the founding of New China to the end of the First Five-Year Plan, China's agricultural development was on the rise. In the late 1950s, however, the situation began to deteriorate. Judging from the relationship between population, arable land and grain output, the problems in China's agricultural production were becoming more and more prominent. From 1957 to 1978, the national population increased by about 300 to 400 million, of which the increase of agricultural population accounted for more than 60% of the total population increase. During the same period, the arable land area nationwide did not increase with the population growth but decreased due to the basic construction land and other reasons. Although the total grain output increased, the national per capita possession of grain was not fundamentally improved, agricultural labor productivity was extremely low, and poverty was widespread in rural areas.

The main reason is that since the late 1950s, the People's Commune Movement had led to the over-centralization of agricultural operation and management, serious egalitarianism in distribution, and other drawbacks, which seriously dampened farmers' enthusiasm for production and offset the state's input in agriculture to a large extent, resulting in slow or even stagnant agricultural development.

At that time, there was a great contradiction between the backward state of China's agriculture and the people's need to improve their lives and the goals of the Four Modernizations. How should China fundamentally overcome the drawbacks of over-centralization in production management? How should China fully mobilize the initiative of farmers in production? These were unavoidable practical problems.

During the autumn planting period in 1978, Anhui, a major agricultural province, suffered a severe drought. The Anhui Provincial Party Committee adopted the strategy of "lending land to tide over shortage", that is, to lend collective land to farmers during a special period and let them cultivate it by themselves, so as to survive the disaster with the harvest. This practice was actually the predecessor of "fixed farm output quotas by household". Then, 18 farmer households in Xiaogang Village, Fengyang County, initiated the practice of "work contracted to households", that is, paying enough to the state and the collective and keeping the rest for themselves. This practice greatly mobilized farmers' enthusiasm for production. In the autumn of 1979, the total output of oil crops in Xiaogang Village reached 17 600 kg, far exceeding the task of 150 kg. Figure 7-1 shows the harvest scene in Xiaogang Village.

Figure 7-1 Harvest scene in Xiaogang Village
Photo from *Guangming Daily*

Influenced by the approach of Anhui Province, other provinces relaxed policies and adopted similar approaches. For example, Sichuan Province encouraged production teams to fix farm output quotas for each production unit, and supported the experiment of "determining work according to production and rewarding excess". Guangdong Province generally implemented the operation and management system of "5 Fixes and 1 Prize" in rural community teams.

The bold attempt of fixed farm output quotas by household and work contracted to households in local areas changed the constraint of production relations on agricultural productivity. It was a bold attempt to encourage farmers to practice by giving them autonomy in production and stimulating their enthusiasm for production according to local conditions. However, some people worry that the contract of production and responsibility would disintegrate the rural collective economy and deviate from the direction of socialism.

At the critical moment of 1980, Deng Xiaoping clearly pointed out in his speeches that the method of fixed farm output quotas by household had worked well and changed quickly, and that this practice would not affect the collective economy. He believed that as long as the production develops and the social division of labor and commodity economy in the countryside develops, the low-level collectivization will develop into a high-level collectivization, and the collective economy will be consolidated. Deng Xiaoping's clear statement eliminated people's rigid thinking and fear and promoted the CPC Central Committee's public affirmation and supported for fixed farm output quotas by household and work contracted to households.

In 1980, the CPC Central Committee issued "Several Issues on Further Strengthening and Improving the Agricultural Production Responsibility System", which for the first time broke through the concept for many years that equating the practice of fixing farm output quotas for each household with the division of land and individual management and capitalism and affirmed that such practice under the leadership of production teams would not deviate from the socialist track and there was no danger of the restoration of capitalism. In 1982, the "Central Document No. 1" on rural work was officially issued. It clearly pointed out that all kinds of responsibility systems, including fixing farm output quotas for each household and work contracted to households, were production responsibility systems of the socialist collective economy, reflecting the strong desire of hundreds of millions of farmers to develop socialist agriculture in light of the actual conditions in China's rural areas.

Since then, rural reform had been carried out more rapidly. The rapid spread of the household contract responsibility system fully mobilized farmers' enthusiasm for production and promoted the rapid development of agricultural production. As shown in Table 7-1, the reform began to yield results, with a significant increase in main agricultural products yield and gratifying changes in the rural areas.

Table 7-1 Comparison of China's main agricultural products yield before and after the household contract responsibility system

Index	1977	1978	1979	1980	1981	1982	1983	1984
Grain yield (10 000 tons)	28 272.50	30 476.50	33 211.50	32 055.50	32 502.00	35 450.00	38 727.50	40 730.50
Oil yield (10 000 tons)	401.58	521.79	643.54	769.06	1 020.52	1 181.73	1 054.97	1 190.95

Source: National Bureau of Statistics of the People's Republic of China

After this period of development, the household contract responsibility system kept releasing dividends, and agriculture sustained steady growth. In order to stabilize the public and adapt to the rural market-oriented reform, the CPC Central Committee further clarified and improved the system.

On the one hand, the management form was institutionalized. In 1991, the "CPC Central Committee's Decision on Further Strengthening Agricultural and Rural Work" made it clear that the system of responsibility based on household contracting and the two-tier management system combing unification and division should be stabilized for a long time and constantly enriched and improved as a basic system for China's township collective economy. In 1993, the household contract responsibility system was incorporated into the "Amendment to the Constitution of the People's Republic of China" as a basic system for the rural economy.

On the other hand, the household contract responsibility system was regulated through the contract, and the rights and obligations among various subjects were clarified. In 1993, "Several Policies and Measures on the Development of Agriculture and Rural Economy" proposed that, in order to stabilize the land contracting relationship and encourage farmers to increase their inputs and improve the productivity of the land, the contracting period for arable land will be extended for another 30 years after its original expiry. For land engaged in developmental production, the contract period can be longer. In 2002, the Rural Land Contract Law of the People's Republic of China guaranteed farmers' long-term land contractual management right in a legal form.

7.1.2 Historical Significance and Limitations of Household Contract Responsibility System

As the basic policy of the Party in rural areas, the two-tier management system that combines centralized and decentralized management based on household contract management broke through the defects of the people's commune system, which was large in scale and collective by nature, and highly centralized. On the premise of insisting on collective ownership of the means of production, the land was contracted to farmer households, which established the dominant position of household management and gave farmers sufficient autonomy in production and management and the right to profit. Since then, the relationship between collective and individual rights, which had been confused for many years, has been clearly demarcated in line with the actual situation for the first time. As the operation results were closely linked to the interests of the producers, the disadvantages of "eating from the same big pot" had been overcome, farmers' enthusiasm for production had been fully exerted, the productivity had been greatly liberated, the production efficiency had been significantly improved, and the agricultural output had been increased rapidly.

In summary, the household contract responsibility system solved the problem of low agricultural production efficiency, alleviated the problem of insufficient national grain production and farmers' inability to meet their food and clothing needs, and laid a solid foundation for the following reform and opening up. More importantly, the household contract responsibility system changed the current situation and structure of agricultural production and laid the foundation for the development of agricultural modernization.

The rural land system reform, marked by the household contract responsibility system, did once lead to the economic and social development of the countryside, and the conditions of rural areas were greatly improved in a period of time. However, after the 21st century, although the rural economy was still growing, the gap between urban and rural residents' income as well as urban and rural development was widening. The underlying three reasons were always associated with the household contract responsibility system, which was the cornerstone of rural reform.

First, the small scale of land restricted the scale of agriculture. The land conditions in China are complicated. Meanwhile, the household contract responsibility system required fairness in per capita arable land area and land quality, resulting in fragmentation of the land parcels contracted by farmers and serious fragmentation of farmers' land management. Furthermore, the fragmentation of land scale restricted the realization of large-scale agricultural operations. It not only restricted the production input of farmers objectively, caused the high cost of agricultural products and low economic benefits of individual farmers, which made farmers in a weak position in market competition and difficult to bear the risk of investment failure. It also subjectively restricted the expectation of large-scale production investment of farmers, which in turn restricted the realization of large-scale agricultural operations, forming a vicious circle.

Second, the household contract responsibility system was unable to meet the needs of the development of the market economy. Marketization was one of the basic characteristics of agricultural industrialization management, but the existing decentralized land management combined with small-scale household management made it difficult for farmers to overcome their blindness in production, causing a phenomenon of following the trend, which resulted in a an imbalance between supply and demand of agricultural products.

Third, the transfer of land use rights was not standardized. The state allowed land use rights to be transferred for a fee, which indicated that land can enter the market as a factor of production and optimize allocation with the help of the market. However, the transfer of land use rights lacked a credible market intermediary, and the regulations on the transfer of land use rights, such as the rights and interests, transaction procedures, implementation principles, and pricing methods were also vague, resulting in insufficient land transfer and low land use efficiency.

7.2 Reform of the Agricultural Product Circulation System

Between agricultural production and resident consumption is the circulation of agricultural products. Under the market economy, circulation determines production. The rigidity of the circulation mode of agricultural products will directly affect agricultural production, and then affect agricultural industrialization, farmers' interests, and the construction of new countryside.

After the Third Plenary Session of the 11th CPC Central Committee, while fully implementing the household contract responsibility system in rural areas, the market-oriented reform of the agricultural product circulation system has achieved great success. With the continuous deepening of the commercialization and marketization of China's agriculture, the transformation from traditional agriculture to modern agriculture is accelerating, and the agricultural product circulation system is playing an increasingly important role in promoting the construction of socialist countryside.

7.2.1 Historical Review of the Reform of Agricultural Product Circulation System

Before the reform and opening up, the agricultural product circulation system in China was still the system of a state monopoly for purchasing and marketing in the era of planned economy, that is, all the food needed by the whole society was supplied by the state, and residents obtained grain using grain ration coupons. In addition to grain, the state also implemented fixed quotas of unified purchasing for up to 132 kinds of products such as pigs, eggs, silkworm cocoons and aquatic products. These products were not permitted to be bought or sold freely, and prices were set by the state. All the means of subsistence needed by urban and rural residents were supplied through ration coupons issued by the state. There were more than a dozen types of coupons, which became the second currency. Figure 7-2 shows some of the ration coupons during that period.

Figure 7-2 Ration coupons during the period of the state monopoly for purchasing and marketing
Photo from Jinhua Party history website

During this period, the circulation of agricultural products was subject to strict administrative restrictions, which prevented the free circulation of agricultural products, and the production and sales of agricultural products could not reflect the changes in market demand, resulting in a serious disconnect between agricultural production, processing and circulation and the market. Since 1978, China has gradually explored the reform of the circulation system of agricultural products, which mainly went through the following five stages.

The first stage (1978-1984) is the transition period from a planned economy to a combination of planned regulation and market regulation.

With the implementation of the household contract responsibility system, the circulation system of agricultural products also began to break through the traditional planned economic system. After the Third Plenary Session of the 11th CPC Central Committee, the state carried out a gradual reform to the system of a state monopoly for purchasing and marketing agricultural products. Under the condition that the system of a state monopoly for purchasing and marketing was not fundamentally affected, the prices of agricultural products were raised in a planned way, the varieties of agricultural products subject to state monopoly were gradually reduced, market trade was liberalized, and certain agricultural products were allowed to be purchased and sold freely with the negotiated price.

Since March 1979, the State Council successively raised the purchase prices of 18 major agricultural products, including grain, oil and grease, and cotton. In January 1982, the "National Rural Work Meeting Minutes" clearly pointed out that the agricultural economy "should be dominated by the planned economy, supplemented by market regulation". In January 1983, the CPC Central Committee pointed out in the "Several Issues on the Current Rural Economic Policies" that multi-channel business should be allowed for the products that farmers have completed the fixed quotas and the products that are not subject to unified purchasing by the state according to fixed quotas. In October 1983, the State Council reduced the number of first- and second-category agricultural and sideline products under the control of the Ministry of Commerce from 46 to 21, and the adjusted 25 kinds were changed to the third category, which was regulated by the market. In July 1984, the State Council reduced the number of first- and second-category agricultural and sideline products from 21 to 12. By the end of 1984, the number of agricultural and sideline products subject to unified purchasing by the state according to fixed quotas had been reduced from more than 100 in 1978 to only 38. Among the total amount of agricultural and sideline products sold by farmers, the proportion of those purchased by the state according to fixed quotas at the planned prices decreased from 84.7% in 1978 to 39.4% in 1984.

Corresponding to the narrowing of the scope of the state monopoly for purchasing and marketing was the opening of the market trade. After April 1979, the state relaxed the restrictions on the market trade and stipulated that the third-category agricultural and sideline products and the first- and second-category agricultural and sideline products that had completed the fixed quotas of state purchase, except for cotton, could carry out the free trade with the negotiated purchase price. Figure 7-3 is the commodity market in Qingdao.

Figure 7-3 Commodity market in Qingdao
Photo from Qingdao Daily

The second stage(1984-1992) is the "double-track system" period in which contractual procurement and market purchase coexisted.

With the household contract responsibility system and the liberalization of purchase price of agricultural products, the rural economy developed rapidly and sloved the problem of the long-term shortage of agricultural product supply. In order to prevent the sudden price changes caused by the sudden liberalization of market prices, the state hoped to use the planned price to meet the basic needs of the society, pursue economic stability, and at the same time gave play to the resource allocation function of the market to promote production and alleviate social contradictions.

In January 1985, the CPC Central Committee issued the Ten Policies on Further Invigorating the Rural Economy, stipulating that, except for certain varieties, the state would no longer assign fixed quotas of unified purchasing to farmers. Instead, it would carry out contractual procurement and market purchase respectively according to different circumstances. Grain and cotton were changed to contractual procurement. Live pigs, aquatic products and vegetables in large and medium-sized cities, and in industrial and mining areas were free to be marketed, traded, fluctuated in line with market conditions, and priced based on quality. Till then, except for a few varieties, the system of unified purchasing of agricultural products by state according to fixed quotas had ended.

This was a stage in which the agricultural product circulation system was transformed from a planned economy to a market economy. The reform of the circulation system of agricultural products broke the restrictions on agricultural products in the era of planned economy, greatly enhanced farmers' commodity awareness, and the output and varieties of agricultural products increased rapidly, marking that the reform of agricultural product circulation system entered into a market-oriented step-forward stage.

The third stage(1992-1998)is the transition to a socialist market economy.

With the improvement of agricultural management forms, the main contradiction in agricultural development was that agricultural development did not fully adapt to the socialist market economy. In order to solve this major contradiction, the CPC Central Committee, oriented towards the establishment of a socialist market system in rural areas, continuously reformed the agricultural product circulation system through agricultural policies and promoted the deepening of rural reform and development.

In 1992, China entered the development stage of the socialist market economy, and the reform of the agricultural product circulation system also entered the stage of transformation and development to the socialist market economy from the stage of opening and invigorating, so as to promote the adjustment of agricultural structure. The main goal of this stage was to orient towards a market economy to speed up the reform of the grain circulation system, liberalize grain prices, implement market-based pricing and stabilize the national grain supply.

In 1993, the State Council issued the "Notice on Accelerating the Reform of Grain Circulation System", requiring agricultural products to form a pattern that is dominated by market purchase and sale and supplemented by contractual procurement. The grain coupons were abolished and the 40 year system of the state monopoly for purchasing and marketing was brought to an end, with grain prices fluctuated in line with market conditions. In 1998, the "Decision of the CPC Central Committee on Several Major Issues Concerning Agriculture and Rural Work" adopted by the Third Plenary Session of the 15th CPC Central Committee, which pointed out that it is necessary to further invigorate the circulation of agricultural products and form an open, unified, competitive and orderly market system for agricultural products as soon as possible, provide a favorable market environment for farmers, and ensure the sustainable and stable development of agriculture and rural economy. This also further clarified the goal of building a market system for agricultural products.

At the same time, China was actively building wholesale markets for agricultural and sideline products. From 1992 to 1998, there was a boom in the construction of wholesale markets for agricultural products across the country, and nearly 3 000 wholesale markets for agricultural and sideline products were built, covering a wide range of grain, vegetables, meat and aquatic products. Wholesale markets became an important driving force for the distribution of agricultural products and resource allocation across the country as well as the development of the agricultural economy. Until then, the agricultural product market system with the wholesale markets as the core had been initially established, laying a solid foundation for the deepening reform of the agricultural product circulation system. Figure 7-4 shows a corner of China's agricultural and sideline products wholesale market.

Figure 7-4 A corner of China's agricultural and sideline products wholesale market

The fourth stage(1998-2004)is the comprehensive marketization stage.

The reform of agricultural product circulation system is a necessary condition for the deepening of China's reform and opening up, an important way to gradually establish a socialist market economy, and an important breakthrough to solve the "Three Rural Issues". Starting in 1998, the agricultural product circulation system entered a period of comprehensive reform, and the reform during this period focused on the grain sector. Given the relative surplus of grain, in April 1998, the National Conference on the Reform of the Grain Circulation System was held, proposing the implementation of a system of separating policy-based and commercial grain purchases and sales, improved the grain pricing mechanism, and implemented the sales of grain at a favorable price; in June, China promulgated "three policies and one reform", that is, to purchase farmers' surplus grain at a protective price, and state-owned grain purchase and storage enterprises shall implement sales at a favorable price, and closed operations of grain purchase funds and accelerate reform of state-owned grain enterprises.

Of course, the reform of the agricultural product circulation system was not limited to the sector of grain. The market-oriented reform process of the circulation of all kinds of agricultural products other than grain was continuously promoted, and a relatively stable market-oriented circulation order was gradually formed.

The fifth stage (2004-present) is the formation stage of a diversified agricultural product circulation system.

In 2004, the General Office of the State Council issued the "Opinions on Further Improving the Circulation of Rural Commodities", calling for accelerating the development of wholesale, retail and logistics of agricultural products to invigorate the circulation of agricultural products. In 2005, China's Ministry of Commerce organized "Ten Thousand Villages and Thousands of Townships" market project with the main content of developing a modern rural circulation network. In 2006, China's Ministry of Commerce implemented the "Double-Hundred Market Project" to improve the modernization level of agricultural product circulation enterprises and upgrade the agricultural product wholesale markets. In May 2006, China's Ministry of Commerce approved the "Specification of Constructing and Reconstructing Countryside Stores" to promote and strengthen the construction of a modern circulation system for agricultural products. Today, a diversified agricultural product circulation system has basically taken shape in China.

7.2.2 Achievements and Inspiration of the Reform of Agricultural Product Circulation System

With the advancement of the reform of the agricultural product circulation system, the circulation channel of agricultural products has also changed from the past single type to diversification, forming a multi-channel circulation system and a fair competition market pattern. The institutional changes have greatly stimulated the impetus of the production and circulation of agricultural products. Through the gradual reform of the circulation system of agricultural products, the circulation pattern of agricultural products with the coexistence of various economic sectors, diversified operation modes and multiple circulation channels has been formed.

Generally, the achievements of the reform of China's agricultural product circulation system are reflected in the following four aspects:

First, the circulation of agricultural products has been continuously expanded. Since the reform and opening up, the reform of agricultural product circulation system has maintained the products supply sufficient and varied. As shown in Figure 7-5, the National Bureau of Statistics released that China's total grain output was 304.77 million tons in 1978, and the country's total grain output in 2021 was 682.85 million tons. The output of other daily necessities such as fruits, vegetables and pork also showed exponential growth,

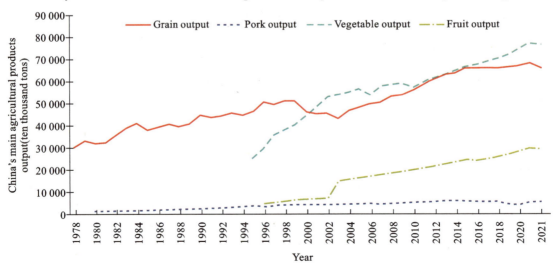

Figure 7-5 Output changes of China's main agricultural products
Data from National Bureau of Statistics of the People's Republic of China

meeting the diversified needs of modern Chinese residents.

Second, the circulation market system of agricultural products has been continuously improved. The market system is the basis, link and channel of the market economy, and the role of the trading market must be fully exerted for the market-orientated development of agriculture. The adequate market conditions can not only improve the efficiency of the trading and circulation of agricultural products, but also increase their returns. Following the reform and opening up, China has basically established an agricultural product market system, including fairs, wholesale markets and retailers, with all kinds of wholesale markets in the pivot, urban and rural farmer's markets as the basis, and direct delivery plus chain supermarkets as supplements, combined with production areas, sales areas and hub markets. Moreover, different markets were connected organically, complementing each other by functions with coordination and linkage, so as to ensure smooth circulation of agricultural products. The developing market system, the improving market function and the strengthening market mechanism have become the immense momentum in boosting China's agriculture.

Third, the macro-economic control mechanism of agricultural product market has been continuously refined. The establishment of the government macro-economic control mechanism is an important means to prevent market blindness. In the process of establishing the market system of agricultural products and cultivating the entities of circulation, the government's macro-economic control mechanism shall play a leading and supporting role. After the reform and opening up, China's central and local governments comprehensively used economic means, legal and administrative approaches as well as price mechanisms to strengthen their ability of macro-economic control over the agricultural product market, and improve their ability and level to deal with emergencies and abnormal market fluctuations. These macro-economic control means have greatly improved circulation environment of China's agricultural products and promoted the development of the agricultural product market.

Fourth, the market entities of the agricultural products have been continuously diversified, and the opening up of the market has been deepened in a phased manner. Since the reform and opening up, market entities of the agricultural products in China have gradually changed from a single pattern of planned economy, featuring state-operated commerce, supply and marketing cooperatives and other commercial organizations, to diversified patterns. This trend has become increasingly obvious. Although the state-operated commerce, supply and marketing cooperatives and other business organizations are becoming less influential in the market circulation of agricultural products, they still play an important role; farmer individuals have been increasingly active; farmer cooperative economic organizations and leading enterprises of agricultural industrialization are becoming more important. Domestic and foreign agricultural product markets are gradually integrated, and the opening up of agricultural product markets has been deepened continuously.

7.3 Experience and Thoughts on China's Rural Reform

By virtue of the rural reform, the rural social productivity has been unprecedentedly unleashed and boosted. The democratic rights of farmers have been fully respected and guaranteed, demonstrating great changes in rural areas. Ultimately, rural reform could not have such achievements without the advantages and safeguards of the socialist system with Chinese characteristics. It is the fundamental system and advantages of socialism with Chinese characteristics that ensure the socialist direction of China's rural reform and lay a political foundation for further deepening rural reform, promoting rural development and implementing the strategy of rural revitalization in the new era. From the perspective of practices regarding China's rural reform, there are four pieces of experience to make great achievements:

First, stick to the Party's centralized and unified leadership over the "Three Rural Issues". Rural reform is the correct choice made by the CPC at the critical moment of historical development, which defines the Chinese-style road of agricultural modernization. At the beginning of rural reform, under the leadership of the CPC Central Committee, by adopting a series of gradual unleashing policies such as popularizing household contract responsibility management, lifting the price regulation of agricultural products, and promoting farmer's employment in non-agricultural sectors, the constraints of the planned economic system were gradually lifted, and the reform dividend was quickly released, which not only mobilized the enthusiasm of farmers, but also optimized the allocation of resources. In the 21st century, the CPC Central Committee proposes to regard the "Three Rural Issues" as the top priority of the whole Party, and constantly promote the theoretical, practical and system innovation of "Three Rural Issues" so as to gradually achieve common prosperity.

Second, continue in the direction of market-oriented reform, optimize the resource allocation mechanism of agricultural modernization and tackle the incentive problem of market entities through market approaches. Practical experience shows that the market-oriented direction must be maintained for rural reform, and comprehensively activating factors, entities and markets through deepening reform can stimulate the endogenous vitality and driving force of rural development. With the market-oriented reform, the relationship between property rights and distribution in rural areas was clarified, promoting the opening up of the market and the flow of factors, improving the price mechanism, and figuring out the function and relationship among farmers, collectives and the governments in the market. Thus, the rural economic system gradually turned to "giving full play to the decisive role of the market in the allocation of resources" and played a key part in liberating and developing rural productive forces, which provided the solid system and mechanism underpinning for agricultural and rural modernization.

Third, follow the general principle of "safeguarding farmer's economic interests and ensuring their political rights" to make sure that farmers are the beneficiaries of rural reform and development. Adhering to this general principle, China has established the position of farmers as the main body in market management by stabilizing and completing the two-layer management system that combines centralized and decentralized management on the basis of household contract management. Through the reform of the system concerning rural labor mobility, farmers were given the rights to migration and employment. By virtue of the reform regarding the operating mechanism of rural collective economic organization and the property rights system, the dominant position of farmers in the development of collective economy has been enhanced. In addition, Chinese rural economy has been rapidly developed on the basis of adhering to collective ownership. Practice shows that treating farmers as the main body and beneficiaries of rural reform and development is the benchmark mainline to promote the coordinated development of rural economy and society, and lays a solid social foundation for the continuous promotion of rural reform and development.

Fourth, pursue the rural reform "methodology" combined grassroots innovation with top-level design. Many major reforms in China, including rural reform originated from grassroots innovation, and then popularized and implemented nationwide through pilot projects. Practice has proved that giving full play to the enthusiasm and creativity of grassroots people and letting them facilitate the reform are often the key points to achieve success. However, relying solely on grassroots innovation is not nearly enough. With the deepening of the reform, the fields involved in the rural reform are becoming extensive, and the deep-seated problems are more complex. Therefore, it is necessary to strengthen the top-level design, clarify the direction of the reform and optimize the implementation paths. From the experience, China must adopt the method of combining bottom-up and top-down to gain successful rural reform, and effectively link grassroots innovation with top-level design through pilot experiments, so as to give full play to farmer's enthusiasm for production.

8 Agricultural Production and Agricultural Industrialization

As the chief architect of China's socialist reform, opening up and modernization construction, Deng Xiaoping put forward the important idea of "Two Leaps" in agricultural reform and development. The first leap is to abolish the people's communes and introduce a responsibility system mainly based on household contract. The second leap is to meet the needs of scientific farming and socialization of production, develop moderate scale business and collective economy. The first leap focuses on changing rural relations of production and promoting the development of productive forces, and the second leap concentrates on promoting agricultural modernization and achieving common prosperity.

As the reform and opening up deepens, China's agricultural development has come to the stage of gradually realizing the "second leap". The rural reform has gradually advanced from the early economic system reform, which mainly focuses on the transformation of agricultural management system and the introduction of market mechanism, to the universal reform covering rural politics, economy, society, culture and ecology, and has made great achievements.

However, China's urban-rural dual economic structure has not been completely broken. Rural land, funds, talents and other resources are still being lost, and the deep-seated problems restricting agriculture and rural development have not yet been resolved. Consequently, it is of great significance to promote rural reform and development.

8.1 Agricultural Modernization in China

The simultaneous promotion of agricultural modernization in the in-depth development of industrialization and urbanization is not only an important content of transforming the mode of economic development and building a moderately prosperous society in all respects, but also an inevitable requirement for improving the comprehensive production capacity of agriculture, increasing farmer's income and building a new socialist countryside.

8.1.1 The Development Process of Agricultural Modernization

Agricultural modernization is not a static process, on the contrary, it is a process of continuous development and evolution. With the different historical backgrounds and technical conditions, the connotation and goal of agricultural modernization show a dynamic change.

From the late 1970s to the early 1990s, it was the stage of agricultural modernization dominated by rural reform and structural change. The establishment and institutionalization of the household contract responsibility system made farmers the masters and promoted the rapid growth of agriculture. After the mid-1980s, the reform of rural economic structure accelerated, and the development of township enterprises absorbed part of the surplus agricultural labor force, which alleviated the contradiction of more rural people and less land to a certain extent. However, due to the constraints of rural labor force leaving the land but not the countryside at that time, the man-land relationship in rural areas had not been actually alleviated, and the increase of agricultural labor productivity was slow.

From the early 1990s to around 2010, it was the stage of agricultural modernization in which farmers were leaving the land and coming out of the village. The rural land transfer market began to develop, and the continuous investment in agriculture steadily promoted the land productivity, coupled with the rapid improvement of agricultural labor productivity due to the substantial improvement of mechanization. The agricultural modernization was moving towards a mode of improving labor productivity.

After 2010, the agricultural development entered a historical transition period. In 2009, the GDP proportion of China's primary industry fell below 10% for the first time. In 2014, the labor force in the primary industry began to account for less than that in the secondary and tertiary industries. In addition, the connotation and function of agriculture changed. The pattern of agricultural development shifted from mainly satisfying food and clothing and improving land productivity to mainly demonstrating rural value and improving rural labor productivity. The agricultural development showed clear characteristics of transformation.

The first manifestation is the intergenerational differentiation of farmers. The "second-generation migrant workers" born in the 1980s and 1990s began to account for the main force of migrant workers in cities. Their behavior showed significant changes between generations in economic and social aspects. The "second-generation migrant workers" not only left the land and villages like the first generation, but also chose to move across provinces and go to eastern regions and large and medium-sized cities for work and business. They are more eager to integrate into the modern urban system. Figure 8-1 shows rural migrant workers in cities.

The second manifestation is that the development of the land market and large-scale operations are poised to boom. In a long period before 2007, the scale of rural land transfer remained stable, and the rural land transfer rate in household contracted farmland area was basically stable between 4.4% and 5.4%. Since 2008, the speed of rural land transfer across the country has accelerated abruptly, and the area of land transfer has expanded year by year. The area of land transfer expanded rapidly from 110 million mu in 2008 to 530 million

Figure 8-1 Rural migrant workers in cities
Photo from Huanqiu.com

mu in 2020.

The third manifestation is the diversity of agricultural business entities. Although farmers are still the main agricultural operators, agricultural business entities have developed in the direction of diversified patterns. Family farms, farmer cooperatives, socialized service organizations engaged in agricultural production trusteeship and various new types of agricultural business entities as well as services entities have developed rapidly. These new types of agricultural entities show new trends different from small rural economy in the application of new technology, more investment in agricultural production, new market hunting, and the integration of modern agriculture chain, etc.

The fourth manifestation is the transition of agricultural development momentum. The modern factor input represented by agricultural machinery has gradually replaced the input of traditional factors such as rural labor force, becoming the new momentum of agricultural development. The total power of agricultural machinery and the overall level of mechanization in plowing, sowing and harvesting of major crops increased significantly. The agricultural production mode was upgraded to the stage of machinery operation and factor matching. Figure 8-2 shows agricultural machinery operation. The technological advances of agriculture have made significant contributions to agricultural production, allocation of agricultural resources as well as diversification and specialization of agricultural products.

Meanwhile, the external environment of agricultural development is more complex. First, the contradiction between people and land is increasingly swelling; second, the negative effects of urban-rural dual economic structure based on the household registration system have become increasingly prominent. Due to China's reality of small farmers in a large country, it is an arduous task for China to realize agricultural modernization. Only by giving full play to the leading role of various forms of moderate scale operation, can the production efficiency of land, capital, labor and other factors be continuously improved,

Figure 8-2 Agricultural machinery operation
Photo from *Economic Daily*

fundamentally ramping up the quality, efficiency and competitiveness of agriculture.

After the 18th National Congress of the CPC, in accordance with the requirements of synchronously promoting agricultural modernization in the in-depth development of industrialization and urbanization, China adheres to the path of agricultural modernization with Chinese characteristics and takes the mode transfer of agricultural development as the main principle, with the guarantee of the effective supply concerning major agricultural products as well as promotion of a sustained and rapid increase in farmer's income being the main objective, and the strengthening of the capacity of comprehensive agricultural production capacity, risk prevention and market competitiveness being the key focus. Efforts shall be made to expedite the specialization, standardization, expansion and intensification of agricultural production and operation, strengthen the support of policies, science and technology, facilities, talents and systems and improve the modern agricultural industry system. Moreover, it is required to raise the level of agricultural modernization, the living standards of farmers and the quality of new rural construction, and provide decisive support for China's modernization.

8.1.2 Major Achievements of Agricultural Modernization

Since the founding of New China, especially since the reform and opening up, China's agricultural modernization process has been advanced continuously, gaining remarkable achievements in agricultural development worldwide. The production capacity of grain and other major agricultural products has been steadily improved, with significant enhancement of the economic efficiency and competitiveness of agriculture, and the income level of farmers have been increased greatly, with continuous strengthening of the capacity for sustainable agricultural development, all of which enables China gradually embark on an agricultural modernization path with Chinese characteristics and make great contributions to the development of world agriculture.

First, the agricultural economy grew steadily, and the comprehensive grain production capacity reached a new height. After the 18th National Congress of the CPC, the grain production of China had been increasing for three consecutive years, with total grain production exceeding 600 million tons for the first time in 2012 and 650 million tons in 2015, and remaining stable at over 650 million tons subsequently. Figure 8-3 describes the changes of total grain production in recent years. According to the data from the World Bank and the Food and Agriculture Organization of the United Nations, China's grain yield reached 6 029 kg per hectare in 2017, comparable to high-income countries. In 2020, per capita grain possessions of China reached 474 kg, had been exceeding the safety line of the international grain standard of 400 kg for 13 consecutive years. China has been fully self-sufficient in grain rations for many consecutive years, feeding about 22% of the world's population with less than 10% of the world's arable land, which makes a world-renowned contribution to food security in China and even the world.

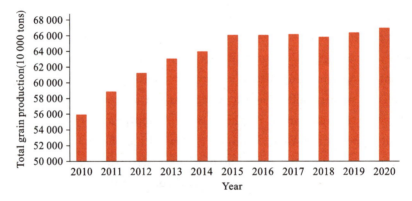

Figure 8-3　Changes in total grain production from 2010 to 2020
Data from National Bureau of Statistics of the People's Republic of China

In addition, China has achieved unprecedented growth in the production of other agricultural products, driven by growth in grain production for successive years. China ranks first in the world in many indicators, such as productions of cereal, wheat, rice, peanut, tea and meat, with cereal, wheat and maize production accounting for over 20% of the world's production, peanut production for over 30% and tea production for over 40%. A diversified growth structure of agricultural products safeguards and optimizes the domestic supply of agricultural products, with the dietary structure of Chinese residents enriched.

Second, the quality and efficiency of agricultural production and operations were steadily enhanced. After years of development, the transformation concerning China's agriculture from a traditional agriculture based on crop farming to a modern agriculture with comprehensive development of agriculture, forestry, animal husbandry and fishery has been achieved, and the development of agriculture has shifted from production-oriented to quality-oriented. In 2020, in China's agriculture, forestry, animal husbandry and fisheries industry, the total output value of agriculture accounted for 52.1%, the total output value of animal husbandry accounted for 29.2%, the total output value of fisheries and forestry gradually increased and accounted for 9.3% and 4.3%, respectively, and the output value of agriculture, forestry, animal husbandry and fisheries professional and auxiliary activities accounted for 5.1%, with the industrial structure further optimized. A modern agricultural industry system with an increasingly reasonable structure of agriculture, forestry, animal husbandry and fishery has been initially established, and the ability for stabilizing and increasing the production of the main grain-producing areas has been enhanced. Moreover, cash crops have been further concentrated in advantageous production areas, and the regional layout of agricultural production has been increasingly optimized.

Third, the conditions of agricultural technology and equipment were improved significantly, and the level of agricultural mechanization, technicalization and informatization was continuously enhanced. Due to the weak foundation of China's agricultural industry in the early years of the founding of New China, the total power of China's agricultural machinery was only 120 million kW in 1978, and the national comprehensive agricultural mechanization rate was only 19.7%. Since the reform and opening up, a historic transformation from relying mainly on human and animal power to relying mainly on mechanical power has been achieved in terms of China's agricultural production mode, with a total national agricultural machinery power of 1.06 billion kW in 2020 as well as an overall level of mechanization in plowing, sowing and harvesting of crops over 70%, among which the overall level of mechanization in plowing, sowing and harvesting of major crops exceeded 80%. Figure 8-4 shows changes in total agricultural machinery power from 2010 to 2020.

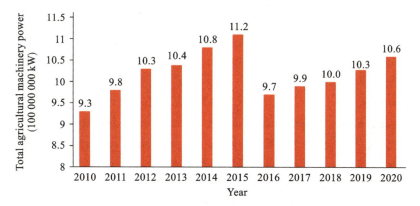

Figure 8-4 Changes in total agricultural machinery power from 2010 to 2020
Data from National Bureau of Statistics of the People's Republic of China

Progress in agricultural science and technology has given a strong impetus to the agricultural modernization. In 1978, the contribution rate of China's agricultural science and technology progress was only 27%, which reached 60.7% in 2020. In addition, the full coverage of improved varieties regarding major crops has basically been achieved, with the area of independently selected varieties exceeding 95%.

The level of informatization in the rural areas increased rapidly, and the digitalization of agricultural production developed initially. Figure 8-5 shows a scene of live broadcasting for rural e-commerce. During the COVID-19 pandemic prevention and control period, the role of rural e-commerce had become even more prominent. According to statistics from the Ministry of Agriculture and Rural Affairs, the coverage rate of China's e-commerce service stations in administrative villages in 2021 was around 80%, and the online retail sales of agricultural products in counties exceeded 300 billion yuan, which grew rapidly. In the field of intelligent agriculture, the digitization of agricultural production is just unfolding, with the construction of the whole industry chain concerning big data for individual products including oilseeds, natural rubber, cotton and soybeans, etc. develops initially, and the application areas of big data systems continue to expand.

Figure 8-5 Rural e-commerce
Photo from GD Today

Fourth, the initial task regarding the reform of rural collective property rights was accomplished, and the collective economy became a new growth point. With the deepening of the supply-side structural reform in China's agriculture, the construction of a modern agricultural management system has also been accelerated, and the nationwide reform of rural collective property rights has basically been completed, with rural assets and resources being greatly revitalized through asset clearance, membership definition, quantification of operational assets, establishment of economic cooperatives and other initiatives. The proportion of the area of rural contracted land transferred has increased significantly, with new development regarding various forms of moderate scale operations achieved, and new types of business entities have been enriched. The number of new types of agricultural business entities has grown rapidly, such as farmers' cooperatives. By the end of 2020, the total number of legally registered farmers' cooperatives in China reached 2.251 million, 5.9 times more than ten years ago, and the overall number has remained stable at over 2.2 million for four consecutive years. There are more than 90 000 leading enterprises nationwide recognized by agricultural industrialization authorities above the county level, including 1 547 national key leading enterprises. The internal energy of rural development has been significantly enhanced, and the collective economy has become a new growth point, laying a solid foundation for achieving the goal of common prosperity.

Fifth, farmers' income grew steadily, and their consumption improved stably. From 2004 to 2020, "seventeen consecutive increases" in farmers' income growth have been accomplished. The growth rate of farmers' income has been continuously higher than that of urban residents' income from 2010 to 2020. In 2020, farmers' per capita disposable income reached 17 131 yuan, achieving the doubling target proposed by the 18th National Congress of the CPC one year ahead of schedule. As shown in Figure 8-6, the ratio of disposable income between urban and rural residents declined steadily, and the income gap narrowed obviously. At the same time, the trend of upgrading rural consumption was obvious. In 2020, the Engel's coefficient of rural residents was 32.7%, of which the proportion of staple food consumption was decreasing year by year, with an increasing proportion of non-staple food consumption as well as growing reasonable dietary structure. On the whole, the proportion of rural residents' expenditure on diet has been declined, while consumption of medical, transport and entertainment has been upgraded and the quality of life has been gradually improved.

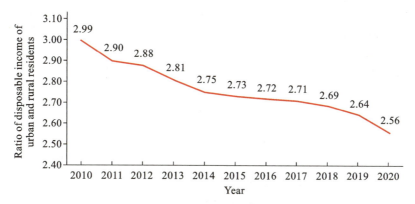

Figure 8-6 Changes in the ratio of disposable income of urban and rural residents from 2010 to 2020
Data from National Bureau of Statistics of the People's Republic of China

By 2020, significant progress was made in agricultural modernization throughout the country. National food security has been effectively guaranteed, and the quality as well as efficiency of the agricultural product supply system has been significantly improved. Besides, the international competitiveness of agriculture has been further enhanced, and the livelihood of farmers has reached an overall well-off level. Agricultural modernization has been basically accomplished in the eastern coastal developed areas, suburbs of large cities, state-owned reclamation areas and national modern agriculture demonstration zones. A production capacity guarantee pattern based on high-standard farmland and supported by functional grain production zones and important agricultural production reserves has been basically established. A modern agricultural industrial system that integrated rotation of grain crop, cash crop and forage crop, the combination of agriculture, forestry, animal husbandry and fishery, consolidation of crop farming, breeding and agriculture production industry, as well as primary, secondary and tertiary industries has been basically constructed.

8.2 Rural Revitalization and the Future Development of China's Agriculture

Agriculture is the basis of the three industries and the foundation of human survival and development, while agricultural products are the most important material means of production for human being. Currently, China has successfully won the tough battle against poverty, built a moderately prosperous society in all respects and eliminated overall absolute poverty in the Chinese countryside. The 14th Five-Year Plan period is the first five-year towards the second centenary goal, the focus of the "Three Rural Issues" has historically shifted to a new situation for comprehensively promoting rural revitalization and further eliminating relative poverty. Promoting the revitalization of rural industries is the primary task of implementing the rural revitalization strategy and an important way to accelerate the construction of a new development pattern and promote the common prosperity of farmers and rural areas.

8.2.1 Implementation Paths of Rural Industrial Revitalization

Among the "five revitalizations" of rural revitalization, industrial revitalization takes the first place, which is the top priority of rural revitalization, an important carrier for industries to transit from development to revitalization, a significant driving force to integrate urban and rural factors, promote rural economic development and stimulate the endogenous power of the countryside, as well as the most effective way to cover the largest area, drive the largest number of people, be the most sustainable, consolidate the results of poverty eradication preventing poverty-returning, and fully complete the task of poverty eradication.

It is a process of tapping the advantages of location, relying on resource endowment, integrating market resources, linking government, farmers, leading enterprises, rural economic cooperative organizations and other entities, adjusting the traditional rural industrial structure, forming a number of modern clustered and symbiotic synergistic industries in rural areas, transforming resource advantages into economic advantages, thereby driving the masses to increase their income and ultimately achieving common prosperity.

In terms of the realization paths of rural industrial revitalization, different models can be adopted in accordance with the local conditions of the region. For regions with a weak industrial base, which generally lack resources and location advantages, the industrial poverty alleviation shall be taken as the primary objective for their industrial revitalization, and a better material and talent foundation for industrial revitalization shall be laid during the implementation of industrial poverty alleviation, with an interface set appropriately in the institutional arrangement. In regions with certain established industrial bases, the development of their industries shall aim to achieve industrial transformation and upgrading, and focus on promoting the integrated development of industries as well as the formation of an industrial integration system. In terms of development models, regions with favorable resource endowment conditions are suitable for an endogenous development model. While in regions with a weak economic base and less obvious resource advantages, strengths from outside including the injection of external capitals, technologies, labor and other production factors as well as strong policy guidance, i. e. an externally induced development model, shall be utilized to effectively promote economic development.

Generally, the prosperity of industry in rural revitalization requires the following three major orientations.

First, adhere to the market orientation, and break institutional barriers to the flow of "people and land" factors.

With respect to the activation concerning the flow of talent factors, the urban-rural economic and social dualistic system shall be broken in the first aspect so as to build a community between urban and rural areas. Policies on education, employment, medical inspection and insurance shall be implemented according to uniform standards, making urban and rural residents enjoy the same public services and bringing urban and rural areas together as a community of shared future in a real sense. In the second aspect, the mechanism of introducing talents shall be explored, and the intensity of personnel training in response to the needs of the industry shall be enhanced, with the mechanism of personnel training innovated. While promoting the return of young rural talents, high-quality talents shall also be gradually attracted to the countryside. Moreover, it is required to help farmers improve the scientific and standardized level of production management, enhance the level of agricultural modernization, and gradually form a skilled and professional workforce, providing an indispensable human capital base for the full realization of agricultural modernization and rural revitalization.

With respect to the activation concerning the flow of the land factor, the nation has expanded empowerment and given rights in the rural land system reform, implementing the parallel separation of land ownership rights, contract rights and management rights, and encouraging the transfer of contracted land to new types of agricultural business entities. With respect to the giving of rights and expansion of empowerment, the land management rights acquired by business entities under transfer contracts shall be equally protected on the premise of protecting collective ownership and farmers' contract rights in accordance with the law, and their stable business expectations shall be guaranteed. With respect to the encouragement of large-scale transfer and operation, it is stressed that new types of agricultural business entities and service entities shall be vigorously cultivated, and the development of various forms of large-scale operations such as land flow transformation and service-driven operation shall be accelerated through various means including transfer of management rights, shareholding cooperation and substitute plowing and sowing, etc.

Second, optimize the industry chain layout and reshape the interest linkage mechanism of the industrial chain.

Each locality needs to adapt to local conditions and choose projects as well as industries that manifest its local characteristics and are in line with local realities and can promote farmers' income growth and prosperity. The industry shall be guided rationally and managed finely to achieve an effective linkage between production and marketing. Regional agricultural brands shall be vigorously shaped and promoted, developing e-commerce and introducing new sales methods such as live-streaming sales, short videos for traffic referral and community marketing. The industrial chain shall be extended gradually, increasing the added value of products, and the integrated development of primary, secondary and tertiary industries shall be promoted with deep processing of primary agricultural products as the main principle, so as to realize the organic integration of agriculture, industry and service industry. Additionally, the value-added level of agricultural products shall be significantly improved, promoting the improvement of farmers' income as well as the realization of common prosperity in urban and rural areas.

In the market competition, the role of new rural cooperative economic organizations shall be brought into play, and the fair, open and equitable benefit distribution mechanism of rural professional cooperative economic organizations shall be used to effectively ensure a steady increase in farmers' income. On this basis, new forms of rural economic organizations shall be actively explored and created, and farmers shall be encouraged and guided to implement group-based professional cooperative business models, so that a community of interests with shared risks for farmers can be formed, effectively guaranteeing the maximization of farmers' interests in the process of commercial production and management of agricultural products.

Third, promote the integration of the three industries and promote industrial prosperity.

Since the integration of the primary, secondary and tertiary industries in China's rural areas are still in its infancy, it is difficult for the three industries to exert a combined effect. It is required to promote diversified industrial prosperity, combine agriculture with secondary and tertiary industries, rely on new types of agricultural business entities, promote internal reorganization and integration of agriculture, facilitate horizontal integration of agricultural operations, and cultivate ecological agriculture as well as facility agriculture. Through leading enterprises, internet platforms and other entities, innovative sharing concepts shall be used to organize and guide the integration of land, labor, technology, capital and other factors with rural industries, breaking down urban-rural barriers, guiding the flow of urban factors to rural areas and promoting the two-way flow of urban and rural factors. The clustering and linkage between industries and vertically integrated development shall be formed so that agriculture extends naturally to secondary and tertiary industries which reverse infiltrate into agriculture, forming a development synergy and creating a multi-functional industrial park that integrates tourism, e-commerce, finance and services.

8.2.2 The Future of China's Agriculture and Rural Areas

In the past five years since the implementation of the "Strategic Plan for Rural Revitalization (2018-2022)", the new development of China's rural industries has been achieved, with the rural ecology demonstrating a new look, and the general farmers' sense of access, happiness and security has been greatly enhanced.

In 2021, national grain production was stable at over 650 billion kg, with an abundant supply of major agricultural products such as cotton, oil and sugar as well as meat, eggs and milk. The contribution rate of agricultural science and technology progress reached 61% in 2021, and the overall level of mechanization in plowing, sowing and harvesting of crops exceeded 72%, indicating an increase of 3.5 and 6 percentage points respectively over 2017. The national conversion rate of agricultural products processing reached 70.6% in 2021, and the primary, secondary and tertiary industries in rural areas were deeply integrated. New industries and new business models such as leisure tourism and rural e-commerce were vigorously developed, and the innovation as well as entrepreneurship in rural areas were booming. The level of green development in agriculture was greatly improved, and the application of chemical fertilizers and pesticides increased negatively for many years, with the comprehensive utilization rate of livestock and poultry manure being reached 76% in 2021. The living environment in rural areas improved significantly, and by the end of 2021, the penetration rate of sanitary toilets in rural China exceeding 70%, and the coverage rate of integrated social service facilities in rural areas increased by more than 40 percentage points compared to 2017. From 2017 to 2021, the per capita disposable income of rural residents nationwide increased by 28.9% in real terms, and the income multiplier difference between urban and rural residents narrowed from 2.71 to 2.5.

In the future, in the face of the current unbalanced and inadequate development of China's rural areas, China will unswervingly continue to comprehensively deepen rural reform, break down institutional barriers that hinder the rural revitalization, co-ordinate urban and rural planning, deepen the land reform, co-ordinate the political, economic, cultural, social, ecological civilization and the Party construction in the rural areas, speed up the modernization of the rural governance system and the governance capability, speed up the modernization of agriculture and the rural areas, and implement industrial prosperity, so as to develop the agriculture, the farmer and the rural area into a promising industry, an attractive occupation and a beautiful home to live and work in the real sense, respectively. By 2035, decisive progress of rural revitalization will be completed in our efforts, with the modernization of agriculture and rural areas basically realized; by 2050, rural areas will be fully revitalized, with strong agriculture, beautiful countryside and rich farmers fully accomplished.

9 Reform of the State-Owned Enterprise System with Chinese Characteristics

State-owned enterprises are the backbone of China's national economy, and the healthy and sustainable development of these enterprises depends on effective enterprise system. As a manifestation of productive relations, the enterprise system changes its form or nature with the development of productive forces. Meanwhile, it reacts on productive forces, influences and sometimes even determines the development of productive forces. The enterprise system is an important part of the basic social economic system and the basic institutional arrangement for achieving the objectives of the basic economic system, and the construction of the state-owned enterprise system is an important part of the formation and development regarding the basic economic system of socialism with Chinese characteristics.

For summarizing the course and experience of the construction concerning the state-owned enterprise system since the founding of New China, the formation of traditional socialist state-owned enterprise system and the exploration of the structural system concerning state-owned enterprises since the reform and opening up can be divided with the reform and opening up as the turning point, which has gone through four stages. First, the exploration of the establishment and adjustment of the state-owned enterprise system under the socialist planned economic system from 1949 to 1978. Second, the decentralization of power and transfer of profits as well as the contract management responsibility system reform in the 1980s after the reform and opening up. Third, the shareholding reform and the modern enterprise system exploration starting from the early 1990s. Fourth, the comprehensive improvement of the modern state-owned enterprise system with Chinese characteristics in the new era since the 18th National Congress of the CPC.

9.1 Establishment of the Socialist Planned Economic System and the State-Owned Enterprise System

The state-owned enterprise system is the most basic component of the whole planned economic system. The period from the founding of New China in 1949 to the period before the reform and opening up in 1978 witnessed the forming and tortuous development of the planned economic system. Since no existed model could be referenced, the exploration in an all-round way from the enterprise ownership system to the internal enterprise governance system was began after the founding of New China, and the state-owned enterprise system of "state-owned and state-operated" form was established. As shown in the Figure 9-1, of the total industrial output in 1957, the state-owned economy accounted for 53.77%, with the collective economy for 19.03%, and the total of private economy, individual economy and joint state-private ownership economy, etc. accounted for 27.2%, with the state-owned economy overwhelmingly dominated. At this point, the socialist public ownership of the means of production was fully established, and the "state-owned and state-operated" system became the most common form of enterprise system in the planned economy period. This unitary enterprise ownership system lasted until the late 1970s.

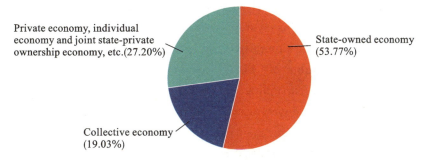

Figure 9-1   The economic proportion of China's total industrial output in 1957

Data from National Bureau of Statistics of the People's Republic of China

9.1.1   Characteristics and Important Constituent System of the State-Owned Enterprise System under the Socialist Public Ownership

At this stage, the development basis of the state-owned enterprise system was the socialist public ownership of the means of production. The rapid establishment of the socialist public ownership of the means of production in China reveals its special political and economic background. At the beginning of the founding of New China, the agriculture was backward and the industrial base was weak. In response to the political and economic blockade by USA and other western countries, decision-making level of the nation chose the development strategy of "giving priority to the growth of heavy industry to drive the development of the whole industrialization so as to realize the rapid growth of the national economy", and accelerated the socialist transformation of the privately owned industrial and commercial enterprises. The rapid establishment of the socialist public ownership of the means of production became the basic institutional arrangement for the implementation of the national development strategy, and the state-owned enterprise system became an endogenous system serving the goal of the national economic system. Moreover, the state-owned enterprises developed rapidly and became overwhelmingly dominant by virtue of the exploration of the realization form of the socialist public ownership.

The industrial administration system characterized by centralization and unification mainly includes the following two levels. At the first level, the central government and local governments implemented the basic principle of unified leadership and hierarchical management in terms of the division regarding administration authority of state-owned enterprises. In 1950, the Government Administration Council of the Central People's Government (which was established in 1949 and ended in 1954) divided the administration of all state-owned factories and enterprises into three categories. The first category were administrated directly by ministries of the central government. The second category were owned by the central government and temporarily entrusted to local governments for administration. The third category were administrated by local governments. The power and responsibility of local governments in developing local industries was properly expanded to boost the development of local industries. A centralized and unified administration system was established. The core of this system was the demands for properly handling the relationship between the Central Committee and local governments. In the early years of the founding of the People's Republic of China, the importance of safeguarding the authority of the central government while expanding the power of local governments to develop local industries and promote the development of local industries was stressed in the system, with centralization and unification as the mainstream. At the second level, the centralized and unified administration system with unified revenue and expenditure as main characteristics in the relationship between the state and state-owned enterprises was implemented. First, unified fiscal revenue and expenditure was implemented. For funds needed by state-owned enterprises, appropriations shall be made from the budgets of the people's governments at various levels in accordance with their affiliations, and excess working funds shall be lent by the People's Bank of China. In addition to paying taxes, state-owned enterprises must also turn over most of their profits to the government. Second, implementation of a material supply and product purchase system based mainly on planned allocation in terms of material supply and product sales was started. Third, a centralized administration system regarding the labor was established, with the personnel of all public enterprises under the unified administration of organization committees at all levels. Fourth, regarding planning, direct planning on state-owned enterprises was conducted, which refers to the mandatory planning administration.

The establishment of the leadership and administration system of state-owned enterprises was an important component of the "state-owned and state-operated" system. Determined by the nature of the socialist public ownership, the relationship between the state and enterprises determined the characteristics and operation mechanism of the state-owned enterprise system to a large extent. Based on the tradition of the supply system of public enterprises in the revolutionary base period before the founding of New China, and on the urgent need of implementing the national industrialization strategy in particular, the leadership and administration system of state-owned enterprises under the planned economic system of the Central Committee was initially established after the founding of New China, including major state-owned enterprises were administrated directly by ministries of the Central Committee. The production and distribution of important industrial products affecting the national economy and the people's livelihood, the vast majority of industrial infrastructure projects and important industrial means of production were uniformly distributed by ministries and commissions of the Central Committee, and enterprises outside the administration of the Central Committee were uniformly administered by local governments. As a whole, the state-owned enterprise system was formed, which consisted of planned economy administration systems including material distribution administration, financial administration, cadre administration and labor wage (welfare) administration.

The factory director responsibility system under the leadership of the Party committee was the internal governance system of state-owned enterprise system at that time. During the First Five-Year Plan period, significant progress was made in the construction of internal governance system of state-owned enterprises. Among them, in the aspects of exploring the internal leadership system of the enterprise, the system of combining the factory director responsibility system and management democratization was mainly implemented, and the purpose of democratic management was achieved by adopting the form of factory management committee. The factory director responsibility system was implemented in the administration work of production. The Party committee was mainly responsible for the political and ideological leadership of the enterprise, and played a role in ensuring and supervising the administration work of production concerning the enterprise, and in leading trade unions, youth leagues and other mass organizations. In September 1956, the report of the Eighth National Congress of the CPC clearly stated that state-owned enterprises shall establish a leadership system with the Party at its core, combining collective leadership with individual responsibility, and all major issues shall be subject to collective discussion and joint decision. This is the first time that the factory director responsibility system under the leadership of the Party committee has been clarified in the development history of China's state-owned enterprises, which is in line with the system of collective leadership of the Party committee that we practice today. In September 1961, the CPC Central Committee formulated and issued the significant "Regulations on the Work of the State-owned Industrial Enterprises (Draft)", clarifying that the state implements the principles of unified leadership and hierarchical administration over state-owned industrial enterprises and clarifying the core factors of the enterprise system such as the factory director responsibility system under the leadership of the Party committee, so as to standardize the basic management of enterprises. While the factory director responsibility system in administration under the leadership of the Party committee was implemented, the workers' congress system was implemented to attract the majority of workers to participate in the democratic management of enterprises. Figure 9-2 shows Wang Lin (third from left), director of Dalian Machine Tool Accessories Factory, studied the quality of the roller shaft with technicians. The main definition of the labor wage system was the establishment of a national unified

Figure 9-2 Wang Lin(third from left), director of Dalian Machine Tool Accessories Factory, studied the quality of the roller shaft with the technicians

Photo from Dalian Machine Tool Group

enterprise wage system, and the main definition of the economic accounting system was the construction of a national unified accounting system, which is embedded in the enterprise system.

9.1.2 Adjustment and Exploration of the State-Owned Enterprise System in the Period of Socialist Planned Economy

Since no existed model could be referenced, twists and turns existed in the exploration of China's state-owned enterprise system during the nearly 30 years from the founding of New China to the reform and opening up. However, the Party and the government were able to draw lessons from their experience and made efforts to correct deviations and mistakes, making two adjustments to the state-owned enterprise system featuring decentralization and centralization.

In 1957, as specified in the "Provisions on Improving the Industrial Management System (Draft)" adopted at the Third Plenary Session of the Eighth CPC Central Committee, the power of management, distribution of materials and profit distribution(use) of some state-owned enterprises was explicitly delegated to local governments and enterprises. In addition, institutional adjustments were made in reducing mandatory plans, simplifying plan formulation procedures, implementing profit sharing between the state and enterprises, and improving enterprise financial and personnel management, etc.

The decentralization enabled state-owned enterprises to obtain a certain degree of operation autonomy, with the operation efficiency of state-owned assets improved. Figure 9-3 shows article on decentralization published by *People's Daily*. However, chaos in economic development and people's life were caused due to overhastiness and excessive decentralization at that time. In addition, local governments lacked experience and ability to manage a large enterprise, failing to implement many systems, and some enterprises revealed chaotic management and low production efficiency. The Central Committee's

Figure 9-3 Article on decentralization published by *People's Daily* on March 23, 1958

control over national economic management was also declining, prompting the Central Committee to take over the management authority again. In the "Temporary Provisions of the CPC Central Committee on Adjusting the Administration System" issued by the CPC Central Committee in January, 1961, centralizing economic management power to the Central Committee, the central office and the provincial (municipality, autonomous region) level and centralizing more power to the Central Committee and the central office in two to three years were proposed. On September 15 of the same year, the CPC Central Committee issued the "Directions of the CPC Central Committee on Current Industrial Issues", emphasizing that the phenomenon of excessive decentralization in the past period of time shall be changed, and more power shall be centralized to the Central Committee (including the central office) to make unified arrangements for human, financial and material resources of the whole country. In fact, the entire economic management system reverted to the "Great Unity" system highly planned and centralized by the Central Committee. Main embodiment of the centralization shows in five ways. First, the power of managing a group of improper decentralized enterprises were centralized uniformly. Second, the planning management authority was centralized uniformly again, changing the practice of "setting two targets" during the "Great Leap Forward" and overcoming the out-of-control phenomenon of planning, and the highly centralized planning system was implemented again. Third, the authority for the administration of capital construction was centralized uniformly, reducing the scale of capital construction, centralizing the power of examination and approval for capital construction, withdrawing the authority for administration of investment plans, tightening the procedures for capital construction and strengthening the supervision over capital construction appropriations. Fourth, the enterprise profit retention system was abolished, centralizing the right to manage financial credit to ensure the financial resources of the Central Committee. Fifth, the materials management authority was centralized uniformly.

9.1.3 Achievements and Limitations of the State-Owned Enterprise System under the Socialist Planned Economic System

The highly planned socialist economic system was based on industries owned by the socialist state, which occupied a dominant position in the national economy. It was an institutional choice in line with the historical situation of low industrial level and simple industrial structure. This state-owned enterprise system played a historic role in the rapid advance of socialist industrialization, market stability, economic recovery and development in the early days of the founding of New China, as well as the rapid catching-up with the industrialized countries. It must be recognized that this enterprise system played an important role in China's industrialization and economic growth. Regarding the advantage of this system, it was easy to centralize production resources and improve the efficiency of factor allocation, but some problems such as overmuch and hidebound controls as well as affected vitality of enterprises also existed. The lack of autonomy and incentive system of the state-owned enterprise under this system was the main defect of the system. The state-owned enterprise became the appendage of the national plan and the tool to carry out the national plan and to implement the catching-up strategy.

In conclusion, a highly centralized planned economic system was established in New China before the reform and opening up in the late 1970s, and "state-owned and state-operated" enterprise system met problems such as lack of dynamics and vitality. However, from a historical perspective, the institutional choice was not accidental. Radically, the "state-owned and state-operated" enterprise system was the endogenous system proposed to realize the country's industrialization strategy, which was the foundation of the whole planned economic system. By 1978, China's gross industrial output increased to 423.1 billion yuan, of which 77.6% were Chinese state-owned enterprises. It is obviously that the state-owned enterprise system makes a great contribution to gross industrial output.

9.2 Exploration for Reform of the State-Owned Enterprise in the Early Stage of the Reform and Opening Up: Decentralization of Power and Transfer of Profits and Contract Management Responsibility System Reform

Under the highly centralized planned economic system, state-owned enterprises were confronted with problems such as low efficiency, large loss and lack of incentives that needed to be solved urgently. The lack of enterprise production and management autonomy led to the rigidity of enterprise organizational structure and short of vitality. Therefore, in order to establish an incentive system suitable for state-owned enterprises, the decision-making level of the CPC Central Committee quickly determined the reform direction of state-owned enterprises with "decentralization of power and transfer of profits" as the core at the beginning of the reform and opening up in 1978. Moreover, the contract management responsibility system, namely the contract system, predominated during this period.

9.2.1 Characteristics and Contents for the Reform of Decentralization of Power and Transfer of Profits

Different from decentralization, the focus of decentralization of power and transfer of profits lied in the reform of expanding enterprise autonomy. It was intended to motivate administrators and workers by releasing part of the revenue control rights to enterprises, and finally increase the interests of administrators, workers and the state altogether. In July 1979, The State Council issued "Several Provisions on Expanding the Autonomy of State-Owned Industrial Enterprises in Operation and Management" and "Provisions on Profit Retention in State-Owned Enterprises" and other supporting documents, putting forward that the enterprise fund system shall be changed into the profit retention system, trying to expand the autonomy of enterprises through the implementation of the profit retention system to endow enterprises with certain rights of distribution, and making efforts to solve the issue of "substitution of government for enterprise administration".

With the support of the Sichuan Provincial Party Government, in October 1978, Sichuan Province took the lead of the pilot projects of "decentralization of power and transfer of profits" in giving six state-owned enterprises a certain degree of operational autonomy in the province, including Ningjiang Machine Tool Plant, Chongqing Iron and Steel Company, Chengdu Seamless Steel Tube Plant, Sichuan Chemical Plant, Xindu County Nitrogen Fertilizer Plant, and Nanchong Silk Manufacturing Factory. Figure 9-4 Shows the Nanchong Silk Manufacturing Factory's workshop before the reform and opening up.

Figure 9-4 The Nanchong Silk Manufacturing Factory's workshop before reform and opening up
Photo from Nanchong Municipal People's Government

In the reform process of decentralization of power and transfer of profits, there were two extremely important supporting measures: replacement of appropriations by loans and replacement of profit delivery by taxes. In terms of credit, the reform of the "replacement of appropriations by loans" was carried out, which refers to the use of appropriations regarding the capital construction by the state changed to loans. In 1979, "replacement of appropriations by loans" was first piloted in Beijing, Shanghai and Guangdong, as well as industries such as textile, light industry and tourism. In 1980, China expanded the scope of the reform, stipulating that all construction projects with independent accounting and the ability to repay loans shall undergo the reform of "replacement of appropriations by loans". From 1985, "replacement of appropriations by loans" had been implemented in all industries across the country. The "replacement of appropriations by loans" played an important role in the reform of the operation mechanism of the state-owned enterprises. The Ministry of Finance no longer allocated funds from the top-down, without the problem of various regions seeking more local investment appropriations from the Ministry of Finance anymore, and the problem of soft budget constraints began to recede gradually.

In 1983, the reform of the "replacement of profit delivery by taxes" was carried out, which refers to the implementation of paying taxes instead of paying profits. Figure 9-5 shows the relevant articles published in the *People's Daily*. The "replacement of profit delivery by taxes" demonstrates the following advantages. First, fixing down the form of paying taxes could avoid the phenomenon of contending for base and proportion while using the methods of profit retention and profit gaining on all-round responsibility. Second, paying the first deduction in the form of taxes to the state after the enterprise realizes its profit ensures the steady growth of national fiscal revenue. Third, decreasing unnecessary administrative intervention by departments and regions on enterprises enables enterprises to arrange their production and operations more independently after paying taxes according

Figure 9-5　The news of the "replacement of profit delivery by taxes" hit the front-page headline of the *People's Daily*

to regulations. Fourth, the state may, in light of the macro-economic needs, adopting measures such as adjusting tax rates and reducing tax burdens to regulate production and distribution and promote the coordinated development of the national economy.

9.2.2 Characteristics and Contents of the Contract Management Responsibility System

"The CPC Central Committee's Decision on Economic Restructuring" adopted by the Third Plenary Session of the 12th CPC Central Committee in October 1984 set the "planned commodity economy based on public ownership" as the target model of the institutional reform at that time. The early decentralization of power and transfer of profits mainly in the form of "profit retention" caused unequal competition among enterprises due to the determination of retention rate and unreasonable market price system, thus failing to achieve the envisaged incentive and restraint effect. In 1986, the contract management responsibility system was widely implemented. The contract management responsibility system is actually a deepening form of "decentralization of power and transfer of profits", with the meaning of "separation of two rights". The contract management responsibility system, as the main form of economic responsibility system adopted by enterprises owned by the whole people at the beginning of the reform, is the initial form of state-owned enterprises transforming from purely production-oriented enterprises to production-and operation-oriented enterprises. Enterprises obtained part of their operation autonomy and residual claims through obligations such as the commitment to turn over profits (taxs), economic benefits, asset value appreciation, technological transformation and self-responsibility for profits and losses. In February 1988, the State Council issued the "Interim Regulations on the Contract Management Responsibility System for Industrial Enterprises Owned by the Whole People", which provided detailed regulations on the contents of enterprise contracting, internal contracting methods, implementation of the responsibility system, and the management system. The Law of the People's Republic of China on Industrial Enterprises Owned by the Whole People issued in April 1988 further enhanced the legal status of the contract management responsibility system. By 1988, 91% of over 9 900 industrial enterprises in the national budget had implemented contracting. Figure 9-6 shows the signing ceremony for Wuxi's pilot implementation of the contract management responsibility system for state-owned enterprises.

9.2.3 Limitations of the Reform of the Contract Management Responsibility System Starting from the Decentralization of Power and Transfer of Profits

The "decentralization of power and transfer of profits" is essentially an adjustment of the relationship between government and enterprises as shareholders of state-owned enterprises, which had a direct impact on the internal governance of state-owned enterprises and led to a number of changes to the governance system of state-owned enterprises. First,

Figure 9-6　Wuxi's pilot implementation of the contract management responsibility system for state-owned enterprises—the labor contract signing site of Wuxi oil pump and nozzle group
Photo from Wuxi Municipal People's Government

the enterprise leadership system was explored, mainly around the relationship among the Party, government, and trade unions within the enterprise. To begin with, it was made clear that state-owned enterprises would implement the factory director responsibility system and the workers' congress system under the leadership of the Party committee. After the large-scale implementation of the contract management responsibility system in 1986, the production and management, and administrative power of factory directors began to be strengthened. Second, a post responsibility system was being established within the enterprise at all levels. In particular, attention began to be paid to how to explore and build a modern enterprise management system suitable for China's national conditions. Third, the reform of the internal wage distribution system was carried out, and new wage systems, such as post wages, post wage allowances, floating wages, bonus withdrawal and distribution, and contract wages, were implemented, so that the total wages of enterprise managers and workers are linked to the economic benefits of the enterprise. The reform of state-owned enterprises from the late 1970s to the early 1990s was mainly a partial reform characterized by limited use of the principle of economic interests, expansion of enterprise autonomy under the framework of the existing planned economy system, and partial economic incentives for enterprises and workers. The decentralization of power and transfer of profits stimulated the enthusiasm of the enterprises and workers and improved the efficiency of the enterprises because it involved control rights and income rights.

The contract management responsibility system partly solved the problems of serious losses, poor management, and insufficient incentives for enterprises. However, it is fair to say that the contract management responsibility system was compromised, transitional and incomplete. Because in this incentive system, the governance structure of enterprises and the incentive structure of entrepreneurs were still imperfect, the independent decision-making power of enterprises was still very limited, the planned economic system had not been broken, and enterprises had not yet become independent legal entities.

The reform of the state-owned enterprise system, which took decentralization of power and transfer of profits as the starting point and the contract management responsibility system as the main form, failed to weaken the enterprise ownership system, but after all, it brought about many positive changes in the structure of control rights, profit distribution structure, and enterprise goals, which were of great significance to the system experiment.

9.3 Reform of State-Owned Enterprises in the Early 1990s: Shareholding System Reform and Modern Enterprise System

In the 1990s, state-owned enterprises were faced with the difficulties of funding and management. There were mainly three problems, namely, the long-term losses caused by the lack of funds, the incentives, and the corporate governance structure of state-owned enterprises. The establishment of the capital market is an inevitable outcome of the reform of China's state-owned enterprises. In 1992, Deng Xiaoping's South Tour Speeches and the 14th CPC National Congress adjusted the original goals of economic restructuring in a timely manner. The report of the 14th CPC National Congress clearly pointed out that the goal of the economic restructuring was to establish and improve the socialist market economic system on the basis of adhering to public ownership and distribution according to work as the mainstay, and other economic sectors and distribution methods as supplements.

9.3.1 The Establishment of Modern Enterprise System under the Shareholding System Reform

From November 11 to 14, 1993, the Third Plenary Session of the 14th CPC Central Committee was held, and the "Decision of the CPC Central Committee on Several Issues Concerning the Establishment of a Socialist Market Economic System" was issued. It made decisions on major issues such as "the transformation of operation mechanisms of the state-owned enterprises and the establishment of a modern enterprise system", and proposed the establishment of a modern enterprise system with "clear property rights, specified powers and responsibilities, separation of government and enterprises, and scientific management". "The Company Law of the People's Republic of China", passed in December 1993, legally regulated the types and basic composition of enterprise organizations under the market economic system, including state-owned enterprises. Taking the Company Law of the People's Republic of China as the basic guideline, state-owned enterprises began to focus on the cultivation of market entities and take property rights as a breakthrough point to carry out enterprise system reform with the corporate system as the main form of realization. From 1994, the State Council selected 100 enterprises in different regions and of various types to carry out pilot projects of the modern enterprise system. Establishing and standardizing the existing joint-stock enterprises in accordance with the requirements of the Company Law of the People's Republic of China became an important task in the reform of state-owned enterprises at that time. Figure 9-7 shows the demonstration meeting for modern enterprise system pilot implementation plan of Guangzhou Shipping (Group) Company. According to incomplete statistics, by the end of 1994, there were 33 000 joint-stock enterprises in China, an increase of 1.52 times over 1993. Among them, there were about 26 600 limited liability companies and 6 326 joint-stock limited companies with a total share capital of 286.756 billion yuan.

Figure 9-7 Demonstration meeting for modern enterprise system pilot implementation plan of Guangzhou Shipping(Group)Company

Photo from COSCO Shipping(Guangzhou)Company

"The Decision of the CPC Central Committee on Some Major Issues of Reform and Development of State-Owned Enterprises" adopted at the Fourth Plenary Session of the 15th CPC Central Committee in September 1999 clearly pointed out that the establishment of a modern enterprise system is an inevitable requirement for the development of socialized mass production and market economy, an effective way to combine public ownership with the market economy, and the direction of state-owned enterprise reform. The corporate system is an effective organization form of the modern enterprise system, and the corporate governance structure is the core of the corporate system. At the same time, the document also specified adhering to the leadership of the Party and giving full play to the political core role of Party organizations in enterprises is a major principle that cannot be shaken at any time; adhering to the principle of "two-way entry" between the Party committee leaders of state-owned enterprises and the board of directors, the board of supervisors, and managers, as well as the governance principle that one person can simultaneously serve as the secretary of the Party committee and the chairman of the board of directors.

9.3.2 The Internal Governance of State-Owned Enterprises under the Modern Enterprise System

During this period, the construction of the internal governance system of state-owned enterprises was mainly to establish a sound and effective corporate governance structure in accordance with the spirit of the CPC central committee on the reform of state-owned enterprises, especially the establishment of a modern enterprise system in large and medium-sized state-owned enterprises. The Company Law of the People's Republic of China played a key role in facilitating the construction of the corporate governance structure of state-owned enterprises in an orderly manner. According to the capital logic, the Company Law of the People's Republic of China determined the power allocation of major matters such as personnel, operation, investment, financial management, profits distribution, and wages at the levels of shareholders, board of directors, board of supervisors, and managers, and established the incentive and balance mechanism for corporate governance. According to the Company Law of the People's Republic of China, the acquisition of the legal person qualifications of corporate enterprises overcame drawbacks that the state as an investor should bear unlimited liability under enterprises owned by the whole people, broke through the limitation of financing scale, and enhanced the mobility of property rights. It allows state-owned capital to get in and out conveniently. In October 2003, the "Decision of the CPC Central Committee on Several Issues Concerning the Improvement of the Socialist Market Economy System" adopted on the Third Plenary Session of the 16th CPC Central Committee proposed to "establish a modern property rights system with clear ownership, specified powers and responsibilities, strict protection, and smooth circulation", hoping to promote the establishment and improvement of an effective corporate governance structure by deepening the reform of property rights and the adjustment of the relationship between government and enterprises and developing a mixed-ownership economy. In 2005, the CPC central committee launched the reform of the split-share structure, which further improved the corporate governance structure of state-owned enterprises by introducing a market-oriented incentive and restraint mechanism, establishing an interest balance and negotiation mechanism, and establishing an effective external supervision and self-discipline mechanism.

9.3.3 Contributions and Limitations of Modern Enterprise System

The reform after 1992 can be regarded as a revolutionary reform of the enterprise system, with the ownership reform as the breakthrough point, the establishment of the corporate governance structure as the center, the state-owned assets supervision system reform as the support, and the cultivation of market entities as the goal. By the end of 2011, more than 90% of the state-owned enterprises nationwide had completed the corporate shareholding reform. The coverage of shareholding system reform in central state-owned enterprises had increased from 30.4% in 2003 to 72% of the total in 2011. With the construction of the modern enterprise system of state-owned enterprises and the deepening of the reform of the state-owned assets supervision system, the economic benefits of state-owned enterprises improved significantly. From 2003 to 2011, the operating income of non-financial state-owned enterprises increased from 10.73 trillion yuan to 39.25 trillion yuan, with an annual growth rate of 17.6%; the net profit increased from 320.23 billion yuan to 1.94 trillion yuan, with an annual growth rate of 25.2%; and taxes paid increased from 836.16 billion yuan to 3.45 trillion yuan, with an annual growth rate of 19.4%. At the end of 2011, the total assets of state-owned enterprises nationwide amounted to 85.37 trillion yuan, and the owner's equity to 29.17 trillion yuan.

The modern enterprise system represented by the shareholding system played a significant role in the independence, standardization, and improvement of corporate governance structure of state-owned enterprises, but the shareholding reform also had drawbacks. Back then, under the imperfect management system of state-owned capital, the shareholding reform of state-owned enterprises had led to the massive loss of state-owned assets, which was rooted in the fact that people with vested interests and internal controllers could sell state-owned assets at a very low price, making a large number of state-owned assets instantly become personal wealth, resulting in great social injustice. Meanwhile, the shareholding system had not completely changed the ownership issues of China's state-owned enterprises.

9.4 Comprehensive Improvement of Modern State-Owned Enterprise System with Chinese Characteristics in the New Era: Mixed-Ownership Reform

After the 18th CPC National Congress, the construction of the modern state-owned enterprise system with Chinese characteristics entered a new era of comprehensive improvement. Its main feature is to strengthen the top-level design and promote the construction of a modern state-owned enterprise system with Chinese characteristics across the board. In November 2013, the Third Plenary Session of the 18th CPC Central Committee adopted the "Decision of the CPC Central Committee on Several Major Issues Concerning Comprehensively Deepening Reforms", which pointed out the direction of the reform of state-owned enterprises in the new era: actively developing the mixed-ownership economy, strengthening the supervision of state-owned assets with a focus on capital management, and promoting the state-owned enterprises to improve the modern enterprise system; defining the specific requirements of the modern state-owned enterprise system, such as improving the corporate governance structure of state-owned enterprises with coordinated operation and effective checks and balances, establishing a professional manager system, giving full play to the role of entrepreneurs, and deepening the reform of internal labor, personnel, and distribution systems. Subsequently, the CPC central committee issued a series of documents including "Guiding Opinions on Deepening the Reform of State-Owned Enterprises" to provide further directions on the improvement of the corporate governance structure of enterprises, strengthening the leadership of the Party, the development of a mixed-ownership economy, employee shareholding, category-based reform and assessment and state-owned assets management system reform. The 19th CPC National Congress and the Fourth Plenary Session of the 19th CPC Central Committee more clearly stressed the core contents of the reform of state-owned enterprises, such as the development of the mixed-ownership economy, the improvement of the modern state-owned enterprise system with Chinese characteristics, and the formation of a state-owned assets supervision system with a focus on capital management. The top-level design of the reform of state-owned enterprises in the new era is the elevation of the 20-year experience of modern state-owned enterprise system construction since 1992, and it is in line with the new stage of the construction of the modern state-owned enterprise system with Chinese characteristics.

9.4.1 The Characteristics and Main Contents of the Construction of Modern State-Owned Enterprise System with Chinese Characteristics in the New Era

Taking the mixed-ownership reform as the starting point, improving the effectiveness of the corporate governance structure is an important feature of the construction of the modern state-owned enterprise system with Chinese characteristics in the new era. After the 18th CPC National Congress, the mixed-ownership reform was raised to an important position. In September 2015, the State Council issued the "Opinions of the State Council on the Development of Mixed-Ownership Economy in State-Owned Enterprises".

At the present stage, the main contents of improving the modern state-owned enterprise system include promoting the reform of the corporate shareholding system, improving the corporate governance structure, establishing a classified and tiered management system for enterprise leaders, implementing the wage distribution system reform, deepening the internal personnel system reform, and strengthening the leadership and construction of the Party, etc. Among them, embedding the enterprise Party organization into corporate governance structure and letting it play the role of leadership core and political core is an important innovation in the construction of the modern enterprise system in the new era. Xi Jinping, General Secretary of the CPC Central Committee pointed out that adhering to the Party's leadership over state-owned enterprises is a major political principle that must be followed consistently. The establishment of modern enterprise system is the direction of state-owned enterprise reform and must also be followed consistently. The two "consistencies" are also fundamental principles for the construction of the modern state-owned enterprise system with Chinese characteristics.

9.4.2 The Constituent System of the Construction of Modern State-Owned Enterprise System with Chinese Characteristics in the New Era

Classified reform and classified governance are new strategies to promote the construction of the modern enterprise system in state-owned enterprises. With the basic premise of promoting reform on tailored policies for enterprises, according to the strategic positioning and development goals of state-owned capital, as well as the role, development status, and needs of state-owned enterprises in economic and social development, state-owned enterprises are divided into commercial and public welfare types to carry out function definition and classified governance and specify different development directions, supervision methods, responsibilities and missions, and assessment content. The detailed information can be seen in Table 9-1.

Table 9-1 Different types of state-owned enterprises adopt different corporate governance structures

Classification of state-owned enterprises	Corporate governance structure
Commercial state-owned enterprises whose main business is in fully competitive industries and fields	Representatives of state-owned capital contributors or investment and operation companies can only implement the strict "separation of two rights" in accordance with the principle of "managing capital", and contributors can only assume responsibility and participate in corporate governance as shareholders
Commercial state-owned enterprises whose main business is in important industries and key areas related to national security and the lifeline of the national economy, and mainly undertake certain special tasks	While "managing capital", state-owned capital contributors pay attention to the situation of enterprises serving the national strategy, ensuring national security and national economic operation, developing forward-looking strategic industries, and completing special tasks through legal procedures
Commercial state-owned enterprises in natural monopoly industries	The governance structure is optimized mainly around deepening marketization, paying attention to the organic combination of economic benefits and social benefits
Public welfare state-owned enterprises	Corporate governance structure is established in the form of sole state-owned capital or diversified investors (Non-state-owned enterprises can participate in operations through purchasing services, franchising, entrusting, etc., but they do not hold shares as investors or participate in corporate governance). External supervision shall be strengthened by increasing information disclosure and accepting social supervision

In line with the need of improving the corporate governance structure, reforming and improving the management system of state-owned assets is an important channel for the construction of the modern state-owned enterprise system with Chinese characteristics in the new era. The "Decision of the CPC Central Committee on Major Issues Concerning Comprehensively Deepening Reforms" of the Third Plenary Session of the 18th CPC Central Committee, the report of the 19th CPC National Congress, and the "Decision of the CPC Central Committee on Several Major Issues Concerning Upholding and Improving Socialism with Chinese Characteristics and Modernizing the State Governance System and Capacity" of the Fourth Plenary Session of the 19th CPC Central Committee all emphasized the importance of improving the management system of state-owned assets and reforming the authorized operation system of state-owned capital. The reform of the state-owned assets supervision system and the authorized operation system of state-owned capital is essentially a reform of the principal-agent relationship of state-owned capital, as well as a reform of the government-enterprise relationship and the government-capital relationship. Promoting the reorganization and establishment of state-owned capital investment and operation companies is an important measure to reform the state-owned capital management system with a focus on state-owned capital management and serve the current construction of the modern enterprise system. "Government—institution (department) performing the duties of state-owned capital contributors—state-owned capital investment and operation company—state-owned enterprise" will become a common pattern in the state-owned capital entrusting chain. From the perspective of institutional arrangement, the state-owned capital investment and operation company plays a key role of "bridging" in the entrusting chain of state-owned capital. In particular, it can effectively isolate the direct connection between state-owned capital contributors and production and operation entities, further separate ownership and management rights, and establish a new state-owned assets governance system with capital management as the main line.

The internal management system is an important part of the modern state-owned enterprise system with Chinese characteristics, and the "labor, personnel, and distribution" system is a very critical part of it. Policy documents such as the "Decision of the CPC Central Committee on Major Issues Concerning Comprehensively Deepening Reforms" of the Third Plenary Session of the 18th CPC Central Committee and the "Guiding Opinions on Deepening the Reform of State-Owned Enterprises" issued by the CPC Central Committee have put forward clear requirements for the reform of "labor, personnel and distribution" system of state-owned enterprises. In recent years, in order to enhance the vitality and competitiveness of enterprises, efforts have been made to build a market-oriented labor, personnel, and income distribution mechanism in which all kinds of personnel can be demoted as well as promoted, dismissed as well as recruited, and income can be increased as well as decreased.

9.4.3 Achievements in the Construction of Modern State-Owned Enterprise System with Chinese Characteristics in the New Era

After the 18th CPC National Congress, the overall improvement and promotion of modern state-owned enterprise system with Chinese characteristics achieved good institutional performance. By the end of 2018, the corporate restructuring of central state-owned enterprises had been completed in an all-round way. With the steady advancement of the mixed-ownership reform, listed companies have become the main operating entities of the central state-owned enterprises, according to the High-Quality Development Report of Central Enterprises released in 2019, with 65% of the assets of central state-owned enterprises, 61% of operating income, and 88% of total profits coming from listed companies. The overall improvement of the enterprise system brought an improvement in the performance of state-owned enterprises. In 2021, the total operating income of state-owned and state-holding enterprises nationwide reached 75.55 trillion yuan, a year-on-year increase of 18.5%. Among them, the central state-owned enterprises accounted for 41.73 trillion yuan, a year-on-year increase of 17.7%; local state-owned enterprises contributed 33.83 trillion yuan, a year-on-year increase of 19.5%. The profit of state-owned enterprises totaled 4.52 trillion yuan, a year-on-year increase of 30.1%, of which central state-owned enterprises totaled 2.86 trillion yuan, a year-on-year increase of 27%, and local state-owned enterprises totaled 1.66 trillion yuan, a year-on-year increase of 35.9%.

10 Industrialization Process and Urban Development

Industrialization is an industry-driven process in which a country or region's per capita income increases and its industrial structure changes from agriculture-led to industry-led. In essence, it is the process in which the combination of a series of important production factors in the national economy undergoes successive breakthrough changes from lower to higher levels, thereby driving economic growth. From the perspective of modernization theory, industrialization can be regarded as economic modernization. One relatively common interpretation of modernization is the historical process of human society transforming from a traditional society to a modern society, and the driving force of social change is economic growth and structural change, which is known as industrialization. This means that the essence of modernization is the process of modern social change driven by industrialization. Therefore, to achieve modernization, a country needs to start and promote its industrialization process.

To sum up the course of industrialization with Chinese characteristics since the founding of the People's Republic of China, it has gone through three stages. The first stage is the formation of China's socialist industrialization path from the 1950s to the 1970s. The second stage is the socialist industrialization after the reform and opening up to the beginning of 21st century. The third stage is the construction of socialist industrialization with Chinese characteristics in the new era. Closely related to the construction of industrialization is the development of China's urbanization.

10.1 The Formation of Socialist Industrialization Path

The path of socialist industrialization after the founding of the People's Republic of China can be summed up in one sentence as "a path of industrialization characterized by a high degree of state centralization, with priority given to the development of the heavy industry". Influenced by the Soviet model and the international environment at that time, China, as a latecomer, had a good reason to choose such a path in order to achieve industrialization and economic catch-up in a short period of time. The "Common Program of the Chinese People's Political Consultative Conference", adopted at the First Plenary

Session of the Chinese People's Political Consultative Conference on September 29,1949, also clearly stated that we should focus on the planned resumption of development of heavy industry to create the basis for the industrialization of the country and at the same time restore and increase the production of light industry to meet the consumption needs of the people. After the founding of the People's Republic of China, China embarked on magnificent industrialization, but the process of industrialization was very tortuous.

10.1.1 The National Economic Recovery Period: A Development Strategy that Prioritizes Heavy Industry

The period of the new democratic society from October 1949 to 1952 saw the implementation of an economic policy of confiscating bureaucratic capital, the completion of the task of national economic recovery, and the establishment of a highly centralized economic management system in its infancy, laying the foundations for large-scale national industrialization.

First of all, the dominant position of the state-owned industry was established and a highly centralized planned economic system for the industrial economy was set up. In 1949, the state-owned industrial output value accounted for 26.2% of the China's gross industrial output value and 41.3% of China's gross output value of large-scale industries, becoming the leading force in the national economy. In March 1950, the Government Administration Council promulgated the "Decision on Unifying National Financial and Economic Work" (as shown in Figure 10-1), marking the initial formation of a financial and economic management system based on centralization and unification. The highly centralized planned economic system of the industrial economy has two levels. At the first level, the management authority over industry was under unified leadership and hierarchical management between the central and local governments. The second level, in terms of the relationship between the state and the state-owned enterprises, unified revenue and expenditure was implemented in finance, a material supply and product purchase system based on planned allocation was implemented for material supply and product sales, and the labor force was under unified administration of national organization committees at all levels, and mandatory plans were implemented for state-owned enterprises.

Furthermore, giving priority to heavy industry was the main development strategy for the industry at the time. As a large country, China had to build its own independent industrial system. China's heavy industry base, which all started from scratch, was particularly weak. Around 1949, China was only able to manufacture some light industrial products, "not even a car, an airplane, a tank, or a tractor". In order to rapidly change the situation of a weak heavy industry base and to strengthen the comprehensive national strength, especially the national defense strength to cope with the severe international situation, China has chosen a strategy of prioritizing the development of the heavy industry.

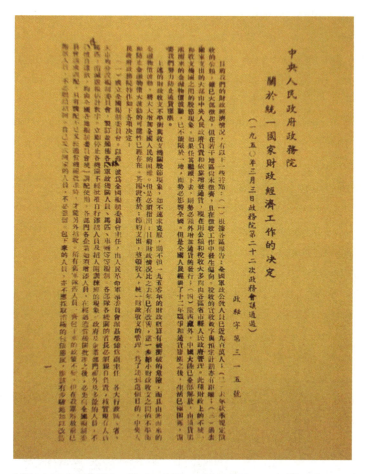

Figure 10-1 Photo of "Decision on Unifying National Financial and Economic Work" promulgated in March 1950

10.1.2 Initial Industrialization in the Transition to Socialism: 156 Key Projects

The transition period between 1953 and 1956 was from a new democratic society to a socialist society. Centering around the general line of the transition period of "one industrialization and three transformations", China introduced 156 key industrial projects during the First Five-Year Plan period, initially laying the foundation for the industrialization of New China. The First Five-Year Plan was a great success and a highly centralized planned economic system gradually took shape during this period.

As a late-comer in pursuing industrialization, China was eager to get rid of its backwardness. In February 1951, the expanded meeting of the Political Bureau of the CPC Central Committee decided to implement the First Five-Year Plan from 1953 and requested the Government Administration Council to start all the preparatory work for the formulation of the plan. In the second half of 1952, the formulation of the First Five-Year Plan began in earnest. The guiding principle of giving priority to the development of heavy industry was clearly manifested from the beginning of the preparation of the first long-term economic construction plan of New China. After the recovery of the national economy and nearly a year of gestation, the general line of the transition period was formally introduced in September 1953. In the same year, the First Five-Year Plan was launched. At the end of 1953, "the Struggle to Mobilize All Forces to Build Our Country into a Great Socialist State—Outline for the Study and Propaganda of the Party's General Line of the Transition Period" clearly put forward "socialist industrialization" and stressed that "developing the country's heavy industry to establish the foundation for national industrialization and national defense modernization" was "the central link to realize socialist industrialization". New China chose a route of industrialization that prioritizes heavy industry for many reasons, and one of the most fundamental reasons was that China's heavy industrial base was too weak, and the possible adverse effects of this fact were constantly strengthened by successive years of wars and foreign invasions.

The 156 Key Projects is a collective name for a series of major heavy industrial projects built with the assistance of the Soviet Union during China's First Five-Year Plan period. Among the 156 key projects, the 150 projects actually implemented were mainly in the seven major industries of energy, metallurgy, chemistry, machinery, light industry, medicine, and military industry, all of which belong to the heavy industry sector or the means of production sector. For example, Figure 10-2 is the Shenyang Aircraft Research Institute and Figure 10-3 is North China Pharmaceutical Plant. Industrial capital construction with the 156 Key Projects as the main focus was the center of the First Five-Year Plan.

Figure 10-2 Studied aircraft manufacturing at Shenyang Aircraft Research Institute under the guidance of Soviet experts

Photo from Aviation Industry Corporation of China

Figure 10-3 North China Pharmaceutical Plant invested by government during the First Five-Year Plan period

Photo from China National Pharmaceutical Group

In the First Five-Year Plan, the investment in the industrial sector was as high as 31.32 billion yuan, accounting for 40.9%, reflecting the central position of industrial construction in the plan. The First Five-Year Plan specifies that in the investment in industrial capital construction, 88.8% goes to the manufacturing of means of production and 11.2% to the manufacturing of means of consumption. The proportionality of investment must be determined in accordance with the principle of limited growth of the means of production, and the specific proportionality in each period of development should, in turn, take into account the specific conditions at that time. Prioritize the growth of means of production, that is, give priority to heavy industry. The 156 Key Projects have not only enabled China to form a relatively complete industrial system in a relatively short period of time, but also significantly narrowed the gap with the world's frontier of industrial productivity, which is of great historical significance in safeguarding national security and promoting economic growth.

10.1.3 Industrialization During the "Great Leap Forward" and the National Economic Adjustment Period

On the basis of the brilliant achievements of the First Five-Year Plan and the basic completion of the Three Socialist Transformations, the CPC Central Committee decided to implement the Second Five-Year Plan from 1958 to 1962, requiring continued industrial construction focusing on heavy industry and the establishment of a solid foundation for China's socialist industrialization. During the Second Five-Year Plan period, the construction of industrial sectors such as metallurgy, machine manufacturing, electricity, coal, and building materials was further developed and strengthened, and the design and manufacturing technologies of modern large-scale equipment for metallurgy, mining, power stations, and petrochemicals were conquered. Due to the excessive haste in the development of the steel industry, the "Great Leap Forward" movement was even launched from 1958 to 1960 to speed up the development of the steel industry so that the output of steel and other major industrial products could catch up with or exceed that of the United Kingdom and USA, resulting in a high rate of unqualified steel production and a serious disproportion in the national economy. Figure 10-4 shows the situation of the large-scale steelmaking during that period.

Figure 10-4 Large-scale steelmaking during the "Great Leap Forward" period
Photo from ScienceNet.cn

In December 1964, Zhou Enlai delivered his government work report at the First Session of the Third National People's Congress of the People's Republic of China, clearly stating the two-step strategy: "Generally, the main task of developing the national economy in the future is to build China into a great socialist country with modern agriculture, modern industry, modern national defense, and modern science and technology within a relatively short historical period, so as to catch up with and surpass the world's advanced level." In January 1975, Zhou Enlai reiterated the goal of the Four Modernizations and the two-step strategy in his government work report at the First Session of the Fourth National People's Congress.

10.1.4 Achievements and Summary

In general, during this period, the core of the industrialization path was to prioritize the rapid development of heavy industry, characterized by the government as the main investor and the state's mandatory planning as a means of allocating resources. On this premise, the Party continued to explore the correct handling of the proportional relationship of the national economy and the relationship between agriculture, light industry, and heavy industry, and gradually established an independent and relatively complete industrial system and national economic system, accumulating experience for the rapid industrialization process after the reform and opening up, and laying a good material and human resource base, especially the heavy industry base, which powerfully broke through the imperialist blockade, guaranteed the country's economic dependence and national defense security, and also laid a solid economic and technological foundation for China to develop into a world manufacturing power during the period of reform and opening up.

The major achievements of socialist industrialization in the nearly 30 years after the founding of the People's Republic of China can be summarized as follows. First, the stability of the state power was consolidated. The national defense industry was gradually built up from scratch, and a number of new industrial bases were built. In particular, the "Two Bombs and One Satellite" were successfully launched. Second, a dependent and relatively complete industrial system was established within a relatively short period of time. From 1949 to 1978, China's gross industrial output value increased from 14 billion yuan to 423.7 billion yuan. Among them, light industry output value increased from 10.3 billion yuan to 182.6 billion yuan and heavy industry output value increased from 3.7 billion yuan to 241.1 billion yuan. In 1978, the gross industrial output value, light industry output value, and heavy industry output value were respectively 30.3 times, 17.7 times and 65.2 times that of 1949. At comparable prices, the gross industrial output value in 1978 was 29.8 times that of 1949, with an average annual growth rate of 12.4%. Third, the national economy had gradually improved and there had been significant growth in economic development. Compared with 1952, when the economic recovery was completed, the major industrial products grew significantly in 1980, including cotton yarn production increased by 3.5 times to 2.93 million tons; raw coal production increased by 8.4 times to 620 million tons; electricity generation increased by 40 times to over 300 billion kWh; crude oil production reached over 1 trillion tons; steel production reached over 37 million tons and the output value of the machinery industry increased by 53 times to over 127 billion yuan.

10.2 Industrialization under the Socialist Market Economic System after the Reform and Opening Up

In the mid-to-late 1970s, China embarked on an ambitious course of reform and opening up in the face of a softening international political environment. By utilizing international capital, markets and resources, taking full advantage of the abundant labor force, low wages and manufacturing costs, and seizing the opportunity of restructuring the global industrial division of labor, China's industry has witnessed a period of rapid growth and has rapidly developed into an important manufacturing base in the world. Driven by the reform and opening up, industrialization in this period went through a stage of exploring the direction of the socialist market economy from 1978 to 1991 and a stage of construction and improvement of the socialist market economy from 1992 to 2012.

10.2.1 The Stage of Exploring the Direction of the Socialist Market Economy

At this stage, with 1984 as the boundary, the entire economic system reform went through a process of shifting of focus from rural areas to urban areas, from agriculture to industry, and the adjustment of the proportion of the light and heavy industries. At the beginning of the reform and opening up, the strategy of giving priority to the heavy industry was no longer suitable as it was not in line with China's comparative advantages at the time, and it was imperative to change the development strategy of giving priority to heavy industry.

In 1978, the Third Plenary Session of the 11th CPC Central Committee decided to shift the focus of the Party's work to socialist modernization from January 1979 and proposed to give local enterprises and industrial and agricultural enterprises more autonomy in their operation and management under the guidance of a unified national plan. China entered a new period of reform and opening up. During this period, the industrialization was adjusted from the Fifth Five-Year Plan to the Seventh Five-Year Plan, as shown in Figure 10-5. In April 1979, the Central Work Conference formulated the policy of "adjusting, reforming, rectifying and improving" the national economy within three years. In the early 1980s, the policy of prioritizing the development of the light textile industry was introduced to accelerate the development of the light industry and adjust the proportional relationship between light and heavy industries and the internal structure of the heavy industry. The shift in the development focus of the light and heavy industries was in line with China's resource endowment conditions of scarce capital and abundant labor at the beginning of reform and opening up. The industrial sector has generally carried out structural adjustment and technological transformation, and the industry sector has developed rapidly. The proportion of industrial output has steadily increased, among which the light industry has developed rapidly, accounting for an increased share, while the proportion of agriculture output has consistently declined. On the whole, China's industrial structure became more reasonable. Driven by the opening up to the outside world, the regional distribution of the economy also changed dramatically. Institutional, capital, and technological factors clustered

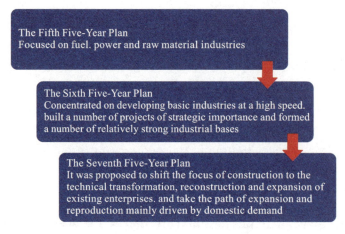

Figure 10-5 Key tasks of industrialization from the Fifth Five-Year Plan to the Seventh Five-Year Plan

in the east, and labor factors also began to migrate to the east, resulting in a "wave of migrant workers" from the west to the east and from the inland to the coast that lasted for many years, and industries along the eastern coast began to rise.

10.2.2 The Stage of the Construction and Improvement of the Socialist Market Economy

Marked by Deng Xiaoping's South Tour Speeches in 1992 and the 14th National Congress of the CPC, the socialist market economy entered a stage of construction and improvement. In 1993, the Third Plenary Session of the 14th CPC Central Committee adopted the "Decision of the CPC Central Committee on Several Issues Concerning the Establishment of a Socialist Market Economic System", proposed to establish a socialist market economic system in which the market plays a fundamental role in the allocation of resources under the macro-control of the state and adhere to the policy of public ownership as the mainstay and the joint development of various economic components. It also proposed to take the factor market as the focus of market system cultivation and thence entered the stage of comprehensively building and continuously improving the socialist market economy. The rapid industrialization process at this stage showed the following characteristics.

First, the shift of consumer focus was transferred to consumer durables, which reflected the characteristics of heavy-chemical industry dominance, contributed to the rapid upgrading of the economic structure and the shift in China's industrial structure from labor-intensive to capital-intensive. In 1996, China's commodity market had largely ended the shortage status; by the beginning of the 21st century, China had developed a huge industrial production capacity and significant price competitiveness, becoming an important processing and manufacturing base in the world.

Second, the strategy of low-cost export-oriented industrialization yielded great results. In particular, after China's accession to the WTO in 2001, China made full use of its comparative advantages to actively participate in the division of labor in the global value chain, deeply integrated into economic globalization, promoted industrial upgrading through "learning by doing", and rapidly promoted its economic growth and industrialization process. China rapidly became a global processing and manufacturing center for labor-intensive industries such as textiles and clothing, consumer electronics, etc. and industrial chain links, making a huge contribution to world economic growth.

Third, local governments played an important role in promoting industrialization. In terms of national strategies, coordinated regional development has gradually become the leading strategy for the regional layout of China's industrialization, and major strategic initiatives such as the development of the western regions, the rise of central regions, and the revitalization of the old industrial bases in the northeast began to be implemented and continuously promoted. At the same time, the central government promoted the reform of decentralization of power and transfer of profits; implementing the reform of the central and local tax distribution system; delegating land assignment rights to city and county governments. This gave local governments two important tools that can be of great use in expanding local investment and strengthening investment attraction. Local governments, as new market entities with Chinese characteristics, directly led local enterprises, used local resources and planned strategic layouts to compete with other regions in the market for accelerated industrialization. The work of local governments to promote industrialization mainly included three aspects: formulating and implementing regional medium and long-term development strategic plans; establishing different types of industrial development zones and industrial parks; carrying out various forms of investment promotion activities in an all-round way. In the practice of such kind of development and competition, a rich variety of industrialization models have been created, such as the "Pearl River Delta Model", the "Southern Jiangsu Model", the "Jinjiang Model" and the "Wenzhou Model", which played a unique role in the rapid advance of industrialization in China.

Fourth, after solving the scale problem, the focus of China's industrial development strategy and policies began to shift to high-quality development such as improving innovation capacity, environmental quality, and economic benefits. In 2002, the 16th National Congress of the CPC proposed "to find a new industrialization path with high scientific and technological content, good economic benefits, low resource consumption, low environmental pollution and the full play of human resource advantages". In 2007, the 17th National Congress of the CPC wrote the Scientific Outlook on Development into the Party's constitution and proposed to "accelerate the transformation of the economic development mode and promote the optimization and upgrading of industrial structure" with regard to industrial development, which involves the development of a modern industrial system, vigorously promoting the integration of information technology and industrialization, and pushing the large industries to grow stronger.

10.2.3 Achievements and Summary

After the reform and opening up, China entered a stage when the industrialization process developed the fastest and the industry's international status improved the fastest, with obvious characteristics of "compressed industrialization". In a few decades, China has completed the industrialization process that developed countries have gone through for hundreds of years, which has strongly supported the great leap of the Chinese people from standing up to becoming rich and strong. The industrial production capacity of China is continuously improving and the international competitiveness of the industry is increasing.

During this period, the path of industrialization under the socialist market economic system with Chinese characteristics was actively explored and established, and the focus of industrialization strategies and policies gradually shifted to the fundamental role of the market in allocating resources, low-cost export orientation, the construction of an open economy and continuous optimization and upgrading of the industrial structure based on the laws of industrial evolution. China's industrialization achieved unprecedented rapid development and created a miracle of economic growth.

10.3 Construction of Socialist Industrialization with Chinese Characteristics since 2012

Since the 18th National Congress of the CPC, socialism with Chinese characteristics has entered a new era. China has achieved a series of innovations in theories and policies on economic reform and development and has made significant achievements in industrialization.

In 2015, the Fifth Plenary Session of the 18th CPC Central Committee focused on adapting to, grasping, and leading the new normal of economic development, and clearly put forward the people-centered development ideology and proposed the new philosophy of innovative, coordinated, green, open, and shared development. China's industrialization path began to transform towards an innovation-driven, inclusive, sustainable, and high-quality industrialization. In particular, innovation is continued to be taken as the first driving force for development to accelerate the building of an innovation-driven country. By continuously optimizing the innovation ecology and increasing investment in scientific research and innovation, new industries, new business forms, and new models have flourished, and new progress has been made in building an innovation-driven country. In November 2015, the supply-side structural reform became the main line of China's economic work. In subsequent years, phased policies were established such as "cutting overcapacity, reducing excess inventory, deleveraging, lowering costs, and strengthening areas of weakness", "cutting ineffective supply, fostering new growth drivers, and reducing costs" and "consolidating, strengthening, upgrading and ensuring unimpeded flows", which have greatly promoted the transformation and upgrading of China's industrial structure in an advanced, green and intelligent direction, deepened the process of China's industrialization and improved the quality of its industrialization. In the new era, in response to the regional imbalance in China's industrialization process, the CPC Central Committee has launched a series of major regional development strategies to accelerate the new people-centered urbanization strategy, which promoted the synchronized development of new industrialization, information technology application, urbanization, and agricultural modernization.

10.3.1 Characteristics of the Construction of Socialist Industrialization with Chinese Characteristics

The prominent feature of industrialization during this period was the implementation of the new development philosophy to accelerate the strategic adjustment of the economic structure, transform and upgrade the manufacturing industry, and improve the overall quality and international competitiveness of the industry. It is mainly manifested in three aspects: the first is to give priority to information technology application in the national economy and society to vigorously develop the manufacturing capacity of electronic information products and new components; the second is to rely on infrastructure and major projects to revitalize the equipment manufacturing industry and improve the overall level of research and development and design of major technology and equipment, supporting core components, processing and manufacturing, and system integration; the third is to cultivate strategic emerging industries and accelerate the upgrading of high-tech industries from low-end links such as processing and assembly to medium and high-end links such as research and development and advanced manufacturing.

10.3.2 Industrialization Process and Strategic Orientation in the New Development Stage

The 19th National Congress of the CPC put forward a new journey to build a modern socialist country in an all-round way and made a strategic plan to achieve the second centenary goal in two stages to promote new progress in China's socialist modernization drive. In the first stage, socialist modernization and new industrialization will be largely realized by 2035, and the per capita GDP will reach the level of moderately developed countries. Then on this basis, in the second stage, China will be built into a great modern socialist country by the middle of this century. In October 2020, the Fifth Plenary Session of the 19th CPC Central Committee adopted the "Recommendations of the Central Committee of the CPC for Formulating the 14th Five-Year Plan for National Economic and Social Development and Long-Range Objectives Through the Year 2035". It proposed to adhere to the core position of innovation in China's overall modernization construction, unswervingly boost China's strength in manufacturing, quality, cyberspace and digital development, promote the upgrading of the industrial base and the modernization of the industrial chain, and improve the quality, benefits and core competitiveness of the economy. The above arrangements have defined the historical position of China's industrialization and the tasks and objectives of China's industrialization in the new era of realizing new industrialization and building a world industrial power. In order to achieve the objective of basically realizing new industrialization and building a world industrial power as scheduled, and to provide strong support for realizing modernization and building a great modern socialist country, Chinese industry must face various weaknesses and challenges, fully implement the new development philosophy, focus on solving core technical challenges, improving its position in the international division of labor, and enhancing its capacity for green and low-carbon development, and on the basis of continuing to increase total volume, accelerate the upgrading of traditional industries, the cultivation of emerging industries, and the growth of advanced manufacturing industries, and strive to improve the quality of development. There are three strategic orientations in the industrialization path in the new stage of development.

First, work hard on innovation and technology, vigorously promote the innovation-driven development strategy, tackle key problems in core technologies and follow the path of innovation-driven industrialization. China's industrial innovation and development should give full play to its advantages of a complete industrial system, the largest manufacturing industry in the world, and a new national system, develop and expand advanced manufacturing industry based on research and development and design, and systematically enhance the independent innovation capacity of the manufacturing industry. In particular, at the global level, it is necessary to respond to global scientific and technological progress, accelerate efforts in solving core technology difficulties in the fields of integrated circuits, computer numerical control machine tools, robots, intelligent equipment, digital technology, and industrial software, break through bottlenecks in key basic materials, core basic components, advanced basic processes, and industrial technology foundations, and promote the application of new technologies such as the Internet of Things (IoT), big data, and robotics in industry, so as to achieve breakthroughs in strategic emerging industries and cutting-edge technology industries, occupy the commanding heights of future industrial competition, and achieve self-reliance in technology. Therefore, it is necessary to clearly define the goal orientation of science and technology innovation policies, strengthen the long-term support capacity of national strategic needs, strengthen guidance and support for key core technology research organizations, improve the social system led by the government and closely linked and effectively interacted with all innovation subjects, promote continuous improvement and upgrading of key core technologies by adopting more methods such as long-term procurement by the public sector and stimulating commercial demand, and play a more active role in the creators and promoters of key core technology markets.

Second, work on the division of labor in the industrial chain, actively respond to new adjustments in the international division of labor, enhance the status of international division of labor, and build an independent and controllable industrial chain. At present, due to the growing anti-globalization and protectionism, the international division of labor system is undergoing new adjustments. The status and added value of research and development, design, and advanced manufacturing are increasing, and the industry still has a strong internal impetus to organize production in a globalized way. As the world's second-largest economy and the largest manufacturer, China is an indispensable part of the international division of labor. China should actively respond to new adjustments brought about by the international industrial division of labor, properly respond to the regionalization trend of the global industrial chain, create internal impetus for moving up the value chain such as research and development, design, and advanced manufacturing, strengthen weak links in the industrial chain, promote the integrated development of information technology application, intelligent technology, network technology and other next-generation technologies with advanced manufacturing industries, strengthen the digital and intelligent transformation of small and medium-sized manufacturing enterprises, promote the specialized division and integrated development between small to medium-sized enterprises and large enterprises, enhance the cohesiveness of the industrial chain, thereby enhancing China's position in the global production network. At the same time, in terms of policies, efforts will be made to expand market access, improve the supporting conditions for the production and collaboration of supply of factors, and increase the attraction to advanced manufacturing capital, technology, and talents from developed countries such as USA. In cutting-edge fields such as high-end equipment and core components, biopharmaceuticals, and next-generation semiconductor materials, international competitiveness could be improved by forming a professional collaboration system in which research and development, design, and manufacturing are closely intertwined and interdependent, and actively participating in global industrial division of labor and technical cooperation.

Third, establish the concept of low-carbon development, accelerate the green transformation of the development pattern, build a low-carbon industrial system, and improve the capacity for low-carbon development. Low-carbon development has become a globally accepted concept. Nowadays, all countries around the world have been actively promoting this concept. The large-scale industrial economy has kept China's resource and energy consumption and pollution emissions at a high level for many years, and the pressure on the ecological environment has soared. In 2020, China announced that it would strive to make its carbon dioxide emissions reach a peak before 2030, and achieve carbon neutrality before 2060. To this end, China should advocate the concept of green and low-carbon development, accelerate the application of green and low-carbon technologies, enhance the capacity for green and low-carbon development, vigorously adopt low-carbon technologies and process equipments, develop low-carbon industries, build a low-carbon industrial system, improve low-carbon development policies in key industries, explore a low-carbon transition strategy that is technically feasible and economically affordable, and follow a green development path of carbon peak and deep decarbonization.

10.3.3 Achievements and Summary

In summary, the industrialization path in this period is guided by the new philosophy of innovative, coordinated, green, open and shared development. The industrialization strategy and policy put more emphasis on the synchronized development of new industrialization, urbanization, information technology application, and agricultural modernization, and more emphasis on meeting the requirements of innovation-driven, inclusive, and sustainable industrialization. As China has gradually shifted from high-speed growth to high-quality development, its industrialization strategy has also shifted from high-speed industrialization to high-quality industrialization. Guided by the new development philosophy, accelerating the construction of a new development pattern has become a major task for the Communist Party of China to explore the path of industrialization with Chinese characteristics in the new development stage.

10.4 Urban Development in China since the Reform and Opening Up: Industrialization and Urbanization

Since the reform and opening up, the relationship between China's industrialization and urbanization has generally gone through three stages. The first stage is from the late 1970s to the early 1990s when rural industrialization rose rapidly, a large number of township enterprises were established and expanded, and the development of urbanization run parallel with the process of industrialization on the whole. The second stage is from the early 1990s to around 2012. As most township enterprises carried out property rights reform and enterprise restructuring, rural industrialization has shifted to urban industrialization, and the industrialization process in the eastern coastal cities has accelerated. Industrialization development has boosted the process of urbanization. The third stage is after the 18th National Congress of the CPC. China adhered to a new urbanization path with Chinese characteristics, and while accelerating urbanization, more attention was paid to the improvement of urbanization quality. Industrialization and urbanization tend to develop in an integrated manner.

10.4.1 Urban System Reform (1979-1991)

The reform and opening up started a new journey of urbanization in China. From 1979 to 1991, a phased path of urbanization gradually took shape in China. This period was characterized by the successive introduction of the rural system reform and urban system reform. Before the reform and opening up, China's urbanization was always suppressed under the strict control of the planning system. At the beginning of the reform and opening up, rural system reform formed a "push" for urbanization, and urban system reform provided a "pull" for urbanization.

On the basis of the reform of the rural economic system kicked off by the Third Plenary Session of the 11th CPC Central Committee in 1978, the "CPC Central Committee's Decision on Economic Restructurings" adopted by the Third Plenary Session of the 12th CPC Central Committee in 1984 initiated the urban system reform, and the focus of economic reform shifted from rural areas to cities. In particular, township enterprises flourished, and the nearby urbanization dominated by small towns has become the mainstream. Figure 10-6 shows a township enterprise's workshop during that time. The urban and rural trading markets were prosperous; 14 coastal port cities were further opened to the outside world; a large number of farmers "departed farming and left native land to work in factories and move to cities", forming a model of many small-scale urbanized towns. Achievements of urbanization during this period include an increase in the number of

Figure 10-6   Liming Farm Grain and Cotton Processing Plant in Zonghan Township, Cixi County is the earliest township enterprise in China

Photo from ifeng. com

cities from 216 in 1979 to 479 in 1991, an increase in the urban population from 184.95 million in 1979 to 312.03 million in 1991, and an increase in the urbanization rate from 18.96% in 1979 to 26.94% in 1991.

Generally, the economic system reform at this stage became the leading force in China's urbanization, and urbanization and industrialization were still parallel on the whole. The non-public economy developed rapidly; the market system continued to develop; the national macro-control system based on economic, legal, and administrative means gradually took shape. The series of achievements of city-centered economic system reform created a favorable economic environment for the further development of urbanization. However, restrictions of the household registration system, housing system, urban employment and social welfare system still existed, and the urban-rural dualistic structure, with a distinct feature of "departing farming without leaving native land", did not change fundamentally. Most of the surplus rural labor force could only flow into small towns nearby, resulting in a phenomenon that the urbanization rate of the permanent resident population was higher than that of the registered population, which showed a trend of gradual expansion. The gate of cities was still not fully opened to rural residents, and the period of rapid urbanization had yet really arrived.

10.4.2   Urbanization Process under the Socialist Market Economic System (1992-2012)

On the basis of the accumulation before the reform and opening up and the exploration at the beginning of the reform and opening up, China's urbanization ushered in a period of rapid development with the gradual establishment and improvement of the framework of the socialist market economic system framework from 1992 to 2012. This stage is characterized by the establishment of the socialist market economic system, the issuance of a series of new policies for the coordinated development of different sizes of cities and small towns as well as for encouraging and supporting farmers to work in cities, the further deepening of urban system reform, and the rapid progress and development of the urbanization.

The reform of the socialist market economic system is a large-scale systematic project. It mainly includes the reform of the household registration system, the reform of housing marketization, the reform of the rural land system, and the reform of the human resources market from the perspective of urbanization. In terms of the reform of household registration system, the issuance of the "Pilot Program for the Reform of the Household Registration System in Small Towns" (1997) and the "Opinions on Promoting the Reform of the Household Registration System in Small Towns" (2001) marked that the reform of the household registration system began to be carried out in small towns in an all-round way and gradually expanded to small and medium-sized cities. In terms of the market-oriented reform of urban housing, through the "Decision of The State Council on Deepening the Reform of the Urban Housing System" (1994), the "Notice of The State Council on Further Deepening the Reform of the Urban Housing System and Accelerating Housing Construction" (1998), and the "Notice of The State Council on Promoting the Sustainable and Healthy Development of the Real Estate Market" (2003) and other documents, China gradually established a general commodity housing market in which the majority of households buy or rent, and at the same time continued to improve the government-subsidized housing system. In terms of the reform of the rural land system, China accelerated the registration and certification of rural collective land ownership and established and improved the market for the transfer of land contract management rights on the basis of long-term and stable land contracting and management. In terms of human resources market reform, the "Outline of the Tenth Five-Year Plan for National Economic and Social Development of the People's Republic of China" (2001) clearly proposed to cancel unreasonable restrictions on rural labor force working in urban areas, and guide the orderly flow of surplus rural labor force between urban and rural areas and between regions. Later on, various departments intensively introduced policies to encourage surplus rural labor force to work in cities, abolished all kinds of unreasonable charges, and gradually established an employment service system.

At this stage, the gap between industrialization rate and urbanization rate gradually decreased. The urbanization rate was 40.53% and the industrialization rate was 40.29% in 2003, indicating that industrialization provided a strong impetus for rapid urbanization. The urbanization rate increased to 53.1% in 2012. From the perspective of the scale of urbanization, the permanent urban population increased from 321.75 million to 721.75 million from 1992 to 2012, with an average of 20 million rural population moving to urban areas every year. From the perspective of urbanization forms, the urbanization of the registered population and the urbanization of the non-registered population, mainly migrant workers, coexisted, and both showed a trend of gradual expansion. By 2012, the total number of rural migrant workers in China was 262.61 million, including 163.36 million outside migrant workers, and 99.25 million local migrant workers. It can be seen that with the gradual improvement of the market economic system, China was shifting from more local urbanization to more remote urbanization. In particular, the economically developed eastern regions and the big cities in the central and western regions were rapidly becoming more attractive to the migrant population.

There is no denying that China also faced many prominent problems in the process of rapid urbanization, such as low land use efficiency, prominent "semi-urbanization" problems, intensifying urban-rural inequality and social contradictions, unreasonable urban distribution and scale structure, widespread "urban diseases" and serious ecological and environmental problems. These problems inevitably required the transformation of the urbanization mode.

10.4.3　New Urbanization with Chinese Characteristics(2013 to Present)

In 2012, the 18th National Congress of the CPC Clearly put forward the concept of new urbanization. In November 2013, the Decision of the CPC Central Committee on Several Major Issues Concerning Comprehensively Deepening Reform adopted at the Third Plenary Session of the 18th CPC Central Committee clearly stated that China should stick to the path of new urbanization with Chinese characteristics, which marked that China's urbanization had entered a new stage of development. This stage is the people-centered new urbanization stage, which is characterized by accelerating urbanization, while paying more attention to the improvement of urbanization quality.

Since the reform and opening up, China's urbanization level has been greatly improved, but the urbanization development model of "emphasizing material aspect over people" has become unsuitable, and it is imperative to change the urbanization mode. As China's economy is facing the strategic task of transformation and upgrading, urbanization has also reached a new crossroad. The new urbanization stage is a new stage of development in which the scientific development system and mechanism and policy system of urbanization are constantly improved by comprehensively deepening reform in all fields. In terms of the reform of the household registration system, the Opinions on Further Promoting the Reform of the Household Registration System(2014) issued by the State Council clearly stated that a unified urban and rural household registration system should be established. Several Opinions of the State Council on Further Promoting the Construction of New Urbanization(2016) further proposed that the residential permit system should be fully implemented and the residential permit should be unified with basic public services. In April 2019, the National Development and Reform Commission proposed in the Key Tasks of New Urbanization Construction in 2019 that restrictions on household registration in type Ⅱ large cities with a permanent urban population of 1 million to 3 million should be completely abolished. In terms of housing market reform, the government should adhere to the position that "housing is for living in, not speculation," and gradually build a housing system featuring multiple suppliers and various channels of support that encourages both housing rentals and purchases. In terms of rural land system reform, the establishment and improvement of the system of "separating rural land ownership rights, contract rights, and management rights" for contracted rural land have established a basic institutional framework and policy basis for guiding the orderly transfer of land, protecting farmers' rights and interests, and forming a unified urban and rural construction land market.

The achievement of urbanization at this stage is the urbanization rate increased from 54.49% to 64.72% from 2013 to 2021, with an average annual growth rate of 2.17%. The quality of urbanization in the new urbanization stage has improved significantly. For example, the gap between the urbanization rate of the registered population and the urbanization rate of the permanent resident population have reduced for the first time since the Thirteenth Five-Year Plan. In 2021, the urbanization rate of the resident population was 46.7%, which is 1.3 percentage points higher than the previous year, and 0.83 percentage points higher than the increase of the urbanization rate of the resident population. Meanwhile, as the state encourages and supports outside migrant workers to return to their hometowns to start businesses and seek employment, the growth scale of migrant workers began to decline, as shown in Table 10-1.

Table 10-1 Statistics on the outside and local migrant workers from 2013 to 2021

Indicator	2013	2014	2015	2016	2017	2018	2019	2020	2021
Outside migrant workers (10 000 people)	16 610	16 821	16 884	16 934	17 185	17 266	17 425	16 959	17 172
Growth of outside migrant workers(%)	1.7	1.3	0.4	0.3	1.5	0.5	0.9	−2.7	1.3
Local migrant workers (10 000 people)	10 284	10 574	10 863	11 237	11 467	11 570	11 652	11 601	12 079
Growth of local migrant workers(%)	3.6	2.8	2.7	3.4	2.0	0.9	0.7	−0.4	4.1

Sources: Statistical Bulletins on National Economic and Social Development in 2013-2021

It can be seen that the proportion of local urbanization was relatively increasing, and China's urbanization is developing towards the trend of paying equal attention to local and remote urbanization. In terms of the layout of urbanization, the new urbanization emphasizes rational layout, large cities leading small ones, coordinated development, with urban agglomeration as the mainstay, to build an urban pattern of coordinated development of cities of different sizes and small towns.

11 China's Macro-Economic Policies and Fiscal and Taxation System

The Third Plenary Session of the 11th CPC Central Committee held in December 1978 initiated the historical process of China's reform and opening up and modernization. Two elementary clues run through this historical process. The first one is the reform of the economic system, that is, establishing institutions and mechanisms that can effectively improve the efficiency of resource allocation and promote economic development through reform and opening up. The other is to explore a development pattern suitable for China's national conditions and find a path to achieve industrialization and modernization. The evolution of the macro-economic policies can be roughly divided into 3 important stages in this historical process. The first stage, from 1978 to 1991, took the transformation of the economic system as the background with the main line of curbing overheated economy. The second stage, from 1992 to 2011, took the establishment and improvement of the socialist market economic system as the background with the main line of effectively expanding domestic demand and responding to external shocks. The third stage, since 2012, has taken comprehensively deepening reform as the background with the main line of adapting to the new normal of economic development and promoting supply-side structural reform. After more than 40 years of painstaking exploration, China's macro-economic policies have been developed and improved in practice, its macro-economic management capacity has been constantly improved, and a macro-economic management system with Chinese characteristics has gradually taken shape.

11.1 The Evolution of China's Macro-Economic Policies

11.1.1 Macro-Economic Control During the Economic Transformation Period (1978-1991)

The Third Plenary Session of the 11th CPC Central Committee was held in December 1978, and then China embarked on a new voyage of reform and opening up. The Government Work Report of 1978 pointed out that, "Planned economy is a basic feature of the socialist economy. We must put economic activities on the path of planned and proportional development. Drawing up plans must follow the mass line; both central and local authorities shall strengthen investigation and research, ensure comprehensive balance, establish plans on a positive and reliable basis, and direct human, material and fiscal resources to where they are most needed, so as to ensure coordinated development of all sectors of the national economy." Therefore, from the late 1970s to the early 1980s, "planned and proportional" and "comprehensive balance" were the main concepts guiding China's macro-economic control.

As the disadvantages of the traditional planned economic system were gradually exposed, how to correctly deal with the relationship between planned economy and market regulation became the key, and market regulation and the law of value began to be valued. The 12th National Congress of the CPC held in 1982 officially proposed to "implement the principle that planned economy shall be the predominance and market regulation shall be the auxiliary". This was the first time that the term "market" was used in important documents of the Party, which was a breakthrough in the barrier of planned economy and a major event in China's economic restructuring. In October 1984, the Third Plenary Session of the 12th CPC Central Committee adopted the "CPC Central Committee's Decision on Economic Restructuring", which stated that we should break through the traditional concept of opposing the planned economy with the commodity economy and recognize that the socialist planned economy must consciously be based on and apply the law of value, and was a planned commodity economy based on public ownership. This document took the socialist commodity economy as the reform goal, and the role of the market was recognized to a certain extent. The initial stage of China's market reform was also the embryonic stage of indirect regulation, and the government began to focus on the introduction of economic means in regulation.

11.1.2 Macro-Economic Control During the Establishment Period of Market Economic System(1992-2011)

11.1.2.1 The Initial Establishment of the Trinity System of Macro-Economic Control (1992-1996)

The socialist market economic system was established after Deng Xiaoping's South Tour Speeches in 1992. Macro-economic control gradually focused on maintaining the basic balance of economic aggregate, while emphasizing structural optimization, economic development and social progress. By establishing the trinity system of macro-economic control with Chinese characteristics, with coordination and clear division of labor among planning, monetary and fiscal functions and implementing a proactive fiscal policy and a prudent monetary policy, China achieved steady economic development. Many studies have shown that after the mid-1990s, China's economy changed its previous operating situation of ups and downs, but achieved smooth fluctuations at a moderate-high level on the whole.

"The Decision of the CPC Central Committee on Several Issues concerning the Establishment of a Socialist Market Economic System", issued at the Third Plenary Session of the 14th CPC Central Committee in November 1993, elaborated on the main tasks, policy means and institutional system of macro-economic control. The Decision pointed out, "The main tasks of macro-economic control are to maintain the basic balance of the economic aggregate, promote the optimization of the economic structure, guide the sustained, rapid and sound development of the national economy, and promote all-round social progress. Economic means are mainly adopted in macro-economic control. In the near future, China will make major strides in reforming the fiscal and taxation, financial, investment and planning systems, establish a mechanism for coordination and restraint among planning, monetary and financial aspects, and strengthen comprehensive coordination in economic operations". So far, the system of macro-economic control with Chinese characteristics has taken shape initially. In terms of the control objectives, in addition to aggregate balance, structural optimization, economic development and social progress were also emphasized. In terms of control means, the leading role of market-oriented means was emphasized, and the improvement of the quality of macro-economic control was promoted by means of institutional reform. In terms of the control system, it was required to establish a trinity system of macro-economic control with coordination and clear division of labor among planning, monetary and fiscal functions. This system includes both conventional fiscal and monetary policies and strategic planning focusing on medium and long-term development, reflecting distinctive Chinese characteristics. Under the system of macro-economic control with Chinese characteristics, China's economy successfully achieved a "soft landing" in 1996, with a GDP growth of 9.7% and inflation under control. The consumer price index fell back to 102.8 in 1997, and the exchange rate between USD and RMB stabilized at 1∶8.3. By the end of 1997, China's foreign exchange reserves reached 139.9 billion USD, and the RMB was convertible under the current account.

11.1.2.2　The Formation of Aggregate Demand Management Framework(1997-2002)

With the outbreak of the Asian financial crisis in 1997, China's macro-economic situation underwent an unprecedented fundamental change, with new phenomena such as credit contraction, deflation and insufficient demand. This indicated that China's economic system reform has promoted some phase-specific and fundamental changes in the macro-economic system, and the economy has changed from supply constraint to demand constraint. In this period, how to cope with external shocks, effectively expand domestic demand, and then stabilize economic growth and ensure employment was the primary goal of macro-economic control. Accordingly, since 1998, the long-term tightening policy of macro-economic policies has been transformed into an expansionary one, "proactive fiscal policy" and "prudent monetary policy" have been implemented, and the aggregate demand management framework has gradually taken shape. It was mainly manifested in the following aspects:

First, the development stage of China's economy has undergone a fundamental shift, and expanding domestic demand and managing aggregate demand have become the main focus of macro-economic control. The Central Economic Work Conference in 1998 stated that, "Expanding domestic demand and the domestic market is the basic foothold and long-term strategic policy of China's economic development." The report of the 16th National Congress of the CPC in 2002 continued to emphasize that "expanding domestic demand is the long-term and basic foothold for China's economic development. We shall stick to the policy of expanding domestic demand and implement macro-economic policies in accordance with the situation".

Second, proactive fiscal policy has played a crucial role in aggregate demand management. When the monetary policy cannot play a full role, the proactive fiscal policy play a key role in expanding domestic demand. Strengthening the coordination of fiscal and monetary policies can take advantage of the short time lag of fiscal policy and revitalize idle resources to increase output. And monetary policy can provide the necessary liquidity to prevent an economic panic, and to complement fiscal policy.

Third, closely monitoring and guarding against policy risks. China has always attached great importance to implementing the idea of comprehensive balance in its macro-economic management activities. Since the Seventh Five-Year Plan, maintaining the respective and comprehensive balance of finance, credit, material and foreign exchange has become an important principle in macro-economic management activities. In addition, the central government also introduced a series of measures, such as the separate operation of financial institutions and five-level classification of loans, to actively guard against financial risks.

In short, during this period, the government resolutely implemented a proactive fiscal policy and avoided a rapid increase in the government debt ratio by promoting economic growth. The fiscal expenditure multiplier of China's economy in this period was quite high, and the fiscal policy effectively played a positive role in promoting economic growth. Certainly, the proactive fiscal policy in recent years was implemented in a special environment. Once the economy is out of the trough, the proactive fiscal policy shall be withdrawn at an appropriate time. Otherwise, the principle of comprehensive balance will be deviated, leading to structural imbalance and economic distortion. According to relevant research, since 2003, China has successfully realized the transformation from a proactive fiscal policy to a prudent one by implementing the fiscal stabilization measures of increasing fiscal revenue as the predominance and reducing fiscal expenditure as the auxiliary.

11.1.2.3 Improvement of the System of Macro-Economic Control(2003-2011)

The 16th National Congress of the CPC in 2002 proposed that "in the first 20 years of this century, all efforts shall be focused on building a moderately prosperous society of a higher level in an all-round way to benefit over 1 billion people". The Decision of the CPC Central Committee on Several Issues Concerning the Improvement of the Socialist Market Economic System adopted at the Third Plenary Session of the 16th CPC Central Committee in 2003 defined the goal of deepening reform and aroused the enthusiasm of local governments to accelerate development. In some local areas, the investment in fixed assets began to heat up, especially the real estate investment. After the accession to the WTO, the export of foreign trade increased rapidly, and a "double surplus" of current account and capital account occurred (Figure 11-1). The foreign exchange reserves kept increasing, the central bank passively purchased foreign exchange and continuously released the base money, and the RMB liquidity increased rapidly, creating conditions for the expansion of investment. In 2004, China's economy emerged from the shadow of deflation, with new phenomena of investment expansion and energy supply shortage. Therefore, "proactive fiscal policy" faded in favor of "prudent fiscal policy". At the same time, the central bank repeatedly stressed the continued implementation of "prudent monetary policy", and introduced some austerity measures. The relevant policy-making department adopted the principle of "maintaining expenditures in some areas while reducing them in others with a discriminative treat", and adopted the way of tapping the brakes to regulate the economic operation.

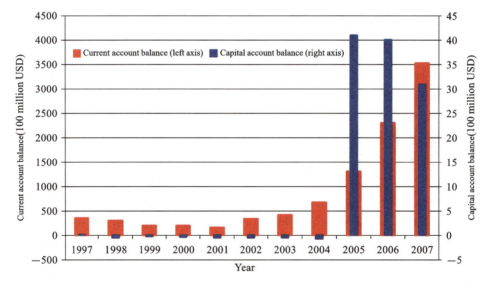

Figure 11-1 Changes of China's Net Export Value from 1997 to 2007 (100 Million USD)

Reprinted from "The Evolution an Innovation of China's Macro-Economic Policies since the Reform and Opening Up", which was published in *Management World* in 2018 and authored by Wang Yiming.

In the fourth quarter of 2008, the global financial crisis was further aggravated. In November of the same year, the Chinese government proposed to implement a proactive fiscal policy and moderately loose monetary policy, and successively introduced a series of stimulus measures in response to the fact that the economic growth slowed down significantly but the price increase was still high. The first is to take 10 measures to further expand domestic demand and promote steady and fast economic growth, and plan to increase investment by about 4 trillion yuan over the next two years, focusing on five aspects including agriculture, rural areas and farmers, transportation and other infrastructure, and energy conservation and emission reduction. The second is to launch a plan to revitalize 10 industries, including the light industry, automobile, steel and electronic information industry, to contain and reverse the decline in industrial growth. The third is to increase financial support for economic development. Since September 2008, the benchmark interest rate and deposit-reserve ratio have been cut five and four times respectively to promote the steady growth of money and credit. The fourth is to put forth effort to promote employment, increase support for agriculture and benefits for farmers, and expand resident consumption demand. Through the implementation of the comprehensive package plan, China quickly reversed the trend of rapid economic decline and became the first major economy in the world to recover.

The central government is increasingly experienced and skilled in macro-economic control, and pays special attention to the appropriate pre-adjustment and fine-tuning of contraction during periods of prosperity. In practice, when the economy shows signs of overheating, the central government often makes several small adjustments in a timely, appropriate and rhythmic manner, so that each regulation has a certain process of digestion and absorption. Proper regulation during periods of prosperity prevented the emergence of large bubbles, thus avoiding the wild fluctuations of China's economy. It can be seen that "managing prosperity" is a major feature of China's macro-economic control.

11.1.3 Supply-Side Structural Reform(2012 to Present)

Since 2013, China's economic development has entered a new normal. The challenges posed by the "shift" of economic growth, the "pains" of structural adjustment and the "digestion" of previous policies(the three-period superimposed) have contributed to the sustained and healthy development of the economy. Under the new normal, the thought of China's macro-economic control made a major breakthrough. While appropriately expanding aggregate demand, supply-side structural reform became the main line of macro-economic control. In practice, "pursuing progress while ensuring stability" has become the basic principle and general tone of macro-economic control in the new era.

11.1.3.1 New Exploration and Practice of Macro-Economic Control Under the New Normal

At the end of 2012, China gradually withdrew from the comprehensive anti-crisis policy track. Macro-economic imbalances gradually shifted from general imbalances to structural imbalances, and the economy entered a new normal. First, the speed of economic growth began to shift from high to medium-high speed into the shift period. Second, the long-term accumulated structural contradictions gradually emerged, manifested as the structural imbalance of supply and demand, and China's economy entered the painful period of structural adjustment. Third, the excess M2(broad money) supply was formed by the anti-crisis stimulus policies after the second half of 2008, which brought the rapid rise of M2/GDP (see Figure 11-2). Financial risks accumulated constantly and China's economy

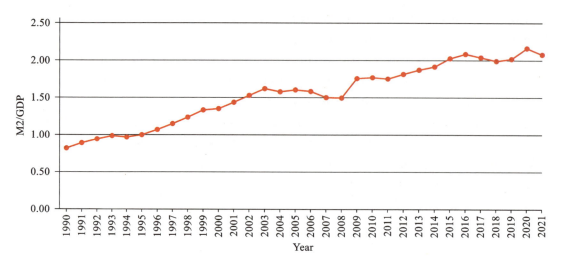

Figure 11-2 Changes of M2/GDP from 1990 to 2021
Data form National Bureau of Statistics of the People's Republic of China

entered the digestion period of previous policies. The economy entered a new track of "the three-period superimposed".

The Central Economic Work Conference in 2014 further clarified that, "To understand, adapt to and guide the new normal is the major logic of China's economic development at present and in the years to come." Therefore, the new normal is a strategic judgment and an accurate summary of the new stage of China's economic development. The new normal contains new driving forces for development. To discover, tap and make good use of these driving forces, it is necessary to carry out a thorough reform of the traditional mode of development, carry out a sweeping reform of the distorted economic structure, and make timely adjustments to those parts of the regulatory system that do not meet the requirements of the new normal.

In the face of the new situation and challenges at home and abroad, especially the downward pressure on the economy, China made innovations in macro-economic control. In 2013, the central government put forward the concept of "range-based regulation", which calls for keeping the direction, intensity and pace of macro-economic control in a proper range, maintaining the "lower limit" for stable growth and employment, and the "upper limit" for preventing inflation, so as to promote economic transformation and upgrading within such a proper range. In 2014, "targeted regulation" was proposed, which means that instead of taking strong short-term stimulus measures, key areas and key links shall be focused on, and market forces shall be more used. China successively implemented targeted tax cuts and general fee cuts for small and micro businesses, expanded the pilot program of replacing business tax with value-added tax, and actively adopted targeted cuts to required reserve ratios and targeted re-lending measures to increase support for weak links in economic development. In 2015, the central government proposed to implement "well-timed regulation" in a more precise manner, emphasizing policy options and response plans, grasping the timing and intensity of the introduction of regulation measures, and constantly improving the level of well-timed decision-making. The "range-based regulation", "targeted regulation" and "well-timed regulation" reflect the new exploration and practice of the central government in innovating and improving macro-economic control.

11.1.3.2 Supply-Side Structural Reform

The Third Plenary Session of the 18th CPC Central Committee held in November 2013 was a meeting of great significance when China's reform entered a critical period and pivotal stage. "The Decision of the CPC Central Committee on Several major Issues Concerning Comprehensively Deepening Reform" adopted at the meeting emphasized that "the market shall play a decisive role in resource allocation and the government shall play its role better". This is a major theoretical innovation of milestone significance, a major breakthrough in understanding the laws of the market economy, and a theoretical preparation for promoting supply-side structural reform.

At the end of 2015, the CPC Central Committee made a major decision to promote supply-side structural reform. While appropriately expanding aggregate demand, strengthening supply-side structural reform shall be focused on. This is a major plan for China's economic development and work focus, and it is the main line of China's macro-economic control in the new era. Macro-economic control shall first give full play to the leading role of supply-side structural reform in improving efficiency and optimizing the structure, and focus on promoting the "five priority tasks" strategy, namely cutting overcapacity, reducing excess inventory, deleveraging, lowering costs, and strengthening areas of weakness.

Driven by supply-side structural reform, the price level of China's industries with overcapacity gradually returned to equilibrium, and the supply and demand situation improved significantly. However, due to the excessive intervention of the government and the insufficient role of the market mechanism, various structural contradictions still exist. Therefore, the Central Economic Work Conference in 2018 emphasized that China must unswervingly focus on supply-side structural reform, adopt more reform measures, make more use of market-based and law-based means, and work hard on "consolidating, strengthening, upgrading, and ensuring unimpeded flows". In other words, the vitality of micro entities, improvement of the industrial chain and smoothness of the circulation of the national economy shall be promoted based on consolidating the achievements of the "five priority tasks" to promote high-quality economic development.

Taking supply-side structural reform as the main line does not mean giving up aggregate demand management. Policy makers believe that supply and demand shall not be pitted against each other, nor shall short-term macro stability be pitted against medium- and long-term growth. Appropriate and effective aggregate demand management is an important policy guarantee for the sustained and healthy development of China's economy. In 2018, the government also stressed the need to strengthen counter-cyclical adjustments, continue to implement proactive fiscal policies and prudent monetary policies, and make timely anticipatory adjustment and fine-tuning to stabilize aggregate demand.

11.2 China's Public Fiscal System

Finance is the distribution relationship formed by the government to distribute and redistribute some social products in order to meet the social public needs. Finance distribution is different from market distribution. The former is the distribution of the nation as the main body and the government's participation in the distribution of national income. The following, starting from public finance, introduces the functions of public finance and the characteristics and construction progress of China's fiscal system, expounds the composition of China's fiscal revenue and expenditure and fiscal capacity, and analyzes the process of China's fiscal and taxation systems reform since the reform and opening up.

11.2.1 Functions of China's Public Finance

According to the general provisions of the market economy, the fiscal functions of the Chinese government include four aspects: resource allocation, income distribution, economic regulation and supervision and management.

11.2.1.1 Resource Allocation

The resource allocation function of finance is to centralize a certain number of social resources to form fiscal revenue. On this basis, the government provides public goods or services through the distribution channel of fiscal expenditure. In the market economy, finance is not only the direct distributor of some social resources, but also the regulator of the whole social resource allocation. This characteristic determines that its resource allocation function not only includes the direct allocation of resources, but also involves the indirect regulation of the whole social resources. Finance regulates the allocation of social resources between government departments and non-government departments to make it conform to the requirements of optimizing resource allocation.

11.2.1.2 Income Distribution

The income distribution function of finance means that the government's fiscal revenue and expenditure activities exert influence on the income share of each social member in the social wealth, so as to achieve fair income distribution. If the government does not intervene, the market generally distributes social wealth initially in accordance with factors such as how much the production factors contribute to production. Such distribution may cause a huge income gap. However, the market cannot handle this problem, but only rely on the government to regulate the excessive income gap. This kind of regulation distribution is mainly carried out through two ways: regulating income gap by taxation and transferring payment to subsidize low-income groups.

11.2.1.3 Economic Regulation

The economic regulation function of finance refers to the implementation of specific fiscal policies to promote the realization of goals such as higher employment level, price stability and economic growth. In different stages of economic development, different fiscal policies are implemented to achieve the basic balance between social aggregate supply and aggregate demand. In a period of economic depression, the social aggregate demand is insufficient and the unemployment rate rises. In this situation, the government shall adopt an expansionary fiscal policy to increase fiscal expenditure and reduce taxes at the same time, so as to stimulate the growth of the aggregate demand and reduce the unemployment rate. In a period of economic prosperity, the excess social aggregate demand will cause inflation, thus the government shall adopt tight fiscal policies to reduce fiscal expenditure and increase taxes at the same time, so as to restrain the aggregate demand and ease inflation.

Take the impact of the COVID-19 pandemic in 2020 as an example. The pandemic caused a severe recession in the world economy, a severe hindrance to the cycle of the industrial chain and supply chain, a shrinkage to international trade and investment, and a turmoil in the commodity market. The fiscal policies in China played a key role in stabilizing the economy at this time. First, tax and fee cuts were increased, with a focus on easing the tax burden on micro, small and medium-sized enterprises, individual businesses and enterprises in difficult industries. The burden was expected to be reduced by over 2.5 trillion yuan this year. Second, funds were raised through multiple channels, increasing the fiscal deficit by 1 trillion yuan compared to 2019. Meanwhile, 1 trillion yuan of special government bonds were issued to combat COVID-19 pandemic and the support for the research and development of COVID-19 vaccines and drugs was increased to effectively meet the funding needs. Third, local fiscal difficulties were eased. All the newly increased fiscal deficits and special government bonds were allocated to local governments. At the same time, a special transfer payment mechanism was set up so that the funds can go directly to cities and counties to benefit enterprises and the people. Fourth, the government investment was increased by 1.6 trillion yuan in local government special bonds compared to 2019, and the living environment in rural areas and the public health system were improved by taking epidemic prevention and control as the entry point. This series of fiscal and taxation policies bolster areas of weakness, improve people's livelihood, boost consumption, and expand domestic demand, so as to promote comprehensive economic and social recovery and smooth fiscal operation.

11.2.1.4 Supervision and Management

In the macro-economic control, the department of finance provides basic rules for market competition by establishing sound laws and regulations on fiscal and taxation administration. Also, it should provide timely feedback based on tracking and monitoring macro-economic indicators to offer a decision-making basis for national macro-economic control. For the management of micro-enterprises, the department of finance ensures the national fiscal revenue by standardizing the economic order and strictly implementing the fiscal, taxation and accounting laws and regulations. For the management of the state-owned assets, the department of finance shall, through the preparation of state-owned capital operation budgets, ensure the preservation and appreciation of the state-owned assets, enhance the nation's fiscal resources, and improve the efficiency of fiscal allocation and the level of fiscal management.

11.2.2 The Establishment of Modern Fiscal System

11.2.2.1 The Basic Establishment of Modern Budget Management System

Budget management system with "unify" and "whole process" was preliminarily established. Through the introduction and modification of of the Budget Law of the People's Republic of China, China has formed a double budget system with Chinese characteristics consisting of "four accounts", which basically realizes the unified management for budget revenue. By introducing an accrual based government accounting system, deepening departmental budget reform, vigorously implementing performance budgeting, strengthening fiscal auditing, increasing budget transparency, and experimenting with cross-cycle budgeting, China's budget management has become more scientific and standardized with high transparency, optimized expenditure structure and constantly improved efficiency of capital use. A modern budget management system commensurate with the modernization of the nation's governance system and capacity has been established.

11.2.2.2 Major Progress in the Construction of Modern Taxation System

(1) *The value-added tax system reform has been implemented*

The pilot projects to replace the business tax with value-added tax was carried out in an all-round way, with value-added tax covering all goods and services, and business tax being phased out. On this basis, the value-added tax rate was simplified from four levels to three levels, reducing the overall value-added tax rate. The reform of replacing business tax with value-added tax has connected the deduction chain within the service industry and between secondary and tertiary industries, promoted social division of labor and cooperation, and effectively reduced the tax burden on enterprises.

(2) *The consumption tax system has been continuously improved*

China regulated the scope of consumption tax collection, optimized the structure of tax rates, and improved taxation procedures. China raised the unit consumption tax on refined oil for three times, canceled the consumption tax on small-emission motorcycles, automobile tires and other products, involved batteries and paints in the scope of consumption tax collection, significantly increased the consumption tax on cigarettes, and added consumption tax on ultra-luxury cars, further enhancing the regulation function of consumption tax.

(3) *The resource tax and environmental protection tax reform has been implemented*

China comprehensively carried out the reform of levying a price-based mineral resource tax, carried out a trial reform of a water resource tax, abolished or suspended related fee funds in line with the principle of "abolishing fees and replacing them with taxes", and promulgated and implemented an environmental protection tax law, effectively promoting resource conservation and environmental protection.

(4) The comprehensive and classified combination of the personal income tax system has been established

The implementation of comprehensive taxation on certain labor income, the increase in the standard of basic deductible expenses for some comprehensive income tax, the optimization and adjustment of the tax rate structure, and the establishment of six special additional deduction items, namely children's education, continuing education, medical treatment for serious diseases, housing loan interest, housing rent, and support for the elderly, marked an important step forward in the comprehensive direction of China's personal income tax system.

11.2.2.3 Promotion in Reform of the Central and Local Fiscal Systems

In terms of revenue division, after the replacement of business tax with value-added tax, the distribution ratio of value-added tax between the central and local governments was adjusted from 75 : 25 to 50 : 50. Meanwhile, the collection of consumption tax was moved later, gradually transforming it into a shared tax for the central and local governments, thus ensuring the normal performance of local governments' duties. In terms of transferring payment system, as early as 2014, the proportion of general transfer payments reached 58.2%, close to the reform target of 60%, and after the establishment of the common responsibility and right in 2019, the proportion was close to 90%. The number of special transfer payments was also significantly reduced. Overall, however, due to the difficulty and large scope of the reform, there is an urgent need to further deepen the reform in this area.

11.3 Fiscal Revenue and Expenditure

11.3.1 Public Fiscal Revenue

The public fiscal revenue is the sum of all monetary income obtained by the government from enterprises, families and other social target groups by various fiscal measures, such as taxation, in order to meet the needs of the government's public expenditure, and perform the responsibilities of government's public management, public services and market-oriented management of the national economy.

11.3.1.1 Forms of Public Fiscal Revenue in China

China's public fiscal revenue mainly consists of 2 parts: tax revenue and non-tax revenue.

Tax revenue includes domestic value-added tax, domestic consumption tax, value-added tax on imports and exports of goods, consumption tax on imports and exports of consumer goods, personal income tax, customs duties, farmland occupation tax, tobacco tax and other tax revenue.

Non-tax revenue mainly includes special revenue, revenue from administrative and institutional fees, revenue from confiscation, revenue from state-owned capital operation, revenue from compensated use of state-owned resources(properties) and other revenue.

Take the fiscal data for 2019 and 2020 as an example, as shown in Table 11-1.

Table 11-1 Major items of China's public fiscal revenue in 2019 and 2020

Items	China's public fiscal revenue (100 million yuan)		Proportion (%)	
Year	2019	2020	2019	2020
In total	190 390.08	182 913.88	100.00	100.00
Tax revenue	158 000.46	154 312.29	82.99	84.36
Non-tax revenue	32 389.62	28 601.59	17.01	15.64
Special revenue	7 134.16	7 123.36	3.75	3.89
Revenue from administrative and institutional fees	3 888.07	3 838.65	2.04	2.10
Revenue from confiscation	3 062.09	3 113.87	1.61	1.70
Revenue from state-owned capital operation	7 720.52	1 938.95	4.06	1.06
Revenue from compensated use of state-owned resources (property)	8 061.01	9 934.33	4.23	5.43
Other revenue	2 523.77	2 652.43	1.33	1.45

Sources: *China Statistics Yearbook* 2020 and 2021

(1) *Tax Revenue*

Tax revenue is a way for the government to obtain fiscal revenue by force and free of charge in accordance with the law in order to meet the public needs by virtue of the state power. Tax revenue plays a major role in the fiscal revenue of all countries.

In 2021, China's public fiscal revenue totaled 20 255.464 billion yuan, an increase of 10.7% over the previous year, of which tax revenue reached 17 273.567 billion yuan, accounting for 85.3%. The annual per capita tax burden in China has exceeded 10 000 yuan, or 30 000 yuan for a family of three. Therefore, the taxation system reform has a vital interest for everyone and every family.

(2) *Non-tax Revenue*

Non-tax revenue refers to the fiscal revenue other than tax revenue and government debt revenue levied, collected, withdrawn and raised by the people's governments at all levels and their subordinate departments and units by making use of their administrative power, government credibility, state resources, state-owned assets or the provision of specific public services in accordance with the law. Non-tax revenue includes revenue from administrative and institutional fees, revenue from compensated use of state-owned resources (property), etc.

The basis for the acquisition of various types of non-tax revenue is different. Revenue from administrative and institutional fees, revenue from confiscation and centralized revenue of competent departments are collected by means of administrative power and are mandatory. Revenue from compensated use of state-owned resources (property), and revenue from the operation of state-owned capital are obtained through the ownership of state-owned resources and assets, which reflects the rights and interests of the state as the owner or contributor. Public welfare funds from lottery and revenue from donations accepted in the name of the government are raised on the basis of the government's credibility and follow the principle of voluntariness.

11.3.1.2 Major Tax Items in China

Tax is the most important form of fiscal revenue in every country, which plays an important role in economic operation, resource allocation and income distribution. At present, 18 major taxes exist in China, among which customs duties and tonnage tax are collected by the customs authorities, value-added tax and consumption tax on imports are collected by the customs authorities on behalf of the tax departments, and other taxes are collected by the tax departments. Table 11-2 shows the fiscal tax revenue situation in China from 2017 to 2020.

Table 11-2 Fiscal tax revenue situation in China from 2017 to 2020

(Unit: 100 million yuan)

Items	Year			
	2017	2018	2019	2020
In total	144 369.87	15 6402.86	158 000.46	154 312.29
Domestic value-added tax	56 378.18	61 530.77	62 347.36	56 791.29
Domestic consumption tax	10 255.09	10 631.75	12 564.44	12 028.10
Value-added tax and consumption tax on imports	15 970.67	16 878.97	15 812.34	14 535.50
Value-added tax and consumption tax on exports	−13 870.37	−15 913.93	−16 503.19	−13 628.98
Enterprise income tax	32 177.29	35 323.71	37 303.77	36 425.81
Personal income tax	11 966.37	13 871.97	10 388.53	11 568.26
Resource tax	1 353.32	1 629.90	1 821.64	1 754.76
Urban maintenance and construction tax	4 362.15	4 839.98	4 820.57	4 607.58
Building Tax	2 604.33	2 888.56	2 988.43	2 841.76
Stamp tax	2 206.39	2 199.36	2 462.96	3 087.45
Urban land use tax	2 360.55	2 387.60	2 195.41	2 058.22
Land value increment tax	4 911.28	5 641.38	6 465.14	6 468.51

Continued

Items	Year			
	2017	2018	2019	2020
Vehicle and vessel use tax	773.59	831.19	880.95	945.41
Tonnage tax	50.40	49.78	50.26	53.72
Vehicle purchase tax	3 280.67	3 452.53	3 498.26	3 530.88
Customs duty	2 997.85	2 847.78	2 889.13	2 564.25
Farmland occupation tax	1 651.89	1 318.85	1 389.84	1 257.57
Contract tax	4 910.42	5 729.94	6 212.86	7 061.02
Tobacco tax	115.72	111.35	111.03	108.67
Environmental protection tax	—	151.38	221.16	207.06
Other tax revenue	4.08	0.04	79.57	45.50

Sources: *China Statistical Yearbook* 2018, 2019, 2020 and 2021.

Note: "—" indicates the missing data due to the adjustment of tax items.

11.3.2 Public Fiscal Expenditure

11.3.2.1 The Definition of Public Fiscal Expenditure

Public fiscal expenditure refers to the payment of fiscal funds made by the government to provide public goods and services to meet the common needs of society. It mainly includes expenditures on ensuring the normal operation of state apparatus, maintaining national security and consolidating the construction of political power of governments at all levels; expenditures on public utilities for maintaining social stability, improving the overall quality of the population and enhancing people's living standards; expenditures on public welfare infrastructure construction that is conducive to the improvement of the economic environment and ecological environment with huge external economic effects; expenditures for necessary regulation of macro-economic operation, etc.

11.3.2.2 Classification of Fiscal Expenditure in China

The classification of fiscal expenditure is to reasonably sum up the contents of government expenditure so as to accurately reflect and scientifically analyze the nature, structure, scale and benefit of expenditure. After the reform of the classification of fiscal revenue and expenditure, the current classification of expenditure in China adopts the international practice, that is, both the functional classification of expenditure and the economic classification of expenditure are used to classify fiscal expenditure.

The functional classification of expenditure is classified in accordance with the main functional activities of the government. The items of the functional classification of expenditure include expenditures on general public services, diplomacy, national defense, public security, education, science and technology, culture, tourism, sports and media, social security and employment, health care and medical services, energy saving and environmental protection, community affairs in urban and rural areas, agriculture, forestry and water conservancy, transportation, etc. Table 11-3 shows the fiscal expenditure items by the functional classification of expenditure.

Table 11-3 China's public fiscal expenditure items for 2019 and 2020

Items	Year 2019 Amount (100 million yuan)	Year 2019 Proportion (%)	Year 2020 Amount (100 million yuan)	Year 2020 Proportion (%)
Expenditure for general public services	20 344.66	8.52	20 061.10	8.17
Expenditure for diplomacy	617.50	0.26	515.44	0.21
Expenditure for national defense	12 122.10	5.08	12 918.77	5.26
Expenditure for public security	13 901.93	5.82	13 862.90	5.64
Expenditure for education	34 796.94	14.57	36 359.94	14.80
Expenditure for science and technology	9 470.79	3.97	9 018.34	3.67
Expenditure for culture, sports and media	4 086.31	1.71	4 245.58	1.73
Expenditure for social security and employment	29 379.08	12.30	32 568.51	13.26
Expenditure for health care and medical services	16 665.34	6.98	19 216.19	7.82
Expenditure for energy saving and environmental protection	7 390.20	3.09	6 333.40	2.58
Expenditure for urban and rural communities	24 895.24	10.42	19 945.91	8.12
Expenditure for agriculture, forestry and water conservancy	22 862.80	9.57	23 948.46	9.75
Expenditure for transportation	11 817.55	4.95	12 197.88	4.96
Expenditure for exploration, power and information	4 914.40	2.06	6 066.88	2.47
Expenditure for commerce and services	1 239.70	0.52	1 568.92	0.64
Expenditure for finance	1 615.36	0.68	1 277.39	0.52
Expenditure for assisting other areas	471.31	0.20	448.59	0.18
Expenditure for natural resources and marine meteorology	2 182.70	0.91	2 333.94	0.95
Expenditure for housing security	6 401.19	2.68	7 106.08	2.89
Expenditure for reserves of grain and oil	1 897.11	0.79	2 117.30	0.86
Expenditure for disaster prevention and emergency management	1 529.20	0.64	1 940.66	0.79

Continued

Items	Year			
	2019		2020	
	Amount (100 million yuan)	Proportion (%)	Amount (100 million yuan)	Proportion (%)
Expenditure for interest payment	8 442.53	3.53	9 812.62	3.99
Expenditure for bond issuance	65.64	0.03	77.05	0.03
Other expenditure	1 748.79	0.73	1 737.18	0.71

Sources: *China Statistical Yearbook* 2020 and 2021

From Table 11-3, the three largest public fiscal expenditures in 2019 were education (14.57%), social security and employment (12.30%), and urban and rural communities (10.42%). The three largest public fiscal expenditures in 2020 were education (14.80%), social security and employment (13.26%), and agriculture, forestry and water conservancy (9.75%).

11.3.3 Fiscal Self-Supporting Capacity

The fiscal self-supporting capacity of the government can be measured by the coefficient of fiscal self-supporting capacity, which is the ratio of the fiscal revenue of the corresponding level to the fiscal aggregate expenditure. The coefficient of fiscal self-supporting capacity is a positive number greater than zero. If the coefficient is one, it indicates that the government is just fiscally self-supporting itself and neither can provide transfer payments to other levels of government nor needs other levels of government to provide transfer payments to it. If the coefficient is greater than one, it indicates that the government at this level has sufficient fiscal self-supporting capacity and can make transfer payments to other levels of government in addition to meeting the expenditure at this level. If the coefficient is less than one, it indicates that the government at this level has insufficient fiscal self-supporting capacity and needs to rely on transfer payments from other levels of government.

In recent years, China's fiscal self-supporting capacity has maintained at a high level, but the coefficient has declined. From Table 11-4, the coefficient of national fiscal self-supporting capacity from 2017 to 2020 is between 0.74 and 0.85.

Table 11-4 China's fiscal self-supporting coefficient from 2017 to 2021

Items	Year			
	2017	2018	2019	2020
Public fiscal revenue (100 million yuan)	172 592.77	183 359.84	190 390.08	182 913.88

Continued

Items	Year			
	2017	2018	2019	2020
Public fiscal expenditure (100 million yuan)	203 085.49	220 904.13	238 858.37	245 679.03
Fiscal self-supporting capacity coefficient	0.85	0.83	0.80	0.74

Sources: *Finance Yearbook of China* 2018, 2019, 2020 and 2021

11.4 Restructuring of the Fiscal System

11.4.1 The Period of Market Economy Exploration: Fiscal Contract Responsibility System

After the Third Plenary Session of the 11th CPC Central Committee in 1978, China started reform and opening up, gradually shifting from a planned economy to a market economy. In line with the market-oriented economic system restructuring, China's fiscal system restructuring also reflects the purpose of the central government to implement the decentralization of power and transfer of profits and mobilize the enthusiasm of local governments and China's fiscal system introduces the fiscal contract responsibility system, which includes three specific measures. First, "cutting taxes and yielding profits" to enterprises. By introducing the enterprise fund system, the profit retention system, the first-step substitution of tax payment for profit delivery, the second-step substitution of tax payment for profit delivery, various forms of systems whereby enterprises are responsible for their profits and losses, and contract management responsibility systems. Second, implementing the "multiple taxation system", establishing a taxation system of multiple taxes, multiple links and multiple levels, with turnover tax and income tax as the mainstay, other taxes as auxiliary. Third, using fiscal expenditure to support reform in prices, wages, science and education and other industries.

The fiscal reform measures in this period promoted the establishment of the socialist market economic system. The fiscal reform has given some autonomy to enterprises and local governments, promoting them to play an important role in the development of the market economy. It promoted the government's function from directly organizing social reproduction to formulating market economic rules, serving the production and operation of enterprises and carrying out macro-management of the national economy and society. It also promoted the establishment of a favorable legal environment conducive to the operation of the market economy; improved the socialist market system and operation mechanism, while promoting the prosperity and development of the market for consumer goods, factors of production, labor, finances, and technology.

11.4.2   The Period When the Market Economy was Established: Tax Distribution Fiscal System

The goal of socialist market economic system was established in 1992. The deepening of marketization has made the drawbacks of the fiscal contract responsibility system apparent. First, a variety of "decentralization" and "concession" initiatives has made the "vassal economy" and local protectionism prevail, to a certain extent, contributing to the blockade of the local economy and blind construction. Second, the reduction of the "two proportions" diluted the central government's macro-control ability over the local governments. To this end, from January 1, 1994, the State Council decided to implement the reform of the tax distribution system for all provinces, autonomous regions, municipalities directly under the central government and municipalities with independent planning status.

The main content of the tax distribution system is to divide the scope of fiscal expenditure between the central and local governments on the basis of the division of administrative powers; divide revenue by tax categories and clarify the respective revenue ranges of the central and local governments; set up two sets of central and local tax agencies; establish a system of tax rebates from the central government to local governments. Its significance is embodied in the following aspects. First, it has preliminarily constructed the modern fiscal management system adapted to the market economy. Second, it increased the "two proportions", that is, the proportion of fiscal revenue in GDP and the proportion of central fiscal revenue in that of national. Third, it comprehensively reformed the tax system and set up a new type, realizing unified tax law, fair tax burden, simplified tax system and reasonable decentralization of power, providing institutional guarantee for the operation of the socialist market economy.

11.4.3   The Period of Consolidating the Fundamental Position of the Market: Constructing the Public Fiscal System

With the continuous maturity of the market economy, China gradually built a public fiscal system from 1998 to 2012. In January 2007, China comprehensively implemented the classification reform of government revenue and expenditure in accordance with the principle of "openness and transparency, conforming to national conditions and facilitating operation". For fiscal revenue, the proportion of tax revenue in fiscal revenue decreased, while the revenue of government-managed funds increased in a regular manner. The proportion of real estate related industries in business tax revenue has gradually increased. In terms of fiscal expenditure, China's fiscal expenditure has increased both in absolute and relative terms, reducing the proportion of expenditure on economic affairs and general public services, and gradually increasing expenditure on "agriculture, rural areas, and farmers" as well as education, medical care, employment and social security related to people's livelihood. The improvement of people's livelihood finance, the enhancement of fiscal transparency and the use of fiscal incentive mechanism played an important role in economic development and welfare promotion at this stage.

The achievements of fiscal reform at this stage are mainly reflected in the following aspects. First, the implementation of unified budget management. By actively implementing departmental budgets and strengthening the management of extra-budgetary funds, a four-category budget system and a two-category budget authority division formed. The transparent and efficient allocation of public resources has been promoted, the responsibility of self-revenue and self-balance has been increased, and the transformation of economic and financial development has been facilitated in the direction of relying on scientific and technological progress with low input and high efficiency. Second, improvement of livelihood-oriented finance. This is mainly reflected in the further consolidation and strengthening of the agricultural foundation, the further promotion of equity in education, the continued expansion of basic medical insurance coverage, breakthroughs in the development of the social security system, and the promotion of energy conservation, emission reduction, as well as ecological and environmental protection. Third, the increased equality of market treatment, and the unification of domestic and foreign enterprises income tax. The Enterprise Income Tax Law of the People's Republic of China, effective as January 1, 2008, has realized the "four unifications", which is of great significance to maintaining a good market competition environment.

11.4.4 The Modernization Period of National Governance: Constructing a Modern Fiscal System

"The General Plan for Deepening the Restructuring of the Fiscal and Taxation System" issued in 2014 gave a detailed description of the modern fiscal system and proposed three reform tasks: budget, tax system, division of authority and expenditure responsibility. The construction of the modern fiscal system, through steadier and more intensive budget support, fair and enabling tax system as well as balanced and effective fiscal relations between governments, can effectively promote the growth of emerging economic forms, and properly solve the problem of fiscal funds for government operation and local development. As mentioned before, some progress has been made in the construction of the modern fiscal system, but there is still a gap between the current situation and the target, and the reform still needs to be continued.

In terms of fiscal revenue, the proportion of direct tax still needs to be increased, the tax structure needs to be optimized, and the establishment of local tax systems needs to be accelerated. Among them, the real estate tax can increase the proportion of direct tax, and at the same time can become the local main tax, also promoting the real estate tax is also an important breakthrough in tax reform. At the same time, inheritance and gift taxes shall also be incorporated into planning and justification.

In terms of fiscal expenditure, optimizing the structure of fiscal expenditure requires the further transformation of government functions. At present, China needs to solve not only the problem of development but also the problem of unbalanced and inadequate development. The government needs to participate in economic construction to promote economic development, but more importantly, to improve the efficiency of government expenditure, increase spending on health care, culture, tourism, sports and media, education, social security and employment and other aspects, and increase the proportion of social welfare expenditure.

In terms of the budget system, a modern budget system needs to be established accelerately. This includes improving the unified budget management system; making solid progress to propel budget openness, and using openness and transparency to constrain government behavior. Meanwhile, the government needs to give full play to the advantages of the National People's Congress and auditing supervision, improve the budget accountability system, and make budgets more binding. On the other hand, the scientific budget standards should also be studied and formulated to improve the performance management system, the performance expenditure evaluation system, and to promote the integration of performance and budget management.

In terms of the fiscal system, the key to whether the fiscal system is reasonable is whether it can mobilize the enthusiasm of the central and local governments. The focus of the reform is to clarify the revenue sources and expenditures destinations of local governments, and to focus the attention of local governments focus on promoting economic development and efficient delivery of public goods.

Constructing a modern fiscal system and promoting fiscal modernization are the basis for modernizing national governance, and also the key to constructing a modernized China, achieving the second centenary goal, and coping with various possible shocks in the future. Therefore, the goal of building a modern fiscal system cannot be shaken, and the process still needs to be accelerated.

12 Reform and Establishment of China's Modern Financial System

Since the reform and opening up, China's financial system has developed from the People's Bank of China (the only one bank in the past) into a financial system in line with China's national conditions, with a relatively complete system, flexible mechanism, complete categories, reasonable structure, full functions and effective supervision. While supporting the rapid, healthy and sustainable development of the national economy, it actively promotes marketization, legalization, internationalization and modernization, and makes tremendous achievements that are universally recognized. This provides valuable experience for developing countries to learn from in their financial reform and development.

12.1 The Stage Review of China's Financial System Restructuring

12.1.1 Construction and Standardization of the Socialist Market Economy and Financial System Basic Framework

The Third Plenary Session of the 11th CPC Central Committee established the basic state policy of reform and opening up, marking the beginning of China's transition from a planned economy to a market economy and from a traditional economy to a modern economy. In the distribution pattern of the national economy, residents and enterprises account for an increasing proportion in the fiscal revenue structure, and the role of bank credit is becoming more and more prominent. In addition, in 1985, China fully implemented the policy of "replacement of appropriations by loans", which resulted in the original planned financial system no longer meet the needs of economic development in the new era. In this case, it is necessary to assess the situation and reform the traditional planned financial system of "Great Unity" mode, thus starting the transition from the traditional socialist planned financial system to the socialist market economic financial system. This process is divided into three stages.

12.1.1.1 Introduction of the Basic Structure of the Market Economy and Financial System

In January 1978, the People's Bank of China was separated from the Ministry of

Finance. The original "Great Unity" mode of the People's Bank of China was gradually split up. Bank of China, Agricultural Bank of China, China Construction Bank and Industrial and Commercial Bank of China were established successively as specialized banks, which not only carried out commercial operations, but also undertook national policy businesses. The split and separation of specialized banks from the People's Bank of China created conditions for the transformation of the latter, from a single national bank to a central bank in the market economy condition. In September 1983, the State Council issued the Decision On the People's Bank Of China Exclusively Exercising the Functions of a Central Bank, marking the establishment of the central banking system.

In addition to specialized banks, national joint-stock banks such as Bank of Communications and China CITIC (China International Trust and Investment Corporation) Industrial Bank (now known as China CITIC Bank), local banks and non-bank financial institutions such as Ping An Insurance (Group) Company of China were also established. These institutions began to conduct financial activities in accordance with the requirements of the market economy. At this time, financial markets also began to be established. With the comprehensive development and deepening of China's economic system restructuring, various forms of market financing activities emerged, among which Shanghai Feilo Acoustics Co., Ltd. offered shares to the public during this period (Figure 12-1). The Shanghai Stock Exchange and Shenzhen Stock Exchange were established in 1990 and 1991 respectively. In this way, since 1984, financial markets including bill acceptance and discount market, inter-bank lending market, foreign exchange market and capital market have initially taken shape.

Figure 12-1 Stock of Shanghai Feilo Acoustics Co., Ltd.
Photo from *Securities Times*

12.1.1.2 The Establishment of the Socialist Market Economic and Financial System

In order to implement the spirit of the "Decision of the CPC Central Committee on Several Issues Concerning the Establishment of a Socialist Market Economy" approved at the Third Plenary Session of the 14th CPC Central Committee in 1993, the State Council made a decision on the restructuring of the financial system and made new corresponding arrangements. Since then, China's financial system began to enter a period of restructuring and exploration in line with the socialist market economy.

In accordance with the spirit of the 14th National Congress of the CPC, the market plays a basic role in the allocation of resources under the macro-control of the socialist country, the original specialized banks began to transform into independent commercial banks, and their policy-related business was undertaken by the newly established three policy banks: the China Development Bank, the Export-Import Bank of China and the Agricultural Development Bank of China. The original policy-related and commercial financial business of the People's Bank of China were also stripped away. Now the People's Bank of China only assumes the functions of a central bank, which means that it is responsible for formulating monetary policies, strengthening financial supervision, and implementing macro-control of the financial industry, etc. The promulgation and implementation of the Law of the People's Republic of China on the People's Bank of China and the Law of the People's Republic of China on Commercial Banks in 1995 fundamentally smoothed out the relationship between the central bank, commercial banks and policy banks, and provided the legal guarantee for the People's Bank of China to exercise the functions of the central bank and commercial banks to carry out business activities independently.

Important progress has been made in financial market reform. In the money market, a unified national inter-bank lending market was established in 1996. In the bill market, the People's Bank of China issued the "Measures for Commercial Bills of Exchange" in 1993, and in 1997, it implemented the "Measures for Payment and Settlement", which played an important role in strengthening the management of bills of exchange and promoting the healthy development of commercial bills of exchange. In terms of the capital market, the People's Bank of China has promulgated a series of policies and regulations to rectify and regulate the securities market, actively and steadily develop bond and equity financing, and regulate the issuance and listing of stocks. Regarding the foreign exchange market, the inter-bank foreign exchange market was established in 1994, a managed floating exchange rate system was implemented, and the RMB became a convertible currency under the current account of the balance of payments in 1996.

On the basis of the reform and development of financial institutions and financial markets, the financial system has been constantly improved. First, establishing a new financial macro-control system, transforming commercial banks from separate operation to mixed operation development, and macro-control from direct control to indirect control. Second, important progress has been made in establishing and improving the financial regulatory system. To exercise separate supervision over the financial sector, the China Insurance Regulatory Commission (CIRC, which was with drawn in 2018) established in 1998 and the China Securities Regulatory Commission (CSRC) established in 1992 were responsible for the supervision of the insurance and securities industries respectively, while the People's Bank of China was responsible for the supervision of the banking and trust industries.

During this period, China basically established a financial system framework dominated by state-owned banks and adapted to the socialist market economy. However, in supporting the reform of state-owned enterprises, due to the inertia of the original system and the financial legal system and imperfect supervision system, state-owned banks accumulated a large number of non-performing assets, about 25%-45%. In addition, the Asian financial crisis that broke out in 1997 further enlarged the challenges that both China's economy and finance have to face. The first National Financial Work Conference held that year decided to establish four asset management companies to manage 1.39 trillion yuan of non-performing assets stripped by the four state-owned banks. In fact, China's financial system dominated by state-owned banks played an important role in overcoming the Asian financial crisis and rescuing state-owned enterprises from difficulties.

12.1.1.3 Financial System Governance and Standardized Reform

Since the 16th National Congress of the CPC, China's economic restructuring has entered a new stage, the mode of economic development has changed, and industrialization and urbanization have accelerated. At the same time, China's opening up has entered a new stage after its accession to the WTO. These changes put forward new requirements for the reform of the financial system, and China's financial system has entered a period of governance, rectification and standardization reform.

The reform of financial institutions focused on implementing the spirit of the second National Financial Work Conference in 2002, and China took a series of measures to rectify and standardize state-owned financial institutions. These measures include reforming accounting standards, implementing a five-level classification of loans, continuing to divest non-performing assets from state-owned banks, enriching the capital of state-owned financial institutions and other policies, restructuring the finances of large state-owned financial institutions, completing the shareholding transformation, and actively encouraging large state-owned financial institutions to go public and raising financing at home and abroad.

After 2003, the four state-owned commercial banks completed financial restructuring and shareholding reform and successfully went public. China Life Insurance, PICC[People's Insurance Company (Group) of China] and other state-owned insurance companies also completed restructuring and reform, and successfully went public. After going public, state-owned financial institutions can improve their governance structure according to the requirements of modern enterprise system, pay more attention to financial risk management, and accept the supervision of small and medium investors, which improves the asset quality and overall strength of state-owned financial institutions.

In 2003, China Banking Regulatory Commission (which was withdrawn in 2018) was established, forming a separate supervision pattern of "One Bank, Three Commissions", clarifying the functions of macro-economic control and financial supervision of the People's

Bank of China, and improving the central banking system.

Driven by various reform measures, the financial systems in banking, securities and insurance have been constantly improved, and the financial system dominated by state-owned banks has been developed in a standardized manner. Among them, banking financial institutions developed the fastest. By the end of 2008, the total assets of more than 5 600 banking financial institutions of all kinds reached 62.39 trillion yuan. The financial market also developed rapidly, and the issuance and stock of the bond market increased steadily. According to the 2008 Statistic Bulletin on National Economic and Social Development, China's GDP amounted to 30.07 trillion yuan, by 2008, the stock of bonds was 15.1 trillion yuan, the total market value of stocks was 12.1 trillion yuan, and the total insurance assets were 3.34 trillion yuan, accounting for 50.3%, 40.4% and 11.1% of GDP respectively. The financing function of the capital market has been constantly improved. It is the standardized restructuring of the financial system that has provided the initial foundation for China's financial industry to successfully fight against the 2008 global financial crisis.

12.1.2 Marketization, Internationalization and Diversified Development of the Financial System

With the outbreak of the global financial crisis in 2008, countries around the world were trying to mitigate the impact of the crisis on the economy and society. Among them, the package plan of economic stimulus proposed by the Chinese government in economic development especially requires the financial sector to cooperate with the national macro-economic decision-making, which put forward new requirements and challenges for China's financial system. Before the standardized reform of the financial system was completed, it began to develop toward the direction of marketization, internationalization and diversification.

After the financial crisis, especially after the Third Plenary Session of the 18th CPC Central Committee proposed that "the market shall play a decisive role in allocating resources", the Chinese government has accelerated the pace of financial market-oriented reform. Marketization in the financial sector mainly refers to the marketization of the price of funds, including the marketization of interest rates and exchange rates, so as to reduce the inefficiency and distortion of funds allocation and better serve the real economy.

As China's GDP surpassing Japan's in 2010 and becoming the world's second-largest economy, China's economy has increasingly moved to the center of the world stage, the pace of opening up of the financial industry has accelerated, and the process of internationalization of the financial system has also developed rapidly. The first was the internationalization of the RMB. After the global financial crisis in 2008, the exchange rates of major world currencies such as the USD and the EUR fluctuated greatly, and global cross-border trade settlement was risky. In order to reduce risks, China began to rapidly develop the cross-border trade RMB settlement business in 2009 and play the role of the RMB swap agreement. At the same time, in October 2016, RMB began to join the Special Drawing Rights of the IMF, which greatly accelerated the internationalization of RMB. By the end of 2018, China had signed RMB swap agreements with central banks or monetary authorities of 38 countries and regions, which expanded the international use of RMB. The second was the internationalization of capital markets. On November 17, 2014, the "Shanghai-Hong Kong Stock Connect" was launched. On December 5, 2016, the "Shenzhen-Hong Kong Stock Connect" was officially put into operation, realizing the interconnection of the Shanghai Stock Exchange, Shenzhen Stock Exchange, and The Stock Exchange Hong Kong Limited. The capital markets in China's mainland went international through the connection with The Stock Exchange Hong Kong Limited. The third was the financial system's support for enterprises to "going global". In 2013, President Xi Jinping proposed the Belt and Road Initiative to increase the interconnection between China and Eurasian countries. In 2014, the Silk Road Fund Co., Ltd. was established, and in 2015, the Asian Infrastructure Investment Bank (AIIB) was established. The financial system supports enterprises to find investment opportunities in the construction of the "Belt and Road" initiative and provides corresponding investment and financing services.

On the evening of September 2, 2021, President Xi Jinping announced at the Global Trade in Services Summit of the China International Fair for Trade in Services 2021 to deepen the reform of the New Third Board (China's National Equities Exchange and Quotations) and establish the Beijing Stock Exchange to create the main venue to serve innovative middle and small-sized enterprises. After the establishment of the Beijing Stock Exchange, the exchanges in Beijing, Shanghai and Shenzhen have complementary functions, each with its own characteristics and advantages, which can not only carry a larger financing scale, smooth the capital circulation mechanism, but also build a more powerful credit growth channel for middle and small-sized enterprises. In terms of positioning, it further unblocked the path of direct financing for middle and small-sized enterprises.

12.2 China's Financial System

12.2.1 China's Monetary System and Policies

12.2.1.1 Evolution of China's Monetary System

Over the past 70 more years, with economic development as well as institutional mechanisms transformation, China's monetary system has also developed through constant improvement. This evolution can be roughly divided into two periods.

(1) *The Establishment of the Monetary System of New China* (1949-1978)

In the early days of the founding of the People's Republic of China, the RMB system was a fiduciary money system prepared for commodity materials, issued and circulated as planned, and completely served for planned production, which was coordinated with the planned economy system of "public ownership of all means of production". The People's Bank of China, established in December 1948, was initially aimed to coordinate financial policies and currency issuance in the liberated areas, and its establishment laid the foundation for monetary unification.

After the founding of the People's Republic of China, the People's Bank of China served the highly centralized planned economy system. The institutional arrangement of the RMB was a paper currency system prepared for commodity materials and completely serving the planned production. The issuance and management right of the RMB was unified under the Central People's Government. Under the background of that time, it was conducive to the unification of the RMB market, the planned adjustment of the circulation of the RMB, the state's control of the seigniorage income brought by the issuance of the RMB, and it was easy for the masses to identify, which was coordinated with the special planned economy background at that time.

(2) *Development of Monetary System (since 1978)*

After the reform and opening up in 1978, in coordination with the socialist market economy system of free commodity trading, China gradually realized the legal bank note system issued by the central bank monopoly. The evolution of the RMB system can be divided into the following three stages:

①Continuation of Planned Characteristics(1978-1992)

From the perspective of the RMB issuance system arrangement, along with the reform of the mode of state monopoly for purchasing and marketing of commodities, the People's Bank of China and the Ministry of Finance were set up separately in January 1978, and began to be responsible for absorbing and distributing funds, supervising industrial and commercial enterprises and general credit business. In 1981, China set out to establish an actual central banking system. At this stage, the number of RMB issuance followed the standard of planned issuance in the era of the planned economy, and the RMB issuance was mainly manifested as a "debt repayment" mode, which inevitably resulted in deficit-type inflation.

At this stage, the market economic system was still in the exploratory period, and the macroeconomic system at that time still retained the characteristics of the planed economy. Therefore, the RMB system in this period was jointly decided by the Ministry of Finance and the People's Bank of China, and the transformation of the RMB system was still under exploration.

②Transition from Planned to Market Economy(1992-1994)

After more than ten years of reform in the economic and financial fields, a new order of socialist market economy with an interest incentive mechanism has been established. In order to coordinate with the reform of the socialist market economic system and reduce transaction costs, the issuance system of the RMB has been changed from debt repayment issuance in the fiscal economy era to bank-dominated issuance mode in the banking economy era, giving rise to a brief period characterized by a banking economy. From the perspective of the RMB circulation, China's credit management system was changed into asset-liability ratio management under loan limit control in 1994, and three policy banks were established to separate the policy-related business from the operational business of commercial banks and promote the transformation of specialized banks into commercial banks.

③Continued Deepening of Market-Oriented Reform(since 1994)

After 1994, China focused on developing an export-oriented economy and formulated an exchange rate management system. This system has developed to the present, with China currently implementing a managed floating exchange rate system based on market supply and demand, and adjusted with reference to a basket of currencies. The development of the market economy and the reform of the market exchange mode led to the beginning of drastic reform of the RMB system. The reform at this stage still took the institutional arrangement of the RMB issuance as the breakthrough point. The Law of the People's Republic of China on the People's Bank of China promulgated in 1995, which clarified the independence of the People's Bank of China from the height of the law, explicitly prohibits the department of finance from overdrawing to the central bank to make up the deficit.

At the same time, China has also carried out a series of key reforms in the arrangement of the RMB circulation system. In order to strengthen the authority of the central bank and improve its ability to manage the RMB, the right of provincial branch banks to adjust the size of loans and special loans to the non-financial sector has been abolished. In 1999, the "Regulations of the People's Republic of China on the Administration of RMB" was promulgated, which clarified the current RMB system implemented in China, covering many aspects of the RMB system, including the nature and use of legal reimbursement of RMB, the unit and type of denomination of RMB, the organization, procedure and update method of RMB issuance, the punishment methods for counterfeiting RMB, and the exchange methods of RMB, etc. It is of great significance to confirm the RMB system in legal form for deepening the reform of the RMB system.

12.2.1.2 China's Monetary Policy Instruments

On December 25, 1993, The State Council proposed in the "Decision on Financial System Reform" that one of the goals of China's financial system reform is to establish a macro-control system of the central bank under the leadership of the State Council to independently implement monetary policies. In accordance with the goal of standardization and legalization, the central bank has tried out a market-oriented mode of regulation and control with the goal of improving macro-control. Reserves against deposit, rediscount business and open market operations are the three major monetary policy instruments, and market-oriented regulation is to make full use of the market mechanism and carries out policy regulation at discretion to achieve the macro-control goal of the central bank.

(1) *Reserves Against Deposit*

The "Decision on the People's Bank of China Exclusively Exercising the Functions of a Central Bank" issued by the State Council in 1983 specifically stipulated that the deposits absorbed by banks shall be deposited with the People's Bank of China in proportion. In March 1998, the People's Bank of China reformed the reserves against deposit system by combining the reserve account with the provisions account and setting up a single reserve account. In September 2015, the People's Bank of China reformed the assessment system of reserves against deposit from a point-in-time method to the average method. In this way, abnormal changes near the assessment period are avoided, and the reserves against deposit can play the functions of monetary management and macro-control more steadily and effectively.

(2) *Rediscount Business*

The use of rediscount business for monetary management was also a new development in this period. China had already started the discount business in bill acceptance in the early 1980s. In contrast, rediscount business refers to commercial banks discount to the central bank with unmatured eligible bills. The establishment of rediscount business is conducive to accelerating the velocity of money circulation, thus affecting the amount of money supply. The People's Bank of China issued the "Trial Measures for Rediscount of the People's Bank of China" on April 16, 1986, to regulate the specific operation of rediscount business. The central bank can use the rediscount policy to adjust the credit scale and market supply, and achieve the monetary policy objectives of the central bank through the operation of the bill market.

(3) *Open Market Operations*

The establishment of a socialist market economy also initiated open market operations as a forerunner of monetary policy in China. Since 1998, the People's Bank of China has established the primary dealer system for open market business, selecting a number of commercial banks that can undertake large bond transactions as the trading objects of open market business. Since 1999, open market operations have developed rapidly and have become one of the main instruments for the daily operation of monetary policy of the People's Bank of China. Its main transactions include repurchase transactions, cash bond transactions and the issuance of central bank bills. In September 2002, the People's Bank of China began to issue central bank bills due to the small amount of national bonds and their unreasonable maturity structure, which were not enough to meet the needs of open market operations.

In addition to the development of conventional monetary policy instruments, the central bank has introduced new monetary instruments such as standing lending facility (SLF), medium-term lending facility (MLF) and pledged supplementary lending (PSL) since 2014. This has played a positive role in regulating the liquidity level of the banking system, guiding the trend of profit and abundance in the money market and promoting the reasonable growth of the money supply.

12.2.2 China's Current Financial Institutions

12.2.2.1 China's Current Banking System

Over the past 40 more years of reform and opening up, great changes have taken place in the structure of China's banking system. The long-practiced "great unity" banking system has gradually developed into a diversified financial system, and a financial system with Chinese characteristics has been established, with the People's Bank of China as the central bank, state-owned commercial banks as the mainstay, and various forms of financial institutions coexisting and cooperating separately. This system has been playing an increasingly important role in China's macroeconomic regulation and socialist modernization.

With the rapid economic development since the reform and opening up, China's modern banking system has further formed and developed rapidly. According to the data of *Almanac of China's Finance and Banking* (1987) and *Almanac of China's Finance and Banking* (2010), if estimated by nominal value, the total assets of China's financial institutions were 1 378.484 billion yuan in 1986, and increased to (78 769.054) billion yuan in 2009, an increase of more than 56 times. From 1986 to 2009, the nominal annual growth rate of financial institutions' total assets was 19.23%, of which the growth rate of banking financial assets was 19.20%, and the growth rate of non-banking financial assets was as high as 21.07%, while according to the data of *China Statistical Yearbook* (2010), the average annual nominal growth rate of GDP was 16.44%.

At present, China's financial structure and financial system are being adjusted and optimized along the direction of adapting to the needs of the market economy, and joint-stock commercial banks, city commercial banks, policy banks, security, insurance, trust and various funds have emerged and developed rapidly one after another. On the whole, China's financial depth and total scale are in line with the development of the real economy, and these financial resources well meet the needs of the current economic growth. According to the statistics of the *Almanac of China's Finance and Banking* (2020), by the end of December 2019, the number of financial institutions in China's banking industry had reached 4 595, including 6 large commercial banks, namely Industrial and Commercial Bank of China, Agricultural Bank of China, Bank of China, China Construction Bank, Bank of Communications and Postal Savings Bank of China. Postal Savings Bank of China was listed as a large state-owned commercial bank at the end of 2018; 3 development financial institutions and policy banks, namely China Development Bank, Export-Import Bank of China and Agricultural Development Bank of China; in addition, there were 12 joint-stock commercial banks, 134 city commercial banks, and 18 private banks; regarding rural banking financial institutions, there were 722 rural credit cooperatives, 1 478 rural commercial banks, 28 rural cooperative banks and 41 foreign-funded financial institutions. In order to meet the needs of economic development, a number of enterprise group finance companies, trust companies, financial leasing companies, auto finance companies, asset management companies, money brokerage companies and other financial institutions have also developed rapidly after the reform and opening up. These financial institutions together with banks constitute a diversified banking financial structure.

After China's accession to the WTO, banking reform has been further deepened, interest rates have been gradually liberalized, and the proportion of large commercial banks in the total assets of all banking institutions has decreased. But at the same time, from 2003 to 2019, the total assets of China's banking financial institutions increased by more than 7 times. By the end of 2019, the total assets of banking financial institutions within China were 282.51 trillion yuan, and the total liabilities of banking financial institutions were 258.24 trillion yuan. In terms of types of institutions, large commercial banks, joint-stock commercial banks, rural financial institutions and urban commercial banks have large assets, accounting for 39.1%, 18.0%, 13.2% and 13.2% of the assets of banking financial institutions respectively.

Looking back at the reform and development of the banking system since the founding of the People's Republic of China, in a manner of speaking, the establishment of a modern banking system is the successful outcome of the construction of a socialist market economy and the reform and opening up. China's multi-level and modern banking system is closely integrated with China's actual situation and continuously reforms in practice and innovates in development. Its reform and development have made great contributions to China's economic and social construction. In general, in more than 70 years since the founding of the People's Republic of China, China's banking industry not only effectively supports the rapid development of China's economy, but also explores a road for the development of the banking industry with Chinese characteristics.

12.2.2.2 China's Current Non-bank Financial Institutions

Non-bank financial institutions emerge with the diversification of financial assets and the specialization of financial business, and are an important part of a country's financial system. Non-bank financial institutions mainly include insurance, trust, securities and financial companies, etc., which play an important role in the financial system and economic development.

(1) *Insurance Company*

After the Third Plenary Session of the 11th CPC Central Committee, it was imperative to resume the insurance business. In February 1979, the People's Bank of China held a national branch bank president meeting and proposed to gradually resume the domestic insurance business. In April of the same year, the State Council made a decision to gradually resume the domestic insurance business. In 2001, China formally acceded to the WTO, and promised to abolish the geographical restrictions on foreign insurance companies within five years and open up most of the business. China's insurance market players are becoming increasingly diversified, and the pace of institutional reform of Chinese insurance enterprises is accelerating. Foreign insurance institutions, with high-quality services, perfect products and advanced management experience, have played a demonstration and benchmark role in China's insurance industry, and promote the operation and supervision of China's insurance industry to be in line with the international insurance industry.

Since 2003, major large insurance companies in China's mainland have begun to implement shareholding reform. After the global financial crisis in 2008, the development of China's insurance industry has shown an obvious trend of comprehensive operation, with the integrated development of banking, security, insurance, trust, leasing and funds and other financial businesses. At present, the mixed operation of insurance institutions in China is mainly reflected in two aspects. On the one hand, insurance companies begin to actively extend to other non-insurance financial businesses; on the other hand, other institutions that started from non-insurance financial businesses participate in the insurance market to varying degrees, and the development trend of comprehensive financial operation is becoming increasingly obvious.

After more than 40 years of development since reform and opening up, China's insurance industry and insurance institutions have experienced considerable development. The scale of the industry and the number of institutions have been growing, and the level of operation and management has also been significantly improved. At present, the insurance industry has become an important part of China's financial system, and is playing an increasingly important role in promoting China's economic development and social stability.

In recent years, the basic system construction of China's insurance market and the insurance supervision system have been continuously developed and improved. While continuing to deepen the reform, China has paid more attention to the scientific and coordinated nature of reform, continuously enriched and developed the insurance function, expanded the service fields of the insurance business, and gradually moved towards a more standardized, diversified and international direction.

(2) *Trust Company*

After the reform and opening up, China decided to restore the trust industry. In October 1979, with the approval of the State Council, CITIC was established in Beijing, which was the first financial trust and investment company established after the reform and opening up. Its task was to guide, absorb and use foreign funds to introduce advanced technology and equipment for domestic construction investment. Since then, China's financial trust industry has developed rapidly. Various central ministries and local governments at all levels have set up various forms of trust and investment companies, and the banking system has also set up affiliated trust and investment institutions. After nearly 30 years of stagnation, China's trust industry has recovered rapidly.

By the end of 1982, there were more than 620 trust institutions, including 186 trust departments of the People's Bank of China, 266 of the China Construction Bank, more than 20 of the Agricultural Bank of China, 96 of the Bank of China. Local government and state-owned banks dominate the composition of trust institutions. However, due to the rich variety of investments and high risk appetite of trust companies, the industry has repeatedly experienced disorderly development. As a result, the regulator has carried out six large-scale clean-ups and reorganizations of the trust industry to guide the development of trust business towards standardization.

On August 24, 2010, China Banking Regulatory Commission announced the implementation of the "Measures for the Management of Net Capital of Trust Companies", which linked the scale of trust assets of trust companies with net capital, and implemented a risk control index system with net capital as the core for trust companies. The Trust Law of the People's Republic of China and the "Measures for the Management of Net Capital of Trust Companies" together constitute the main policy basis for the supervision of the trust industry in China, and the operation of trust institutions in China has become more standardized. According to the relevant data of "China Trust Industry Research Report (2018)", by the end of 2017, 68 trust companies in the industry had a total registered capital of 247 463 billion yuan, a total net asset size of 525. 067 billion yuan, and a total revenue of 119. 069 billion yuan.

(3) *Securities Company*

Securities companies are corporate entities that specialize in security trading and can be divided into two types, securities trading companies and a securities registration companies. A securities company in a narrow sense refers to a securities business company, which is an institution that specializes in securities business after it has been approved by the competent authority and obtained a business license from the relevant administration bureau for industry and commerce. It has a membership in a stock exchange and can underwrite the issuance, self-dealing or self-dealing and agent trading of securities. The securities investment of ordinary investors should be carried out through securities dealers.

Between 2011 and 2021, the number of Chinese securities firms has grown from 109 in 2011 to 140 in 2021, an increase of 28. 44%. The operating income of the securities industry also rose, from 135. 95 billion yuan in 2011 to 502. 41 billion yuan in 2021, an increase of 366. 46 billion yuan.

With the continuous development of China's securities business, China's securities industry has diversified development, in which investment banking and asset management business income proportion gradually increased.

Securities companies, as an important part of China's financial market, through increasing the ratio of direct financing and improving the allocation of resources, lay the foundation for the sustainable development of China's financial market.

(4) *Financial Company*

①Finance Company

Finance companies are non-bank financial institutions that provide financial services for enterprises' technological transformation, new product development and product sales, focusing on medium and long-term financial business. China's first enterprise group finance company, Dongfeng Motor Finance Co., Ltd., was established in May 1987. Approved by the head office of the People's Bank of China in September of the same year, Zhongshan Group Finance Co., Ltd. was also established in Nanjing, marking the beginning of the combination of China's industrial capital and financial capital. Up to now, almost all the large enterprise groups in the basic industries related to the national economy and people's livelihood, such as energy and electric power, aerospace, petroleum, chemical industry, iron and steel, metallurgy, machinery manufacturing and other important industries, have had their own finance companies.

②Financial Leasing Company

According to the "Measures for the Administration of Financial Leasing Companies" promulgated by the China Banking Regulatory Commission in 2007, a financial leasing company refers to a non-bank financial institution approved by the China Banking Regulatory Commission that mainly engages in the financial leasing business. Financial leasing business refers to the transaction activity in which the lessor leases the leased property obtained from the supplier to the lessee for possession and use according to the contract, and collects rent from the lessee according to the lessee's selection or recognition of the leased property and the supplier.

As of September 2018, there are 69 financial leasing companies in normal operation in China, mainly engaged in public transportation, urban construction, medical care, aviation, IT and other industries. At the same time, financial leasing companies actively make innovation in terms of capital sources and service models of small and micro enterprise businesses. By the end of 2018, the total number of financing leasing enterprises in China was 11 777, with a registered capital of approximately 3 276. 3 billion yuan and a balance of financial leasing contracts of approximately 6 650 billion yuan.

③Financial Asset Management Company

Financial asset management company are wholly state-owned non-bank financial institutions established by the decision of the State Council to acquire the non-performing loans of state-owned banks and manage and dispose of the assets formed by the acquisition of non-performing loans of state-owned banks. China's four big asset management companies, namely China Huarong Asset Management Co., Ltd., China Great Wall Asset Management Co., Ltd., China Orient Asset Management Co., Ltd., and China Cinda Asset Management Co., Ltd., received the non-performing assets divested from Industrial and Commercial Bank of China, Agricultural Bank of China, Bank of China and China Construction Bank respectively. After 2004, the Ministry of Finance stipulated that asset management corporations shall complete their commercial transformation by the end of 2006, and diversify their business development.

In July 2017, At the National Financial Work Conference, President Xi Jinping emphasized, "Follow the laws of financial development, closely focus on the three tasks of serving the real economy, preventing and controlling financial risks, deepening financial reform... promote a virtuous cycle and healthy development of the economy and finance." In order to better serve the supply-side structural reform of finance, asset management companies shall focus on the core priority tasks of "cutting overcapacity, reducing excess inventory, deleveraging, lowering costs, and strengthening areas of weakness"; focus on the acquisition and disposal of financial non-performing assets to help improve the quality of financial supply; focus on non-financial non-performing assets acquisition business to serve the transformation and upgrading of the real economy; and focus on substantive restructuring means to rescue problem projects and enterprises in crisis.

④Other Financial Companies

With the development of the market economy and the diversification of consumption, auto finance companies, consumer finance companies and money brokerage companies, etc. have emerged one after another.

In conclusion, non-bank financial institutions are the product of financial system development to a certain extent. With the development of the market economy and the deepening of credit relationships, people's demand for financial services tends to be increasingly diversified. The proportion of assets of non-bank financial institutions in financial assets has gradually increased. As the main complement to the banking industry, non-bank financial institutions are an integral part of a country's financial system.

12.2.3 China's Current Financial Market

From the founding of the People's Republic of China in 1949 to reform and opening up, China's financial market developed for a short period of time under the traditional planned economic system. In the early stage of reform and opening up, it was widely believed that the financial market was the product of the capitalist social economy and finance and was incompatible with the socialist system. Since the mid-1980s, for the ideological emancipation and the gradual prosperity of the socialist economy, the originally suppressed financial market gradually recovered its vitality. Not only was the money market enriched, but also the capital market was developed, expanding the space of the financial market and promoting the perfection of the financial market system. Since the beginning of the 21st century, all kinds of financial markets have developed rapidly, the scale has been expanding, the infrastructure has been making solid progress, the market trading system and oversight mechanism have been maturing and improving, and the participants in the market have become increasingly diverse. Up to now, a complete financial market system composed of several sub-markets, such as bill market, inter-bank lending market, stock market, bond market and foreign exchange market, has formed.

The commercial bill market, where the commercial bill is accepted, discounted and rediscounted, is one of the oldest in the development of the money market. The commercial bill is a kind of unsecured credit voucher issued by enterprises in the open market to raise funds, promising to pay the bearer the face value on a specified date. In the commercial bill market, the issuers are mostly large, highly creditworthy, well-funded, and rated companies or enterprises because of the lack of guarantees.

On November 9, 2000, the first institution specializing in bill in China, the Bill Sales Department of the Industrial and Commercial Bank of China, was established in Shanghai, marking that the business mode of bill entered the intensive and professional development track.

Since the beginning of the 21st century, the scale of China's bill market has been expanded rapidly, the bill business has been continued to expand, the market participants have become more diversified, the system and regulations have been gradually improved, the bill risks have been effectively controlled, the marketization level of bill interest rate has been continuously improved, and innovative products have been emerging, therefore, the bill market has been further developed.

The inter-bank lending market is formed by short-term capital lending activities between various financial institutions. It mainly meets the needs of adjusting the long and short positions that often occur in the daily business activities of financial institutions. It is also a window and transmission channel for the central bank to implement the monetary policies.

In January 1996, the People's Bank of China established a national unified inter-bank lending market, which consists of a primary network and a secondary network. On May 17, 1996, the People's Bank of China issued the "Notice on the Cancellation of the Upper Limit Management of Inter-bank Lending Rate", and decided to cancel the upper limit management of inter-bank lending rate from June 1. The lending rate shall be determined by both parties in accordance with the supply and demand of funds in the market. The establishment and trial operation of the national unified inter-bank lending market structure marks that the development of that market in China entered a new era.

In 1998, the People's Bank of China successively approved foreign banks, commercial banks and insurance companies conforming to relevant regulations to become members of the national inter-bank lending market and engage in inter-bank lending business. In 1999, some rural credit cooperatives and securities companies were approved to become members of the national inter-bank lending market and engage in inter-bank lending business. In July 2007, the People's Bank of China promulgated "Measures for the Administration of Inter-bank Lending", which included insurance companies, insurance capital management companies, financial asset management companies, trust companies, auto finance companies, financial leasing companies and other non-bank financial institutions into the scope of participants in the lending market. In recent years, the inter-bank lending market has not only formed a national network, but also gradually developed towards the internationalization with advanced means of communication. The stable and orderly development of the inter-bank lending market not only improves China's money market system, but also promotes the regulatory mechanism reform of China's currency.

Stock is an important form of direct financing for enterprises. The stock market is the market of stock issuance and transaction. In the process of China's economic transformation and enterprise reform, the stock market has become the engine and booster of the marketization of China's economy, and an important way and means of enterprise financing, resource allocation and enterprise reform.

Since the beginning of the 21st century, China's capital market, especially the stock market, has entered a new stage of development. After more than 10 years of exploration, China's stock market entered an important turning point of development, ushering in the most profound institutional reform in history. By the end of 2019, there were 3 777 listed companies in Shanghai and Shenzhen stock exchanges, including 1973 main boards, 943 small and medium-sized enterprises boards, 791 second boards and 70 science and technology innovation boards. The aggregate market value of Shanghai and Shenzhen stock exchanges was 59.29 trillion yuan, and the circulation market value was 48.35 trillion yuan, an increase of 36.33% and 36.65% respectively compared with the end of 2018. The circulation market value accounted for 81.54% of the total market value, increasing 0.19 percentage points compared with the end of 2018. The aggregate market value of Shanghai and Shenzhen stock exchanges accounted for 59.84% of the GDP in 2019, ranking the second in the world after the United States.

With the continuous advancement of the reform of non-tradable shares, the rules and regulations of the stock market became more standardized, and the level of market supervision and market governance structure were improved. The implementation of equity incentives and other measures further improved the competitiveness and quality of listed companies.

In 1981, the State Council decided to resume the issuance of treasury securities to concentrate the fiscal resources of all sectors to carry out socialist modernization and alleviate the problem of national fiscal deficit. Since China resumed issuing national debt, the nation has been exploring and reforming the way of issuing national debt. In 1991, China first tried to issue national debt in the way of underwriting, and initially realized marketization. This marked the formation of the primary market of China's national debt, namely the issuing market mechanism.

Since the beginning of the 21st century, the primary market of China's national debt has been formed, and the degree of its marketization has been continuously improved. The varieties of national debt issued were further diversified. The Ministry of Finance successively introduced new varieties of discounted national debt and interest-bearing national debt, and completed the reform of the paperless accounting system. In terms of maturity, there were not only short-term national debts of 3 and 6 months, but also long-term national debts of 7, 9 and 10 years. A reasonable maturity system of the national debt has been formed. Meanwhile, the frequency of national debt issuance increased greatly. The national debt market not only provides investors with diversified and multi-choice investment tools, but also helps the department of finance to adjust the debt structure, balance the debt burden and relieve the peak pressure of debt repayment.

Since the beginning of the 21st century, China's financial derivatives market has begun to multiply and develop. The number of products has been increasing, and the varieties have been continuously enriched. Financial derivatives have increasingly become an effective means to avoid financial risks and reduce transaction costs. However, compared with developed countries, the current financial derivatives market in China is still in its infancy, and the varieties and scale of financial derivatives are still small.

12.2.4 China's Current Financial Regulatory System

Since 1978, China has maintained strong control over financial resources and the economic field through the financial system arrangement with state-owned banks as the main body, providing broad institutional space and huge cost compensation for China's economic restructuring.

The Central Economic Work Conference held in December 1998 pointed out that, "The main tasks of financial work are to stabilize the currency value, support economic development, and prevent and defuse financial risks". The Conference put forward clear requirements for promoting financial reform, strengthening financial regulation, accelerating legal construction and establishing and improving effective mechanisms to prevent and defuse financial risks, demonstrating China's determination to establish a prudential financial regulatory system that is in line with international standards.

Since 1998, China has adopted a series of measures to build a prudential financial regulatory system, such as implementing a five-level risk-based loan classification system, strengthening the regulation of capital adequacy ratio, resolving huge non-performing assets of state-owned banks, establishing and improving a professional regulatory structure, formulating and improving regulatory laws and regulations, etc., which have gradually strengthened the prudential financial regulatory system and achieved notable results.

At the same time, in the process of building and strengthening the prudential regulatory system, China has created a favorable external environment for the improvement of China's prudential financial regulatory system by deepening the reform of state-owned enterprises and the fiscal system, continuing to promote the opening up of the financial system and the optimization of the financial system structure.

In 2017, the report of the 19th National Congress of the CPC clearly proposed to "improve the two-pillar regulatory framework of monetary policy and macro-prudential policy". In 2020, the Law of the People's Republic of China on the People's Bank of China was overwritten for the first time in 17 years, and the two-pillar framework of "monetary policy and macro-prudential policy" was defined in the law. At this point, the "two-pillar" framework of China's monetary policy has been formally defined, and the two-pillar is the core of understanding the current and the next few years of the thoughts of macro-economic control. On December 31, 2021, the central bank issued the Guidelines on Macro-Prudential Policy (for Trial Implementation), marking another big institutional step forward for China's two-pillar framework. The core content of the Guidelines can be summed up in four aspects. The first is that the goal of the macro-prudential policy is to prevent systemic financial risks; the second is that the leading department for macro-prudential management will coordinate with relevant departments to monitor, identify and evaluate systemic financial risks; the third is that macro-prudential policy tools have the basic attributes of "macro, counter-cyclical and anti-contagion" and the characteristics of "time-varying"; the fourth is the coordination between macro-prudential polices and monetary policies, micro-prudential supervision and other policies.

12.3 Basic Experience of China's Financial System Reform

During the past 70 more years of development, China's financial system has made key contributions to the nation's economic development and the reform and opening up, successfully resisted the impact of two global financial crises, and formed a financial development path with Chinese characteristics. Therefore, China must sum up the experience of the evolution of the financial system to guide the further reform and opening up and the high-quality development of the financial industry. The basic experience of China's financial system over the past 70 more years are as below.

12.3.1 Following the Chinese Path on Financial Reform

The financial system of the New China has made remarkable achievements in the past 70 more years. One of the most important lessons is we need to adhere to the development path with Chinese characteristics. The Chinese government sticked to its own path in the financial reform, introduced the basic structure of the market economy and financial system, developed the financial market step by step in response to the lack of development environment for the capital market in China, and established a financial system dominated by state-owned specialized banks in accordance with the national conditions.

In 1992, the 14th National Congress of the CPC established the socialist market economy system. The financial system began to reform around the establishment of the financial system framework of the socialist market economy, and a financial system dominated by state-owned commercial banks was built. The capital market began to develop and grow, and large state-owned financial institutions assumed the function of allocating financial resources. The shareholding reform of state-owned financial institutions after 2004 mainly adhered to the "state-owned holding", and actively introduced foreign strategic investors to promote the healthy and standardized development of the financial system. The financial reform also ensured that the People's Bank of China was not restricted by foreign banks but adopted independent monetary policies, which not only formed a financial development path with Chinese characteristics, but also set a good example for the financial reform and development of developing countries.

12.3.2　Insisting on Financial Services for the Real Economy

Since its establishment, China's financial system has been operating around the real economy and developing in the service of it. Since reform and opening up, China has made great achievements in economic development, which is inseparable from the financial sector serving the real economy. Financial reform and development are always accompanied by the reform and development of the economic system. In 1985, with the full implementation China's investment and financing system from fiscal allocation to bank loans, finance has begun to replace fiscal policies and become the core of economic resource allocation. The development of state-owned banks from specialized banks to commercial banks and shareholding commercial banks is the result of financial support for the development of real enterprises, which changes with the organizational form and market environment of real enterprises. In the late 1990s, non-performing assets of state-owned commercial banks began to be removed, the governance and rectification of the insurance market and the securities market were made, the market-oriented reform of interest rate and exchange rate was carried out after 2008, and non-bank financial institutions began to rise with the internationalization of RMB. All these measures were institutional arrangements made in financial institutions, markets and products in order to coordinate the relationship between the financial system and the real economy, and were supported policies for financial reform to adapt to the further reform of China's economic system and the market-oriented and international development of real enterprises.

It is the establishment of a financial system dominated by state-owned banks that converts savings absorbed at low cost into investment in real enterprises (state-owned enterprises, private enterprises, etc.). The characteristics of high savings and high investment ensure the combination of labor and capital and promote the development of China's "investment-driven" economic model. After 2008, with the vanishing of China's demographic dividend, China's economy entered a new normal, the investment-driven development began to be driven by innovation, and the financial system shifted its support for the real economy to high-tech industry, green industry and other fields. China gradually opened up the capital market, vigorously developed non-bank financial institutions, and provided diversified financing channels for real enterprises. Meanwhile, in view of the difficulty and high cost of financing in rural areas and small and medium-sized enterprises, the Chinese government put forward policies such as "financial poverty alleviation" and "financial services for small and medium-sized enterprises" to guide the financial sector to serve the real economy. In recent years, it has become a new trend for Chinese enterprises to "go global" with the deepening of opening up. In line with this, China's financial industry also stepped up the pace of opening up. The "internationalization of RMB", "capital account convertibility" and the establishment of the "Silk Road Fund" and the "Asian Infrastructure Investment Bank" in the process of financial internationalization are all basic strategies of the financial system to support real enterprises to go global. Therefore, the fundamental purpose of China's financial industry is to serve the real economy. Only by firmly grasping the concept of "financial services for the real economy" can China ensure the healthy development and continuous growth of its financial industry.

12.3.3 Adhering to the Stable and Orderly Development of Financial Reform

Finance is the core of the economy, so financial stability ensures economic stability. In more than 70 years of the development of New China's financial system, an important piece of experience is to adhere to the stable and orderly development of financial reform.

As for financial institutions, Chinese government supported the development of state-owned financial institutions by setting up access barriers. State-owned banks developed from specialized banks in the 1980s and commercial banks in the 1990s to shareholding banks in the 21st century, all of which were carried out in a stable and orderly manner under the guidance of the central government. China's financial institutions not only provided low-cost capital support to state-owned enterprises, but also promoted the stable development of the national economy, and in the service for the reform of state-owned enterprises, their own organizations also were optimized.

As for the financial market, Chinese government has been cautious about opening up all kinds of financial markets. However, the core of financial market development is to let the market play a key role in the allocation of financial resources, namely financial marketization. The key to financial marketization is the marketization of the interest rate market and exchange rate. Although the pilot programs of interest rate marketization and exchange rate marketization were launched in the 1990s, the real marketization of the interest rate and exchange rate gradually took shape and developed steadily with the marketization, internationalization and diversification of the financial system after the 2008 global financial crisis, and the marketization of interest rate has not been fully implemented.

To sum up, in China's financial system dominated by state-owned banks, state-owned financial institutions have monopolized financial services in the financial market and the reform of financial institutions and the reform of financial marketization have adopted a "passive" reform strategy of gradual and lagging behind economic development, which ensures the stable and orderly development of the financial industry and is conducive to the stable development of the national economy.

12.3.4　Adhering to the Leadership of the CPC on Financial Work

Over the past 70 more years, the New China's financial system has been transformed from zero to one, from disorderly to orderly, from weak to strong, and from closed to open, and another important lesson is adhering to the Party's leadership over financial work. Under the leadership of the Party, the financial reform always adheres to the gradual reform dominated by state-owned banks and state-owned capital, which can correctly handle the relationship between financial reform, economic development and social stability, so as to ensure the healthy development of the financial industry and the political direction of financial reform. Moreover, the financial industry is a high-risk industry, and financial stability is related to the interests of thousands of households. The Party attaches great importance to the stable development of the financial sector, and always insists that the financial sector should serve the real economy and the people. In financial practices, it also focuses on the autonomy, safety and controllability of financial reform and innovation as well as the prevention of systemic financial risks which successfully fended off the impact of the global financial crisis on China's economy and financial markets.

12.4　The Development Trend and Future Prospects of China's Financial System

12.4.1　Current Financial Development Trend in China

At present, China's financial structure is still dominated by banks, which play a major role in social financing. With the continuous promotion of China's financial market-oriented reform and the continuous development of financial innovation, China's financial structure has shown some new features in recent years, which are mainly reflected in the following four aspects.

First, the role and status of financial markets in China's financial system are constantly improving. First of all, from the perspective of policy support, China has always regarded the development of the capital market as an important part of the implementation of national strategies. Since the 18th CPC National Congress, the CPC Central Committee with President Xi Jinping at its core has attached great importance to the work of the capital market, strengthened centralized and unified leadership over the capital market, and made a series of major decisions and plans to make it clear that we shall build a standardized, transparent, open, dynamic and resilient capital market through deepening reform.

Second, the business boundaries of traditional financial institutions are blurring. First of all, the emergence of financial holding groups broke the restrictions on separate financial operations, so the traditional restrictions on separate financial operations no longer exist for these groups. Secondly, financial product innovation blurred the boundaries of financial institutions. Finally, the business of financial institutions continuously crossed and integrated. These strengthened the links between financial institutions and between financial institutions and financial markets.

Third, new financial media and quasi financial institutions developed rapidly. In recent years, with the development of financial innovation and the extensive application of internet technology in the financial field, third-party financial sales, internet crowdfunding and various new financial media have developed rapidly. Combined with traditional financial institutions, these financial media can provide new financial functions and services more conveniently, weaken the boundaries between traditional financial institutions, and strengthen the connections between financial institutions and financial markets.

Fourth, financial institutions are more closely linked to financial markets. With the development of financial markets, financial institutions are increasingly dependent on financial markets in terms of the source and the use of funds. The flow of funds between financial markets and financial institutions becomes more convenient and concealed with the development of new financial institutions and financial instruments.

12.4.2 Current Financial Reform in China

China's finance, like China's economy, faces the challenge of transformation and upgrading, i.e., from a factor-driven to an innovation-driven development model. However, innovation also implies risks. The current financial system in China cannot support innovation effectively, so further reforms are needed, which are mainly reflected in the following three aspects.

The first is to vigorously develop the capital market. The indirect financing financial system with banks as the main body is not conducive to the development of innovative activities. Only through direct financing can innovative behaviors be carried out, especially to provide financial support for the innovative behaviors of small and medium-sized enterprises. Vigorously developing the capital market can increase the financing channels for enterprises, expand the scale of direct financing, improve the efficiency of resource allocation, and strongly support the innovative behaviors of Chinese enterprises.

The second is to vigorously promote financial innovation. The change in economic structure requires the corresponding adjustment of financial structure and needs innovative financial instruments to adapt to economic development. With the development of the comprehensive financial operation trend in China, emerging financial instruments are also developing, and a new round of financial industry layout and competition has begun. China shall combine its own advantages in resource endowment and industrial structure to build the whole financial industry chain and promote finance to better serve the real economy.

The third is to vigorously strengthen financial regulation. The new generation of information technology, represented by artificial intelligence, blockchain, cloud computing and big data, is deeply integrated with finance, giving birth to sci-tech finance. On the one hand, it expands financing channels, reduces financing costs and accelerates the trend of comprehensive operation of the financial industry. On the other hand, it increases all kinds of financial risks. Additionally, with the gradual advance of the opening up of the financial industry, the complexity of China's financial risk monitoring has increased, so the financial regulatory system needs to be transformed to strengthen financial regulation. In particular, it is necessary to strengthen the construction of financial rule of law, strengthen the "penetrating" regulation of the whole process of financial market transactions to improve the ability to identify financial risks, resolutely hold the bottom line of no systemic financial risks, and safeguard China's economic development.

13 The Economic Development Model with Chinese Characteristics

China's economic development model is the product of reform and opening up policy. Since reform and opening up includes two interdependent aspects, namely internal reform and opening up to the outside world, the discussion on the China model should explore the significance of reform and opening up in the context of both China's own and international developments.

The China model has different meanings for Western developed countries and other developing countries. For many developing countries, the significance of the China model lies in whether it can be an alternative to all the other models of modernization that have come before. After World War II, the development model of the world was basically divided into the Soviet model and the Western model. After the collapse of the Soviet model, only the Western model remained. The Western model mainly refers to the capitalist model of USA and Europe. USA emerged as the sole superpower after the end of the Cold War, promoting its "laisser-faire" market economic model, known as the "Washington Consensus". However, neither Europe nor USA has achieved great success in promoting its model. Many developing countries that adopted the Western model have not thus achieved social and economic development and stable operation of democratic politics. In this case, the China model has a very important use for reference for developing countries.

The significance of the China model for China's own development cannot be ignored. From a macro perspective, the most profound significance of reform and opening up lies in the exploration of the nation's development path, including economic, social and political paths. Before China entered its modern history, despite its long history, it was mostly a simple repetition, with agrarian societies and dynastic succession being the most consistent features of thousands of years of history. Only after the contact with Western powers in modern times did China undergo fundamental changes in all aspects. The China model is a developing model and an accumulation of the world and China's own experience.

13.1 The Socialist Market Economic Model with Chinese Characteristics

13.1.1 The Unification of the Well-Functioning Government and the Efficient Market

The government itself is the most important institutional condition in the development of a country. The state of independence and mutual coordination and promotion of an effective market and a well-functioning government is a great practical achievement of the combination of the socialist market with Chinese characteristics and the basic socialist economic system.

China pursued a planned economy before reform and opening up. The economic role of the government was extreme, the market was regarded as part of the capitalist system, and thus its function was also denied. After reform and opening up, China had a different view on the market. Deng Xiaoping argued that capitalism can use the market and so can socialism, which neutralizes the market. Meanwhile, Chinese government vigorously promoted the construction of the market, and all kinds of economic ownership interacted and competed on the same market platform. Exploring the relationship between the market and the government as the main line, and constantly releasing the dividends of reform and system to economic entities, are the key factors for the great achievements of reform and development. Different from what is defined by western mainstream economic theories, the Chinese government is not limited to the functions required by the general market economy, but also undertakes extensive responsibilities such as developing the market system and implementing industrial policies. These more diverse and complex government functions can only be fully and efficiently realized under the background of relying on the basic socialist economic system and driven by the fundamental goal of building a modern socialist country. The functions and roles played by the Chinese government in the whole process of reform and opening up have extremely important leading and guiding significance, specifically including the following aspects.

13.1.1.1 Developing the Market System

From the early stage of reform and opening up to the beginning of the 21st century, the Chinese government focused on product market and price control in developing the market system. In 1983, the State Council issued the "Notice on Strengthening Market and Price Control", which stipulated the business scope and price authority of state-owned, collective and individual businesses. The Notice effectively expanded the production scale of commodities and the channels of market circulation. In 1994, the "Outline of the Plan for National Commodity Market" was issued by the Ministry of Internal Trade (which was reorganized as the National Bureau of Interal Trade in 1998 and was withdrawn in 2000), which established the basic ideas, principles, objectives and procedures for the development of the commodity market, and also pointed out that the commodity market is an important basis for the market system and the key point of the overall planning of the commodity market system is to coordinate the construction and management of important national and regional commodity markets. In 2004, the "Outline for the Construction of the National Commodity Market System" was further issued by Ministry of Commerce, calling on governments at all levels to focus on the establishment of a unified and open modern commodity market system with orderly competition, reasonable distribution and optimized structure to enhance the status of the commodity market in the national economy. Since 2005, with the promotion of a series of policy documents and cultivation measures, the construction of China's commodity market has gradually improved, with more than 97% of goods and services priced by the market in 2020.

In addition to the commodity market, China has also made great achievements in the promotion of production factor markets such as land, labor and capital. For the land market, since the 1980s, a prerequisite for optimizing the allocation of land factor has been created through the separation of land ownership and use rights. A number of documents including the "Interim Regulations Concerning the Assignment and Transfer of the Right to the Use of the State-owned Land in the Urban Areas" were subsequently issued, effectively regulating the land assignment of local governments and improving the efficiency of land resource allocation. As for the labor market, the "three-combination employment policy" proposed in the two documents of "Further Improving Urban Labor Employment" and "Several Decisions on Opening Wider Doors, Invigorating the Economy and Solving the Problem of Urban Employment" has become an important driving force to stimulate the development of the urban labor market. At the same time, farmers became self-employed, rural labor began to flow, and policies restricting labor mobility between urban and rural areas began to loosen. After the 14th National Congress of the CPC in 1992 made it clear that the direction of China's economic restructuring was to establish a socialist market economy, the reform of state-owned enterprises and the development of the private economy promoted the rapid development of the labor market and created a large number of non-agricultural employment opportunities. The successive issuance of Labor Law of the People's Republic of China and the Labor Contract Law of the People's Republic of China guaranteed workers' rights and interests and standardized the order of the labor market. As for the capital market, documents such as the "Notice of the State Council on Further Strengthening the Macro Management of the Securities Market" have been issued since 1992, and the "Several Opinions of the State Council on Further Promoting the Healthy Development of the Capital Market" in 2014 on promoting the healthy development of the capital market was issued. By building a multi-level capital market system, these documents have continuously expanded the investment and financing channels for Chinese enterprises and residents, and actively promoted the development of the real economy.

13.1.1.2 Promoting the Development of Micro-Market Entities

Enterprise is the most basic entity in market activity, and is the micro foundation of market mechanism operation. The key to enhance the vitality of micro entities is to enhance the internal driving force of enterprise development to let them enter the benign development track with self-generating ability. China's basic economic system framework, with public ownership as the mainstay while different forms of ownership continue to develop together, determines that both public and non-public enterprises are important components of the socialist market economy with Chinese characteristics. The continuous release of their operational vitality through reform measures can constitute an important driving force for economic and social development.

In terms of the reform of public enterprises, the Chinese government effectively upgraded the layout and structure of the state-owned economy through institutional innovation at the internal level and strategic restructuring at the overall level. This process can be summarized as follows. First, from 1978 to 1984, the government focused on "decentralization of power and transfer of profits", actively expanded the autonomy of state-owned enterprises, and implemented measures such as two-step replacement of profit delivery by taxes and replacement of government appropriations by loans; second, from 1985 to 1992, it was characterized by the separation of ownership and management rights, with the goal of making state-owned enterprises truly become relatively independent economic entities by adopting specific forms such as contract management responsibility system, system of separating tax from profit, and pilot of shareholding system; third, from 1993 to 2002, in order to promote the state-owned enterprises to establish a modern enterprise system, "invigorating large enterprises while relaxing control over small ones" and strategic restructuring were implemented; fourth, from 2003 to 2013, the State-owned Assets Supervision and Administration Commission of the State Council was set up to implement the reform of non-tradable shares and the board of directors system with the state-owned assets supervision and administration system reform as the main line; fifth, since 2014, the government has emphasized the separation of government and enterprise and the separation of government and assets, developed mixed-ownership enterprises, classified state-owned enterprises, and put forward the distinction between public welfare state-owned enterprises and competitive state-owned enterprises.

In terms of supporting the development of non-public enterprises, the "Opinions of the State Council on Encouraging, Supporting and Guiding the Development of Individual and Private Economy and Other Non-Public Sectors of the Economy" was issued in 2005, which was the first time that a special document on promoting the development of the non-public economy was issued in the name of the central government. The "Opinions of the Central Committee of the CPC and the State Council on Accelerating the Improvement of the Socialist Market Economic System in the New Era" released in 2020 also systematically discussed the relevant policies supporting for the development of non-public enterprises. To summarize, the Chinese government always works hard to eliminate the institutional factors that affect the development of non-public enterprises. In terms of access to factors, approval, access, operation, government procurement and bidding, the Chinese government significantly removes all kinds of obstacles and hidden barriers that restrict the participation of non-public enterprises in market competition, including supporting and guiding non-public enterprises to enter the electric power, oil and gas and other fields, and participate in the implementation of major national strategies and the construction of major projects. Meanwhile, the Chinese government starts to reduce the burden on non-public enterprises by gradually reducing taxes and fees through the reform of replacing business tax with value-added tax, lowering value-added tax rates, and raising the standard for personal income tax and fee deductions. In particular, the government implements a policy of universal tax exemption for small and micro enterprises and technology start-ups.

13.1.1.3 Improving Macro-Governance

Stable macro-economic operation is a necessary condition for economic growth. The goal of macro-governance by the government is to correct the bias of the market economy in spontaneously regulating economic activities, stabilize the expectations of social and economic entities, and finally achieve sustainable economic growth.

Before the supply-side structural reform strategy was proposed at the end of 2015, the Chinese government adopted government intervention and regulation policies advocated by western mainstream economics for a long period of time, and developed more diversified regulation combinations in accordance with specific national conditions. In 1984, the Chinese government proposed that "the more the economy is revitalized, the more importance shall be attached to macro-economic control" and tried to regulate the aggregate social supply and demand, as well as the major proportional relationship between accumulation and consumption and tertiary industry structure through price, tax and credit. After the goal of reforming the socialist market economic system was established in 1992, the government's tools for macro-economic control became more diversified, and the government also focused on the comprehensive coordination among different regulation methods such as tax, price, industry, exchange rate and interest rate. In 1998, in order to cope with the possible deflation caused by the Asian financial crisis, the Chinese government adopted a macro-economic control policy focusing on actively increasing investment and expanding domestic demand, and significantly relaxed the issuance of national debt and credit. In 2007, the government emphasized the guiding role of the national development plan in the positioning of the macro-economic control system, although the coordination role of the national plan with the fiscal and monetary policies was still kept. After the global financial crisis caused by the subprime crisis in USA in 2008, China's economic growth slowed down and its foreign exports even showed negative growth. Therefore, the government implemented the economic stimulus plan represented by the "4-Trillion-Yuan Stimulus Package".

The Chinese government tends to formulate macro-economic control policies from the perspective of Keynesianism to reduce economic fluctuations and maintain price stability. This kind of intervention is based on Keynes' theory of aggregate demand management, so problems of investment and consumption overheating, inflation and economic structural imbalance have occurred to a certain extent in China's economy every now and then. Therefore, at the end of 2015, the Chinese government put forward supply-side structural reform on the premise of continuing to attach importance to expanding domestic demand. This also raised the concept and level of the Chinese government's economic regulation systematically to a new height. The government recognized that the problems of overcapacity and duplication of structure that constrain long-term and stable economic growth, and the problems housing, education, healthcare and providing for the aged that are closely related to people's lives are not only demand-related, but also related to the relative lack of supply of high-quality goods or services.

In the process of reform and opening up, the Chinese government adopted various means to regulate the economy, which effectively maintained steady and healthy economic development on the whole. In the process of constant exploration and adjustment, the means of government regulation are gradually steady, and the methods of administrative intervention are transferred to the methods of economic and legal regulation, shifting from a focus on aggregate indicators of scale to structural proportion indicators. The Chinese government also frequently coordinates the specific economic intervention with the required institutional reform, which is well in line with the operation law of the socialist market economy with Chinese characteristics.

13.1.2 The Mixed-Ownership Economy

Mixed-ownership economy is an economic form in which property rights belong to different owners, and a property system with diversified subjects. In China's specific economic environment, mixed-ownership has macro and micro implications. At the macro level, mixed-ownership refers to the non-singularity of ownership components in China's economy, that is, the basic pattern of coexisting of public and private ownership under the premise of public ownership as the main body. At the micro level, mixed-ownership refers to the non-unitary ownership nature of enterprise investment subjects, that is, the property structure shows a trend of mutual integration of state-owned capital, private capital and foreign capital.

Mixed-ownership reform formed a more compatible ownership operation system arrangement in state-owned enterprises. On the one hand, it promoted the market mechanism to play a positive role in state-owned enterprises with the help of the vitality of non-public ownership. On the other hand, while opening a breakthrough in the reform of state-owned enterprises, it promoted the incremental reform to optimize the development environment of the non-public economy, which is of great significance for giving full play to the comparative advantages of diversified economic components and rational allocation of social resources. As an important form of realization of China's basic socialist economic system, mixed-ownership reform is an important part of the reform of state-owned enterprises, an active exploration of various forms of realization of public ownership, and a major breakthrough in the integration mode of state-owned economy and market economy.

On the basis of the gradual deepening of the mixed-ownership reform, the Third Plenary Session of the 18th CPC Central Committee established the overall spirit to comprehensively deepen the reform. The reform of the economic system entered a critical period, state-owned enterprises entered a period of "comprehensively deepening the reform", and the development of private enterprises also entered a "leap-forward period" under the background of the comprehensive reform of the economic system. Private enterprises are encouraged to actively integrate into the national strategy and actively combine with state-owned capital. With the establishment of the strategic position of mixed-ownership as "an important form of realization of the basic socialist economic system", a series of targeted reform plans marked the deepening and accelerating of mixed-ownership reform into a new cycle. Introducing strategic investors with a high matching degree, high coordination and high identity to participate in governance were focused on Reform of the labor, personnel and distribution systems was carried out, the market-oriented operation mechanism was deeply transferred, and a differentiated employee incentive and distribution mechanism that combines salary incentives with equity incentives was implemented.

13.1.3 The Open Economy

In the 1960s, labor-intensive processing links from developed economies flowed into Asia. China's Hong Kong, China's Taiwan, Singapore and South Korea participated in economic globalization by undertaking labor-intensive processing links and achieved rapid economic growth, known as the "Four Asian Dragons". In the 1980s, the global value chain led by developed countries gradually developed, but the production costs in the "Four Asian Dragons" was high, so there was an urgent need for a new market to undertake labor-intensive industries. China's opening up coincided with the third wave of globalization with the development of the global value chain as the main driving force. The gradual opening up and the market-oriented domestic reform complemented each other and enabled China to gradually integrate into the global economic and trade system.

China's opening up since 1978 has been a historical process of continuous expansion and deepening. At the beginning of reform and opening up, China was an adaptor and integrator of the international economic system, then became a participant and consummate, and then tried to become an advocate and leader of the reform of the international system. In practice, a series of progressive and continuous open economic policies and theories with Chinese characteristics have been formed.

13.2 "China's Miracle" of Economic Growth and Social Development

13.2.1 China's Economic Growth

Since the reform and opening up in 1978, China's economy has experienced more than 40 years of sustained and rapid growth. Its GDP expanded from 367.87 billion yuan in 1978 to 114 923. 7 billion yuan in 2021, with an average annual growth rate of more than 9% after deduction of the price factor, as shown in Figure 13-1. In terms of USD, China surpassed Japan in 2010 in terms of GDP, becoming the world's second largest economy after USA, as shown in Figure 13-2. Its per capita GDP increased from 385 yuan in 1978 to 81 370 yuan in 2021. China has also entered the ranks of upper-middle-income countries from low-income countries, where its per capita income was only 62% of the per capita GDP of low-income countries at the beginning of reform and opening up.

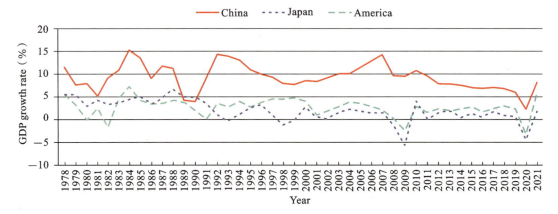

Figure 13-1 GDP growth rates of China, USA, and Japan from 1978 to 2021
Data from World Bank, IMF, National Bureau of Statistics of the People's Republic of China

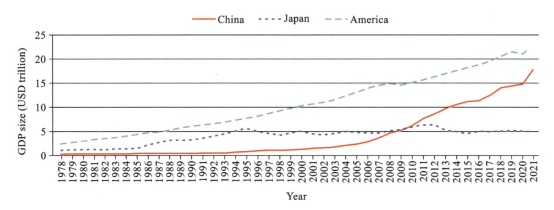

Figure 13-2 Size of GDP(trillions of dollars) in China, USA, and Japan from 1978 to 2021
Data from World Bank, IMF, National Bureau of Statistics of the People's Republic of China

After more than 40 years of rapid development, China has developed into the world's largest manufacturing country, the largest exporter of goods, and the second largest importer of goods after USA. According to China's National Bureau of Statistics, from 2013 to 2021, China's average contribution to world economic growth reached 38.6%, exceeding the combined contribution of the Group of Seven(G7) countries. In 2021, China's GDP reached 17.7 trillion USD, accounting for 18.5% of the world's total GDP and 7.2 percentage points higher than that of 2012. In 2021, China's GDP was equivalent to 77.1% of that of USA, 24.6 percentage points higher than that of 2012, 3.6 times that of Japan and 5.6

times that of India. At the same time, China's per capita gross national income has leaped, reaching 11 890 USD in 2021, double that of 2012. China's output of major industrial and agricultural products ranks among the top in the world. Among them, since 2012, the output of agricultural products such as grains, meat, peanuts and tea, as well as industrial products such as crude steel, coal, power generation capacity, cement, fertilizer, automobiles, microcomputers and mobile phones has remained the first in the world.

Since the implementation of reform and opening up, China's foreign trade and economic cooperation, as a link between the domestic economy and the world economy, has undergone earth-shaking changes and made remarkable achievements. China's foreign trade has made a historic leap forward. "Bringing in" and "going global" strategies have gone hand in hand. Regional economic and trade cooperation has continued to advance, successfully achieving a great transition from closed and semi-closed to all-dimensional opening up, and forming a new pattern of all-round opening up that is all-dimensional, multi-tiered and wide-ranging. Since the 18th National Congress of the CPC, China has steadily promoted the building of a large trade nation, focused on optimizing the business environment, accelerated the implementation of the free trade zone strategy, and actively promoted international cooperation under the "Belt and Road" Initiative.

In 1950, China's import and export of goods amounted to 1.13 billion USD, and in 1977 it was 14.8 billion USD. Over the past 28 years, imports and exports of goods totaled 148.7 billion USD, with an average annual growth rate of less than 10% from a low base figure. In 2004, the imports and exports of goods exceeded 1 trillion USD. In 2007 and 2011, it exceeded 2 trillion and 3 trillion USD respectively. In 2013 and 2021, China's imports and exports of goods exceeded 4 trillion and 6 trillion USD respectively. From China acceded to the WTO in 2001 to 2021, its imports and exports of goods have grown by 12.2% annually during these 20 years.

China's accession to the WTO in 2001 accelerated its integration into the global trading system and became a key node in the development of China's open economy. China has gradually improved the legal system for trade promotion and remedy, and the legal and regulatory system for the protection of intellectual property rights, so as to promote the legalization of foreign economic and trade. These institutional dividends have greatly promoted the development of China's foreign trade and promoted the integration of China's economy with the world economy at a higher level. In 2013, China became the world's largest trading country in goods, realizing the transformation from a "small trading country" to a "large trading country". In 2020, China's total foreign trade rose to 5.3 trillion USD from 4.4 trillion USD in 2012, overtaking USA for the first time to become the world's largest trading country. In 2021, China's total foreign trade reached 6.9 trillion USD.

Since the 18th National Congress of the CPC, China has vigorously implemented the strategy of innovation-driven development, achieved remarkable results in building an innovation-driven country, and greatly enhanced its innovation capacity and international competitiveness. In 2021, China's innovation index ranked 12th in the world, up 22 places from 2012, ranking first among middle-income countries. Since 2012, the number of Chinese companies on the Fortune Global 500 list has continued to grow, and in 2018, it surpassed USA for the first time, ranking first in the world for four consecutive years. In 2021, the number of Chinese companies on the list reached a new peak of 145, 50 more than in 2012, realizing the 19th consecutive year of growth in the number of companies on the list.

13.2.2　China's Experience in Poverty Eradication

On February 25, 2021, General secretary Xi Jinping solemnly proclaimed at National Poverty Eradication Summary and Commendation Conference, China has won a comprehensive victory in its battle against poverty. All 98.99 million rural people living in poverty under the current standard have been lifted out of poverty, all 832 impoverished counties have been lifted out of poverty, and all 128 000 impoverished villages have been lifted out of poverty. Region-wide poverty has been solved, and the arduous task of eliminating absolute poverty has been completed, creating another human miracle that will stand out in history. According to the 2010 poverty line, it is estimated that China's poverty alleviation work over the past 40 more years has lifted more than 700 million people out of poverty and reduced the poverty incidence by more than 93 percentage points. This great miracle reveals the great superiority of China's system and national governance system, proves the scientific and effective nature of the philosophy of targeted poverty alleviation and the specific actions under its guidance, and provides an example for the world's anti-poverty.

The region-wide poverty phenomenon is the most concentrated manifestation of poverty in China for thousands of years. According to the list released by the State Council Leading Group Office of Poverty Alleviation and Development in 2014, the 832 impoverished counties in China involved 22 provinces, autonomous regions and municipalities. Among them, Tibet had the highest coverage rate of impoverished counties, all 74 counties of which were impoverished counties.

Since the 18th National Congress of the CPC, China has made it one of the three tough battles in the decisive period of building a moderately prosperous society in all respects to completely solve the problem of region-wide poverty and absolute poverty. After the entry of the 13th Five-Year Plan, China has further stipulated that the core assessment indicators for poverty alleviation are to ensure that rural poor people are "free from worries over food and clothing and have access to compulsory education, basic medical services and safe housing" by 2020, and at the same time, the increase in per capita disposable income must be higher than the national average, and the main indicators for basic public services must be close to the national average. To this end, China has given full play to its institutional advantage of pooling all its resources to complete major missions. According to statistics, during the poverty alleviation period, the government has invested nearly 1.6 trillion yuan in special poverty alleviation funds, and coupled with the pairing support between regions and the investment of all walks of life in poverty alleviation, the face of impoverished areas has changed dramatically in a short period of time. Significant progress has been made in the construction of infrastructures such as road traffic, hydraulic power, living environment and public facilities such as compulsory education, medical and health services, and the conditions of education, culture and medical care have improved significantly. Problems that have long restricted impoverished areas, such as difficulties in travel, drinking water, housing and medical treatment, have been comprehensively solved.

Since the reform and opening up, China's sustained and rapid development and the increasing sound social security system have contributed to the rapid reduction of the poor population in China. In 2015, China made the decision to resolutely win the fight against poverty, and the central government adjusted the previous poverty alleviation and development model, which focused on regional development, to take targeted poverty alleviation and poverty reduction as the basic strategy. In 2015, the Fifth Plenary Session of the 18th CPC Central Committee clearly put forward the specific deployment of the poverty alleviation project, that is, through a combination of industrial support, relocation and social security assistance, from 2015 to 2020, all 55.75 million registered poor people under the current standard will be lifted out of poverty.

13.2.3 Achievements of Social Security Undertakings

As a basic security system to protect and improve people's livelihood and enhance people's well-being, social security plays a crucial role in promoting social and economic development and people's livelihood. Since 2012, China has carried out an integrated, all-around adjustment and reform of its social security system from social insurance, social assistance and other aspects, achieving steady improvement in the number of people covered and the level of treatment. Social security has achieved remarkable results in poverty alleviation, and its service and security functions have become increasingly complete. At present, there are the following social security systems.

The first is the old-age insurance system. In 2014, China formally established the basic old-age insurance system for urban and rural residents, realizing the overall planning of urban and rural areas at the level of basic old-age insurance. In 2015, a comprehensive reform of the basic old-age insurance system for employees in Party and government offices and public institutions was implemented, so as to unify it with the design and operation mechanism of the basic old-age insurance system for employees in urban enterprises, and improve the fairness of social insurance. In 2018, the central adjustment fund system for the basic old-age insurance fund was officially established, aiming to relieve the pressure on the payment of the basic old-age insurance fund for employees of urban enterprises in different regions. In 2022, it was proposed that individual pensions shall be subject to a fully accumulated individual account system, which promoted the improvement of the third pillar pension system.

The second is medical insurance system and maternity insurance system. Serious illness insurance for urban and rural residents was implemented nationwide in 2015 as a beneficial supplement to the basic medical insurance system, alleviating the possibility that urban and rural residents may fall back into or lead to poverty due to serious illness. In 2016, a unified basic medical insurance system for urban and rural residents was established, realizing the overall planning of basic medical insurance for urban and rural areas. In 2018, the State Council proposed the establishment of the National Healthcare Security Administration, which integrates basic medical insurance, medical assistance and other functions into the institution and implements standardized management. In 2019, China officially merged maternity insurance with basic medical insurance for employees.

The third is long-term care insurance system. In order to meet the long-term care demand brought by the aging, senior population and relieve the payment pressure of basic medical insurance, China has carried out the pilot work of the long-term care insurance system in several cities since 2016.

The fourth is social assistance system. This system mainly includes minimum living allowances, support for people in extreme poverty, special assistance system and temporary assistance system. In 2014, in the top-level design, China for the first time conducted overall management of the above social assistance contents, and the social assistance system was unified and standardized, stepping into the stage of systematic development from decentralization to unification. In 2016, China merged the system of receiving guarantees of food, clothing, medical care, housing and burial expenses for childless and infirm rural residents with the assistance system for urban residents without identification paper, a normal residence permit and a source of income, forming a unified system for supporting the extremely poor in urban and rural areas. In 2021, the concept of distinguishing between urban and rural subsistence allowances was deleted from Measures for Review and of Minimum Subsistence Allowance unified and standardized as minimum subsistence allowance. At this point, the social assistance system has moved from urban-rural segmentation to overall planning.

At the same time, social security undertakings have made great progress. The number of inclusive social security programs continued to increase, and the coverage of insured people continued to expand. First, the expansion and increment of basic insurance have increased simultaneously. By the end of 2021, the number of people covered by China's basic old-age insurance was 1.03 billion. The number of people covered by China's basic medical insurance was 1.36 billion, and the participation rate remained above 95%, and universal medical insurance has been realized. Second, the number of people covered by social assistance and welfare has gradually increased. A total of 46 824 million people in urban and rural areas were entitled to subsistence allowances and assistance benefits for urban and rural people in extreme poverty, ensuring all people eligible for assistance have access to it. The coverage of child welfare has been extended to all children in need, and the level of welfare has been gradually improved. The cost-of-living allowances for people with disabilities in financial difficulty and nursing care subsidies for people with severe disabilities were implemented, and 26 973 million people, accounting for 31.6% of the total number of disabled people, were entitled to treatment.

In addition, the level of social security benefits has continuously improved. First, the level of pension benefits has been raised year by year. Since 2005, China has continuously raised the pension of enterprise employees, and periodically raised the basic pension of residents since the implementation of the old-age insurance for residents. Second, the burden of medical insurance costs has been significantly reduced. The triple system of basic medical insurance, serious disease insurance and medical assistance has benefited 123 million low-income rural people. Third, government subsidies for medical insurance have been steadily increased. The medical insurance subsidy for residents was 240 yuan in 2012 and was raised to 580 yuan in 2021. Fourth, the gap between urban and rural minimum subsistence allowance standard has gradually narrowed.

China's social security has developed from a filling-in type to an inclusive type, and the objects covered by social welfare are more common. Welfare projects have established corresponding service contents around the elderly, the disabled, children and women, and each service content also constitutes a welfare system. The state-led social welfare system plays a positive role in promoting the sharing of economic development results by the whole people.

14 Development Philosophy and Pattern in the New Era

In accordance with the spirit of the Fifth Plenary Session of the 19th CPC Central Committee, China would enter a new stage of development from 2021 onwards. This is a new stage of development for building a modern socialist country in all respects and marching towards the second centenary goal after completing the building of a moderately prosperous society in all respects and achieving the first centenary goal.

Entering such a new stage of development and achieving its goals and tasks are of decisive significance to the great rejuvenation of the Chinese nation. With a history of more than 5 000 years, the Chinese nation has created a splendid civilization and made outstanding contributions to all mankind. After the Opium War, the Chinese people suffered an unprecedented disaster and fell into a miserable situation of poverty and weakness which was at other's disposal. Since then, the rejuvenation of the Chinese nation has become the great dream and unremitting pursuit of generations of descendants. This rejuvenation is a comprehensive revival of the economy, politics, culture, science and technology, military and international status. Its fundamental goal is to achieve the nation prosperous and strong, revitalize the nation and deliver a better life for the people.

The 14th Five-Year Plan period is a new starting point for a new stage of development and an important period for China to achieve greater development. To launch a new stage of development, implement a new development philosophy, and build a new development pattern is of great historical and practical significance as it bears on China's sustained and sound economic and social development and the overall realization of socialist modernization in an all-around way.

14.1 The Proposal and Connotation of the New Development Philosophy

14.1.1 The Connotation of the New Development Philosophy

The Fifth Plenary Session of the 18th CPC Central Committee first put forward the new development philosophy of innovative, coordinated, green, open and shared development.

Through the development of the 13th Five-Year Plan period, the whole Party and society have continuously enriched and improved their understanding and practice of the new development philosophy. During the 14th Five-Year Plan period, in the face of new development situations and tasks, it is even more necessary to firmly implement the new development philosophy.

In the new development philosophy, the key point of innovation-driven development is to solve the problem of the driving force of development, the key point of coordinated development is to solve the problem of unbalanced development, the key point of green development is to solve the problem of harmony between man and nature, the key point of open development is to solve the problem of internal and external linkage of development, and the key point of shared development is to solve the problem of social equity and justice.

From the internal structure, the five aspects of development theory have their own systems and are relatively independent. Innovation-driven development refers to taking innovation as the foundation of development and forming innovation-driven development by establishing an institutional framework supported by innovation. Through innovation, adding new drivers of development, unleashing new demand, creating new supply and providing new impetus for the vigorous development of new technologies and new forms of business. The focus of coordinated development is the coordination between urban and rural areas, the coordination of economy and society, the coordination of new industrialization and information technology, and the coordination of agricultural modernization and urbanization, etc. Green development includes sustainable development and building a resource-saving and environment-friendly society, establishing a legal framework and policy guidance for green and ecological production and consumption, and building a sound economic system for the development of low-carbon, saving and green circulation. Open development includes the need to carry out internal and external coordination, balance imports and exports, combine bringing in and going global, attract capital and technology, develop a high-level of an open economy, and actively participate in economic governance. Shared development includes more effective institutional arrangements, more provision of public services, implementation of poverty alleviation programs, a fairer and more durable social security system, and improving the wellbeing of the people with common development, effectively enhancing the sense of gain, participation and happiness of the people, and constantly promoting common prosperity for all people and realizing all-round human development.

The new development philosophy profoundly reveals the only way to achieve higher quality, more efficient, fairer and more sustainable development. It is a profound change in the overall situation of China's development, a fundamental solution to the situation of China's economic development entering a new normal and the sluggish recovery of the world economy, and a strategic guidance put forward for the prominent problems and challenges facing China's development. The new development philosophy reflects the Party's deepening understanding of the law of economic and social development, and moreover points out China's long-term development thinking, direction and focus, which is strategic, programmatic and leading.

14.1.2 Innovation-Driven Development as the Core

The Chinese people are people with a great spirit of creativity. They have long put forward the idea that, "As heaven maintains vigor through movement, a gentleman should constantly strive for self perfection". China promotes high-quality development, and innovation is the primary driving force for development. At present, China's economic development is in the three-period superimposed, a period of economic growth rate shift, a period of making difficult structural adjustments, and a period of absorbing the effects of previous economic stimulus policies. High-quality development is in line with China's new development situation. China's economic aggregate is now the second largest in the world, the momentum of China's development needs to be stimulated by innovation. In particular, more Chinese "new voices" in key and difficult areas of concern to the world are needed to be heard. Only by capturing the key of innovation can China make steady and long-term progress in high-quality development.

At the same time, the "five development philosophies" is a collection of closely related internal relations. Innovation, as the primary driving force, also plays a leading role in the other four development philosophies. Innovation opens up new space for coordinated development, provides new paths for green development, creates new advantages for open development, and builds new support for shared development.

The philosophy of innovative development with Chinese characteristics in the new era is the persistence and creative development of important ideas such as "Science and technology is the primary productive force", "Innovation sustains the progress of a nation. It is an inexhaustible motive force for the prosperity of a country", and "To construct an innovative country" under the conditions of the new era. To transform the driving force of development, adhering to innovation-driven development and putting innovation at its core are necessary. Only innovators get advance, only innovators are strong, and only innovators win. China is the largest developing country in the world, and development is the foundation and key to solving all problems in China. Innovation is at the top of the "five development philosophies", and it is precisely the key to solving the driving force of development.

14.1.3 Promote Economic Transformation with Green Development

The development of human society is confronted with many problems, including climate change, environmental degradation and resource crisis. Since the beginning of the new century, the United Nations has repeatedly promoted the concept of green development through conferences, initiatives and forums. Countries around the world have responded positively and adopted many effective measures according to their actual conditions. As a major country with important influence in the world, China has responded in a timely manner and listed green development as one of the five development philosophies for the new era, demonstrating its responsibility as a major country.

Since the 18th National Congress of the CPC, China has attached great importance to ecological civilization construction and put forward a series of new ideas, thoughts and strategies. The Fifth Plenary Session of the 19th CPC Central Committee established "new progress in ecological civilization construction" as one of the main goals of China's economic and social development during the 14th Five-Year Plan period, emphasizing "promoting green development and promoting harmonious coexistence between man and nature". This reflects the strategic determination and long-term planning of the Party Central Committee with Comrade Xi Jinping at its core in the construction of ecological civilization, and also provides important guidelines for the construction of ecological civilization in the 14th Five-Year Plan period.

Green development is a necessary condition for sustainability. It represents the people's aspiration for a better life. It focuses on solving the problem of harmonious coexistence between man and nature. Achieving carbon peak and carbon neutrality is an inherent requirement for implementing the new development philosophy, building a new development pattern and promoting high-quality development, and a major strategic decision made by the Party Central Committee in coordination with the overall situation at home and abroad. Promoting the comprehensive green transformation of economic and social development and accelerating the formation of green ways of production and life are major measures to achieve carbon peak and carbon neutrality.

In 2020, China officially announced that it would strive to achieve carbon peak by 2030 and carbon neutrality by 2060. This is also a major strategic decision made by China based on its responsibility to build a community with a shared future for mankind and its inherent requirement to achieve sustainable development. In order to achieve this goal, it is necessary to promote new energy, new materials, environmental protection and other fields, while reducing steel, chemical, construction and other industries, so as to promote the transformation of economic structure and gradually achieve carbon neutrality.

14.2 The Connotation and Characteristics of the New Development Pattern

In the past decade, China has entered a new stage of development with great changes in the global economic environment. The original development model is no longer suitable for the new stage and cannot be sustained. The construction of a new development pattern is a major decision made by the Party Central Committee with Comrade Xi Jinping at its core according to China's development stage, environment and changing conditions, taking into account the current situation. It is also a strategic layout and proactive efforts to grasp the initiative of future development, a major historical task that must be accomplished in the new stage of development, and an important element of Xi Jinping's economic thought.

The new development pattern has rich theoretical connotations, which can be summarized as follows. First, we should set the domestic circulation as the mainstay and ensure that the initiative and control of economic development are firmly in our own hands, which is the core to constructing the new development pattern. Second, we should set expanding domestic demand as the strategic priority and constantly consolidate and enhance China's super-sized market advantages, which is the foundation for building a new development pattern. Third, we should set supply-side structural reform as the main task, by unclogging circulation impediments, removing bottlenecks and constraints, increasing employment and income, and creating demand capacity, which is the key to building a new development pattern. Fourth, we should achieve a high-level of self-reliance and self-improvement, which is the most essential feature of building a new development pattern. Fifth, we should implement opening up to the outside world at a high-level and use the global circulation to improve the efficiency and level of the domestic circulation, which is the basic requirement for building a new development pattern. These five factors are interrelated, interdependent and mutually promoting, forming an organic internal logic system.

14.2.1 Domestic Circulation as the Mainstay

To build a new development pattern, taking the domestic circulation as the mainstay is necessary. This is not only the general law of building an economic power, but also the inevitable choice of China's economic development.

Throughout the history of world economic development, it is a general rule to build an economic power to develop the economy based on the domestic circulation. As the largest developing country in the world, China has achieved the goal of building a moderately prosperous society in all respects. In the future development path, China must continue to take the domestic circulation as the mainstay. China has a population of more than 1.4 billion and a middle-income population of more than 400 million, which are important pillars for China to form a super-sized market advantage. At the same time, the rapid development of urbanization and the increase of farmers' income have also accelerated the formation of China's super-sized market advantages. In 2021, domestic demand contributes 79.1% to China's economic growth, an increase of 4.4 percentage points over 2020. In a manner of speaking, since the global financial crisis in 2008, China's economy has been shifting to the pattern of the domestic circulation as the mainstay. And in the future for a period of time, the potential of domestic demand will continue to be released, and the characteristics of the national economic cycle led by domestic demand will be more significant. On the whole, in the current severe international situation, with the major domestic circulation as the mainstay and giving full play to the advantages of the domestic super-sized market, China can better guard against risks, stabilize growth, seize the initiative in development, and provide a strong guarantee for the sustained and stable development of the Chinese economy.

14.2.2 Expanding Domestic Demand as the Strategic Priority

The sustained and steady growth of domestic demand is the foundation for building a new development pattern with the domestic circulation as the mainstay. Especially in the context of the intensified anti-globalization and the severe impact of COVID-19 pandemic on economic development, the huge scale of market resources is particularly important. The expansion of domestic demand shall not be used only to address financial risks and external shocks in the short term, but be transformed into a sustainable historical process.

There is a realistic possibility for China to take expanding domestic demand as the strategic priority and continuously consolidate and enhance its advantages in the super-sized market. First, stable economic growth will bring greater incremental market demand. With the promotion of the goal of common prosperity, the large growth of middle-income groups will release huge consumer demand, thus promoting the sustained and stable growth of total domestic market demand. Second, the continuous upgrading of residents' consumption structure will also bring new market demand. According to the experience of world economic development, when the per capita GDP reaches 5 000 USD, the consumption structure of residents enters the track of upgrading, and a large number of new market demands are constantly generated. Third, the continuous upgrading of the industrial structure has created huge new market demand. The industrial transformation brought about by the new round of scientific and technological revolution has changed the original mode of production and way of life, and created a large number of new demands in the consumer market. Finally, investment still has plenty of room to grow for below reasons: first, China's level of industrialization is uneven, and accelerating the development of new industries in the central and western regions is bound to bring plenty of investment; second, with the improvement of Chinese residents' consumption level, the transformation and upgrading of traditional industries and the rapid development of the service industry will inevitably attract a large amount of investment; third, the rapid development of a new round of scientific and technological revolution will lead to large-scale investment in new infrastructure, industries and technologies; fourth, large-scale investment is still needed to promote equal access to public services.

14.2.3 Supply-Side Structural Reform as the Main Task

With the continuous consolidation of the advantages of China's super-sized market, in order to build a new development pattern, it is necessary to smooth the domestic circulation, transform the demand of China's super-sized market from potential demand to actual demand, so as to promote the sustained and stable economic growth. To smooth the domestic circulation, supply-side structural reform must be the main task.

The misallocation between supply and demand is not a total supply and demand problem, but a structural problem, whose most obvious feature is the coexistence of overcapacity and excess demand. The main reason for the misallocation between supply and demand is that the upgrading of the supply structure lags behind the upgrading of residents' consumption structure. Since the root cause of the supply-demand misallocation lies on the supply side, it is the key to solving the main social contradiction to accelerate the supply-side structural reform, smooth the domestic circulation, and unclog bottlenecks and reconnect disrupted links of production, distribution, circulation and consumption. To build a new development pattern, the supply-side structural reform as the mainstay must be deepened to strengthen the elasticity of the supply system, so as to achieve a high-level of economic dynamic balance.

14.2.4 Scientific and Technological Innovation as a Powerful Driving Force

Achieving a high-level of self-reliance and self-improvement is the most essential feature of building a new development pattern. In the final analysis, competition among countries is competition in science and technology, in specific, competition in key and core technologies. Only by independently mastering key and core technologies can the smooth flow of domestic circulation be fundamentally achieved and the mainstay position of domestic circulation be established.

First, to achieve the domestic circulation, scientific and technological innovation must be relied on. General Secretary Xi Jinping clearly pointed out that the boost of domestic circulation and international circulation also needs the strength of science and technology, to ensure the security and stability of the industrial and supply chain. Second, scientific and technological innovation is the key to expanding domestic demand. Under the new situation of household consumption upgrading, expanding domestic demand not only requires the control of demand, but also relies on supply-side structural reform. Only by accelerating scientific and technological innovation and using new technologies to form new industries, new types of business, new models and new products can more products and services be created, thus continuously promoting the expansion of domestic demand. Third, scientific and technological innovation is the key to promoting supply-side structural reform. On the one hand, the transformation of traditional industries to meet people's needs for a better life by improving the variety of products and services, quality satisfaction and brand recognition requires accelerating the digital transformation of traditional industries; on the other hand, accelerating the development of service industries and promoting the upgrade of lifestyle services to high quality and diversity depends on accelerating the digitalization and intelligentization of service industries, which also requires independent innovation of technologies.

14.2.5 High-Level Opening Up as a Basic Requirement

In building a new development pattern, while establishing the major domestic circulation as the mainstay, opening up in a wider scope, in broader fields and at deeper levels must also be implemented, to promote positive interplay between domestic circulation and international circulation. If China wants to gain advantages, take the initiative and win the future, it needs to rely on its advantages in the super-sized market and implement a more active strategy of opening up on a global scale.

The domestic circulation cannot be separated from a more open international circulation. From the perspective of effectively giving play to the two forces at home and abroad to promote high-quality economic development, China must attract global resource factors through the domestic circulation to make up for its own factor shortcomings, which requires actively promoting the coordinated development of domestic circulation and international circulation. At the same time, the international circulation must be based on the domestic circulation. In order to smoothly promote high-level opening up and overcome the countercurrents and dangerous shoals encountered by economic globalization, it is necessary to take the domestic circulation as the fundamentals, give full play to the advantages of the domestic super-sized market, and better grasp the initiative and rule-making power to participate in the global economy. In addition, the international circulation has also played a role in improving the efficiency and level of the domestic circulation. To accelerate China's development into a manufacturing, science and technology, human resources, trade and digital power, the overall situation at home and abroad must be balanced to make good use of both domestic and international markets and resources, close loopholes, remedy deficiencies, strengthen weak links, and enhance advantages. The level of opening up must be constantly raised to improve the efficiency and level of the domestic circulation, and build new strengths for China's development.

All in all, building a new development pattern is a major strategic decision made on the basis of changes in China's development stage, environment and conditions; it is a strategic choice for upgrading China's economic development in keeping with the times; and it is a strategic choice to shape China's new advantages in international cooperation and competition. Building a new development pattern is an important element of Xi Jinping's economic thought. An accurate and scientific understanding of the theoretical logic of the new development pattern is important for the comprehensive interpretation of the scientific and theoretical system of Xi Jinping's economic thought. Building a new development pattern helps China to achieve a balance between domestic and foreign development and deal with the risks brought by the external environment through a controllable domestic circulation, thus promoting China's own development and the development of the global economy, and providing a new idea for solving the economic relations between China and the world.

参考文献
References

1 中国经济的自然条件和基础
Natural Conditions and Foundation of the Chinese Economy

[1] Zheng J. Impact of Climate Change on Chinese Economy[C]//Zhang Y, Volodina T, Hou R. Proceedings of the 1st International Symposium on Innovation Management and Economics(ISIME 2021). [S. l.]: Atlantis Press, 2021: 189-193.

[2] 陈宜瑜, 丁永建, 佘之祥, 等. 中国气候与环境演变评估(Ⅱ): 气候与环境变化的影响与适应、减缓对策[J]. 气候变化研究进展, 2005, 1(2): 51-57. DOI: 10.3969/j.issn.1673-1719.2005.02.001.

[3] 蒋茂荣, 范英, 夏炎, 等. 中国高铁建设投资对国民经济和环境的短期效应综合评估[J]. 中国人口·资源与环境, 2017, 27(2): 75-83. DOI: 10.3969/j.issn.1002-2104.2017.02.012.

[4] 李炳元, 潘保田, 韩嘉福. 中国陆地基本地貌类型及其划分指标探讨[J]. 第四纪研究, 2008, 28(4): 535-543. DOI: 10.3321/j.issn:1001-7410.2008.04.004.

[5] 秦大河, 丁一汇, 苏纪兰, 等. 中国气候与环境演变评估(Ⅰ): 中国气候与环境变化及未来趋势[J]. 气候变化研究进展, 2005, 1(1): 4-9. DOI: 10.3969/j.issn.1673-1719.2015.01.002.

[6] 姚玉璧, 王毅荣, 李耀辉, 等. 中国黄土高原气候暖干化及其对生态环境的影响[J]. 资源科学, 2005, 27(5): 146-152. DOI: 10.3321/j.issn:1001-7588.2005.05.023.

[7] 中国地图出版社. 中国地图集[M]. 3版. 北京: 中国地图出版社, 2022.

[8] 赵济. 新编中国自然地理[M]. 北京: 高等教育出版社, 2015.

2 中国经济的历史发展(1949年以前)
Historical Development of the Chinese Economy (Before 1949)

[1] 巴里·诺顿. 中国经济: 适应与增长[M]. 安佳, 译. 2版. 上海: 上海人民出版社, 2020.

[2] 王曙光. 中国经济: 北京大学课堂讲录[M]. 北京: 北京大学出版社, 2020.

3 中国经济的发展和探索(1949—1978年)
Development and Exploration of the Chinese Economy (1949-1978)

[1] 巴里·诺顿. 中国经济: 适应与增长[M]. 安佳, 译. 2版. 上海: 上海人民出版社, 2020.

[2] 何伟.《中华人民共和国经济史(1949—90年代初)》评介[J].经济学动态,1995(1):72.
[3] 黄群慧.中国共产党领导社会主义工业化建设及其历史经验[J].中国社会科学,2021(7):4-20,204.
[4] 苏晓云.毛泽东"推广"农村人民公社的价值诉求[J].现代哲学,2012(4):41-53.DOI:10.3969/j.issn.1000-7660.2012.04.007.
[5] 田居俭.社会主义改造:毛泽东领导新中国经济建设的成功创举[J].党的文献,2011(4):59-65.

4 中国经济的改革和转型(1978年以后)
Reform and Transformation of the Chinese Economy (after 1978)

[1] 陈会广.中国农村土地制度变迁的理论与经验研究述评[J].甘肃行政学院学报,2010(4):16.DOI:10.3969/j.issn.1009-4997.2010.04.010.
[2] 顾功耘,李波.论国有企业改革的重大转变及其法制方略[J].法学,1995(10):26-30,11.
[3] 黄金生.深圳特区40年:为什么要定名为"经济特区"[J].决策探索,2020(19):60-63.DOI:10.3969/j.issn.1003-5419.2020.19.027.
[4] 王延中."世界工厂"与我国国际劳务合作[J].管理世界,2002(9):64-70.
[5] 赵国良.以调整为中心,稳步进行经济改革——对四川经济改革中几个问题的探讨[J].财经科学,1981(2):6-10,29.

5 改革开放以来中国的经济与社会发展
Economic and Social Development in China since the Reform and Opening Up

[1] 华尔特·惠特曼·罗斯托.从起飞进入持续增长的经济学[M].贺力平,等,译.成都:四川人民出版社,1988.
[2] 黄群慧,李芳芳,等.中国工业化进程报告(1995～2020)[M].北京:社会科学文献出版社,2020.
[3] 周振华.现代经济增长中的结构效应[M].上海:上海三联书店,1995.

6 中国的对外开放与国际贸易
Opening Up to the Outside World and International Trade of China

[1] 国家发展和改革委员会国际合作中心对外开放课题组.中国对外开放40年[M].北京:人民出版社,2018.
[2] 杨逢珉,汪五一.中国对外贸易[M].北京:北京大学出版社,2015.
[3] 余振,王净宇.中国对外贸易发展70年的回顾与展望[J].南开学报(哲学社会科学版),2019(4):36-47.

7 中国的农村改革
   Rural Reform in China

[1] 蔡荣,虢佳花,祁春节.农产品流通体制改革:政策演变与路径分析[J].商业研究,2009(8):4-7.DOI:10.3969/j.issn.1001-148X.2009.08.002.

[2] 邓曦泽.家庭联产承包责任制成功的原因、普遍机制及其走势——从"唯利是图"到"义利兼顾"[J].农业经济问题,2014,35(9):74-87,111-112.

[3] 邓正阳.论农村土地产权制度与家庭联产承包责任制[J].社会主义研究,2016(1):98-104.

[4] 黄少安.改革开放40年中国农村发展战略的阶段性演变及其理论总结[J].经济研究,2018,53(12):4-19.

[5] 孔祥智,涂圣伟,史冰清.中国农村改革30年:历程、经验和前景展望[J].教学与研究,2008(9):19-25.DOI:10.3969/j.issn.0257-2826.2008.09.003.

[6] 刘守英.农村土地制度改革:从家庭联产承包责任制到三权分置[J].经济研究,2022,57(2):18-26.

[7] 罗玉辉.新中国成立70周年中国农村改革历史脉络、经验总结和未来发展[J].现代经济探讨,2019(10):125-132.DOI:10.3969/j.issn.1009-2382.2019.10.017.

[8] 彭海红.中国农村改革40年的基本经验[J].中国农村经济,2018(10):107-118.

[9] 宋瑛.我国农产品流通体制演进回顾及思考[J].商业时代,2014(7):10-11.DOI:10.3969/j.issn.1002-5863.2014.07.004.

[10] 魏后凯,刘长全.中国农村改革的基本脉络、经验与展望[J].中国农村经济,2019(2):2-18.

[11] 张兰,冯淑怡.建党百年农村土地制度改革的基本历程与历史经验[J].农业经济问题,2021(12):4-15.

[12] 周振,孔祥智.新中国70年农业经营体制的历史变迁与政策启示[J].管理世界,2019,35(10):24-38.DOI:10.3969/j.issn.1002-5502.2019.10.004.

8 农业生产与农业产业化
   Agricultural Production and Agricultural Industrialization

[1] 蔡继明.乡村振兴战略应与新型城镇化同步推进[J].人民论坛·学术前沿,2018(10):76-79.DOI:10.16619/j.cnki.rmlixsqy.2018.10.007.

[2] 陈锡文.论农业供给侧结构性改革[J].中国农业大学学报(社会科学版),2017,34(2):5-13.

[3] 陈锡文.实施乡村振兴战略,推进农业农村现代化[J].中国农业大学学报(社会科学版),2018,35(1):5-12.

[4] 苟安经.新时代我国的"三农"问题与应对策略[J].农业经济,2018(9):26-28.DOI:10.3969/j.issn.1001-6139.2018.09.010.

[5] 顾益康,邵峰.全面推进城乡一体化改革——新时期解决"三农"问题的根本出路[J].

中国农村经济,2003(1):20-26,44.

[6] 韩一军,姜楠,赵霞,等.我国农业供给侧结构性改革的内涵、理论架构及实现路径[J].新疆师范大学学报(哲学社会科学版),2017,38(5):34-40,2.

[7] 贺立龙,刘丸源.巩固拓展脱贫攻坚成果同乡村振兴有效衔接的政治经济学研究[J].政治经济学评论,2022,13(2):110-146.DOI:10.3969/j.issn.1674-7542.2022.02.007.

[8] 黄承伟.推进乡村振兴的理论前沿问题[J].行政管理改革,2021(8):22-31.DOI:10.3969/j.issn.1674-7453.2021.08.003.

[9] 姜长云,杜志雄.关于推进农业供给侧结构性改革的思考[J].南京农业大学学报(社会科学版),2017,17(1):1-10,144.

[10] 孔祥智.农业供给侧结构性改革的基本内涵与政策建议[J].改革,2016(2):104-115.

[11] 李实,陈基平,滕阳川.共同富裕路上的乡村振兴:问题、挑战与建议[J].兰州大学学报(社会科学版),2021,49(3):37-46.DOI:10.13885/j.issn.1000-2804.2021.03.004.

[12] 刘合光.乡村振兴战略的关键点、发展路径与风险规避[J].新疆师范大学学报(哲学社会科学版),2018,39(3):25-33.

[13] 孙圣民,陈家炜.城乡融合背景下如何实现涉农政策的精准聚焦——基于"三农"要素变化的动态分析[J].理论学刊,2022(2):74-83.DOI:10.3969/j.issn.1002-3909.2022.02.009.

[14] 唐任伍.新时代乡村振兴战略的实施路径及策略[J].人民论坛·学术前沿,2018(3):26-33.DOI:10.16619/j.cnki.rmltxsqy.2018.03.004.

[15] 王胜,吴大兵.中国共产党对"三农"问题的百年探索、经验与展望[J].农村经济,2021(7):1-10.

[16] 魏后凯,姜长云,孔祥智,等.全面推进乡村振兴:权威专家深度解读十九届五中全会精神[J].中国农村经济,2021(1):2-14.

[17] 文丰安.全面实施乡村振兴战略:重要性、动力及促进机制[J].东岳论丛,2022,43(3):5-15.

[18] 项继权,周长友."新三农"问题的演变与政策选择[J].中国农村经济,2017(10):13-25.

[19] 谢芬.新时代中国"三农"问题演变及破解思路[J].农村经济,2019(6):15-21.

[20] 杨建利,邢娇阳.我国农业供给侧结构性改革研究[J].农业现代化研究,2016,37(4):613-620.DOI:10.13872/j.1000-0275.2016.0071.

[21] 张涛,赵磊.城乡发展一体化:解决"三农"问题的根本路径[J].农村经济,2017(10):24-29.

[22] 朱鹏华.新中国70年城镇化的历程、成就与启示[J].山东社会科学,2020(4):107-114.

9 中国特色的国有企业制度改革
Reform of the State-Owned Enterprise System with Chinese Characteristics

[1] 何瑛,杨琳.改革开放以来国有企业混合所有制改革:历程、成效与展望[J].管理世界,

2021,37(7):44-60,4. DOI:10.3969/j. issn.1002-5502.2021.07.004.
[2] 林毅夫,蔡昉,李周.充分信息与国有企业改革[M].上海:上海人民出版社,1997.
[3] 綦好东,彭睿,苏琪琪,等.中国国有企业制度发展变革的历史逻辑与基本经验[J].南开管理评论,2021,24(1):108-119.

10 工业化进程与城市发展
Industrialization Process and Urban Development

[1] 陈健,郭冠清.政府与市场:对中国改革开放后工业化过程的回顾[J].经济与管理评论,2021(3):20-30. DOI:10.13962/j. cnki.37-1486/f.2021.03.002.
[2] 当代中国研究所.中华人民共和国史稿:第1卷(1949—1956)[M].北京:人民出版社,2012.
[3] 黄群慧.中国共产党领导社会主义工业化建设及其历史经验[J].中国社会科学,2021(7):4-20,204.
[4] 刘戒骄,孙琴.中国工业化百年回顾与展望:中国共产党的工业化战略[J].中国经济学人,2021,16(5):2-31.
[5] 卢福财,马绍雄,徐斌.新中国工业化70年:从起飞到走向成熟[J].当代财经,2019(10):3-14.
[6] 毛泽东.关于中华人民共和国宪法草案(一九五四年六月十四日)[M]//毛泽东.毛泽东著作选读.北京:人民出版社,1986.
[7] 汪海波,刘立峰.新中国工业经济史[M].3版.北京:经济管理出版社,2017.
[8] 习近平.习近平谈治国理政:第2卷[M].北京:外文出版社,2017.
[9] 张培刚.农业与工业化:上卷[M].武汉:华中工学院出版社,1984:82.
[10] 中国经济增长与宏观稳定课题组.城市化、产业效率与经济增长[J].经济研究,2009(10):4-21.
[11] 郑玉歆.全要素生产率的测度及经济增长方式的"阶段性"规律——由东亚经济增长方式的争论谈起[J].经济研究,1999(5):55-60.

11 中国的宏观经济政策和财税体制
China's Macro-Economic Policies and Fiscal and Taxation System

[1] 北京大学中国经济研究中心宏观组.货币政策乎?财政政策乎?——中国宏观经济政策评析及建议[J].经济研究,1998(10):11-19.
[2] 陈诗一,陈登科.经济周期视角下的中国财政支出乘数研究[J].中国社会学,2019(8):111-129,206-207.
[3] 程谦,等.财政制度变迁与政策选择:基于经济体制转型期的研究[M].北京:中国财政经济出版社,2006.
[4] 董昀.中国宏观调控思想七十年演变脉络初探——基于官方文献的研究[J].金融评论,2019(5):15-37,116.

[5] 范从来.论通货紧缩时期货币政策的有效性[J].经济研究,2000(7):24-31.
[6] 龚浩,李丽珍,王晓.中国现代财政制度构建的目标、进程与现状评估[J].经济体制改革,2021(1):129-135.
[7] 郭庆旺,贾俊雪.中国潜在产出与产出缺口的估算[J].经济研究,2004(5):31-39.
[8] 郭庆旺,贾俊雪.稳健财政政策的非凯恩斯效应及其可持续性[J].中国社会学,2006(5):58-67,206.
[9] 韩琪,陈福中.中国经济概论[M].3版.北京:清华大学出版社,2019.
[10] 韩文秀.买方市场条件下的宏观调控[J].管理世界,1998(5):22-31.
[11] 华而诚.中国经济的软着陆:1992—1997[M].北京:中国财政经济出版社,1997.
[12] 李炜光,任晓兰.财政社会学源流与我国当代财政学的发展[J].财政研究,2013(7):36-39.DOI:10.3969/j.issn.1000-8772.2016.12.192.
[13] 马金华,薛迪.改革开放四十年中国财税体制改革回顾与展望[J].财政监督,2018(8):5-9.
[14] 王一鸣.改革开放以来我国宏观经济政策的演进与创新[J].管理世界,2018,34(3):1-10.DOI:10.3969/j.issn.1002-5502.2018.03.001.
[15] 现代财政体制的内涵和外延[J].中国总会计师,2021(1):39-41.
[16] 现代财政体制建设的现状[J].中国总会计师,2021(1):41-42.
[17] 殷剑峰.二十一世纪中国经济周期平稳化现象研究[J].中国社会科学,2010(4):56-73,221.
[18] 中共中央文献研究室.十五大以来重要文献选编[M].北京:人民出版社,2000.
[19] 中国社会科学院经济所宏观课题组.寻求更有效的财政政策——中国宏观经济分析[J].经济研究,2000(3):3-15,79.
[20] 国家统计局.中国统计年鉴(2018)[M].北京:中国统计出版社,2018.
[21] 国家统计局.中国统计年鉴(2019)[M].北京:中国统计出版社,2019.
[22] 国家统计局.中国统计年鉴(2020)[M].北京:中国统计出版社,2020.
[23] 国家统计局.中国统计年鉴(2021)[M].北京:中国统计出版社,2021.
[24] 国家统计局.中华人民共和国2021年国民经济和社会发展统计公报[J].中国统计,2022(3):9-26.

12 中国现代金融体系的改革与建立
Reform and Establishment of China's Modern Financial System

[1] 戴金平,张成祥.我国渐进式金融改革:发展与修正[J].南开学报(哲学社会科学版),2014(5):49-57.
[2] 孙力军,齐春宇.渐进式改革、金融控制与经济增长[J].经济学家,2015(3):47-55.
[3] 谭小芬,李昆.多举措扩大跨境贸易人民币结算[N].中国证券报,2019-05-14(A03).
[4] 吴敬琏.当代中国经济改革教程[M].2版.上海:上海远东出版社,2015:229.
[5] 张健华.中国金融体系[M].北京:中国金融出版社,2010:15-17.
[6] 周小川.金融改革发展及其内在逻辑[J].中国金融.2015(19):11-17.

13 中国特色的经济发展模式
The Economic Development Model with Chinese Characteristics

[1] 何瑛,杨琳.改革开放以来国有企业混合所有制改革:历程、成效与展望[J].管理世界,2021,37(7):44-60,4. DOI:10.3969/j.issn.1002-5502.2201.07.004.

[2] 洪俊杰,商辉.中国开放型经济发展四十年回顾与展望[J].管理世界,2018,34(10):33-42. DOI:10.3969/j.issn.1002-5502.2018.10.005.

[3] 刘晓梅,曹鸣远,李歆,等.党的十八大以来我国社会保障事业的成就与经验[J].管理世界,2022,38(7):37-48. DOI:10.3969/j.issn.1002-5502.2002.07.004.

[4] 卢福财,王守坤.历史脉络与实践视野下的有为政府——中国特色社会主义政治经济学的核心命题[J].管理世界,2021(9):77-89. DOI:10.3969/j.issn.1002-5002.2021.09.021.

[5] 汪三贵,曾小溪.从区域扶贫开发到精准扶贫——改革开放 40 年中国扶贫政策的演进及脱贫攻坚的难点和对策[J].农业经济问题,2018(8):40-50.

[6] 张宇燕.中国对外开放的理念、进程与逻辑[J].中国社会科学,2018(11):30-41.

[7] 郑子青,郑功成.消除贫困:中国奇迹与中国经验[J].中共中央党校(国家行政学院)学报,2021,25(2):39-48.

[8] 郑永年.国际发展格局中的中国模式[J].中国社会科学,2009(5):20-28,204.

[9] 中央党校"中国特色社会主义政治经济学研究"课题组.中国特色社会主义政治经济学对西方经济学理论的借鉴与超越——学习习近平总书记关于中国特色社会主义政治经济学的论述[J].管理世界,2017(7):1-16.

14 新时代的发展理念与发展格局
Development Philosophy and Pattern in the New Era

[1] 黄泰岩.构建新发展格局的理论逻辑[N].经济日报,2022-04-21(10).

[2] 刘云山.牢固树立和自觉践行五大发展理念[J].党建,2015(12):8-11.

[3] 习近平.习近平谈治国理政[M].北京:外文出版社,2014.

[4] 习近平.习近平谈治国理政:第 2 卷[M].北京:外文出版社,2017.

[5] 习近平.习近平谈治国理政:第 3 卷[M].北京:外文出版社,2020.

[6] 张莹云.深刻理解创新在"五大发展理念"中的核心地位[J].产业与经济论坛,2020,19(1):10-11. DOI:10.3969/j.issn.1673-5641.2020.01.003.